READINGS
IN MARKETING
TODAY

READINGS
IN MARKETING
TODAY

John T. Mentzer
Virginia Polytechnic Institute and State University

Forrest S. Carter
Michigan State University

67916

HARCOURT BRACE JOVANOVICH, PUBLISHERS
San Diego   New York   Chicago   Atlanta   Washington, D.C.
London   Sydney   Toronto

ISBN: 0-15-575814-4
Library of Congress Catalog Card Number: 84-81745
Printed in the United States of America

Copyrights and acknowledgments appear on pages 451–452,
which constitute a continuation of the copyright page.

Preface

The articles selected for this book fall into three categories. Articles in Parts One and Two emphasize a theoretical base for key marketing concepts. They elaborate on important topics—such as the role of marketing in the economy, the marketing concept, market segmentation, and strategic planning—beyond the level of discussion typically given in principles texts. By gaining a deeper understanding of how and why these concepts were developed, the student will be better able to turn theory into practice.

Parts Three through Six provide how-to discussions on the development and implementation of marketing-mix strategies. These articles provide guidelines for appropriate managerial actions in various situations for the areas of products, distribution, promotion, and pricing.

Part Seven demonstrates how the theories, concepts, and management guidelines are actually applied. The articles illustrate how companies and other organizations have addressed their marketing problems and opportunities, allowing the student to observe the results of putting theory into practice.

Each part of this book begins with a discussion of its purpose, its learning objectives, and the contribution that each article makes to the achievement of the objectives. Thus, the student will know at the outset where he or she is going and how to get there. Also each article begins with a brief summary. The questions at the end of each article will stimulate the student's thinking and may be used for class discussions. In addition, the test bank for the Fourth Edition of *Marketing Today* includes multiple-choice questions based on these articles.

Although *Readings in Marketing Today* is specifically designed to be integrated with the principles text *Marketing Today*, it would be a valuable supplement to any of the other leading principles texts or it could be used alone to enhance the understanding of marketing concepts. The following table provides a key that links each of the articles in this book to appropriate chapters in the Fourth Edition of *Marketing Today*.

v

CHAPTERS IN TEXTBOOK
AND RELATED ARTICLES IN READER

Marketing Today	Readings in Marketing Today	
Chapter No.	Part No.	Selection No.
1	One	1, 5
2	One	5
3	One Two Seven	4 5 5
4	Two	2
5	One Two	2, 3, 4 1, 2, 3
6	Two	3
7	Two	4
8	Three Four Seven	1 3, 5 6
9	Three	2, 3
10	Two Four Seven	2 2 4
11	Four	1, 4
12	Four	5
13	Four	4
14	Four	1, 5
15	Five	1
16	Five	2, 3
17	Five	4, 5
18	Six	5
19	Six	1, 2, 3, 4
20	Seven	2
21	Seven	1, 3, 4
22	Seven	1, 5

John T. Mentzer
Forrest S. Carter

Contents

TWO

THREE

3

5

Price-Cost Planning   352
C. Davis Fogg and Kent H. Kohnken

SEVEN

Other Marketing Considerations   367

1

Marketing Issues   369
Stephen Greyser

2

Market Expansion Strategies in Multinational Marketing   377
Igal Ayal and Jehiel Zif

3

Responsible Marketing in an Expanded Marketing Concept   396
Leland L. Beik and Warren A. French

4

Strategies for Introducing Marketing into Nonprofit Organizations   408
Philip Kotler

5

Are You Really Planning Your Marketing?   424
Leon Winer

6

Coke's Big Marketing Blitz   440
Business Week

PART ONE

What Is Marketing?

Marketing is a basic, dynamic aspect of social behavior, and everyone participates in or is affected by some type of marketing activity. Ironically, the pervasiveness of marketing and the widespread familiarity with some marketing activities make it difficult to characterize the term in a single definition. The consequences of applying marketing principles are often confused with the underlying principle; for example, selling and advertising are often considered synonymous with marketing rather than components of marketing. The articles in Part One characterize marketing and will provide a better understanding of the meaning of the term.

The first article, "Marketing: The New Priority," gives an overview of the problems facing American firms and those expected to occur in the future and of the key role that marketing plays in the solution to those problems. Students should gain some appreciation of how important marketing is and how some firms are using marketing to solve the complex problems of their competitive environment.

"Marketing Myopia," the second article, is an important conceptual paper that helped usher in the era of the "marketing concept." The marketing concept focuses the firm's resources on the satisfaction of customer needs, and satisfying those needs becomes the primary objective of all its operations. The articles "Putting Customer Demands First" and "Behind the Profit Squeeze at the New York Times" provide examples of successful implementations of the marketing concept.

Finally, the many perspectives of marketing and the broad scope of its impact on society are discussed and placed in a useful and systematic framework in "The Nature and Scope of Marketing." The student is not provided with a single, all-encompassing definition of marketing, but rather a model that uses three basic dimensions to classify marketing activities.

The overall purpose of Part One is to provide different perspectives on what marketing entails. The variety of these perspectives will allow the reader to look beyond those functional areas that are usually visible to consumers and discover the fundamentals of marketing.

1

MARKETING: THE NEW PRIORITY

Business Week

This selection presents marketing as the key ingredient for success. Several examples are given of firms seeking to satisfy market demand and perform the associated marketing tasks.

Question: What do John Sculley and James J. Morgan have in common? Answer: Each is an experienced, highly regarded consumer goods marketer who has recently moved to a top job at a large corporation. Sculley, an alumnus of PepsiCo Inc., is now president of Apple Computer Inc. Morgan, who came from Philip Morris Inc., is chairman of Atari Inc. In the past, Apple and Atari had concentrated more on developing new technologies than on understanding the dynamics of the marketplace—and suffered because of it. The recruitment of Sculley and Morgan is one of the more visible signs that marketing has become the new corporate priority.

Vast economic and social changes have made better marketing an imperative. Realization of that fact has set off a near free-for-all in recruiting circles for successful marketers, now hotter prospects for high-level jobs than executives with financial experience. Companies of every stripe are looking for managers, presidents, or chief executive officers who can not only develop long-term product strategies but also instill an entrepreneurial spirit into corporations that, more often than not, practice risk-avoidance.

NO BEAN COUNTERS. Says Gerard R. Roche, chairman of Heidrick & Struggles, a top recruiting firm: "Nobody wants bean counters now. Everybody wants a president with marketing experience—someone who knows about product life cycles and developing product strategies." James R. McManus, chairman of Marketing Corp. of America, a consulting firm, agrees: "Today, companies realize that their raw material, labor, and physical-

3

resource costs are all screwed down and that the only option for dramatic improvement will come from doing a better marketing job."

As companies define marketing more clearly, they no longer confuse it with advertising, which uses media to let consumers know that a certain product or service is available. In essence, marketing means moving goods from the producer to the consumer. It starts with finding out what consumers want or need, and then assessing whether the product can be made and sold at a profit. Such decisions require conducting preliminary research, market identification, and product development; testing consumer reaction to both product and price; working out production capacities and costs; determining distribution; and then deciding on advertising and promotion strategies.

Simple as those steps may sound, many of them were all but forgotten in the 1970s, when inflation kept sales pacing upward and marketing was of secondary importance. Corporate strategies emphasized acquisitions, cash management, or the pursuit of overseas markets. Then came the recession, with its stranglehold on consumer spending, and companies were forced into trying to understand what made the domestic marketplace tick. They soon discovered that demographic and lifestyle changes had delivered a death blow to mass marketing and brand loyalty. A nation that once shared homogeneous buying tastes had splintered into many different consumer groups—each with special needs and interests.

The emergence of this fragmented consumer population, together with an array of economic factors—intense international competition, the impact of rapid technological change, the maturing or stagnation of certain markets, and deregulation—has altered the shape of competition. "If you have to change how to compete, then all of a sudden marketing is a very important function," says Robert D. Buzzell, a Harvard University School of Business Administration professor who specializes in strategic market planning.

RALLYING CRY.   Robert L. Barney, chairman and CEO of Wendy's International Inc., understands this all too well. "The main thrust today is taking business away from the competition, and that fact, more than any other, is modifying our business," he explains. To pick up market share, the fast-food and hamburger chain is trying to build up its breakfast and dinner business, to achieve greater store efficiencies, and to introduce a slew of new products that will attract a broader spectrum of consumers. Wendy's has not only raised its ad budget by 45% but also increased its marketing staff to 70 from 10 five years ago. "You have to out-execute the competition, and that's why marketing is more important than ever before," asserts Barney.

The realization that marketing will provide the cutting edge in the 1980s not only has hit well-known packaged goods marketers—such as Procter &

Gamble, Coca-Cola, and General Foods—but is affecting industries that used to be protected from the vagaries of consumer selling by regulatory statutes. Airlines, banks, and financial-services groups are looking for ways to grow and prosper in an environment of product proliferation, advertising clutter, escalating marketing costs, and—despite advances in research and testing—a dauntingly high rate of new-product failures.

With marketing the new priority, market research is the rallying cry. Companies are trying frantically to get their hands on information that identifies and explains the needs of the powerful new consumer segments now being formed. Kroger Co., for example, holds more than 250,000 consumer interviews a year to define consumer wants more precisely. Some companies are pinning their futures to product innovations, others are rejuvenating timeworn but proven brands, and still others are doing both.

Unquestionably, the companies that emerge successfully from this marketing morass will be those that understand the new consumer environment. In years past, the typical American family consisted of a working dad, a homemaker mom, and two kids. But the 1980 census revealed that only 7% of the 82 million households then surveyed fit that description. Of those families that reported children under the age of 17, 54% of the mothers worked full- or part-time outside their homes. Smaller households now predominate: More than 50% of all households comprise only one or two persons.

MEN ALONE.   Even more startling, and most overlooked, is the fact that 24% of all households are now headed by singles. This fastest-growing segment of all—up some 80% over the previous decade—expanded mainly because the number of men living alone increased. Some 20% of households include persons 65 or older, a group that will grow rapidly. Already, almost one out of six Americans is over age 55.

These statistics are significant to marketers. "It means that the mass market has splintered and that companies can't sell their products the way they used to," says Laurel Cutler, executive vice-president for market planning at Leber Katz Partners, an advertising agency that specializes in new products. "The largest number of households may fall into two-wage-earner grouping, but that includes everyone from a manicurist to a Wall Street type—and that's really too diverse in lifestyle and income to qualify as a mass market." Cutler foresees "every market breaking into smaller and smaller units, with unique products aimed at defined segments."

Even the auto makers agree. "We've treated the car market as a mass one, but now I'm convinced that concept is dead," says Lloyd E. Reuss, general manager of General Motors Corp.'s Buick Motor Div. Reuss now believes in target marketing: specific products and ads aimed at selected groups.

CANNED HEALTH.   Despite this segmentation, there is enormous common interest in convenience, service, health, cost, and quality. Some companies have already translated these desires into successful products. Makers of soft drinks sell caffeine- and sugar-free products to health- and calorie-conscious consumers. Diet and low-salt foods have found a small but growing number of takers, and so too have high-quality frozen entrées. Robert A. Fox, the first marketing-oriented CEO in Del Monte Corp.'s 65-year history, has wasted little time getting the company into fancy frozen-food products. And he has repositioned its existing line of canned vegetables and fruits as low-salt and low-sugar items.

Philadelphia's ARA Services Inc. offers the patrons of its workplace cafeterias the option of picking up full dinners for consumption at home. It has also acquired a day-care operation and expanded the number of centers from 40, in 1980, to more than 150. "Changing demographics have a tremendous influence on the services we provide," affirms Joseph Neubauer, ARA's CEO. He says the changes have given marketing "one of the key roles—if not the key one—in corporate strategy."

As families and dwellings grow smaller, the need for more compact products and packages grows more pressing. General Electric Co. downsized its microwave oven and then modeled it to hang beneath kitchen cabinets, thereby freeing valuable counter space. The result: GE went from an also-ran in this category to a strong No. 2.

HOW-TO DATA.   Yet many new consumer segments are not being mined. Men, for instance, are probably the most ignored of all buying groups—especially for household items. A recent study by Langer Associates Inc. found that men living alone are indeed interested in furniture, cooking, and cleaning and resented their "domestic dummy" stereotype. What they wanted, and what they were not getting, was straightforward how-to information from peer figures.

Teenagers, too, have become a much larger shopping force. A Yankelovich, Skelly & White Inc. poll, undertaken with *Seventeen* magazine, found that nearly 75% of teenage girls with working mothers now regularly shop for groceries. Yet few companies try to reach this group to sell anything but games, records, and clothes.

Many companies still gear their products and ads to 18-to-34-year-olds, who dominated the marketplace of the 1970s but have been supplanted in power and size by the 25-to-45-year-olds [see Figure 1]. "Youth reflected everything we did as a culture for a long time, but that's not where the bulge is today," says Paula Drillman, executive vice-president and director of research at McCann-Erickson Inc.

This means that companies must sell to an older, better-educated consumer who regards the marketplace with a jaundiced eye. Drillman, for one, believes that this skepticism accounts for the slow growth of brands in such industries as liquor. "The shopper is saying, 'Why should I pay so much more for Smirnoff when all I do is put it in a glass and mix it with something? Vodka is vodka is vodka.'"

This indifference to brands is partly the result of the massive proliferation of consumer goods. In an attempt to fire up sales, companies have been swamping the market with new products and line extensions backed by ads, coupons, giveaways, and sweepstakes. For instance, of the 261 varieties of cigarettes for sale today, about half are 10 years old or less.

ME, TOO. This huge influx of products has shifted the balance of power from manufacturers to retailers. Lawrence C. Burns, a partner with the Cambridge

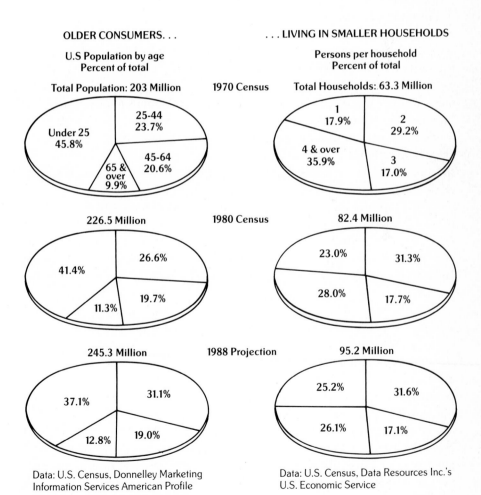

OLDER CONSUMERS. . .

U.S Population by age
Percent of total

Total Population: 203 Million

Under 25
45.8%

25-44
23.7%

45-64
20.6%

65 & over
9.9%

226.5 Million

41.4%

26.6%

19.7%

11.3%

245.3 Million

37.1%

31.1%

19.0%

12.8%

1970 Census

1980 Census

1988 Projection

. . . LIVING IN SMALLER HOUSEHOLDS

Persons per household
Percent of total

Total Households: 63.3 Million

1
17.9%

2
29.2%

4 & over
35.9%

3
17.0%

82.4 Million

23.0%

31.3%

28.0%

17.7%

95.2 Million

25.2%

31.6%

26.1%

17.1%

Data: U.S. Census, Donnelley Marketing Information Services American Profile

Data: U.S. Census, Data Resources Inc.'s U.S. Economic Service

FIGURE 1 *The Changing Market*

Group, a Chicago firm of marketing consultants, finds that "stores are eliminating slow movers and won't take on any new products unless they are assured of good inventory turns and margins. They want proof that a product really is a success, and the only way companies can provide that is through more regional roll-outs and more test marketing."

But achieving those affirmative results is more difficult because so many of the offerings are basically parity items. Says Robert E. Jacoby, chairman and CEO of Ted Bates Worldwide Inc.: "We seem to be experiencing a never-ending flow of me-too products or line extensions, which makes it difficult to make a unique claim about the product." Roy Grace, chairman and executive creative director of Doyle Dane Bernbach Inc., seconds that view. He comments, "If a new technology appears, most companies can quickly copy it or acquire it. So it's really hard to gain a competitive advantage."

Examples of this difficulty abound. Aseptic packaging, a technology for putting food and drinks in specially prepared foil or cardboard pouches that require no refrigeration, has been embraced by nearly all juice makers during the past 18 months. And after the Food & Drug Administration ruled last summer that aspartame, a natural sweetener, could be used in soft drinks, all the major manufacturers raced to reformulate their diet brands to include it. Even Procter & Gamble Co. is easing up on its age-old philosophy of testing a product for years and bringing it to market only when convinced that some claim of superiority can be made. P&G has rushed its Citrus Hill brand into the spurting orange-juice category, even though it admits it cannot make any unique claims for the juice.

The result is a vicious cycle. With the plethora of new choices, products have much shorter life spans, so a steady flow of new items is needed to keep sales curving upward. "The number of entrants in a given category has increased, and the implication is that there is greater market segmentation and shorter product life cycles," points out Derwyn F. Phillips, executive vice-president at Gillette North America. "And we find ourselves really working hard at projecting a given brand's life cycle—when the bell curve is likely to peak and the point at which it is no longer intelligent to support a given brand."

Phillips says that Gillette is now trying to speed up new-product development to prevent its combined market share in a category from shrinking. Half of the company's $2.2 billion revenues last year came from products that did not exist five years ago.

Despite advances in the technology of testing, the level of new-product casualties remains astonishingly high. Two out of three new entries still fail—the same proportion as in the 1960s—while the cost of introducing a new item has skyrocketed. An outlay of some $50 million is needed to launch a national brand in a major category. P&G is said to be spending almost $100 million to roll out Citrus Hill orange juice.

ANALYSIS PARALYSIS.   At those odds and prices, companies are understandably wary about committing themselves to high-risk endeavors. They are demanding more research, more strategic planning, and more "review" committees to weed out problems. More often than not, however, the result of all these checks is total confusion and inactivity. Ellen I. Metcalf, a senior consultant with Arthur D. Little Inc., reports: "In some companies, you can spend six weeks going through psychographics, trend-line analysis, quarterly consumer reports, scanner data from grocery products—rooms just full of data. Then you ask, 'How do you use this information?' And they say they don't know what to do with it."

Ad agencies, in particular, resent the analysis-paralysis climate. "There are more and more people [at a company] who can say no and very few who can say yes," laments Barry Loughrane, president and CEO of Doyle Dane. This risk-avoidance atmosphere worries Allen G. Rosenshine, chairman and CEO of ad agency Batten Barton Durstine & Osborn Inc. "Everyone has developed a corporate timidity." That, along with the B-school mentality—quantify everything, take few chances—is threatening the entrepreneurialism that companies need if they are to grow, he feels.

But the outlook may not be altogether bleak. Enlightened companies have recognized the challenge and are radically overhauling their operations to put more emphasis on marketing, seeking top marketing executives, and changing the nature and scope of their jobs. Lester B. Korn, chairman of Korn/Ferry International, says he recently filled the top marketing slot at a major consumer goods company—a $350,000-a-year post that typifies the trend to give marketing more clout. "Companies want marketing executives to be responsible for total business results—they're putting the profit-and-loss in with the job—and that's a big step forward from the past, when they had only been responsible for volume and share growth," he says. Companies hope to create a culture that encourages more risk-taking, accepts some failures, and rewards success.

The hottest companies to recruit from are P&G, Johnson & Johnson, Philip Morris, General Foods, and Thomas J. Lipton—large, disciplined consumer product marketers with broad product lines. "These companies teach their people how to create profitable product lines in brutally competitive industries, and their consistency is what makes them so attractive," says J. Gerald Simmons, president of Handy Associates Inc.

SUPPORT SYSTEMS.   Some executive-search specialists express reservations, however, about placing a P&Ger. "Their support system is just so strong that they end up working for the system rather than being creative," says David S. Joys, executive vice-president of Russell Reynolds Associates Inc. "Many clients prefer that a P&G executive go to another company first, and then they'll go after him."

Today, most companies believe that their brightest chances for success in coming years will hinge on the development of innovative products aimed at specific consumer niches. But because of the risks, they are trying to direct development efforts toward producing related items in order to achieve economies of scale and a greater overall market share. "You have to go into areas where you have some right to be in that category," says McManus of Marketing Corp. "Companies that go with a product in search of a market or one that has no fit with their existing businesses are doomed to a bloody nose."

Hershey Foods Corp. learned that very lesson when it tried to get into the canned-frosting business. Hershey's problem: It did not have a cake mix to support its frosting, unlike its chief competitors, General Mills, P&G, and Pillsbury. These rivals discounted the frosting and made up the difference on the cake batter. Hershey, with no companion product to fall back on, had to discount its product to stay in the market. "The competition was suicidal, and while we could have stayed in the market, it wouldn't have been prudent," says Jack Dowd, Hershey Chocolate Co.'s vice-president for new-product development. "But you've got to have the right to fail."

The company has recouped with its new Hershey's chocolate milk, packaged in a rich brown container that makes chocoholics drool in anticipation. Hershey had planned to have the chocolate milk in four markets by the end of the year, but strong demand has already put it in 12 cities, and the figure is growing.

HANG WITH IT.   To minimize the risk of failure with new products, experts make several recommendations. "Companies need to have a high-level executive who will champion the new creation—hang with it—and move fast," says Cutler of Leber Katz, which since 1969 has helped clients develop 10 major brands, including Vantage brand cigarettes, with no failures. "It's vital to get a pilot product up quickly, test consumers' reactions to it, refine it, and get it going."

Speed, however, is not the hallmark of many companies. Up to seven years can elapse between the time a new product is proposed and its nationwide distribution. A product developed in 1976 may meet with wholly different market conditions when it finally makes its debut in 1983. "Developing a new product is like shooting a duck," observes Gary W. McQuaid, marketing vice-president at Hershey's. "You can't shoot it where it is; you've got to shoot it where it's going to be."

Aiming too far ahead of the market is just as risky, of course. But for some companies, such as auto makers, the lengthy time it takes to develop a new product leaves no choice. "When we commit to a car, we're four years away from production," says F. James McDonald, GM's president. "How many people today know what they want four years from now? We really have to roll some dice."

The task of understanding and predicting consumer behavior has led to a nearly insatiable hunger for market research. But experts in the field caution companies about switching from one new technique to another, and they suggest that keeping a steady information base will allow for more accurate projections and comparisons with previous years. Cutler believes that new products often misfire because they "are assigned to junior people at either the company or agency level, since the most experienced people do not want to take their eyes off the main brands. But it is imperative that the team have broad knowledge and have clout—in order to see the new product through review committees and then to get it on the shelf."

Given the slim odds for scoring a new-product hit, many executives are trying to breathe new life into dying brands. "There are dozens of older brands lying around that have been neglected over the years," says Chester Kane, president of Kane, Bortree & Associates, a new-product consulting group. "Companies must discover ways to make them viable for today's consumer."

RIGHT GUARD REBORN. Gillette is trying for just such a comeback with its Right Guard deodorant, which dropped from a huge 25% share of the deodorant market in the mid-1960s to 8% today. The company was loath to let the bronze-canned brand die, since it had produced $500 million in profits during its 23-year life span. For the past two years, all departments—research, marketing, research and development, manufacturing, sales, and finance—as well as the product's ad agency, Young & Rubicam Inc., have been getting together monthly to coordinate plans for rejuvenating Right Guard. Last June, Gillette put the deodorant into new, bold-stripe containers and began a $28.2 million ad campaign—the most expensive in the company's 82 years. Gillette says the deodorant sales are running 14% higher than planned.

Whether a product is new, old, or rejuvenated, the task facing all marketers is to differentiate it from competitors' offerings. The consumer must be made aware of its usefulness and given a reason to choose it over all other brands. "The financial-services companies are having trouble with this," remarks Russell Reynolds' Joys. "They all want a product portfolio that matches the competitors' offerings, but they also must come up with unique products—carrying higher gross margins—for the salesmen to really focus on."

Federated Department Stores Inc. is grappling with these issues. Fearful that its core department stores were losing their identity with consumers because of the rapid growth of designer labels and discounters, it has set up a buying office for the purpose of creating private-label goods that would be sold only in its better stores. As a first step, the company has brought out a line of sheets and towels under the "Home Concept" name. The idea is to develop unique, high-quality merchandise that carries a higher profit margin and is different from anything a consumer could buy at a rival department store or discounter—even a Federated-owned one, such as Gold Circle Stores.

Advertising plays a major role in carving out distinct identities for consumer products. The push is on for harder-hitting, product-selling ads and the increased use of sales-promotion devices, such as direct mail and rebates. Broadcast television is still the preferred medium, because cable is not yet in enough homes, and viewership data are still too sketchy to make it efficient as an audience-target device. However, specialty publications are getting more play from companies that wish to reach a particular market group—usually a working population that may not have the time to read more general media or watch TV.

NUKES AND BAGELS. Furthermore, companies are consolidating their accounts at a few full-service agencies, rather than letting a number of agencies handle various brands. They are doing this on the theory that the more important an account is to an agency, the higher the quality of attention the client is likely to receive. Then, too, that policy promotes efficiency and more unified marketing, especially for companies that sell overseas. To capitalize on the consolidation trend, Bates has centralized in New York its operations for key multinational clients, including Colgate-Palmolive Co. and Mars Inc. The strategy is to develop "benchmark ads" that can be launched in the U.S. and then adapted for use all over the world.

The need to reorganize corporate priorities to meet the changing marketplace has caused several companies—quietly and almost surreptitiously—to start their own in-house venture-capital operations. Companies such as Seagrams, R. J. Reynolds, and Gillette have begun either funding or acquiring small, diverse businesses in market segments that hold promise. By experimenting in areas as disparate as nuclear medicine (Seagrams) and bagel chains (Reynolds), these companies can explore the intricacies of the medical or fast-food businesses—categories that are likely to become increasingly important—with little risk.

Gillette North America's just-begun ventures council—composed of its domestic divisional presidents and three corporate executives—has been charged with ferreting out opportunities, not necessarily in the consumer packaged-goods area. "The level of maturity of some of our businesses says to us that it is very important that we invest dollars today to grow higher-yield businesses for tomorrow," says Gillette's Phillips. "We are trying to motivate people inside and outside the company to help us develop new opportunities for the future."

QUESTIONS

1. What environmental and economic factors have helped initiate the recent emphasis on marketing?
2. Define "marketing," "advertising," and "selling." Distinguish each term from the others.
3. Now that marketing is the major priority of many firms, what are these firms doing differently?
4. Why are successful new products so important to the marketing process?
5. What objectives and management perspective should marketing-oriented chief executive officers have?

2

MARKETING MYOPIA

Theodore Levitt

*The need to focus on customer needs
rather than on products is substantiated
in this article. The success and growth
of a firm is linked to its ability to define
its business broadly and in terms of
benefits provided to customers.*

Every major industry was once a growth industry. But some that are now riding a wave of growth enthusiasm are very much in the shadow of decline. Others which are thought of as seasoned growth industries have actually stopped growing. In every case the reason growth is threatened, slowed, or stopped is *not* because the market is saturated. It is because there has been a failure of management.

FATEFUL PURPOSES.   The failure is at the top. The executives responsible for it, in the last analysis, are those who deal with broad aims and policies. Thus:

The railroads did not stop growing because the need for passenger and freight transportation declined. That grew. The railroads are in trouble today not because the need was filled by others (cars, trucks, airplanes, even telephones), but because it was *not* filled by the railroads themselves. They let others take customers away from them because they assumed themselves to be in the railroad business rather than in the transportation business. The reason they defined their industry wrong was because they were railroad-oriented instead of transportation-oriented; they were product-oriented instead of customer-oriented.

Hollywood barely escaped being totally ravished by television. Actually, all the established film companies went through drastic reorganizations. Some simply disappeared. All of them got into trouble not because of TV's inroads but because of their own myopia. As with the railroads, Hollywood defined its business incorrectly. It thought it was in the movie business when it was actually in the entertainment business. "Movies" implied a specific, limited product. This produced a fatuous contentment which from the beginning led producers to view TV as a threat. Hollywood scorned and rejected TV when it should have welcomed it as an opportunity—an opportunity to expand the entertainment business.

Today TV is a bigger business than the old narrowly defined movie business ever was. Had Hollywood been customer-oriented (providing entertainment), rather than product-oriented (making movies), would it have gone through the fiscal purgatory that it did? I doubt it. What ultimately saved Hollywood and accounted for its recent resurgence was the wave of new young writers, producers, and directors whose previous successes in television had decimated the old movie companies and toppled the big movie moguls.

There are other less obvious examples of industries that have been and are now endangering their futures by improperly defining their purposes. I shall discuss some in detail later and analyze the kind of policies that lead to trouble. Right now it may help to show what a thoroughly customer-oriented management *can* do to keep a growth industry growing, even after the obvious opportunities have been exhausted; and here there are two examples that have been around for a long time. They are nylon and glass—specifically, E. I. duPont de Nemours & Company and Corning Glass Works.

Both companies have great technical competence. Their product orientation is unquestioned. But this alone does not explain their success. After all, who was more pridefully product-oriented and product-conscious than the erstwhile New England textile companies that have been so thoroughly massacred? The DuPonts and the Cornings have succeeded not primarily because of their product or research orientation but because they have been thoroughly customer-oriented also. It is constant watchfulness for opportunities to apply their technical knowhow to the creation of customer-satisfying uses which accounts for their prodigious output of successful new products. Without a very sophisticated eye on the customer, most of their new products might have been wrong, their sales methods useless.

Aluminum has also continued to be a growth industry, thanks to the efforts of two wartime-created companies which deliberately set about creating new customer-satisfying uses. Without Kaiser Aluminum & Chemical Corporation and Reynolds Metals Company, the total demand for aluminum today would be vastly less.

ERROR OF ANALYSIS.   Some may argue that it is foolish to set the railroads off against aluminum or the movies off against glass. Are not aluminum and glass naturally so versatile that the industries are bound to have more growth opportunities than the railroads and movies? This view commits precisely the error I have been talking about. It defines an industry, or a product, or a cluster or know-how so narrowly as to guarantee its premature senescence. When we mention "railroads," we should make sure we mean "transporation." As transporters, the railroads still have a good chance for a very considerable growth. They are not limited to the railroad business as such (though in my opinion rail transportation is potentially a much stronger transportation medium than is generally believed).

What the railroads lack is not opportunity, but some of the same managerial imaginativeness and audacity that made them great. Even an amateur like Jacques Barzun can see what is lacking when he says:

"I grieve to see the most advanced physical and social organization of the last century go down in shabby disgrace for lack of the same comprehensive imagination that built it up. [What is lacking is] the will of the companies to survive and to satisfy the public by inventiveness and skill."[1]

Shadow of Obsolescence

It is impossible to mention a single major industry that did not at one time qualify for the magic appellation of "growth industry." In each case its assumed strength lay in the apparently unchallenged superiority of its product. There appeared to be no effective substitute for it. It was itself a runaway substitute for the product it so triumphantly replaced. Yet one after another of these celebrated industries has come under a shadow. Let us look briefly at a few more of them, this time taking examples that have so far received a little less attention:

Dry cleaning—This was once a growth industry with lavish prospects. In an age of wool garments, imagine being finally able to get them safely and easily clean. The boom was on.

Yet here we are 30 years after the boom started and the industry is in trouble. Where has the competition come from? From a better way of cleaning? No. It has come from synthetic fibers and chemical additives that have cut the need for dry cleaning. But this is only the beginning. Lurking in the wings and ready to make chemical dry cleaning totally obsolescent is that powerful magician, ultrasonics.

Electric utilities—This is another one of those supposedly "no-substitute" products that has been enthroned on a pedestal of invincible growth. When the incandescent lamp came along, kerosene lights were finished. Later the water wheel and the steam engine were cut to ribbons by the flexibility, reliability, simplicity, and just plain easy availability of electric motors. The prosperity of electric utilities continues to wax extravagant as the home is converted into a museum of electric gadgetry. How can anybody miss by investing in utilities, with no competition, nothing but growth ahead?

---

[1] Jacques Barzun, "Trains and the Mind of Man," *Holiday*, February 1960, p. 21.

But a second look is not quite so comforting. A score of nonutility companies are well advanced toward developing a powerful chemical fuel cell which could sit in some hidden closet of every home silently ticking off electric power. The electric lines that vulgarize so many neighborhoods will be eliminated. So will the endless demolition of streets and service interruptions during storms. Also on the horizon is solar energy, again pioneered by nonutility companies.

Who says that the utilities have no competition? They may be natural monopolies now, but tomorrow they may be natural deaths. To avoid this prospect, they too will have to develop fuel cells, solar energy, and other power sources. To survive, they themselves will have to plot the obsolescence of what now produces their livelihood.

Grocery stores—Many people find it hard to realize that there ever was a thriving establishment known as the "corner grocery store." The supermarket has taken over with a powerful effectiveness. Yet the big food chains of the 1930s narrowly escaped being completely wiped out by the aggressive expansion of independent supermarkets. The first genuine supermarket was opened in 1930, in Jamaica, Long Island. By 1933 supermarkets were thriving in California, Ohio, Pennsylvania, and elsewhere. Yet the established chains pompously ignored them. When they chose to notice them, it was with such derisive descriptions as "cheapy," "horse-and-buggy," "cracker-barrel storekeeping," and "unethical opportunists."

The executive of one big chain announced at the time that he found it "hard to believe that people will drive for miles to shop for foods and sacrifice the personal service chains have perfected and to which Mrs. Consumer is accustomed."[2] As late as 1936, the National Wholesale Grocers convention and the New Jersey Retail Grocers Association said there was nothing to fear. They said that the supers' narrow appeal to the price buyer limited the size of their market. They had to draw from miles around. When imitators came, there would be wholesale liquidations as volume fell. The current high sales of the supers was said to be partly due to their novelty. Basically people wanted convenient neighborhood grocers. If the neighborhood stores "cooperate with their suppliers, pay attention to their costs, and improve their service," they would be able to weather the competition until it blew over.[3]

It never blew over. The chains discovered that survival required going into the supermarket business. This meant the wholesale destruction of their huge investments in corner store sites and in established distribution and merchandising methods. The companies with "the courage of their convic-

---

[2] For more details see M. M. Zimmerman, *The Super Market: A Revolution in Distribution* (New York, McGraw-Hill Book Company, Inc., 1955), p. 48.

[3] Ibid., pp. 45–47.

tions" resolutely stuck to the corner store philosophy. They kept their pride but lost their shirts.

SELF-DECEIVING CYCLE.   But memories are short. For example, it is hard for people who today confidently hail the twin messiahs of electronics and chemicals to see how things could possibly go wrong with these galloping industries. They probably also cannot see how a reasonably sensible business-man could have been as myopic as the famous Boston millionaire who 50 years ago unintentionally sentenced his heirs to poverty by stipulating that his entire estate be forever invested exclusively in electric streetcar securities. His posthumous declaration, "There will always be a big demand for efficient urban transportation," is no consolation to his heirs who sustain life by pumping gasoline at automobile filling stations.

Yet, in a casual survey I recently took among a group of intelligent business executives, nearly half agreed that it would be hard to hurt their heirs by tying their estates forever to the electronics industry. When I then confronted them with the Boston streetcar example, they chorused unani-mously, "That's different!" But is it? Is not the basic situation identical?

In truth, *there is no such thing* as a growth industry, I believe. There are only companies organized and operated to create and capitalize on growth opportunities. Industries that assume themselves to be riding some automatic growth escalator invariably descend into stagnation. The history of every dead and dying "growth" industry shows a self-deceiving cycle of bountiful expansion and undetected decay. There are four conditions which usually guarantee this cycle:

1. The belief that growth is assured by an expanding and more affluent population.
2. The belief that there is no competitive substitute for the industry's major product.
3. Too much faith in mass production and in the advantages of rapidly declining unit costs as output rises.
4. Preoccupation with a product that lends itself to carefully controlled scientific experimentation, improvement, and manufacturing cost reduction.

I should like now to begin examining each of these conditions in some detail. To build my case as boldly as possible, I shall illustrate the points with reference to three industries—petroleum, automobiles, and electronics—particularly petroleum, because it spans more years and more vicissitudes. Not only do these three have excellent reputations with the general public and also enjoy the confidence of sophisticated investors, but their managements have become known for progressive thinking in areas like financial control, product research, and management training. If obsolescence can cripple even these industries, it can happen anywhere.

Population Myth

The belief that profits are assured by an expanding and more affluent population is dear to the heart of every industry. It takes the edge off the apprehensions everybody understandably feels about the future. If consumers are multiplying and also buying more of your product or service, you can face the future with considerably more comfort than if the market is shrinking. An expanding market keeps the manufacturer from having to think very hard or imaginatively. If thinking is an intellectual response to a problem, then the absence of a problem leads to the absence of thinking. If your product has an automatically expanding market, then you will not give much thought to how to expand it.

One of the most interesting examples of this is provided by the petroleum industry. Probably our oldest growth industry, it has an enviable record. While there are some current apprehensions about its growth rate, the industry itself tends to be optimistic.

But I believe it can be demonstrated that it is undergoing a fundamental yet typical change. It is not only ceasing to be a growth industry, but may actually be a declining one, relative to other business. Although there is widespread unawareness of it, I believe that within 25 years the oil industry may find itself in much the same position of retrospective glory that the railroads are now in. Despite its pioneering work in developing and applying the present-value method of investment evaluation, in employee relations, and in working with backward countries, the petroleum business is a distressing example of how complacency and wrongheadedness can stubbornly convert opportunity into near disaster.

One of the characteristics of this and other industries that have believed very strongly in the beneficial consequences of an expanding population, while at the same time being industries with a generic product for which there has appeared to be no competitive substitute, is that the individual companies have sought to outdo their competitors by improving on what they are already doing. This makes sense, of course, if one assumes that sales are tied to the country's population strings, because the customer can compare products only on a feature-by-feature basis. I believe it is significant, for example, that not since John D. Rockefeller sent free kerosense lamps to China has the oil industry done anything really outstanding to create a demand for its product. Not even in product improvement has it showered itself with eminence. The greatest single improvement—namely, the development of tetraethyl lead— came from outside the industry, specifically from General Motors and DuPont. The big contributions made by the industry itself are confined to the technology of oil exploration, production, and refining.

ASKING FOR TROUBLE.   In other words, the industry's efforts have focused on improving the *efficiency* of getting and making its product, not really on improving the generic product or its marketing. Moreover, its chief product has continuously been defined in the narrowest possible terms, namely, gasoline, not energy, fuel, or transportation. This attitude has helped assure that:

- Major improvements in gasoline quality tend not to originate in the oil industry. Also, the development of superior alternative fuels comes from outside the oil industry, as will be shown later.
- Major innovations in automobile fuel marketing are originated by small new oil companies that are not primarily preoccupied with production or refining. These are the companies that have been responsible for the rapidly expanding multipump gasoline stations, with their successful emphasis on large and clean layouts, rapid and efficient driveway service, and quality gasoline at low prices.

Thus, the oil industry is asking for trouble from outsiders. Sooner or later, in this land of hungry inventors and entrepreneurs, a threat is sure to come. The possibilities of this will become more apparent when we turn to the next dangerous belief of many managements. For the sake of continuity, because this second belief is tied closely to the first, I shall continue with the same example.

IDEA OF INDISPENSABILITY.   The petroleum industry is pretty much persuaded that there is no competitive substitute for its major product, gasoline— or if there is, that it will continue to be a derivative of crude oil, such as diesel fuel or kerosene jet fuel.

There is a lot of automatic wishful thinking in this assumption. The trouble is that most refining companies own huge amounts of crude oil reserves. These have value only if there is a market for products into which oil can be converted—hence the tenacious belief in the continuing competitive superiority of automobile fuels made from crude oil.

This idea persists despite all historic evidence against it. The evidence not only shows that oil has never been a superior product for any purpose for very long, but it also shows that the oil industry has never really been a growth industry. It has been a succession of different businesses that have gone through the usual historic cycles of growth, maturity, and decay. Its overall survival is owed to a series of miraculous escapes from total obsolescence, of last-minute and unexpected reprieves from total disaster reminiscent of the Perils of Pauline.

PERILS OF PETROLEUM.   I shall sketch in only the main episodes.

First, crude oil was largely a patent medicine. But even before that fad ran out, demand was greatly expanded by the use of oil in kerosene lamps. The prospect of lighting the world's lamps gave rise to an extravagant promise of growth. The prospects were similar to those the industry now holds for gasoline in other parts of the world. It can hardly wait for the underdeveloped nations to get a car in every garage.

In the days of the kerosene lamp, the oil companies competed with each other and against gaslight by trying to improve the illuminating characteristics of kerosene. Then suddenly the impossible happened. Edison invented a light which was totally nondependent on crude oil. Had it not been for the growing use of kerosene in space heaters, the incandescent lamp would have completely finished oil as a growth industry at that time. Oil would have been good for little else than axle grease.

Then disaster and reprieve struck again. Two great innovations occurred, neither originating in the oil industry. The successful development of coal-burning domestic central-heating systems made the space heater obsolescent. While the industry reeled, along came its most magnificent boost yet—the internal combustion engine, also invented by outsiders. Then when the prodigious expansion for gasoline finally began to level off in the 1920s, along came the miraculous escape of a central oil heater. Once again, the escape was provided by an outsider's invention and development. And when that market weakened, wartime demand for aviation fuel came to the rescue. After the war the expansion of civilian aviation, the dieselization of railroads, and the explosive demand for cars and trucks kept the industry's growth in high gear.

Meanwhile, centralized oil heating—whose boom potential had only recently been proclaimed—ran into severe competition from natural gas. While the oil companies themselves owned the gas that now competed with their oil, the industry did not originate the natural gas revolution, nor has it to this day greatly profited from its gas ownership. The gas revolution was made by newly formed transmission companies that marketed the product with an aggressive ardor. They started a magnificent new industry, first against the advice and then against the resistance of the oil companies.

By all the logic of the situation, the oil companies themselves should have made the gas revolution. They not only owned the gas; they also were the only people experienced in handling, scrubbing, and using it, the only people experienced in pipeline technology and transmission, and they understood heating problems. But, partly because they knew that natural gas would compete with their own sale of heating oil, the oil companies pooh-poohed the potentials of gas.

The revolution was finally started by oil pipeline executives who, unable to persuade their own companies to go into gas, quit and organized the spectacularly successful gas transmission companies. Even after their success became painfully evident to the oil companies, the latter did not go into gas transmission. The multibillion dollar business which should have been theirs went to others. As in the past, the industry was blinded by its narrow preoccupation with a specific product and the value of its reserves. It paid little or no attention to its customers' basic needs and preferences.

The postwar years have not witnessed any change. Immediately after World War II the oil industry was greatly encouraged about its future by the rapid expansion of demand for its traditional line of products. In 1950 most companies projected annual rates of domestic expansion of around 6% through at least 1975. Though the ratio of crude oil reserves to demand in the Free World was about 20 to 1, with 10 to 1 being usually considered a reasonable working ratio in the United States, booming demand sent oil men searching for more without sufficient regard to what the future really promised. In 1952 they "hit" in the Middle East; the ratio skyrocketed to 42 to 1. If gross additions to reserves continue at the average rate of the past five years (37 billion barrels annually), then by 1970 the reserve ratio will be up to 45 to 1. This abundance of oil has weakened crude and product prices all over the world.

UNCERTAIN FUTURE.   Management cannot find much consolation today in the rapidly expanding petrochemical industry, another oil-using idea that did not originate in the leading firms. The total United States production of petrochemicals is equivalent to about 2% (by volume) of the demand for all petroleum products. Although the petrochemical industry is now expected to grow by about 10% per year, this will not offset other drains on the growth of crude oil consumption. Furthermore, while petrochemical products are many and growing, it is well to remember that there are nonpetroleum sources of the basic raw material, such as coal. Besides, a lot of plastics can be produced with relatively little oil. A 50,000-barrel-per-day oil refinery is now considered the absolute minimum size for efficiency. But a 5,000-barrel-per-day chemical plant is a giant operation.

Oil has never been a continuously strong growth industry. It has grown by fits and starts, always miraculously saved by innnovations and developments not of its own making. The reason it has not grown in a smooth progression is that each time it thought it had a superior product safe from the possibility of competitive substitutes, the product turned out to be inferior and notoriously subject to obsolescence. Until now, gasoline (for motor fuel, anyhow) has escaped this fate. But, as we shall see later, it too may be on its last legs.

The point of all this is that there is no guarantee against product obsolescence. If a company's own research does not make it obsolete, another's will. Unless an industry is especially lucky, as oil has been until now, it can easily go down in a sea of red figures—just as the railroads have, as the buggy whip manufacturers have, as the corner grocery chains have, as most of the big movie companies have, and indeed as many other industries have.

The best way for a firm to be lucky is to make its own luck. That requires knowing what makes a business successful. One of the greatest enemies of this knowledge is mass production.

Production Pressures

Mass-production industries are impelled by a great drive to produce all they can. The prospect of steeply declining unit costs as output rises is more than most companies can usually resist. The profit possibilities look spectacular. All effort focuses on production. The result is that marketing gets neglected.

John Kenneth Galbraith contends that just the opposite occurs.[4] Output is so prodigious that all effort concentrates on trying to get rid of it. He says this accounts for singing commercials, desecration of the countryside with advertising signs, and other wasteful and vulgar practices. Galbraith has a finger on something real, but he misses the strategic point. Mass production does indeed generate great pressure to "move" the product. But what usually gets emphasized is selling, not marketing. Marketing, being a more sophisticated and complex process, gets ignored.

The difference between marketing and selling is more than semantic. Selling focuses on the needs of the seller, marketing on the needs of the buyer. Selling is preoccupied with the seller's need to convert his product into cash, marketing with the idea of satisfying the needs of the customer by means of the product and the whole cluster of things associated with creating, delivering, and finally consuming it.

In some industries the enticements of full mass production have been so powerful that for many years top management in effect has told the sales departments, "You get rid of it; we'll worry about profits." By contrast, a truly marketing-minded firm tries to create value-satisfying goods and services that consumers will want to buy. What it offers for sale includes not only the generic product or service, but also how it is made available to the customer, in what form, when, under what conditions, and at what terms of trade. Most important, what it offers for sale is determined not by the seller but by the buyer. The seller takes his cues from the buyer in such a way that the product becomes a consequence of the marketing effort, not vice versa.

LAG IN DETROIT.   This may sound like an elementary rule of business, but that does not keep it from being violated wholesale. It is certainly more violated than honored. Take the automobile industry.

Here mass production is most famous, most honored, and has the greatest impact on the entire society. The industry has hitched its fortune to the

---

[4]*The Affluent Society* (Boston, Houghton Mifflin Company, 1958), pp. 152–160.

relentless requirements of the annual model change, a policy that makes customer orientation an especially urgent necessity. Consequently the auto companies annually spend millions of dollars on consumer research. But the fact that the new compact cars are selling so well in their first year indicates that Detroit's vast researches have for a long time failed to reveal what the customer really wanted. Detroit was not persuaded that he wanted anything different from what he had been getting until it lost millions of customers to other small car manufacturers.

How could this unbelievable lag behind customer wants have been perpetuated so long? Why did not research reveal consumer preferences before customers' buying decisions themselves revealed the facts? Is that not what consumer research is for—to find out before the fact what is going to happen? The answer is that Detroit never really researched the customer's wants. It only researched his preferences between the kinds of things which it had already decided to offer him. For Detroit is mainly product-oriented, not customer-oriented. To the extent that the customer is recognized as having needs that the manufacturer should try to satisfy, Detroit usually acts as if the job can be done entirely by product changes. Occasionally attention gets paid to financing, too, but that is done more in order to sell than to enable the customer to buy.

As for taking care of other customer needs, there is not enough being done to write about. The areas of the greatest unsatisfied needs are ignored, or at best get stepchild attention. These are at the point of sale and on the matter of automotive repair and maintenance. Detroit views these problem areas as being of secondary importance. That is underscored by the fact that the retailing and servicing ends of this industry are neither owned and operated nor controlled by the manufacturers. Once the car is produced, things are pretty much in the dealer's inadequate hands. Illustrative of Detroit's arm's-length attitude is the fact that, while servicing holds enormous sales-stimulating, profit-building opportunities, only 57 of Chevrolet's 7,000 dealers provide night maintenance service.

Motorists repeatedly express their dissatisfaction with servicing and their apprehensions about buying cars under the present selling setup. The anxieties and problems they encounter during the auto buying and mainte-nance processes are probably more intense and widespread today than 30 years ago. Yet the automobile companies do not *seem* to listen to or take their cues from the anguished consumer. If they do listen, it must be through the filter of their own preoccupation with production. The marketing effort is still viewed as a necessary consequence of the product, not vice versa, as it should be. That is the legacy of mass production, with its parochial view that profit resides essentially in low-cost full production.

WHAT FORD PUT FIRST.   The profit lure of mass production obviously has a place in the plans and strategy of business management, but it must always *follow* hard thinking about the customer. This is one of the most important lessons that we can learn from the contradictory behavior of Henry Ford. In a sense Ford was both the most brilliant and the most senseless marketer in American history. He was senseless because he refused to give the customer anything but a black car. He was brilliant because he fashioned a production system designed to fit market needs. We habitually celebrate him for the wrong reason, his production genius. His real genius was marketing. We think he was able to cut his selling price and therefore sell millions of $500 cars because his invention of the assembly line had reduced the costs. Actually he invented the assembly line because he had concluded that at $500 he could sell millions of cars. Mass production was the *result* not the cause of his low prices.

Ford repeatedly emphasized this point, but a nation of production-oriented business managers refuses to hear the great lesson he taught. Here is his operating philosophy as he expressed it succinctly:

"Our policy is to reduce the price, extend the operations, and improve the article. You will notice that the reduction of price comes first. We have never considered any costs as fixed. Therefore we first reduce the price to the point where we believe more sales will result. Then we go ahead and try to make the prices. We do not bother about the costs. The new price forces the costs down. The more usual way is to take the costs and then determine the price; and although that method may be scientific in the narrow sense, it is not scientific in the broad sense, because what earthly use is it to know the cost if it tells you that you cannot manufacture at a price at which the article can be sold? But more to the point is the fact that, although one may calculate what a cost is, and of course all of our costs are carefully calculated, no one knows what a cost ought to be. One of the ways of discovering . . . is to name a price so low as to force everybody in the place to the highest point of efficiency. The low price makes everybody dig for profits. We make more discoveries concerning manufacturing and selling under this forced method than by any method of leisurely investigation."[5]

PRODUCT PROVINCIALISM.   The tantalizing profit possibilities of low unit production costs may be the most seriously self-deceiving attitude that can afflict a company, particularly a "growth" company where an apparently assured expansion of demand already tends to undermine a proper concern for the importance of marketing and the customer.

---

[5] Henry Ford, *My Life and Work* (New York, Doubleday, Page & Company, 1923), pp. 146–147.

The usual result of this narrow preoccupation with so-called concrete matters is that instead of growing, the industry declines. It usually means that the product fails to adapt to the constantly changing patterns of consumer needs and tastes, to new and modified marketing institutions and practices, or to product developments in competing or complementary industries. The industry has its eyes so firmly on its own specific product that it does not see how it is being made obsolete.

The classical example of this is the buggy whip industry. No amount of product improvement could stave off its death sentence. But had the industry defined itself as being in the transportation business rather than the buggy whip business, it might have survived. It would have done what survival always entails, that is, changing. Even if it had only defined its business as providing a stimulant or catalyst to an energy source, it might have survived by becoming a manufacturer of, say, fanbelts or air cleaners.

What may some day be a still more classical example is, again, the oil industry. Having let others steal marvelous opportunities from it (e. g., natural gas, as already mentioned, missile fuels, and jet engine lubricants), one would expect it to have taken steps never to let that happen again. But this is not the case. We are now getting extraordinary new developments in fuel systems specifically designed to power automobiles. Not only are these developments concentrated in firms outside the petroleum industry, but petroleum is almost systematically ignoring them, securely content in its wedded bliss to oil. It is the story of the kerosene lamp versus the incandescent lamp all over again. Oil is trying to improve hydrocarbon fuels rather than develop *any* fuels best suited to the needs of their users, whether or not made in different ways and with different raw materials from oil.

Here are some things which nonpetroleum companies are working on:

- Over a dozen such firms now have advanced working models of energy systems which, when perfected, will replace the internal combustion engine and eliminate the demand for gasoline. The superior merit of each of these systems is their elimination of frequent, time-consuming, and irritating refueling stops. Most of these systems are fuel cells designed to create electrical energy directly from chemicals without combustion. Most of them use chemicals that are not derived from oil, generally hydrogen and oxygen.

- Several other companies have advanced models of electric storage batteries designed to power automobiles. One of these is an aircraft producer that is working jointly with several electric utility companies. The latter hope to use off-peak generating capacity to supply overnight plug-in battery regeneration. Another company, also using the battery approach, is a medium-size electronics firm with extensive small-battery experience that it developed in connection with its work on hearing aids. It is collaborating with an automobile manufacturer. Recent improvements arising from the need for high-powered miniature power storage plants in rockets have put us within reach of a relatively small battery capable of withstanding great overloads or surges of power. Germanium diode applications and batteries using sintered-plate and nickel-cadmium techniques promise to make a revolution in our energy sources.

● Solar energy conversion systems are also getting increasing attention. One usually cautious Detroit auto executive recently ventured that solar-powered cars might be common by 1980.

As for the oil companies, they are more or less "watching developments," as one research director put it to me. A few are doing a bit of research on fuel cells, but almost always confined to developing cells powered by hydrocarbon chemicals. None of them are enthusiastically researching fuel cells, batteries, or solar power plants. None of them are spending a fraction as much on research in these profoundly important areas as they are on the usual run-of-the-mill things like reducing combustion chamber deposit in gasoline engines. One major integrated petroleum company recently took a tentative look at the fuel cell and concluded that although "the companies actively working on it indicate a belief in ultimate success . . . the timing and magnitude of its impact are too remote to warrant recognition in our forecasts."

One might, of course, ask: Why should the oil companies do anything different? Would not chemical fuel cells, batteries, or solar energy kill the present product lines? The answer is that they would indeed, and that is precisely the reason for the oil firms having to develop these power units before their competitors, so they will not be companies without an industry.

Management might be more likely to do what is needed for its own preservation if it thought of itself as being in the energy business. But even that would not be enough if it persists in imprisoning itself in the narrow grip of its tight product orientation. It has to think of itself as taking care of customer needs, not finding, refining, or even selling oil. Once it genuinely thinks of its business as taking care of people's transportation needs, nothing can stop it from creating its own extravagantly profitable growth.

"CREATIVE DESTRUCTION." Since words are cheap and deeds are dear, it may be appropriate to indicate what this kind of thinking involves and leads to. Let us start at the beginning—the customer. It can be shown that motorists strongly dislike the bother, delay, and experience of buying gasoline. People actually do not buy gasoline. They cannot see it, taste it, feel it, appreciate it, or really test it. What they buy is the right to continue driving their cars. The gas station is like a tax collector to whom people are compelled to pay a periodic toll as the price of using their cars. This makes the gas station a basically unpopular institution. It can never be made popular or pleasant, only less unpopular, less unpleasant.

To reduce its unpopularity completely means eliminating it. Nobody likes a tax collector, not even a pleasantly cheerful one. Nobody likes to interrupt a trip to buy a phantom product, not even from a handsome Adonis or a seductive Venus. Hence, companies that are working on exotic fuel substitutes which will eliminate the need for frequent refueling are heading directly into the outstretched arms of the irritated motorist. They are riding a wave of inevitability, not because they are creating something which is technologically superior or more sophisticated, but because they are satisfying a powerful customer need. They are also eliminating noxious odors and air pollution.

Once the petroleum companies recognize the customer-satisfying logic of what another power system can do, they will see that they have no more choice about working on an efficient, long-lasting fuel (or some way of delivering present fuels without bothering the motorist) than the big food chains had a choice about going into the supermarket business, or the vacuum tube companies had a choice about making semiconductors. For their own good the oil firms will have to destroy their own highly profitable assets. No amount of wishful thinking can save them from the necessity of engaging in this form of "creative destruction."

I phrase the need as strongly as this because I think management must make quite an effort to break itself loose from conventional ways. It is all too easy in this day and age for a company or industry to let its sense of purpose become dominated by the economies of full production and to develop a dangerously lopsided product orientation. In short, if management lets itself drift, it invariably drifts in the direction of thinking of itself as producing goods and services, not customer satisfactions. While it probably will not descend to the depths of telling its salesmen, "You get rid of it; we'll worry about profits," it can, without knowing it, be practicing precisely that formula for withering decay. The historic fate of one growth industry after another has been its suicidal product provincialism.

Dangers of R&D

Another big danger to a firm's continued growth arises when top management is wholly transfixed by the profit possibilities of technical research and development. To illustrate I shall turn first to a new industry—electronics—and then return once more to the oil companies. By comparing a fresh example with a familiar one, I hope to emphasize the prevalence and insidiousness of a hazardous way of thinking.

MARKETING SHORTCHANGED.   In the case of electronics, the greatest danger which faces the glamorous new companies in this field is not that they do not pay enough attention to research and development, but that they pay *too much* attention to it. And the fact that the fastest growing electronics firms owe their eminence to their heavy emphasis on technical research is completely beside the point. They have vaulted to affluence on a sudden crest of unusually strong general receptiveness to new technical ideas. Also, their success has been shaped in the virtually guaranteed market of military subsidies and by military orders that in many cases actually preceded the existence of facilities to make the products. Their expansion has, in other words, been almost totally devoid of marketing effort.

Thus, they are growing up under conditions that come dangerously close to creating the illusion that a superior product will sell itself. Having created a successful company by making a superior product, it is not surprising that management continues to be oriented toward the product rather than the people who consume it. It develops the philosophy that continued growth is a matter of continued product innovation and improvement.

A number of other factors tend to strengthen and sustain this belief:

1. Because electronic products are highly complex and sophisticated, managements become top-heavy with engineers and scientists. This creates a selective bias in favor of research and production at the expense of marketing. The organization tends to view itself as making things rather than satisfying customer needs. Marketing gets treated as a residual activity, "something else" that must be done once the vital job of product creation and production is completed.

2. To this bias in favor of product research, development, and production is added the bias in favor of dealing with controllable variables. Engineers and scientists are at home in the world of concrete things like machines, test tubes, production lines, and even balance sheets. The abstractions to which they feel kindly are those which are testable or manipulatable in the laboratory, or, if not testable, then functional, such as Euclid's axioms. In short, the managements of the new glamour-growth companies tend to favor those business activities which lend themselves to careful study, experimentation, and control—the hard, practical realities of the lab, the shop, the books.

What gets shortchanged are the realities of the *market*. Consumers are unpredictable, varied, fickle, stupid, shortsighted, stubborn, and generally bothersome. This is not what the engineer-managers say, but deep down in their consciousness it is what they believe. And this accounts for their concentrating on what they know and what they can control, namely, product research, engineering, and production. The emphasis on production becomes particularly attractive when the product can be made at declining unit costs. There is no more inviting way of making money than by running the plant full blast.

Today the top-heavy science-engineering-production orientation of so many electronics companies works reasonably well because they are pushing into new frontiers in which the armed services have pioneered virtually assured markets. The companies are in the felicitous position of having to fill, not find markets; of not having to discover what the customer needs and wants, but of having the customer voluntarily come forward with specific new product demands. If a team of consultants had been assigned specifically to design a business situation calculated to prevent the emergence and development of a customer-oriented marketing viewpoint, it could not have produced anything better than the conditions just described.

STEPCHILD TREATMENT.   The oil industry is a stunning example of how science, technology, and mass production can divert an entire group of companies from their main task. To the extent the consumer is studied at all (which is not much), the focus is forever on getting information which is designed to help the oil companies improve what they are now doing. They try to discover more convincing advertising themes, more effective sales promotional drives, what the market shares of the various companies are, what people like or dislike about service station dealers and oil companies, and so forth. Nobody seems as interested in probing deeply into the basic human needs that the industry might be trying to satisfy as in probing into the basic properties of the raw material that the companies work with in trying to deliver customer satisfactions.

Basic question about customers and markets seldom get asked. The latter occupy a stepchild status. They are recognized as existing, as having to be taken care of, but not worth very much real thought or dedicated attention. Nobody gets as excited about the customers in his own backyard as about the oil in the Sahara Desert. Nothing illustrates better the neglect of marketing than its treatment in the industry press.

The centennial issue of the *American Petroleum Institute Quarterly,* published in 1959 to celebrate the discovery of oil in Titusville, Pennsylvania, contained 21 feature articles proclaiming the industry's greatness. Only one of these talked about its achievements in marketing, and that was only a pictorial record of how service station architecture has changed. The issue also contained a special section on "New Horizons," which was devoted to showing the magnificent role oil would play in America's future. Every reference was ebulliently optimistic, never implying once that oil might have some hard competition. Even the reference to atomic energy was a cheerful catalogue of how oil would help make atomic energy a success. There was not a single apprehension that the oil industry's affluence might be threatened or a suggestion that one "new horizon" might include new and better ways of serving oil's present customers.

But the most revealing example of the stepchild treatment that marketing gets was still another special series of short articles on "The Revolutionary Potential of Electronics." Under that heading this list of articles appeared in the table of contents:

- "In the Search for Oil"
- "In Production Operations"
- "In Refinery Processes"
- "In Pipeline Operations"

Significantly, every one of the industry's major functional areas is listed, *except* marketing. Why? Either it is believed that electronics holds no revolutionary potential for petroleum marketing (which is palpably wrong), or the editors forgot to discuss marketing (which is more likely, and illustrates its step-child status).

The order in which the four functional areas are listed also betrays the alienation of the oil industry from the consumer. The industry is implicitly defined as beginning with the search for oil and ending with its distribution from the refinery. But the truth is, it seems to me, that the industry begins with the needs of the customer for its products. From that primal position its definition moves steadily back-stream to areas of progressively lesser importance, until it finally comes to rest at the "search for oil."

BEGINNING & END. The view that an industry is a customer-satisfying process, not a goods-producing process, is vital for all businessmen to understand. An industry begins with the customer and his needs, not with a patent, a raw material, or a selling skill. Given the customer's needs, the industry develops backwards, first concerning itself with the physical *delivery* of customer satisfactions. Then it moves back further to *creating* the things by which these satisfactions are in part achieved. How these materials are created is a matter of indifference to the customer, hence the particular form of manufacturing, processing, or what-have-you cannot be considered as a vital aspect of the industry. Finally, the industry moves back still further to *finding* the raw materials necessary for making its products.

The irony of some industries oriented toward technical research and development is that the scientists who occupy the high executive positions are totally unscientific when it comes to defining their companies' overall needs and purposes. They violate the first two rules of the scientific method—being aware of and defining their companies' problems, and then developing testable hypotheses about solving them. They are scientific only about the convenient things, such as laboratory and product experiments.

The reason that the customer (and the satisfaction of his deepest needs) is not considered as being "the problem" is not because there is any certain belief that no such problem exists, but because an organizational lifetime has conditioned management to look in the opposite direction. Marketing is a stepchild.

I do not mean that selling is ignored. Far from it. But selling, again, is not marketing. As already pointed out, selling concerns itself with the tricks and techniques of getting people to exchange their cash for your product. It is not concerned with the values that the exchange is all about. And it does not, as marketing invariably does, view the entire business process as consisting of a tightly integrated effort to discover, create, arouse, and satisfy customer needs. The customer is somebody "out there" who, with proper cunning, can be separated from his loose change.

Actually, not even selling gets much attention in some technologically minded firms. Because there is a virtually guaranteed market for the abundant flow of their new products, they do not actually know what a real market is. It is as if they lived in a planned economy, moving their products routinely from factory to retail outlet. Their successful concentration on products tends to convince them of the soundness of what they have been doing, and they fail to see the gathering clouds over the market.

Conclusion

Less than 75 years ago American railroads enjoyed a fierce loyalty among astute Wall Streeters. European monarchs invested in them heavily. Eternal wealth was thought to be the benediction for anybody who could scrape a few thousand dollars together to put into rail stocks. No other form of transportation could compete with the railroads in speed, flexibility, durability, economy, and growth potentials.

As Jacques Barzun put it, "By the turn of the century it was an institution, an image of man, a tradition, a code of honor, a source of poetry, a nursery of boyhood desires, a sublimest of toys, and the most solemn machine—next to the funeral hearse—that marks the epochs in man's life."[6]

Even after the advent of automobiles, trucks, and airplanes, the railroad tycoons remained imperturbably self-confident. If you had told them 60 years

---

[6] Jacques Barzun, "Trains and the Mind of Man," *Holiday,* February 1960, p. 20.

ago that in 30 years they would be flat on their backs, broke, and pleading for government subsidies, they would have thought you totally demented. Such a future was simply not considered possible. It was not even a discussable subject, or an askable question, or a matter which any sane person would consider worth speculating about. The very thought was insane. Yet a lot of insane notions now have matter-of-fact acceptance—for example, the idea of 100-ton tubes of metal moving smoothly through the air 20,000 feet above the earth, loaded with 100 sane and solid citizens casually drinking martinis— and they have dealt cruel blows to the railroads.

What specifically must other companies do to avoid this fate? What does customer orientation involve? These questions have in part been answered by the preceding examples and analysis. It would take another article to show in detail what is required for specific industries. In any case, it should be obvious that building an effective customer-oriented company involves far more than good intentions or promotional tricks; it involves profound matters of human organization and leadership. For the present, let me merely suggest what appear to be some general requirements.

VISCERAL FEEL OF GREATNESS.   Obviously the company has to do what survival demands. It has to adapt to the requirements of the market, and it has to do it sooner rather than later. But mere survival is a so-so aspiration. Anybody can survive in some way or other, even the skid-row bum. The trick is to survive gallantly, to feel the surging impulse of commercial mastery; not just to experience the sweet smell of success, but to have the visceral feel of entrepreneurial greatness.

No organization can achieve greatness without a vigorous leader who is driven onward by his own pulsating *will to succeed*. He has to have a vision of grandeur, a vision that can produce eager followers in vast numbers. In business, the followers are the customers.

In order to produce these customers, the entire corporation must be viewed as a customer-creating and customer-satisfying organism. Management must think of itself not as producing products but as providing customer-creating value satisfactions. It must push this idea (and everything it means and requires) into every nook and cranny of the organization. It has to do this continuously and with the kind of flair that excites and stimulates the people in it. Otherwise, the company will be merely a series of pigeonholed parts, with no consolidating sense of purpose or direction.

In short, the organization must learn to think of itself not as producing goods or services but as *buying customers*, as doing the things that will make people *want* to do business with it. And the chief executive himself has the inescapable responsibility for creating this environment, this viewpoint, this attitude, this aspiration. He himself must set the company's style, its direction, and its goals. This means he has to know precisely where he himself wants to go, and to make sure the whole organization is enthusiastically aware of where that is. This is a first requisite of leadership, for *unless he knows where he is going, any road will take him there.*

If any road is okay, the chief executive might as well pack his attaché case and go fishing. If an organization does not know or care where it is going, it does not need to advertise that fact with a ceremonial figurehead. Everybody will notice it soon enough.

Retrospective Commentary

Amazed, finally, by his literary success, Isaac Bashevis Singer reconciled an attendant problem: "I think the moment you have published a book, it's not any more your private property. . . . If it has value, everybody can find in it what he finds, and I cannot tell the man I did not intend it to be so." Over the past 15 years, "Marketing Myopia" has become a case in point. Remarkably, the article spawned a legion of loyal partisans—not to mention a host of unlikely bedfellows.

Its most common and, I believe, most influential consequence is the way certain companies for the first time gave serious thought to the question of what businesses they are really in.

The strategic consequences of this have in many cases been dramatic. The best-known case, of course, is the shift in thinking of oneself as being in the "oil business" to being in the "energy business." In some instances the payoff has been spectacular (getting into coal, for example) and in others dreadful (in terms of the time and money spent so far on fuel cell research). Another successful example is a company with a large chain of retail shoe stores that redefined itself as a retailer of moderately priced, frequently purchased, widely assorted consumer specialty products. The result was a dramatic growth in volume, earnings, and return on assets.

Some companies, again for the first time, asked themselves whether they wished to be masters of certain technologies for which they would seek markets, or be masters of markets for which they would seek customer-satisfying products and services.

Choosing the former, one company has declared, in effect, "We are experts in glass technology. We intend to improve and expand that expertise with the object of creating products that will attract customers." This decision has forced the company into a much more systematic and customer-sensitive look at possible markets and users, even though its stated strategic object has been to capitalize on glass technology.

Deciding to concentrate on markets, another company has determined that "we want to help people (primarily women) enhance their beauty and sense of youthfulness." This company has expanded its line of cosmetic products, but has also entered the fields of proprietary drugs and vitamin supplements.

All these examples illustrate the "policy" results of "Marketing Myopia." On the operating level, there has been, I think, an extraordinary heightening of sensitivity to customers and consumers. R&D departments have cultivated a greater "external" orientation toward uses, users, and markets—balancing thereby the previously one-sided "internal" focus on materials and methods; upper management has realized that marketing and sales departments should be somewhat more willingly accommodated than before; finance departments have become more receptive to the legitimacy of budgets for market research and experimentation in marketing; and salesmen have been better trained to listen to and understand customer needs and problems, rather than merely to "push" the product.

A Mirror, Not a Window

My impression is that the article has had more impact in industrial-products companies—perhaps because the former had lagged most in customer orientation. There are at least two reasons for this lag: (1) industrial-products companies tend to be more capital intensive, and (2) in the past, at least, they have had to rely heavily on communicating face-to-face the technical character of what they made and sold. These points are worth explaining.

Capital-intensive businesses are understandably preoccupied with magnitudes, especially where the capital, once invested, cannot be easily moved, manipulated, or modified for the production of a variety of products—e.g., chemical plants, steel mills, airlines, and railroads. Understandably, they seek big volumes and operating efficiencies to pay off the equipment and meet the carrying costs.

At least one problem results: corporate power becomes disproportionately lodged with operating or financial executives. If you read the charter of one of the nation's largest companies, you will see that the chairman of the finance committee, not the chief executive officer, is the "chief." Executives with such backgrounds have an almost trained incapacity to see that getting "volume" may require understanding and serving many discrete and sometimes small market segments, rather than going after a perhaps mythical batch of big or homogeneous customers.

These executives also often fail to appreciate the competitive changes going on around them. They observe the changes, all right, but devalue their significance or underestimate their ability to nibble away at the company's markets.

Once dramatically alerted to the concept of segments, sectors, and customers, though, managers of capital-intensive businesses have become more responsive to the necessity of balancing their inescapable preoccupation with "paying the bills" or breaking even with the fact that the best way to accomplish this may be to pay more attention to segments, sectors, and customers.

The second reason industrial products companies have probably been more influenced by the article is that, in the case of the more technical industrial products or services, the necessity of clearly communicating product and service characteristics to prospects results in a lot of face-to-face "selling" effort. But precisely because the product is so complex, the situation produces salesmen who know the product more than they know the customer, who are more adept at explaining what they have and what it can do than learning what the customer's needs and problems are. The result has been a narrow product orientation rather than a liberating customer orientation, and "service" often suffered. To be sure, sellers said, "We have to provide service," but they tended to define service by looking into the mirror rather than out the window. They *thought* they were looking out the window at the customer, but it was actually a mirror—a reflection of their own product-oriented biases rather than a reflection of their customers' situations.

A Manifesto, Not a Prescription

Not everything has been rosy. A lot of bizarre things have happened as a result of the article:

- Some companies have developed what I call "marketing mania"—they've become obsessively responsive to every fleeting whim of the customer. Mass production operations have been converted to approximations of job shops, with cost and price consequences far exceeding the willingness of customers to buy the product.

- Management has expanded product lines and added new lines of business without first establishing adequate control systems to run more complex operations.

- Marketing staffs have suddenly and rapidly expanded themselves and their research budgets without either getting sufficient prior organizational support or, thereafter, producing sufficient results.

- Companies that are functionally organized have converted to product, brand, or market-based organizations with the expectation of instant and miraculous results. The outcome has been ambiguity, frustration, confusion, corporate infighting, losses, and finally a reversion to functional arrangements that only worsened the situation.

- Companies have attempted to "serve" customers by creating complex and beautifully efficient products or services that buyers are either too risk-averse to adopt or incapable of learning how to employ—in effect, there are now steam shovels for people who haven't yet learned to use spades. This problem has happened repeatedly in the so-called service industries (financial services, insurance, computer-based services) and with American companies selling in less-developed economies.

"Marketing Myopia" was not intended as analysis or even prescription; it was intended as manifesto. It did not pretend to take a balanced position. Nor was it a new idea—Peter F. Drucker, J. B. McKitterick, Wroe Alderson, John Howard, and Neil Borden had each done more original and balanced work on "the marketing concept." My scheme, however, tied marketing more closely to the inner orbit of business policy. Drucker—especially in *The Concept of the Corporation* and *The Practice of Management*—originally provided me with a great deal of insight.

My contribution, therefore, appears merely to have been a simple, brief, and useful way of communicating an existing way of thinking. I tried to do it in a very direct, but responsible, fashion, knowing that few readers (customers), especially managers and leaders, could stand much equivocation or hesitation. I also knew that the colorful and lightly documented affirmation works better than the tortuously reasoned explanation.

But why the enormous popularity of what was actually such a simple preexisting idea? Why its appeal throughout the world to resolutely restrained scholars, implacably temperate managers, and high government officials, all accustomed to balanced and thoughtful calculation? Is it that concrete examples, joined to illustrate a simple idea and presented with some attention to literacy, communicate better than massive analytical reasoning that reads as though it were translated from the German? Is it that provocative assertions are more memorable and persuasive than restrained and balanced explanations, no matter who the audience? Is it that the character of the message is as much the message as its content? Or was mine not simply a different tune, but a new symphony? I don't know.

Of course, I'd do it again and in the same way, given my purposes, even with what more I now know—the good and the bad, the power of facts and the limits of rhetoric. If your mission is the moon, you don't use a car. Don Marquis's cockroach, Archy, provides some final consolation: "an idea is not responsible for who believes in it."

QUESTIONS

1. What is "marketing myopia"?
2. Give a few examples of firms (not listed in the article) that suffer from marketing myopia.

3. Explain the self-deceiving cycle and the conditions that foster it.
4. What are the negative aspects of an intensive research-and-development process directed at increasing profits?
5. How should a firm define its business in order to avoid marketing myopia?

3

PUTTING CUSTOMER DEMANDS FIRST

Business Week

*This selection relates how the Reliance
Electric Company demonstrated
the success that can follow
the implementation of the
marketing concept.*

If there is a Golden Rule of marketing, Harvard professor Theodore Levitt summed it up in his landmark book, *Innovation in Marketing*. The successful company, he wrote, makes what the customer and market need, not what the company's machinery is set up to make. The only trouble is that like most Golden Rules, this one tends to be forgotten.

Reliance Electric Co. is one company that suffered just such a memory lapse. For years, the 66-year-old Cleveland manufacturer of industrial motors, drives, and measuring equipment concentrated only on the quality of its products, at the expense of its markets and their needs. This week, Reliance is now in the final phases of reorganizing and restructuring its whole approach to the customer along the lines that Levitt proposed. The shift, which began three years ago, has helped Reliance double its average annual growth rate to 8%–10%. Next week, Reliance will release figures for its 1970 fiscal year. While earnings will probably dip below last year's $17.4-million, reflecting the general business downturn, sales are expected to reach a new record of more than $320-million. "When we discovered the opportunities we had walked right by, we shook our heads and wondered how we could have been so stupid," admits Lewis J. Carr, vice president of industrial drives.

OLD LESSON. In a sense, Reliance is relearning a lesson it once practiced. Just after World War I, the company designed a new line of direct current motors after spending a full year just asking customers what they wanted. "Those machines became No. 1 on the hit parade," says Carr, "and they put Reliance on the map."

Over the years, however, Reliance gradually lost touch with its markets. At first, that did not prevent the company from building popular drives, including one standout success in the 1940s. "Somebody just guessed right," Carr admits, "and people bought it. After that, we decided we knew what people wanted without asking them." Unfortunately, the guesses were not always right. "We came out with quality products," says Carr, "but they didn't set the world on fire."

In the late 1950s, for instance, Reliance engineers designed what they thought to be an ultra-futuristic drive. It relied on a complex system of vacuum tubes to convert incoming alternating current power to direct current. But customers decided the drive was too complicated for most plant electricians to understand or fool with. It also proved too sensitive to the moisture, dirt, and temperature adversities of a plant environment. So what looked revolutionary in the lab flopped on the market.

OBSOLESCENT PRODUCTS.   Such mistakes began taking their toll. "As lesser companies in the industry fell by the wayside in the early '60s," says Carr, "somebody other than Reliance picked up their business"—primarily, General Electric Co. At that point, Reliance's annual growth rate hovered around 4%, equal to the industry average but far below that of GE and other progressive specialty manufacturers.

Then, in 1965, Hugh D. Luke took over as Reliance president, and the company began hiring consultants to study what had gone wrong. The chief conclusion: While many of the company's motors were among the best in the field, customers did not need—and obviously did not want to pay for— some of the built-in features. The paper industry, for instance, wanted the best insulation to protect its motors from corrosion. But it did not need the special safeguards that the mining industry required to prevent dust from clogging bearings.

In the new-product area, Reliance similarly came to realize that it was missing out completely on other important markets. "Our product development was simply an extension of our current lines of products and current capabilities," Luke says. One typically neglected market was for the revolutionary a.c. inverter drive, the first drive to use a variable-speed a.c. motor in a practical way. Reliance had preferred to stick with the traditional d.c. motor it had always built. Luke claims that by failing to develop radically new products to meet rapidly changing markets, a product-oriented company easily "extrapolates its existing products right into obsolescence."

AIMLESS SALES FORCE.   At the same time, one of the company's consultants, McKinsey & Co., revealed that Reliance had drifted into a loose and casual relationship with its sales force. This, in turn, widened the gap between company and markets. "The sales offices were selling the things they found easiest to sell," says Luke, "and that's typical of a product-oriented company." This was especially true when Reliance acquired a new company. The salesmen of that company often pushed only their own products and not all of the Reliance products.

Even worse, Reliance was losing potential customers who still pictured the company as a small producer of electrical drives—when, in fact, it had grown enormously by acquiring other makers of drives and motors, and by diversifying through the acquisition of such companies as Dodge Mfg. Corp. (power transmission equipment) and Toledo Scale Corp. (weighing and measuring equipment). "We had made several good acquisitions," Luke says, "but a lot of people didn't know they were now part of our total capability." In one case, a major rubber company turned to Reliance for the design of a computerized plant, then went to a larger company to equip it. "We weren't big enough in their eyes," says Luke, "because we hadn't gotten the word to them about our capabilities."

BRIGHTENING THE IMAGE.   In 1967, Reliance started getting the word out. Since then, the company has spent more than $1-million just to create and promote a broader and clearer corporate image. As a starter, it forked out $150,000 for a name change (from Reliance Electric & Engineering Co.) and a new logo, which features a bold and slanted "R." This is intended to suggest a big, progressive company and avoid reference to one type of product.

Another $500,000 went into a special advertising campaign ("The man from Reliance has only one engineered drive for you . . . the one you need"), created by Cleveland's Gregory, Inc. The ad campaign and a $225,000 public relations effort began billing Reliance in larger terms as a company with "fresh ideas in automation"—one that could tackle any automation need, including those not covered by existing products.

Reliance backed up the new image with major organizational changes. Small divisions that had grown up around specific products were consolidated into large divisions organized more around markets. For instance, four motor divisions that had been organized by motor sizes were lumped into one catch-all division. The theory was that a certain market may need many sizes of motors and that one division could now handle the market's entire motor requirements.

MEETING CHALLENGES.   As part of the same realignment, Reliance followed a McKinsey suggestion and set up an industrial marketing department with 12 specialists called market managers. They oversee the company's 31 markets and feed engineers, product managers, and others information about shifting requirements in those industries. "They have to eat and sleep with their markets," explains Carr.

At the same time, the sales force in the industrial drives group, the company's largest sector, has been increased 40%, to 264, and the entire sales operation was reshuffled for better central direction. Salesmen long unaccustomed to corporate directives now talk up total company capabilities, not just favorite products.

Reliance engineers and manufacturing executives receive the same market stress. In a product-oriented company, says Luke, manufacturing men frequently resist salesmen who suggest entirely new products to meet a customer's need. "You always hear engineers telling salesmen to sell what they already have," he says. "Now we tell manufacturing, 'Don't come back and say you can't design a product to fit a new market need. Tell us instead what it takes to build it.'"

To back up the salesman and manufacturing executive, market research has been beefed up and redirected to study and predict long-term market needs for revolutionary new products. "Before," says Carr, "if the market suddenly demanded pink ashtrays, we would make them. Now we anticipate market needs well in advance rather than react to immediate demands."

One key market-forecasting tool is an annual symposium on "Automation and Society," that Reliance began cosponsoring with the University of Georgia last year. The first two symposia, which cost Reliance $125,000, brought together representatives from universities, industry, labor, and government to discuss solutions to problems created by automation.

SALES JUMP.   Out of all this effort and energy, Carr now feels that some of his company's products are virtually tailor-made for certain industries. In the food industry alone, Reliance claims to have doubled its market share of electric-motor sales simply by cleaning up the motor it made. "The motor we were selling to the food companies was designed to be sturdy even in heavy industries and without regard for sanitation," remarks E. L. Bronold, the company's market manager for that industry. "It had a lot of crud collectors—fins and recesses where dirt could collect." Seeing that such a motor did not fit the needs of an industry demanding easy-to-clean equipment, Bronold encouraged engineers to build a new motor, one with smooth contours and without pockets to collect dirt.

As Reliance continues to sharpen its marketing focus, Luke projects sales of more than $500-million by 1974—a jump of nearly 70% from 1969. "It is essential and inevitable," Luke claims, "that industry turn increasingly to automation." And it is just as inevitable, he adds, that Reliance will be there to serve the market, rather than being there to be served by the market.

QUESTIONS

1. What type of corporate orientation did Reliance Electric Company have before implementing the marketing concept?
2. How did Reliance integrate its total efforts toward consumer satisfaction?

4

BEHIND THE
PROFIT SQUEEZE AT
THE NEW YORK TIMES

Business Week

*Just having the best product does not
insure success. Unless the product
satisfies the real needs of some group of
consumers the firm will not thrive. This
statement is vividly illustrated by this
article. The New York Times, generally
regarded as one of the best newspapers
in the world, had major problems until it
began addressing the needs of its
customers.*

In 1963 when Arthur Ochs "Punch" Sulzberger took over the family
business—the *New York Times*—the nation's most prestigious newspaper was
riding a wave of prosperity. So the soft-spoken Sulzberger was content to
ignore some obvious problems on the paper and let nature take its course,
even though Sulzberger bore the titles of publisher of the paper and chief
executive of the parent New York Times Co.

Under this loose rein, the paper's pervasive management and marketing
shortcomings festered and became much worse. The result is that the financial
health of the *Times* has seriously deteriorated. Editorially and politically, the
newspaper has also slid precipitously to the left and has become stridently
antibusiness in tone, ignoring the fact that the *Times* itself is a business—and
one with very serious problems.

Clobbered by the recession, pretax earnings of the *Times* plunged 58% last
year to $4.6 million on revenues of $269.6 million. Helped along by this
year's recovery, the *Times* made up that decline in the first six months, boosting
earnings 60% over the same period a year ago. Beneath the short-term ebb
and flow of earnings, however, there are deeper troubles that have long-

range implications. During the past five years, circulation has slipped 1%, while advertising linage fell 7%. Over-all last year, revenues of the parent Times Co. rose a mere 5% to $408.9 million, while net income tumbled 37% to $12.8 million. For the first six months, revenues increased 11% and net income, only 5.9%.

Sulzberger, 50, grandson of the late Adolph S. Ochs who started many of the traditions of the *Times* after he purchased the paper in 1896, is now trying to turn the ailing company around. With unaccustomed forcefulness, Sulzberger is even surprising many members of the *Times*. Says one editorial staffer of the paper, which is known for its unflagging resistance to change: "The big story at the *New York Times* these days is the movement of the publisher into all aspects of the paper, including editorial. It's the first time."

Some *Times* watchers even speculate that the family may eventually sell the paper, unless Sulzberger is able to raise its return on investment to a level comparable with the company's other properties—which range from magazines and books to broadcasting. Sulzberger vehemently denies that he has heard any such talk either within his family or among his management. "We have argued what the return should be," he says—then quickly backs off from giving any specific numbers. As for family dissatisfaction, Sulzberger adds: "I'm the leader of the part of the family that's dissatisfied with the return."

Some of the problems at the *Times* are the same ones worrying virtually all big-city newspapers. Costs of production, paper, and distribution are skyrocketing at the same time that television and other competing media are grabbing a growing chunk of advertising budgets. As an added worry, suburban newspapers are stealing a growing number of readers and advertisers from big-city dailies.

An Identity Crisis

On top of these problems, the *Times* faces a slew of headaches all its own. Even before Sulzberger inherited his job, following the death of his brother-in-law, Orvil E. Dryfoos, the *Times* had been a managerial nightmare. There was no organizational structure, merely a group of warring factions and fiefdoms working against each other. Admits Sulzberger: "We were organized like a forest of bamboo trees. Everything went straight up the organization to one person and nothing ever came together anywhere." A newspaper consultant who knows the *Times* claims, "The *Times* is a prototypical, family-run business that simply outgrew family control." Then he adds, "The only answer is decisive and knowledgeable management that is able to make its decisions stick."

That is the role that Sulzberger has carved out for himself. Grudgingly and belatedly, the newspaper that previously refused to change is now going in some dramatic new directions. Under Sulzberger, the basic look of the *Times* is changing; next month the paper will shift from its traditional eight-column makeup to a more readable six columns for news and nine for advertising. The sales department is going through a shake-up. Internal management is being modernized to include the first use of budgets, planning, a group profit-center concept, and a centralized corporate structure. Editorial operations also are being consolidated.

Yet inside and outside the *Times*, there is lively argument over whether Sulzberger is decisive enough—or savvy enough—to make all the changes that are needed. Puffing on a black briar pipe and smiling pleasantly, Sulzberger looks more like an economics professor than head of one of the most powerful newspapers in the world. "I've never seen him lose his temper," says James C. Goodale, one of Sulzberger's three executive vice-presidents. "He is very mild, and he tries to get people to work together without forcing anything on them."

The mildness that Goodale admires creates doubts among members of the financial community. "He's just not an aggressive businessman," says Joan Lappin, a respected newspaper analyst for Dreyfus Corp. "He wants to be left alone to be publisher. But unfortunately his name is Sulzberger, and he has to run the company."

Running the company means resolving an identity crisis that grips the *Times* like an iron claw. Sulzberger suggests the dilemma himself when he first tells a visiting reporter, "Our real problem today is to be noncompetitive with what is out there, to provide something that readers can get only in the *Times*." This means heavy national and international coverage of a type that nobody else does. With this kind of news emphasis, some of the paper's top executives see the *Times* evolving into a national newspaper. Then in almost the next breath, Sulzberger claims that the *Times* is evolving from a big-city daily into a regional daily. This would mean more suburban news coverage. That kind of contradiction leads at least one New York advertising executive to ask "whether the *Times* really knows what it wants to be."

The Search for Profits

While they may not be coming to grips yet with the *Times's* identity crisis, Sulzberger and his top lieutenants are beginning to alter some of the hidebound traditions that have stifled the *Times* for years. These traditions caused some colossal errors of judgment all through the 1950s and 1960s. During that period, the paper remained aloof while many of its readers migrated to the suburbs. From their new homes, many of these former *Times* readers switched to local newspapers that reported on local taxes, school budgets, and other suburban happenings that directly affected them. Many advertisers switched right along with them. At the same time, the population mix of New York City, the core of the *Times's* circulation, changed with the tremendous growth in the numbers of blacks and Hispanics, fewer of whom read newspapers, and older citizens who do not buy many of the things advertised in newspapers.

Because the *Times* neglected the growing suburban markets, *Newsday,* a Garden City (N.Y.) daily, was able to prosper in rich, populous Long Island, while the *Bergen Record* did the same in northern New Jersey. North of New York City, even the Westchester Rockland Group of Gannett Co., though weak in editorial coverage, grew rapidly and prospered. Along with these suburban papers, New York's *Daily News,* the *Times's* top remaining competitor in the city, also grew fat on the suburban migration by expanding its suburban coverage.

In the booming Long Island market, weekday editions of *Newsday* now go into 62% of all households, the *Daily News* 31%, and the *Times* only 11%. Within the over-all New York metropolitan market, which covers a 50-mi. radius out of New York City, the daily *Times* reaches only 14% of total households, or roughly one-third of the *Times's* target audience of 2.3 million higher-income families.

This marketing oversight—plus steadily rising costs—finally caught up with the *Times* in the late 1960s and helped send profit margins tumbling. From a 6.5% return on sales in 1968, the parent company's profit margins dipped to 4.2% in 1970 and 3.2% in 1971. Last year the pretax margin on the newspaper alone slipped to a bare 1.7%.

With pressures already beginning to build in 1968, Times Co. went public that year and began diversifying, hoping to add some higher-margin businesses. Sulzberger and the rest of the family now own 70% of the parent company's controlling class of stock, plus 37% of the noncontrolling stock traded on the American Stock Exchange. Thus Sulzberger has strong incentive to turn the company around. From $53 in 1968, the company's stock has slipped to $14.50 per share this week, a slide that clearly upsets the rest of the family.

Like many other corporate diversification efforts, the one at Times Co. has had as many disappointments as successes. Says one source close to the company: "There was no strong sense of corporate direction or objectives." Of the diversification, Goodale admits, "It went slowly at first. We spent a lot of money on internal development that didn't pan out too well." Then, on some outside acquisitions, Goodale adds, "we were unable to pull off some big deals we should have."

The biggest single deal was the acquisition of 14 properties from Cowles Communications Inc. in 1970 for $52 million worth of stock (now worth only $37.7 million) and the assumption of $15 million of Cowles's debt. This became the cornerstone of the Times Co.'s diversification. Altogether, the company added five consumer magazines (*Family Circle, Golf Digest, Golf World, Tennis, Hockey*), eight medical and dental magazines, 13 daily and weekly newspapers in Florida and North Carolina, a television station in Memphis, three book publishing operations, and several other communications businesses.

As it searched for new properties, the company gained a reputation for paying too much on some acquisitions. When the *Times* bought the *Wilmington* (N.C.) *Star-News* last year, it reportedly paid well over $10 million for a newspaper with a circulation of only 34,500. Based on earnings potential, some other members of the industry considered the same acquisition worth about $8.5 million. Washington Post Co. had offered only $10 million.

Those Costly Contracts

While Times Co. struggled with diversification, an even bigger problem began rearing its head: a series of costly union contracts climaxed by a disastrous settlement in 1970 with the International Typographical Union. This contract provided a 42% wage increase over three years. Times Co. reaped additional criticism because the *Times*'s editorial pages had blasted other industries for granting much smaller wage increases.

In 1973, when new contract negotiations came up, the *Times* finally stood firm—but only because it was up against the wall. "The thing that broke the ice with the union," says Sulzberger, "was the realization that we could sit down with paper and pencil and plot ourselves right out of business with the wrong kind of settlement." In the 1973 bargaining, the union agreed to a 7% wage boost spread over 10 years and gradual automation of many of its jobs. In return, union members then working at the *Times* received lifetime job guarantees.

By then, Sulzberger was feeling plenty of heat from family shareholders as well as outsiders. This led to his first major moves to reform the company's jumbled management structure. One by one, he replaced many top executives, either retiring or nudging them quietly aside. To help eliminate fiefdoms, he consolidated jobs and departments and created a clearer organizational tree. The first level under Sulzberger now consists of three executive vice-presidents: Goodale, 43, an attorney who oversees corporate affairs; Walter Mattson, 44, who is general manager of the *Times*; and Sydney

Gruson, 59, head of all subsidiary operations. These three are in turn delegating authority.

With tighter lines of responsibility, Sulzberger has also set up the company's first use of budgets, planning, and group profit centers. "Before this," says Goodale, "we had something called a budget. But it was really just a document to add up what people thought they would spend each year." Sulzberger adds, "There was no concern among any *Times* departments as to whether they had a profit or a loss. That was the concern of the publisher. The division people never saw any numbers at all."

Sulzberger has moved far more slowly to solve the problem of growing suburban competition. This is the biggest and most crucial challenge facing big-city dailies and is starting to change their whole approach to circulation. In the past, newspaper circulation used to be a numbers game—and still is, to some degree. But the numbers must add up to something. "Circulation just for the sake of circulation is no longer that important," says Reg Murphy, editor and publisher of the *San Francisco Examiner*. The buzzword is "productive" circulation. Unlike a few years ago, says Thomas Vail, editor and publisher of the Cleveland *Plain Dealer*, "you have to show advertisers that the people taking the paper are buying things. It could come down to having a healthy business with less readers." This demands more and better market research, more part-run sections aimed at higher-income suburbs, and a tighter bead on both readers and competitors. "We found we are competing against 57 different papers in Cuyahoga County alone," says William A. Holcombe, business manager for the *Cleveland Press*. From the reader's standpoint, adds Holcombe, "We're trying to find out what the best role of the newspaper is."

Asked about the loss of the *Times*'s own suburban market, a former ad salesman for the paper still shakes his head in disbelief. "The *Times* could have owned the suburbs, if it had only gone after them," he says.

In the last five years, Long Island's *Newsday*—purchased by Los Angeles-based Times Mirror Co. in 1970—boosted its circulation 6% and its ad linage 31%. From a standing start in 1972, *Newsday*'s Sunday circulation is now up to 438,781. That puts Sunday *Newsday* into 55% of Long Island households, compared with 49% for the Sunday *Daily News* and only 18% for the Sunday *Times*. Even among the *Times*'s main target audience, households earning $20,000 or more a year, *Newsday* beats out the *Times* in weekday penetration: 65% vs. 42% for the *Times*. Among those same households, the Sunday *Times* is still ahead of Sunday *Newsday*, with 57% of the market compared with 44% for *Newsday*. "But we'll catch the Sunday *Times* soon enough," vows William Attwood, *Newsday*'s publisher. "We're only in our fifth year on a Sunday edition, and we're gaining all the time."

At the *Bergen Record*, which now puts out four separate editions for the single county it covers, Publisher Malcolm A. Borg claims the key is a tightly concentrated market and "community identity."

With its new regional emphasis, the *Times* audience is moving in the other direction and becoming increasingly dispersed. This makes it harder and costlier to reach. Since 1960, the *Times's* daily circulation in the city has slipped from 51% of the total to 39%. Along the way, suburban circulation has risen from 28% to 36%, while circulation beyond the metropolitan market has increased from 21% to 25%.

To build a bigger and steadier circulation base, nearly all metropolitan dailies are pushing for more home-delivery customers. Yet, so far, the *Times* is barely holding its own—if that. Right now, home delivery accounts for only 28% of the *Times's* daily city circulation and 50% of suburban readers. And it is slipping. Late last year, a huge promotional campaign for home delivery helped increase "voluntary" subscriptions 25% over 1974. Yet total home-delivery circulation still fell 6% for the year.

Targeting the Readers

Up to now, the biggest roadblock in any such campaign has been the *Times's* lack of solid market research. Past research was haphazard and never accurately pinpointed what "target" readers and nonreaders were all about. "Until you know that, you can't really build the kind of circulation you want," stresses Philip Thompson, the *Times's* new director of market research. This year, the *Times* expanded its market research budget 80%. Along with more polls and probes, the *Times* is also computerizing the analysis of everything from home-delivery complaints to circulation penetration by Zip code and census tract.

A recovery in circulation—if it comes—might help advertising. At the *Times* and other large metropolitan newspapers, advertising always tended to sell itself. "But the days of waltzing into some store and asking for an ad are over," says Robert C. Nelson, general manager of the *Detroit News*. The competition is keen—and getting more so. John Kimball, retail ad manager for the *Detroit Free Press*, notes: "In the last few years, we have nearly doubled our sales staff with young and aggressive people who have been trained in the approach used by the broadcast people." The *Washington Post* and several other big dailies are even training "media representatives" to help advertisers design total campaigns that include newspapers, broadcast, and other media. "At the same time," says Mark J. Meagher, *Post* general manager, "we make the case for the *Post*."

At the *New York Times*, however, there has been a conspicuous lack of such combativeness. Because of poor middle-level management, the ad department went through a morale-crushing period that dragged on for six or eight years. *Times* salesmen, typically lackluster and unaggressive, grew even more so. "They spent most of their time on the phone letting advertisers know they couldn't get into the paper rather than going out and selling," Sulzberger admits. During the worst of this period, internal tensions triggered a wave of resignations and dismissals. "It was difficult when our best guys got offered jobs other places," Sulzberger concedes. "They didn't see where they were going here. We ran pretty dry on good talent."

Fred D. Thompson, former president of *Family Circle*, is now trying to set things right. Named *Times* advertising vice-president last year, Thompson is adding new training programs, sales aids, the paper's first sales incentive system, and tighter middle-level management. As a not-so-subtle hint, Thompson even printed up Christmas aprons for his ad managers. Playing on the *Times* slogan for classified ads, they read: "I got my job through *The New York Times*—Now I have to work to keep it."

The Bread-and-Butter Ads

So far, few outside see much change. Richard Olsen, senior vice-president of Vitt Media International Inc., in New York, still rates *Times* salesmen near the bottom. "They have always been inflexible and unresponsive to agency problems," says Olsen. "And that certainly hasn't changed. If I were Fred Thompson, I'd be very, very concerned."

Among Thompson's concerns, the biggest of all is probably retail advertising, the bread and butter of every metropolitan newspaper. Last year, the *Times* ran about 30 million lines of retail advertising at roughly $2 a line, 20 million lines of classified at $3 a line, and 20 million lines of general advertising at $4 a line.

But that retail volume is draining off into suburban papers. While the *Times*'s total retail linage dropped 4% in the last five years, retail linage spurted 39% at *Newsday*, 17% at the *Bergen Record*, and 18% at the *White Plains Reporter Dispatch* in Westchester County. During that same period, Abraham & Straus cut its *Times* ad linage 10%, B. Altman 23%, Gimbel 26%, Alexanders 46%, Macy 49%, and Franklin Simon 64%.

To help hold onto retail advertising, most metropolitan dailies are adding part-run suburban sections. This way, they can chop out some of their waste circulation, offer lower ad rates, and pick up more small advertisers. Once a week, for instance, the *Daily News* now produces three separate editorial and advertising sections for Queens alone. In its New Jersey edition, which averages 12 pages of state news each day, the *News* even substitutes New Jersey editorials and a separate New Jersey front page. "Instead of being a single, mass paper with little suburban appendages," says Editor Michael O'Neill, "we are becoming several different and distinct papers."

Cutting Some Ad Losses

The *Times* itself is proceeding more slowly. While it prints a daily half page or so of New Jersey news just for New Jersey readers, the *Times*'s only part-run advertising, other than classified, is carried in a small Wednesday food section and two local Sunday feature sections. One Sunday section goes to New Jersey, the other to Long Island, and a third is being considered for Westchester County. These sections help make up some of the ad losses in the full-run edition. For the first five months of this year, full-run retail linage continued dropping—down 3%. Meantime, part-run retail linage jumped 34%. Part-run ads now make up 8% of the *Times*'s total linage, compared with 50% for the *Daily News*.

Like other papers around the country, the *Times* is also launching special weekly ad sections in the full-run edition. The first is "Weekend," a regional entertainment guide published every Friday. Since its debut in April, "Weekend" has lifted Friday circulation 5% and Friday ad linage 20%.

"However, we are not rushing pell-mell into these sections," stresses Managing Editor A. M. Rosenthal. "They must have journalistic validity." Rosenthal still carries the scars of the Brooklyn/Long Island/Queens section, forerunner of the Sunday Long Island section. "It was a disaster," says Rosenthal—"cheap and shoddy." He adds, "The business people carried the day on that one, and I think they lived to regret it."

As managing editor, Rosenthal must also grapple with one of the paper's most worrisome concerns: a long-term erosion of editorial quality. As a start, some costly editorial duplication has been cut by combining daily and Sunday news staffs under Rosenthal. To make the paper easier to read, Rosenthal is now dividing the daily paper into as many as four sections. And when the *Times* switches next month from an eight-column makeup to six columns for news and nine for ads, it will improve readability and reduce paper costs 5%.

Insiders claim, however, that these are only cosmetic touches that fail to get at deeper troubles. "Even beyond the normal morale problems you find in every big-city newsroom," says an editor of a rival paper, "there are sharp divisions on the editorial side." While Sulzberger denies it, others claim that he has been concerned about the paper's political swing to the left. According to these sources, this concern exploded into the open recently when Sulzberger and John B. Oakes, head of the editorial page, collided over an editorial on the city's financial mess. One answer to that mess, the editorial claimed, was a hefty tax increase for business. "Something like that," muses a Wall Street analyst, "could put the *Times* right out of business." This disagreement may have been behind Sulzberger's recent decision to create revolving memberships on the editorial board and to replace Oakes, who retires from the board next January, with Max Frankel.

New-Venture Disappointments

Amid the growing pressures on both the editorial and business side of the *Times*, the parent company had hoped to gain some relief through diversification. Instead, many of these new ventures have only added to the burden. While the company's pretax profit margins continue high in broadcasting (26%) and smaller newspapers (21%), they are slipping on the magazines, down from 9.7% in 1972 to 7.2% last year. In June, the company dumped one of the biggest disappointments, its eight medical and dental magazines. Following a *Times* series on medical incompetence, the group's flagship magazine lost $500,000 in pharmaceutical advertising. This only reinforced an earlier decision to unload the group, which was sold to Harcourt Brace Jovanovich Inc. The Times Co. is also trying to sell another disappointment, its music-publishing operation, acquired in 1973 for an estimated $4 million.

Last year's biggest profit drain was the *Times'*s major equity investments in newsprint production. Because of a strike that shut down two of the company's three newsprint mills for the entire fourth quarter, equity earnings tumbled 69% to $2.3 million. "Yet with the rising costs of newsprint," says one Wall Street source, "these equity interests could become one of the company's most profitable investments. They'll come back."

But will the *Times* itself? "All of us are watching the *Times* with great interest," says *Newsday*'s Attwood. "But don't forget," he adds, "we're all trying to become more competitive"—suggesting that the *Times* may fall even further behind, regardless of how much it changes. Sulzberger, of course, is determined this will not happen. "I'm not positive there are any single answers for big-city newspapers," he says. "But I do know that as long as you fulfill a need, there is a place out there for you." Among all its problems and the worsening state of its financial and editorial quality, the trick for the *Times* will be finding that place—and then filling it.

QUESTIONS

1. Describe the two markets a newspaper must serve and the potential conflicts that might arise between them.
2. How should the New York Times define its business?
3. What additional steps could the newspaper take to increase profits?

5

THE NATURE AND SCOPE OF MARKETING

Shelby D. Hunt

The objective of this article was to analyze the long-standing controversy over whether marketing is a science. The conceptual model that the author of this article develops for the scope of marketing provides a useful tool for viewing the many aspects of marketing and for approaching the study of the marketing discipline.

During the past three decades, two controversies have overshadowed all others in the marketing literature. The first is the "Is marketing a science?" controversy sparked by an early JOURNAL OF MARKETING article by Converse entitled "The Development of a Science of Marketing."[1] Other prominent writers who fueled the debate included Bartels, Hutchinson, Baumol, Buzzell, Taylor, and Halbert.[2] After raging throughout most of the '50s and '60s, the controversy has since waned. The waning may be more apparent than real, however, because many of the substantive issues underlying the marketing science controversy overlap with the more recent "nature of marketing" (broadening the concept of marketing) debate. Fundamental to both con-

---

[1] Paul D. Converse, "The Development of a Science of Marketing," JOURNAL OF MARKETING, Vol. 10 (July 1945), pp. 14–23.

[2] Robert Bartels, "Can Marketing Be a Science?"JOURNAL OF MARKETING, Vol. 15 (January 1951), pp. 319–328; Kenneth D. Hutchinson, "Marketing as a Science: An Appraisal," JOURNAL OF MARKETING, Vol. 16 (January 1952), pp. 286–293; W. J. Baumol, "On the Role of Marketing Theory," JOURNAL OF MARKETING, Vol. 21 (April 1957), pp. 413–419; Robert D. Buzzell, "Is Marketing a Science?" *Harvard Business Review*, Vol. 41 (January-February 1963), pp. 32–48; Weldon J. Taylor, "Is Marketing a Science? Revisited," JOURNAL OF MARKETING, Vol. 29 (July 1965), pp. 49–53; and M. Halbert, *The Meaning and Sources of Marketing Theory* (New York: McGraw-Hill Book Co., 1965).

troversies are some radically different perspectives on the essential characteristics of both *marketing* and *science*.

The purpose of this article is to develop a conceptual model of the scope
of marketing and to use that model to analyze (1) the approaches to the study
of marketing, (2) the "nature of marketing" controversy, and (3) the marketing
science debate. Before developing the model, some preliminary observations
on the controversy concerning the nature of marketing are appropriate.

The Nature of Marketing

What is marketing? What kinds of phenomena are appropriately termed
marketing phenomena? How do marketing activities differ from nonmarketing
activities? What is a marketing system? How can marketing processes be
distinguished from other social processes? Which institutions should one refer
to as marketing institutions? *In short, what is the proper conceptual domain of the
construct labeled "marketing"?*

The American Marketing Association defines marketing as "the performance of business activities that direct the flow of goods and services from
producer to consumer or user."[3] This position has come under attack from
various quarters as being too restrictive and has prompted one textbook on
marketing to note: "Marketing is not easy to define. No one has yet been able
to formulate a clear, concise definition that finds universal acceptance."[4]

Although vigorous debate concerning the basic nature of marketing has
alternately waxed and waned since the early 1900s, the most recent controversy probably traces back to a position paper by the marketing staff of the
Ohio State University in 1965. They suggested that marketing be considered
"the process in a society by which the demand structure for economic goods
and services is anticipated or enlarged and satisfied through the conception,
promotion, exchange, and physical distribution of goods and services."[5] Note
the conspicuous absence of the notion that marketing consists of a set of
business activities (as in the AMA definition). Rather, they considered marketing
to be a *social process*.

Next to plunge into the semantical battle were Kotler and Levy. Although

---

[3] Committee on Terms, *Marketing Definitions: A Glossary of Marketing Terms* (Chicago: American Marketing Assn., 1960).

[4] Stewart H. Rewoldt, James D. Scott, and Martin R. Warshaw, *Introduction to Marketing Management* (Homewood, Ill.: Richard D. Irwin, 1973), p. 3.

[5] Marketing Staff of the Ohio State University, "Statement of Marketing Philosophy," JOURNAL OF MARKETING, Vol. 29 (January 1965), pp. 43–44.

they did not specifically propose a new definition of marketing, Kotler and Levy in 1969 suggested that the concept of marketing be broadened to include nonbusiness organizations. They observed that churches, police departments, and public schools have products and customers, and that they use the normal tools of the marketing mix.. Therefore, Kotler and Levy conclude that these organizations perform marketing, or at least marketing-like, activities. Thus,

> the choice facing those who manage nonbusiness organizations is not whether to market or not to market, for no organization can avoid marketing. The choice is whether to do it well or poorly, and on this necessity the case for organizational marketing is basically founded. [6]

In the same issue of the JOURNAL OF MARKETING, Lazer discussed the changing boundaries of marketing. He pleaded that: "What is required is a broader perception and definition of marketing than has hitherto been the case—one that recognizes marketing's societal dimensions and perceives of marketing as more than just a technology of the firm." [7] Thus, Kotler and Levy desired to broaden the notion of marketing by including not-for-profit organizations, and Lazer called for a definition of marketing that recognized the discipline's expanding societal dimensions.

Luck took sharp issue with Kotler and Levy by insisting that marketing be limited to those business processes and activities that ultimately result in a *market* transaction. [8] Luck noted that even thus bounded, marketing would still be a field of enormous scope and that marketing specialists could still render their services to nonmarketing causes. Kotler and Levy then accused Luck of a new form of myopia and suggested that, "The crux of marketing lies in a *general idea of exchange* rather than the narrower thesis of market transactions." [9] They further contended that defining marketing "too narrowly" would inhibit students of marketing from applying their expertise to the most rapidly growing sectors of the society.

Other marketing commentators began to espouse the dual theses that (1) marketing be broadened to include nonbusiness organizations, and (2) marketing's societal dimensions deserve scrutiny. Thus, Ferber prophesied

---

[6]Philip Kotler and Sidney J. Levy, "Broadening the Concept of Marketing," JOURNAL OF MARKETING, Vol. 33 (January 1969), p. 15.

[7]William Lazer, "Marketing's Changing Social Relationships," JOURNAL OF MARKETING, Vol. 33 (January 1969), p. 9.

[8]David Luck, "Broadening the Concept of Marketing—Too Far," JOURNAL OF MARKETING, Vol. 33 (July 1969), p. 54.

[9]Philip Kotler and Sidney Levy, "A New Form of Marketing Myopia: Rejoinder to Professor Luck," JOURNAL OF MARKETING, Vol. 33 (July 1969), p. 57.

that marketing would diversify into the social and public policy fields.[10] And Lavidge sounded a similar call to arms by admonishing marketers to cease evaluating new products solely on the basis of whether they *can* be sold. Rather, he suggested, they should evaluate new products from a societal perspective, that is, *should* the product be sold?

> The areas in which marketing people can, and must, be of service to society have broadened. In addition, marketing's functions have been broadened. Marketing no longer can be defined adequately in terms of the activties involved in buying, selling, and transporting goods and services.[11]

The movement to expand the concept of marketing probably became irreversible when the JOURNAL OF MARKETING devoted an entire issue to marketing's changing social/environmental role. At that time, Kotler and Zaltman coined the term *social marketing*, which they defined as "the design, implementation and control of programs calculated to influence the acceptability of social ideas and involving considerations of product planning, pricing, communication, distribution, and marketing research."[12] In the same issue, marketing technology was applied to fund raising for the March of Dimes, health services, population problems, and the recycling of solid waste.[13] Further, Dawson chastised marketers for ignoring many fundamental issues pertaining to the social relevance of marketing activities:

> Surely, in these troubled times, an appraisal of marketing's actual and potential role in relation to such [societal] problems is at least of equal importance to the technical aspects of the field. Yet, the emphasis upon practical problem-solving within the discipline far outweighs the attention paid to social ramifications of marketing activity.[14]

---

[10]Robert Ferber, "The Expanding Role of Marketing in the 1970's," JOURNAL OF MARKETING, Vol. 34 (January 1970), pp. 29–30.

[11]Robert J. Lavidge, "The Growing Responsibilites of Marketing," JOURNAL OF MARKETING, Vol. 34 (January 1970), p. 27.

[12]Philip Kotler and Gerald Zaltman, "Social Marketing: An Approach to Planned Social Change," JOURNAL OF MARKETING, Vol. 35 (July 1971), p. 5.

[13]JOURNAL OF MARKETING, Vol. 35 (July 1971): William A. Mindak and H. Malcolm Bybee, "Marketing's Application to Fund Raising," pp. 13–18; Gerald Zaltman and Ilan Vertinsky, "Health Services Marketing: A Suggested Model," pp. 19–27; John U. Farley and Harold J. Leavitt, "Marketing and Population Problems," pp. 28–33; and William G. Zikmund and William J. Stanton, "Recycling Solid Wastes: A Channels-of-Distribution Problem," pp. 34–39.

[14]Leslie Dawson, "Marketing Science in the Age of Aquarius," JOURNAL OF MARKETING, Vol. 35 (July 1971), p. 71.

Kotler has since reevaluated his earlier positions concerning broadening the concept of marketing and has articulated a "generic" concept of marketing. He proposes that the essence of marketing is the *transaction*, defined as the exchange of values between two parties. Kotler's generic concept of marketing states: "Marketing is specifically concerned with how transactions are created, stimulated, facilitated and valued."[15] Empirical evidence indicates that, at least among marketing educators, the broadened concept of marketing represents a *fait accompli*. A recent study by Nichols showed that 95% of marketing educators believed that the scope of marketing should be broadened to include nonbusiness organizations. Similarly, 93% agreed that the marketing goes beyond just economic goods and services, and 83% favored including in the domain of marketing many activities whose ultimate result is not a market transaction.[16]

Although the advocates of extending the notion of marketing appear to have won the semantical battle, their efforts may not have been victimless. Carman notes that the definition of marketing plays a significant role in directing the research efforts of marketers. He believes that many processes (e.g., political processes) do not involve an exchange of values and that marketing should not take such processes under its "disciplinary wing."[17] Bartels has also explored the so-called identity crises in marketing and has pointed out numerous potential disadvantages to broadening the concept of marketing. These *potential* disadvantages include: (1) turning the attention of marketing researchers away from important problems in the area of physical distribution, (2) emphasizing methodology rather than substance as the content of marketing knowledge, and (3) an increasingly esoteric and abstract marketing literature. Bartels concluded: "If 'marketing' is to be regarded as so broad as to include both economic and noneconomic fields of application, perhaps marketing as originally conceived will ultimately reappear under another name."[18]

Similarly, Luck decries the "semantic jungle" that appears to be growing in marketing.[19] Citing conflicting definitions of *marketing* and *social marketing* in

---

[15] Philip Kotler, "A Generic Concept of Marketing," JOURNAL OF MARKETING, Vol. 36 (April 1972), p. 49.

[16] William G. Nichols, "Conceptual Conflicts in Marketing," *Journal of Economics and Business*, Vol. 26 (Winter 1974), p. 142.

[17] James M. Carman, "On the Universality of Marketing," *Journal of Contemporary Business*, Vol. 2 (Autumn 1973), p. 14.

[18] Robert Bartels, "The Identity Crisis in Marketing," JOURNAL OF MARKETING, Vol. 38 (October 1974), p. 76.

[19] David J. Luck, "Social Marketing: Confusion Compounded," JOURNAL OF MARKETING, Vol. 38 (October 1974), pp. 2–7.

the current literature, Luck suggests that this semantic jungle has been impeding the efforts of marketers to think clearly about their discipline. He has challenged the American Marketing Association to create a special commission to clear up the definitional problems in marketing. Finally, a recent president of the American Marketing Association set the development of a consistent standard definition of marketing as a primary goal of the association. [20]

Three questions appear to be central to the "nature [broadening the concept] of marketing" controversy. First, what kinds of phenomena and issues *do* the various marketing writers perceive to be included in the scope of marketing? Second, what kinds of phenomena and issues *should* be included in the scope of marketing? Third, how can marketing be defined to both systematically encompass all the phenomena and issues that should be included and, at the same time, systematically exclude all other phenomena and issues? That is, a good definition of marketing must be both properly inclusive and exclusive. To rigorously evaluate these questions requires a conceptual model of the scope of marketing.

The Scope of Marketing

No matter which definition of marketing one prefers, the scope of marketing is unquestionably broad. Often included are such diverse subject areas as consumer behavior, pricing, purchasing, sales management, product management, marketing communications, comparative marketing, social marketing, the efficiency/productivity of marketing systems, the role of marketing in economic development, packaging, channels of distribution, marketing research, societal issues in marketing, retailing, wholesaling, the social responsibility of marketing, international marketing, commodity marketing, and physical distribution. Though lengthy, this list of topics and issues does not exhaust the possibilities. Not all writers would include all the topics under the general rubric of marketing. The point deserving emphasis here, however, is that different commentators on marketing would *disagree* as to which topics should be excluded. The disagreement stems from fundamentally different perspectives and can best be analyzed by attempting to develop some common ground for classifying the diverse topics and issues in marketing.

The most widely used conceptual model of the scope of marketing is the familiar "4 Ps" model popularized by McCarthy in the early '60s. [21] The

---

[20]Robert J. Eggert, "Eggert Discusses Additional Goals for His Administration, Seeks Help in Defining Marketing," *Marketing News*, September 15, 1974.

[21]E. J. McCarthy, *Basic Marketing* (Homewood, Ill.: Richard D. Irwin, 1960).

model is usually represented by three concentric circles. The inner circle contains the consumer, since this is the focal point of marketing effort. The second circle contains the marketing mix ("controllable factors") of price, place, promotion, and product. Finally, the third circle contains the uncontrollable factors of political and legal environment, economic environment, cultural and social environment, resources and objectives of the firm, and the existing business situation. As is readily apparent, many of the subject areas previously mentioned have no "home" in the 4 Ps model. For example, where does social marketing or efficiency of marketing systems or comparative marketing belong?

During a presentation at the 1972 Fall Conference of the American Marketing Association, Kotler made some observations concerning the desirability of classifying marketing phenomena using the concepts of *micro*, *macro*, *normative*, and *positive*.[22] These observations spurred the development of the conceptual model detailed in Table 1. The schema proposes that all marketing phenomena, issues, problems, models, theories, and research can be categorized using the three categorical dichotomies of (1) profit sector/ nonprofit sector, (2) micro/macro, and (3) positive/normative. The three categorical dichotomies yield $2 \times 2 \times 2 = 8$ classes or cells in the schema. Thus, the first class includes all marketing topics that are micro-positive and in the profit sector. Similarly, the second class includes all marketing activities that are micro-normative and in the profit sector, and so on throughout the table.

Some definitions are required to properly interpret the schema presented in Table 1. *Profit sector* encompasses the study and activities of organizations or other entities whose stated objectives include the realization of profit. Also applicable are studies that adopt the *perspective* of profit-oriented organizations. Conversely, *nonprofit* sector encompasses the study and perspective of all organizations and entities whose stated objectives do not include the realization of profit.

The *micro/macro* dichotomy suggests a classification based on the level of aggregation. *Micro* refers to the marketing activities of individual units, normally individual organizations (firms) and consumers or households. *Macro* suggests a higher level of aggregation, usually marketing systems or groups of consumers.

The *positive/normative* dichotomy provides categories based on whether the focus of the analysis is primarily descriptive or prescriptive. *Positive* marketing adopts the perspective of attempting to describe, explain, predict, and

---

[22]These observations were apparently extemporaneous since they were not included in his published paper: Philip Kotler, "Defining the Limits of Marketing," in *Marketing Education and the Real World*, Boris W. Becker and Helmut Becker, eds. (Chicago: American Marketing Assn., 1972).

Table 1

THE SCOPE OF MARKETING

	Positive	Normative

Micro	(1) Problems, issues, theories, and research concerning:
	  a. Individual consumer buyer behavior
	  b. How firms determine prices
	  c. How firms determine products
	  d. How firms determine promotion
	  e. How firms determine channels of distribution
	  f. Case studies of marketing practices
		(2) Problems, issues, normative models, and research concerning how firms *should*:
		  a. Determine the marketing mix
		  b. Make pricing decisions
		  c. Make product decisions
		  d. Make promotion decisions
		  e. Make packaging decisions
		  f. Make purchasing decisions
		  g. Make international marketing decisions
		  h. Organize their marketing departments
		  i. Control their marketing efforts
		  j. Plan their marketing strategy
		  k. Apply systems theory to marketing problems
		  l. Manage retail establishments
		  m. Manage wholesale establishments
		  n. Implement the marketing concept

Macro	(3) Problems, issues, theories, and research concerning:
	  a. Aggregate consumption patterns
	  b. Institutional approach to marketing
	  c. Commodity approach to marketing
	  d. Legal aspects of marketing
	  e. Comparative marketing
		(4) Problems, issues, normative models, and research concerning:
		  a. How marketing can be made more efficient
		  b. Whether distribution costs too much
		  c. Whether advertising is socially desirable
		  d. Whether consumer sovereignty is desirable

Profit Sector

Table 1 (continued)

	Positive	Normative
Macro	f. The efficiency of marketing systems g. Whether the poor pay more h. Whether marketing spurs or retards economic development i. Power and conflict relationships in channels of distribution j. Whether marketing functions are universal k. Whether the marketing concept is consistent with consumers' interests	e. Whether stimulating demand is desirable f. Whether the poor should pay more g. What kinds of laws regulating marketing are optimal h. Whether vertical marketing systems are socially desirable i. Whether marketing should have special social responsibilities

Nonprofit Sector

	Positive	Normative
Micro	(5) Problems, issues, theories, and research concerning: a. Consumers' purchasing of public goods b. How nonprofit organizations determine prices c. How nonprofit organizations determine products d. How nonprofit organizations determine promotion e. How nonprofit organizations determine channels of distribution f. Case studies of public goods marketing	(6) Problems, issues, normative models, and research concerning how nonprofit organizations *should*: a. Determine the marketing mix (social marketing) b. Make pricing decisions c. Make product decisions d. Make promotion decisions e. Make packaging decisions f. Make purchasing decisions g. Make international marketing decisions (e.g., CARE) h. Organize their marketing efforts i. Control their marketing efforts j. Plan their marketing strategy k. Apply systems theory to marketing problems

Table 1 *(continued)*

	Positive	Normative

Macro	(7) Problems, issues, theories, and research concerning:
	  a. The institutional framework for public goods
	  b. Whether television advertising influences elections
	  c. Whether public service advertising influences behavior (e.g., "Smokey the Bear")
	  d. Whether existing distribution systems for public goods are efficient
	  e. How public goods are recycled
		(8) Problems, issues, normative models, and research concerning:
		  a. Whether society should allow politicians to be "sold" like toothpaste
		  b. Whether the demand for public goods should be stimulated
		  c. Whether "low informational content" political advertising is socially desirable (e.g., ten-second "spot" commercials)
		  d. Whether the U.S. Army should be allowed to advertise for recruits

understand the marketing activities, processes, and phenomena that actually exist. This perspective examines *what is*. In contrast, normative marketing adopts the perspective of attempting to prescribe what marketing organizations and individuals ought to do or what kinds of marketing systems a society ought to have. That is, this perspective examines what *ought to be* and what organizations and individuals *ought to do*.

Analyzing Approaches to Marketing

An examination of Table 1 reveals that most of the early (circa 1920) approaches to the study of marketing reside in cell 3: profit sector/macro/positive. The institutional, commodity, and functional approaches analyzed existing (positive) business activities (profit sector) from a marketing systems (macro) perspective. However, not all the early marketing studies were profit/macro/positive. Weld's 1920 classic *The Marketing of Farm Products* not only examined existing distribution systems for farm commodities, but also attempted to evaluate such normative issues as: "Are there too many middlemen in food marketing?"[23] Thus, Weld's signally important work was both

---

[23]L. D. H. Weld, *The Marketing of Farm Products* (New York: Macmillan, 1920).

profit/macro/positive and profit/macro/normative. Similarly, the Twentieth Century Fund study *Does Distribution Cost Too Much?* took an essentially profit/macro/normative perspective.[24] Other important works that have combined the profit/macro/positive and the profit/macro/normative perspectives include those of Barger, Cox, and Borden.[25]

Although the profit/micro/normative (cell 2) orientation to marketing can be traced at least back to the 1920s and the works of such notables as Reed and White,[26] the movement reached full bloom in the early 1960s under proponents of the *managerial approach* to marketing, such as McCarthy.[27] The managerial approach adopts the perspective of the marketing manager, usually the marketing manager in a large manufacturing corporation. Therefore, the emphasis is micro and in the profit sector. The basic question underlying the managerial approach is: "What is the optimal marketing mix?" Consequently, the approach is unquestionably normative.

During the middle 1960s, writers such as Lazer, Kelley, Adler, and Fisk began advocating a *systems approach* to marketing.[28] Sometimes the systems approach used a profit/micro/normative perspective and simply attempted to apply to marketing certain sophisticated optimizing models (like linear and dynamic programming) developed by the operations researchers. Other writers used the systems approach in a profit/macro/positive fashion to analyze the complex interactions among marketing institutions. Finally, some used the systems approach in a profit/macro/normative fashion:

> The method used in this book is called the general systems approach. In this approach the goals, organization, inputs, and outputs of marketing are examined to determine how efficient and *how effective marketing is.* Constraints, including competition and government, are also studied because they affect both the level of efficiency and the kinds of effects obtained.[29]

---

[24] Paul W. Stewart, *Does Distribution Cost Too Much?* (New York: Twentieth Century Fund, 1939).

[25] Harold Barger, *Distribution's Place in the Economy Since 1869* (Princeton: Princeton University Press, 1955); Reavis Cox, *Distribution in a High Level Economy* (Englewood Cliffs, N.J.: Prentice-Hall, 1965); and Neil Borden, *The Economic Effects of Advertising* (Chicago: Richard D. Irwin, 1942).

[26] Virgil Reed, *Planned Marketing* (New York: Ronald Press, 1930); and P. White and W. S. Hayward, *Marketing Practice* (New York: Doubleday, Page & Co., 1924).

[27] Same reference as footnote 21.

[28] William Lazer and Eugene Kelley, "Systems Perspective of Marketing Activity," in *Managerial Marketing: Perspectives and Viewpoints*, rev. ed. (Homewood, Ill.: Richard D. Irwin, 1962); Lee Adler, "Systems Approach to Marketing," *Harvard Business Review*, Vol. 45 (May-June, 1967); and George Fisk, *Marketing Systems: An Introductory Analysis* (New York: Harper & Row, 1967).

[29] Fisk, same reference as footnote 28, p. 3.

During the late 1960s, the *environmental approach* to marketing was promulgated by writers such as Holloway, Hancock, Scott, and Marks.[30] This approach emphasized an essentially descriptive analysis of the environmental constraints on marketing activities. These environments included consumer behavior, culture, competition, the legal framework, technology, and the institutional framework. Consequently, this approach may be classified as profit/macro/positive.

Two trends are evident in contemporary marketing thought. The first is the trend toward *social marketing* as proposed by Kotler, Levy, and Zaltman[31] and as promulgated by others.[32] Social marketing, with its emphasis on the marketing problems of nonprofit organizations, is nonprofit/macro/normative. The second trend can be termed *societal issues*. It concerns such diverse topics as consumerism, marketing and ecology, the desirability of political advertising, social responsibility, and whether the demand for public goods should be stimulated.[33] All these works share the common element of *evaluation*. They attempt to evaluate the desirability or propriety of certain marketing activities or systems and, therefore, should be viewed as either profit/macro/normative or nonprofit/macro/normative.

In conclusion, it is possible to classify all the approaches to the study of marketing and all the problems, issues, theories, models, and research usually considered within the scope of marketing using the three categorical dichotomies of profit sector/nonprofit sector, positive/normative, and micro/macro. This is not meant to imply that reasonable people cannot disagree as to which topics should fall within the scope of marketing. Nor does it even imply that reasonable people cannot disagree as to which cell in Table 1 is most

---

[30]Robert J. Holloway and Robert S. Hancock, *The Environment of Marketing Behavior* (New York: John Wiley & Sons, 1964); Robert J. Holloway and Robert S. Hancock, *Marketing in a Changing Environment* (New York: John Wiley & Sons, 1968); and Richard A. Scott and Norton E. Marks, *Marketing and Its Environment* (Belmont: Wadsworth, 1968).

[31]Kotler and Levy, same reference as footnote 6; Kotler and Zaltman, same reference as footnote 12; and Kotler, same reference as footnote 15.

[32]Mindak and Bybee, same reference as footnote 13; Farley and Leavitt, same reference as footnote 13; Zikmund and Stanton, same reference as footnote 13; Carman, same reference as footnote 17; and Donald P. Robin, "Success in Social Marketing," *Journal of Business Research*, Vol. 3 (July 1974), pp. 303–310.

[33]Lazer, same reference as footnote 7; Dawson, same reference as footnote 14; David S. Aaker and George Day, *Consumerism* (New York: Free Press, 1971); Norman Kangun, *Society and Marketing* (New York: Harper & Row, 1972); Frederick E. Webster, Jr., *Social Aspects of Marketing* (Englewood Cliffs, N.J.: Prentice-Hall, 1974); Reed Moyer, *Macro-Marketing* (New York: John Wiley & Sons, 1972); John R. Wish and Stephen H. Gamble, *Marketing and Social Issues* (New York: John Wiley & Sons, 1971); Ross L. Goble and Roy Shaw, *Controversy and Dialogue in Marketing* (Englewood Cliffs, N.J.: Prentice-Hall, 1975); Ronald R. Gist, *Marketing and Society* (New York: Holt, Rinehart & Winston, 1971); and William Lazer and Eugene Kelley, *Social Marketing* (Homewood, Ill.: Richard D. Irwin, 1973).

appropriate for each issue or particular piece of research. For example, a study of the efficiency of marketing systems may have *both* positive and normative aspects; it may both *describe* existing marketing practices and *prescribe* more appropriate practices. Rather, the conceptual model of the scope of marketing presented in Table 1 provides a useful framework for analyzing fundamental differences among the various approaches to marketing and, as shall be demonstrated, the nature of marketing and marketing science controversies.

Analyzing the Nature of Marketing and Marketing Science

The previous discussion on the scope of marketing now enables us to clarify some of the issues with respect to the "nature [broadening the concept] of marketing" controversy and the "Is marketing a science?" debate. Most marketing practitioners and some marketing academicians perceive the entire scope of marketing to be profit/micro/normative (cell 2 of Table 1). That is, practitioners often perceive the entire domain of marketing to be the analysis of how to improve the decision-making processes of marketers. This perspective is exemplified by the definition of marketing Canton has suggested[34] and, somewhat surprisingly, by the definition proffered by Kotler in the first edition of *Marketing Management*: "Marketing is the analyzing, organizing, planning, and controlling of the firm's customer-impinging resources, policies, and activities with a view to satisfying the needs and wants of chosen customer groups at a profit."[35]

Most marketing academicians would chafe at delimiting the entire subject matter of marketing to simply the profit/micro/normative dimensions. Most would, at the very least, include all the phenomena, topics, and issues indicated in the top half of Table 1 (that is, cells 1 through 4). Kotler and others now wish to include in the definition of marketing *all* eight cells in Table 1.

Other fields have experienced similar discipline-definitional problems. Several decades ago, a debate raged in philosophy concerning the definition of philosophy and philosophy of science. Some philosophers chose a very narrow definition of their discipline. Popper's classic rejoinder should serve to alert marketers to the danger that narrowly circumscribing the marketing discipline may trammel marketing inquiry:

---

[34]Irving D. Canton, "A Functional Definition of Marketing," *Marketing News*, July 15, 1973.

[35]Philip Kotler, *Marketing Management* (Englewood Cliffs, N.J.: Prentice-Hall, 1967), p. 12.

. . . the theory of knowledge was inspired by the hope that it would enable us not only to know more about knowledge, but also to contribute to the advance of knowledge—of scientific knowledge, that is. . . . Most of the philosophers who believe that the characteristic method of philosophy is the analysis of ordinary language seem to have lost this admirable optimism which once inspired the rationalist tradition. Their attitude, it seems, has become one of resignation, if not despair. They not only leave the advancement of knowledge to the scientists: they even define philosophy in such a way that it becomes, by definition, incapable of making any contribution to our knowledge of the world. The self-mutilation which this so surprisingly persuasive definition requires does not appeal to me. There is no such thing as an essence of philosophy, to be distilled and condensed into a definition. *A definition of the word "philosophy" can only have the character of a convention, of an agreement; and I, at any rate, see no merit in the arbitrary proposal to define the word "philosophy" in a way that may well prevent a student of philosophy from trying to contribute,* qua *philosopher, to the advancement of our knowledge of the world.*[36]

Four conclusions seem warranted. First, definitions of the nature of marketing differ in large part because their authors perceive the total scope of marketing to be different portions of Table 1. Second, there is a growing consensus that the total scope of marketing should appropriately include all eight cells of Table 1. Third, it may be very difficult to devise a definition of marketing that would both systematically *include* all eight cells of Table 1 and, at the same time, systematically *exclude* all other phenomena. Especially difficult will be the task of including in a single definition both the normative dimensions of the *practice* of marketing and the positive dimensions of the *discipline* or *study* of marketing.

The fourth conclusion deserves special emphasis and elaboration. There is now a consensus among marketers that most nonprofit organizations, such as museums, zoos, and churches, engage in numerous activities (pricing, promoting, and so forth) that are very similar to the marketing activities of their profit-oriented cousins. There is also consensus that the marketing procedures that have been developed for profit-oriented organizations are equally applicable to nonprofit concerns. These are the two major, substantive issues involved in the debate over the nature (broadening the concept) of marketing. On these two issues there now exists substantial agreement.

The remaining two points of *disagreement* among marketers concerning the nature of marketing are minor when compared to the points of agreement.

---

[36] Karl R. Popper, *The Logic of Scientific Discovery* (New York: Harper & Row, 1959), p. 19. (Emphasis added.)

Issue one is essentially whether the activities of nonprofit organizations should be referred to as *marketing* activities or *marketing-like* activities. Given the agreement among marketers concerning the two previously cited substantive issues, the problem of distinguishing between marketing activities and marketing-like activities must be considered trivial to the extreme. The second issue on which disagreement exists concerns developing a definition of marketing. Although certainly nontrivial in nature, on this issue marketers would be well advised to take a cue from the discipline of philosophy, which has been around much longer and has yet to develop a consensus definition. That is, the discipline of marketing should not be overly alarmed about the difficulty of generating a consensus *definition* of marketing as long as there appears to be a developing consensus concerning its total *scope*.

The preceding analysis notwithstanding, there does remain a major, unresolved, substantive issue concerning the nature of marketing. Although *marketers* now recognize that nonprofit organizations (1) have marketing or marketing-like problems, (2) engage in marketing or marketing-like activities to solve these problems, and (3) can use the marketing policies, practices, and procedures that profit-oriented organizations have developed to solve marketing problems, we must candidly admit that most *nonmarketers* have yet to perceive this reality. Sadly, most administrators of nonprofit organizations and many academicians in other areas still do not perceive that many problems of nonprofit organizations are basically marketing in nature, and that there is an extant body of knowledge in marketing academia and a group of trained marketing practitioners that can help resolve these problems. Until administrators of nonprofit organizations perceive that they have marketing problems, their marketing decision making will inevitably suffer. Thus, the major *substantive* problem concerning broadening the concept of marketing lies in the area of *marketing* marketing to nonmarketers.

Is Marketing a Science?

Returning to the "Is marketing a science?" controversy, the preceding analysis suggests that a primary factor explaining the nature of the controversy is the widely disparate notions of marketing held by the participants. The common element shared by those who hold that marketing is not (and cannot) be a science is the belief that the entire conceptual domain of marketing is cell 2: profit/micro/normative. Hutchinson clearly exemplifies this position:

> There is a real reason, however, why the field of marketing has been slow
> to develop an unique body of theory. It is a simple one: marketing is not a
> science. It is rather an art or a practice, and as such much more closely

resembles engineering, medicine and architecture than it does physics, chemistry or biology. The medical profession sets us an excellent example, if we would but follow it; its members are called "practitioners" and not scientists. It is the work of physicians, as it is of any practitioner, to apply the findings of many sciences to the solution of problems. . . . It is the drollest travesty to relate the scientist's search for knowledge to the market research man's seeking after customers.[37]

If, as Hutchinson implies, the entire conceptual domain of marketing is profit/micro/normative, then marketing is not and (more importantly) probably *cannot* be a science. If, however, the conceptual domain of marketing includes both micro/positive and macro/positive phenomena, then marketing *could* be a science. That is, if phenomena such as consumer behavior, marketing institutions, marketing channels, and the efficiency of systems of distribution are included in the conceptual domain of marketing (and there appears to be a consensus to so include them), there is no reason why the study of these phenomena could not be deserving of the designation *science*.

Is marketing a science? Differing perceptions of the scope of marketing have been shown to be a primary factor underlying the debate on this question. The second factor contributing to the controversy is differing perceptions concerning the basic nature of science, a subject that will now occupy our attention.

The Nature of Science

The question of whether marketing is a science cannot be adequately answered without a clear understanding of the basic nature of science. So, what is a science? Most marketing writers cite the perspective proposed by Buzzell. A science is:

> . . . a classified and systematized body of knowledge, . . . organized around one or more central theories and a number of general principles, . . . usually expressed in quantitative terms, . . . knowledge which permits the prediction and, under some circumstances, the control of future events.[38]

Buzzell then proceeded to note that marketing lacks the requisite central theories to be termed a science.

Although the Buzzell perspective on science has much to recommend it, the requirement "organized around one or more central theories" seems overly

---

[37] Hutchinson, same reference as footnote 2.

[38] Buzzell, same reference as footnote 2, p. 37.

restrictive. This requirement confuses the *successful culmination* of scientific efforts with *science itself*. Was the study of chemistry not a science before discoveries like the periodic table of elements? Analogously, would not a pole vaulter still be a pole vaulter even if he could not vault fifteen feet? As Homans notes, "What makes a science are its aims, not its results."[39] The major purpose of science is to discover (create? invent?) laws and theories to explain, predict, understand, and control phenomena. Withholding the label *science* until a discipline has "central theories" would not seem reasonable.

The previous comments nowwithstanding, requiring a science to be organized around one or more central theories is not completely without merit. There are strong *honorific* overtones in labeling a discipline a science.[40] These semantical overtones are so positive that, as Wartofsky has observed, even areas that are nothing more than systematized superstition attempt to usurp the term.[41] Thus, there are treatises on such subjects as the "Science of Numerology" and the "Science of Astrology." In part, the label *science* is conferred upon a discipline to signify that it has "arrived" in the eyes of other scientists, and this confirmation usually occurs only when a discipline has matured to the extent that it contains several "central theories."[42] Thus, chronologically, physics achieved the status of science before psychology, and psychology before sociology. However, the total conceptual content of the term *science* is decidedly not just honorific. Marketing does not, and should not, have to wait to be knighted by others to be a science. How, then, do sciences differ from other disciplines, if not by virtue of having central theories?

Consider the discipline of chemistry—unquestionably a science. Chemistry can be defined as "the science of substances—their structure, their properties, and the reactions that change them into other substances."[43] Using chemistry as an illustration, three observations will enable us to clarify the distinguishing characteristics of sciences. First, a science must have a distinct subject matter, a set of real-world phenomena that serve as a focal point for investigation. The subject matter of chemistry is *substances*, and chemistry attempts to understand, explain, predict, and control phenomena related to substances. Other disciplines, such as physics, are also interested in sub-

---

[39] George C. Homans, *The Nature of Social Science* (New York: Harcourt, Brace & World, 1967), p. 4.

[40] Ernest Nagel, *The Structure of Science* (New York: Harcourt, Brace & World, 1961), p. 2.

[41] Marx W. Wartofsky, *Conceptual Foundations of Scientific Thought* (New York: Macmillan Co., 1968), p. 44.

[42] Thomas S. Kuhn, *The Structure of Scientific Revelations* (Chicago: University of Chicago Press, 1970), p. 161.

[43] Linus Pauling, *College Chemistry* (San Francisco: W. H. Freeman & Co., 1956), p. 15.

stances. However, chemistry can meaningfully lay claim to being a separate science because physics does not *focus on* substances and their reactions.

What is the basic subject matter of marketing? Most marketers now perceive the ultimate subject matter to be the *transaction*. Some subscribe to the *narrower thesis of marketing* and wish to delimit the basic subject matter to the *market* transaction. Other propose the *liberalized thesis of marketing* and wish to include within the subject matter of marketing all transactions that involve any form of *exchange of values* between parties.

Harking back to the chemistry analogue, marketing can be viewed as the *science of transactions*—their structure, their properties, and their relationships with other phenomena. Given this perspective, the subject matter of marketing would certainly overlap with other disciplines, notably economics, psychology, and sociology. The analysis of transactions is considered in each of these disciplines. Yet, only in marketing is the transaction the focal point. For example, transactions remain a tangential issue in economics, where the primary focus is on the allocation of scarce resources.[44] Therefore, the first distinguishing characteristic is that any science must have a distinct subject matter. Given that the transaction is the basic subject matter of marketing, marketing would seem to fulfill this requirement. Note that this conclusion is *independent* of whether one subscribes to the narrower or more liberal thesis of marketing.

A distinct subject matter alone is not sufficient to distinguish sciences from other disciplines, because all disciplines have a subject matter (some less distinct than others). The previously cited perspective of chemistry provides a second insight into the basic nature of science. Note the phrase, "their structure, their properties, and their reactions." Every science seeks to describe and classify the structure and properties of its basic subject matter. Likewise, the term *reactions* suggests that the phenomena comprising the basic subject matter of chemistry are presumed to be systematically interrelated. Thus, another distinguishing characteristic: *Every science presupposes the existence of underlying uniformities or regularities among the phenomena that comprise its subject matter. The discovery of these underlying uniformities yields empirical regularities, lawlike generalizations (propositions), and laws.*

Underlying uniformities and regularities are necessary for science because (1) a primary goal of science is to provide responsibly supported explanations of phenomena,[45] and (2) the scientific explanation of phenomena requires the existence of laws or lawlike generalizations.[46] Uniformities and regularities are

---

[44] Richard H. Leftwich, *The Price System and Resource Allocation* (New York: Holt, Rinehart & Winston, 1966), p. 2.

[45] Same reference as footnote 40, p. 15.

[46] Carl G. Hempel, *Aspects of Scientific Explanation* (New York: Free Press, 1965), pp. 354–364.

also a requisite for theory development since theories are systematically related sets of statements, *including some lawlike generalizations*, that are empirically testable.[47]

The basic question for marketing is not whether there presently exist several "central theories" that serve to unify, explain, and predict marketing phenomena, as Buzzell suggests. Rather, the following should be asked: "Are there underlying uniformities and regularities among the phenomena comprising the subject matter of marketing?" This question can be answered affirmatively on two grounds—one *a priori* and one empirical. Marketing is a discipline that investigates human behavior. Since numerous uniformities and regularities have been observed in other behavioral sciences,[48] there is no *a priori* reason for believing that the subject matter of marketing will be devoid of uniformities and regularities. The second ground for believing that the uniformities exist is empirical. The quantity of scholarly research conducted on marketing phenomena during the past three decades probably exceeds the total of *all* prior research in marketing. Substantial research has been conducted in the area of channels of distribution. Also, efforts in the consumer behavior dimension of marketing have been particularly prolific. Granted, some of the research has been less than profound, and the total achievements may not be commensurate with the efforts expended. Nevertheless, who can deny that *some* progress has been made or that *some* uniformities have been identified? In short, who can deny that there exist uniformities and regularities interrelating the subject matter of marketing? I, for one, cannot.

The task of delineating the basic nature of science is not yet complete. Up to this point we have used chemistry to illustrate that all sciences involve (1) a distinct subject matter and the description and classification of that subject matter, and (2) the presumption that underlying the subject matter are uniformities and regularities that science seeks to discover. The chemistry example provides a final observation. Note that "chemistry is the *science of*. . . ." This suggests that sciences can be differentiated from other disciplines by the method of analysis. At the risk of being somewhat tautologous: sciences employ a set of procedures commonly referred to as the scientific method. As Bunge suggests, "No scientific method, no science."[49] The historical significance of the development and acceptance of the method of science cannot be overstated. It has been called "the most significant intellec-

---

[47] Richard S. Rudner, *The Philosophy of Social Science* (Englewood Cliffs, N.J.: Prentice-Hall, 1966), p. 10; and Shelby D. Hunt, "The Morphology of Theory and the General Theory of Marketing," JOURNAL OF MARKETING, Vol. 35 (April 1971), pp. 65–68.

[48] Bernard Berelson and Gary Steiner, *Human Behavior: An Inventory of Scientific Findings* (New York: Harcourt, Brace & World, 1964).

[49] Mario Bunge, *Scientific Research I: The Search for System* (New York: Springer-Verlag, 1967), p. 12.

tual contribution of Western civilization."[50] Is the method of science applicable to marketing?

Detailed explication of the scientific method is beyond the scope of this article and is discussed elsewhere.[51] Nevertheless, the cornerstone requirement of the method of science must be mentioned. The word *science* has its origins in the Latin verb *scire*, meaning "to know." Now, there are many ways *to know* things. The methods of tenacity, authority, faith, intuition, and science are often cited.[52] The characteristic that separates scientific knowledge from other ways to "know" things is the notion of *intersubjective certification*.

Scientific knowledge, in which theories, laws, and explanations are primal, must be *objective* in the sense that its truth content must be *intersubjectively certifiable*.[53] Requiring that theories, laws, and explanations be empirically testable ensures that they will be intersubjectively certifiable since different (but reasonably competent) investigators with differing attitudes, opinions, and beliefs will be able to make observations and conduct experiments to ascertain their truth content. "Science strives for objectivity in the sense that its statements are to be capable of public tests with results that do not vary essentially with the tester."[54] Scientific knowledge thus rests on the bedrock of empirical testability.

There is no reason whatsoever to presume that the scientific method of analysis is any less appropriate to marketing phenomena than to other disciplines. Similarly, scholarly researchers in marketing, although sometimes holding rather distorted notions concerning such topics as the role of laws and theories in research, seem to be at least as technically proficient as researchers in other areas. Finally, although some marketing researchers continue to cite "proprietary studies" as evidentiary support for their positions, the extent of this practice is now extremely small.

In summary, sciences (1) have a distinct subject matter drawn from the real world which is described and classified, (2) presume underlying uniformities and regularities interrelating the subject matter, and (3) adopt intersubjectively certifiable procedures for studying the subject matter. This

---

[50] Charles W. Morris, "Scientific Empiricism," in *Foundations of the Unity of Science*, Vol. 1, Otto Newrath, Rudolf Carnap and Charles Morris, eds. (Chicago: University of Chicago Press, 1955), p. 63.

[51] Shelby D. Hunt, *Marketing Theory: Conceptual Foundation of Research in Marketing* (Columbus, Ohio: Grid Publishing Co., 1976).

[52] Morris R. Cohen and Ernest Nagel, *Logic and the Scientific Method* (New York: Harcourt, Brace & World, 1934), p. 193.

[53] Same reference as footnote 36, p. 44.

[54] Carl G. Hempel, "Fundamentals of Concept Formation in Empirical Science," in *Foundations of the Unity of Science*, Vol. 2, Otto Newrath, ed. (Chicago: University of Chicago Press, 1970), p. 695.

perspective can be appropriately described as a consensus composite of philosophy of science views on science.[55] For example, Wartofsky suggests that a science is

> . . . an organized or systematic body of knowledge, using general laws or principles; that it is knowledge about the world; and that it is that kind of knowledge concerning which universal agreement can be reached by scientists sharing a common language (or languages) and common criteria for the *justification* of knowledge claims and beliefs.[56]

Is Marketing a Science? A Conclusion

The scope of the area called marketing has been shown to be exceptionally broad. Marketing has micro/macro dimensions, profit sector/nonprofit sector dimensions, and positive/normative dimensions. Reasonable people may disagree as to which combination of these dimensions represents the *appropriate* total scope of marketing, although a consensus seems to be developing to include all eight cells in Table 1. If marketing is to be restricted to *only* the profit/micro/normative dimension (as many practitioners would view it), then marketing is not a science and could not become one. All sciences involve the explanation, prediction, and understanding of phenomena.[57] These explanations and predictions frequently serve as useful guides for developing normative decision rules and normative models. Such rules and models are then *grounded* in science.[58] Nevertheless, any discipline that is *purely* evaluative or prescriptive (normative) is not a science. At least for marketing academe, restricting the scope of marketing to its profit/micro/normative dimension is unrealistic, unnecessary, and, without question, undesirable.

Once the appropriate scope of marketing has been expanded to include at least some *positive* dimensions (cells 1, 3, 5, and 7 in Table 1), the explanation,

---

[55] See, for example: Nagel, same reference as footnote 40, p. 4; May Brodbeck, *Readings in the Philosophy of the Social Sciences* (New York: Macmillan Co., 1968), pp. 1–11; Richard B. Braithwaite, *Scientific Explanation* (Cambridge: Cambridge University Press, 1951), pp. 1–21; B. F. Skinner, *Science and Human Behavior* (New York: Macmillan Co., 1953), pp. 14–22; Rudner, same reference as footnote 47, pp. 7–9; Abraham Kaplan, *The Conduct of Inquiry* (Scranton, Pa.: Chandler Publishing Co., 1964), p. 32; Popper, same reference as footnote 36, pp. 44–48; and Hempel, same reference as footnote 54, p. 672.

[56] Same reference as footnote 41, p. 23.

[57] Nagel, same reference as footnote 40, p. 15; Henry E. Kyburg, Jr., *Philosophy of Science* (New York: Macmillan Co., 1968), p. 3; Carl G. Hempel, "The Theoretician's Dilemma," in *Aspects of Scientific Explanation* (New York: Free Press, 1965), p. 173; and Nicholas Rescher, *Scientific Explanation* (New York: Free Press, 1970), p. 4.

[58] Mario Bunge, *Scientific Research II: The Search for Truth* (New York: Springer-Verlag, 1967), p. 132.

prediction, and understanding of these phenomena could be a science. The question then becomes whether the study of the positive dimensions of marketing has the requisite characteristics of a science. Aside from the strictly honorific overtons of *nonmarketers* accepting marketing as a science, the substantive characteristics differentiating sciences from other disciplines have been shown to be (1) a distinct subject matter drawn from the real world and the description and classification of that subject matter, (2) the presumption of underlying uniformities and regularities interrelating the subject matter, and (3) the adoption of the method of science for studying the subject matter.

The *positive* dimensions of marketing have been shown to have a subject matter properly distinct from other sciences. The marketing literature is replete with description and classification. There have been discoveries (however tentative) of uniformities and regularities among marketing phenomena. Finally, although Longman deplores "the rather remarkable lack of scientific method employed by scientists of marketing,"[59] researchers in marketing are at least as committed to the method of science as are researchers in other disciplines. Therefore, the study of the *positive* dimensions of marketing can be appropriately referred to as *marketing science.*

---

[59] Kenneth A. Longman, "The Management Challenge to Marketing Theory," in *New Essays in Marketing Theory*, George Fisk, ed. (Boston: Allyn & Bacon, 1971), p. 10.

The author wishes to gratefully acknowlege the constructive criticisms of earlier drafts of this article by Professors George W. Brooker and John R. Nevin, both of the University of Wisconsin-Madison.

QUESTIONS

1. Summarize the arguments for and against broadening the definition of marketing.
2. Describe the difference between micro and macro marketing perspectives and between positive and normative marketing perspectives.
3. Into what category of marketing's scope would a managerial marketing approach be placed?
4. Describe your views on whether marketing is a science.

PART TWO

Markets and
Their Characteristics

The development of effective marketing strategies begins with the customer. In order for marketers to create and manage exchange processes, they must have a thorough understanding of (1) what benefits customers desire, (2) what decision processes customers use to acquire these benefits, and (3) what value customers place on these benefits. Once this level of understanding of the customer is obtained, markets can be matched to the firm's resources and competitive strengths through the segmentation process, and targeted strategies can be developed.

Consumer behavior, like all human behavior, is a complex phenomenon affected by several factors and influences. An individual's culture, economic status, social environment, and personality are but a few of the influences on his or her needs, motives, attitudes, or methods of decision making. The first article in Part Two, "How Marketers Can Better Understand Consumers," provides a critical review of the type of information or factors that can be used to understand or predict buyer behavior. Suggestions are also provided for what type of information might prove to be most helpful to marketers in their planning processes. An example of how consumer profiles can be used by a firm is provided in the second article, "The ATM-Prone Consumer: A Profile and Implications." An important customer group, other than consumers, is composed of industrial buyers. The third article, "A Model of Industrial Buyer Behavior," describes a model that enables marketers to understand the complex factors and procedures that influence buying decisions in the industrial sector.

The focus of the last two articles is market segmentation, that is, the process of structuring the market into distinct groups such that members of each group are as homogeneous as possible in terms of product needs, personal characteristics, and response to marketing stimuli, while the group remains large enough to be profitable. The more precisely the profitable segments can be defined, the more effective the marketing strategies can become, because the firm will be better able to target its efforts specifically to the set of needs and characteristics of each segment.

This last point is the primary objective of the article "Market Segmentation as a Competitive Strategy," which asserts that merely identifying homogeneous segments is not sufficient and that the true value of segmentation is not realized until effective competitive strategies are derived. The development of such strategies requires matching competitors' offerings with the usual evaluations of the firm's offerings and customer needs.

The success of attempts to understand customers, to segment markets, and to develop strategies depends a great deal on the quality of the information used. Marketing research is the systematic process of collecting and processing information for marketing decisions. The final article, "How Research Relates to Marketing Process," describes the important role this activity plays in various stages of marketing planning.

The articles in Part Two attempt to provide an understanding of what data on customers should be obtained, how to obtain that data, and how to use that data to exploit opportunities or thwart competitive threats. Specifically, the objectives are to provide:

1. An appreciation of the important relationship between knowing one's market and the ultimate success of a marketing strategy,
2. A set of guidelines for implementing a market segmentation procedure, and
3. An appreciation of the role marketing research plays in developing marketing strategies.

1

HOW MARKETERS CAN BETTER UNDERSTAND CONSUMERS

Priscilla A. La Barbera
Larry J. Rosenberg

This article contends that conventional sources of consumer information, such as market surveys, sales data, and consultants, become more inadequate as consumers become more sophisticated in their acquisition and use of products. It describes ways that marketing managers can augment their traditional sources to better understand their markets.

Consumerism affects nearly every corporation. Pro-consumer government regulations pose problems, but what really exasperates executives is trying to understand changing consumer demands. Marketing research studies, sales data, market intelligence reports, and advice from numerous consultants have not provided sufficient information for marketing decisions. Although business has not given up on these conventional approaches, some firms are tapping new sources, with solid results.

- The Boston-based supermarket chain Stop and Shop credits its consumer advisory boards with several successful operational and policy changes—such as decreasing the number of package sizes stocked and installing aisle warmers in the frozen food section.
- Whirlpool Corporation acknowledges that its "cool line," a toll-free telephone system for consumer use, has measurably reduced product and service complaints.
- Through its consumer affairs division, Prudential Insurance produced a buyer's guide to make life insurance policies more comprehensible.

● When top executives of Southern Airways stood in the reservation lines of airports to hear complaints, such problems as cold in-flight coffee and inadequate flight information were corrected.

Approaches such as these can put companies in touch with consumers. In the 1960s, the gap supposedly was narrowed by the ambitious development of information systems to monitor consumer behavior and other market activity. While firms with these sophisticated systems often generated consumer-oriented marketing strategy, they faltered in identifying many genuine consumer needs, aspirations, and complaints. The consequences were attacks by consumer advocates, adverse publicity in the media, waves of government regulation, and increased consumer distrust of business.

We believe that companies of all sizes can do more to gain insight into the real world of consumers. After an appraisal of the conventional ways of monitoring consumers, we examine other sources. Next, we describe how firms can construct a system of approaches to better understand their consumers.

Progressive marketing has as its primary goal the recognition of the consumer viewpoint. Therefore, information on consumer behavior and the extent to which a firm is satisfying consumers must underlie marketing decisions. Conventional sources are necessary but have limitations.

Managers clearly attribute great importance to *market performance data.* Indicators such as sales volume, sales growth, and market share provide excellent feedback and are used directly in profit calculations. But they can measure only so much. While sales figures indicate customer acceptance in a given time period, they tell little about the degree of satisfaction.[1] They generally exclude such factors as brand loyalty, supply availability, and competitive alternatives, which can affect future sales and market share.

Marketing research is a specialized organization function by which information about consumers and the firm's activities in the marketplace is gathered and analyzed. Research spending has grown dramatically among major marketers in response to competitive pressure and government and consumer demands.[2] But would consumerism be as entrenched today if marketing researchers had more accurately read the consumer and social climates? Most marketing research remains project oriented and concerned primarily with competitive considerations, rarely with real consumer needs.[3]

---

[1] John A. Howard and James Hulbert, *Advertising and the Public Interest: A Staff Report to the Federal Trade Commission* (Chicago, Ill.: Crain Communications Inc., 1973), p. 3.

[2] "Research Outlays Show Sharp Increase: Harden," *Advertising Age,* 2 May 1977, p. 22.

[3] David A. Aaker and George S. Day, "Corporate Responses to Consumerism Pressures," *Harvard Business Review* 50 (November-December 1972): 118.

Because *sales representatives* meet with present and prospective customers, they have the potential for delivering timely and valuable information for managerial decision making. However, problems can arise if heavy demands are placed on sales personnel. Moreover, good sales people can be poor feedback reporters.[4]

Marketing consultants possess acknowledged and objective expertise. Through them the marketing manager can keep in touch with trends, explore customer problems, and seek advice on courses of action. The limitation of many consultants is their orientation toward market trends rather than the consumer interest. Rumblings of consumer discontent may be glossed over.

As an informal data source, *surrogate consumers* include an executive's family, friends, and secretary. For example, a spouse complains about a recent shopping experience at the executive's store or about the performance of a product at home. Such opinions can have a dramatic influence because of the personal relationship and ease of communicating with executives. But these surrogates are not representative of consumers who encounter a distant and faceless corporate bureaucracy.

Another Generation to the Rescue

In recent years, some firms recognized the weaknesses of the conventional information mix and tried other ways of reaching consumers and letting them reach the firm. As a result, a new generation of sources took shape, enhancing corporate sensitivity to the consumer's changing world and leading to pro-consumer marketing strategies. These sources include face-to-face inter-action with customers, consumer advisory boards, voluntary consumer communication, consumer affairs units, and consumer-oriented consultants. Here is how they improve the corporate capacity to listen.

CONSUMER ORIENTED. They zero in on the consumers' world, rather than on more impersonal market variables (segments, shares, and trends).

MORE DIRECT. They speak directly to consumers rather than relying on filtered data and interpretations of less direct sources.

MORE ANTICIPATORY. They more effectively identify consumer interests in the early stages, in constrast to sources dealing mainly with consumer reactions to marketing actions.

---

[4] Thomas M. Rohan, "Getting (and Using) Good Feedback From Salesmen," *Industry Week*, 19 January 1976, pp. 24–30.

MORE AWARE.   They possess a keener capacity for tapping consumer feelings, rather than just thoughts.

DISSATISFACTION SENSITIVE.   They stand a better chance of registering consumer dissatisfaction, all too often overlooked by the traditional sources.

GOVERNMENT AND CONSUMER INFLUENCED.   They recognize the effect on consumers of the government-consumer advocate coalition, as distinct from the effect of competitors and intermediaries.

Some of the newer consumer sources have surfaced or are flourishing in a particular industry. However, we are convinced that all these corporate links to consumers can be used effectively by almost any large firm. This simply involves grasping the nature of the information source and adapting it to the organization's situation.

EXPERIENCING WHAT CONSUMERS EXPERIENCE.   Most large organizations shield executives from contact with consumers. This isolation is compounded when subordinates insulate executives from bad news, especially in the early stages. To break out of the corporate cocoon, some managers *seek interaction with customers*. Either voluntarily or because of company policy, these managers ride repair trucks, answer telephones, wait on customers, and stand in lines—without identifying themselves. They seek out customers' opinions of the company's products or service. With an eye on consumerist critics, executives can benefit from feeling firsthand many of the frustrations their customers experience.

For example, Avis's chairman, Winston J. Morrow, Jr., gets in line with customers waiting for cars at airports and sometimes steps behind the counter to check out customer reactions. McDonald's Corporation executives eat regularly at company fast-food outlets. Signs ordering people to move to the "next position" were removed from all outlets following chairman Ray Kroc's experience and statement: "It's up to us to move to the customer."

The opportunity for senior executives to gather field information may be limited. Some executives prefer the VIP treatment. Even when executives visit service outlets, a typical experience may elude them—if they are recognized or if employees are notified prior to the visit. To prevent this, several companies use a spotter service to check on product or service performance.

MEETING THE BOARD OF CONSUMERS.   One way several companies have let consumers in is through the *consumer advisory board*, sometimes called a customer council. The same cross-section of a firm's customers meets with executives periodically as a group to air feelings and share suggestions. Companies view these regional and local boards as communication opportunities rather than research vehicles. Nonetheless, experiencing the content and intensity of comments can help executives understand consumers.

Sound objectives for a consumer advisory board come from Stop and Shop Companies: (1) make store personnel aware of what consumers are thinking; (2) elicit the consumer's impression of store operations, merchandising, and prices; (3) give consumers an opportunity to voice their complaints and to hear the experts explain the situation; (4) act as a sounding board for proposed products and policies; and (5) glean ideas to improve operations at all levels.[5]

Consumer advisory boards work well for firms with products that consumers buy frequently. This explains their growing popularity among mass-merchandising retailers, especially supermarket chains. One major insurance firm has a board for its automobile insurance customers, but has held off launching one for its life insurance policyholders. The success of these boards in retailing should tempt firms in other industries to consider adapting them to their own use.

A typical consumer advisory board has ten to twenty members who meet with lower- to upper-level executives every few months. Selection criteria vary among firms. The first Stop and Shop board roster consisted of prominent women active in clubs, educational groups, and the like. Increasingly, companies pursue a board comprised of diverse consumers—by age, income, education, ethnicity, and race. Board members rarely receive payment, although they may receive travel reimbursement, lunch, and gifts.

The board meeting involves a round table of consumers and executives. The consumers express their views and offer suggestions; the executives submit proposals and explain corporate conditions. Executives and board members establish the meeting's agenda. The minutes of board meetings go to managers for possible action before the next board meeting.

At first glance the consumer advisory board resembles a focus group— often used for qualitative market research. The focus group is different because it has a professional moderator to direct the dialogue and encourage opinions on a specific issue from a homogeneous group (usually of "typical" homemakers). The name of the sponsoring firm is withheld or revealed only near the end.

Evaluating the effectiveness of consumer advisory boards reveals benefits and difficulties. Stop and Shop executives generally laud its board's role, although they admit to being stymied in obtaining a group of representative consumers.

Keeping the same board membership session after session poses a

---

[5] Dorothy Haase Kuper and Stephen A. Greyser, "The Stop and Shop Consumer Board of Directors," Intercollegiate Case Clearing House, No. 1-571-058, 1970, pp. 4–5.

dilemma for management. On the positive side, members gain confidence about speaking out and become knowledgeable about corporate operations. The risk comes when the "friendly adversaries" begin to feel like "company people," sympathizing with the firm's viewpoint rather than criticizing its practices. Rotating a minority of the board's membership each year can help.

A further problem with consumer advisory boards is related to member suggestions that the company cannot implement. Supermarket boards have objected to long, slow-moving check-out lines, but already slim profits and high wages of clerks prevent corrective action. Furthermore, managers of frequently criticized departments may become discouraged by the impossibility of fully pleasing customers. Another problem arises when management becomes more concerned with the board receiving publicity than with its consumer information value.

HEARING CONSUMER COMPLAINTS AND QUESTIONS.   Thanks to consumerism, the public finds it easier to inquire, complain, suggest, and even praise. Many firms have realized the value of this *voluntary consumer communication*. Not only can consumers have their problems addressed or their questions answered, but also the information they provide is vital for decision making.

While most consumers nurse their complaints in silence, others contact business by letter, phone call, or visit. Many airlines, hotels, and restaurants encourage this by providing reply cards soliciting opinions. Several appliance and automobile producers promote their toll-free telephone "cool lines." A few firms, such as General Electric, regularly conduct surveys on customer dissatisfactions.[6]

The organizational units handling customer complaints often prepare duplicate copies of a complaint before it is resolved, dispatching copies to appropriate departments or executives. This makes information available for investigation, alerts corporate counsel to a specific grievance that could lead to litigation or a government inquiry, and provides an early warning of problems whose prompt solution could avert further complaints, bad publicity, or a product recall. Even if complaints turn out to be due to consumer error, an early signal can be crucial. Complaint letters tipped off Pillsbury and General Foods to exploding pots, failing cakes, unjelled gelatin, and "ground glass" in biscuits (acutally crystallized sugar from excessive moisture during production). This let them swiftly pinpoint product code dates and recall lots from store shelves.

---

[6] Robert W. Pratt, "The Index of Consumer Satisfaction and Corporate Marketing Policy," in *Proceedings of the Third Annual Conference of the Association for Consumer Research* (November 1972): 742–45.

On a monthly or quarterly basis, summaries give the volume and breakdown of complaints—Trans World Airlines has 400 categories for detailed analysis. Several large firms have computerized the processing and analysis of complaint data. At many, annoyance with complaints is giving way to more positive feelings.

Furthermore, complaint data can make management aware of otherwise undiscovered attitudes toward the firm's goods and service. Consumer complaint reports have led to improvements in the physical product, packaging, advertising, distribution, and quality control programs.[7]

Management should heed the important message of consumers requesting more information. Consumer questions indicate deficiencies in advertising, labeling, or point-of-sale material. Missing and misunderstood information can scare away buyers. In comparison to sales reports and marketing research, this information is quick and inexpensive.

However, management must exercise caution in using voluntary consumer communication to make marketing decisions. First, complaint patterns can mislead. After a product improvement in General Mill's long-established Bisquick brand appeared, the consumer complaint rate soared. Because technical and consumer testing had convinced management of the net benefit of the change, the company stayed with the modification. A subsequent upturn in sales justified its patience.

Relying on voluntary consumer communication as a barometer of consumer satisfaction leads to a second risk. The interpretation of a consumer communication can be incorrect when a complaint actually is a result of personal problems. Also, the wording or phrasing can obscure the depth of dissatisfaction. To fully use consumer feedback, marketers must probe the roots of consumer discontent, especially with follow-up surveys.[8]

HEEDING YOUR OWN CONSUMER SPECIALIST. Called by various names, a corporate *consumer affairs unit* attempts to improve the firm's relations with consumers, making it more responsive to their interests. The nature of its activities varies with the line of business, funds and staff available, consumer target, and the company's general consumer policy.[9] Typically, it will: (1) resolve and analyze customer communication; (2) develop and disseminate

[7]C. L. Kendall and Frederick A. Russ, "Warranty and Complaint Policies: An Opportunity for Marketing Management," *Journal of Marketing* 39 (April 1975): 36–43.

[8]Mary Gardiner Jones, "The Consumer Affairs Office: Essential Element in Corporate Policy and Planning," *California Management Review* 20 (Summer 1978): 65–66.

[9]Milton L. Blum, John B. Stewart, and Edward W. Wheatley, "Consumer Affairs: Viability of the Corporate Response," *Journal of Marketing* 38 (April 1974): 13–19.

better information to consumers on the purchase and use of company products or services; (3) serve as an internal consumer advocate and consultant; and/or (4) provide liaison with consumer organizations.[10]

The effectiveness of consumer affairs units rests on their credibility in the eyes of the organization. Because most of these units are new, antagonizing other divisions would ruin their potential effect. At Prudential Insurance, the consumer affairs staff works quietly to disseminate its viewpoint throughout the company. Technical people (such as actuaries) are assigned to the staff for a few years. Once educated to the consumer view, they rejoin their original units to spread the word. J. C. Penney's consumer affairs director says she does not want herself or her department singled out. Instead, her department tries to share in corporate decision making, providing information just as the finance and sales departments do.

The impact of consumer affairs units can be heightened through formal involvement with representatives of corporate operating divisions. RCA established a consumer council three years ago to get all divisions to see their common interest in relating to consumers and stop blaming one another for problems.

To become an effective representative of the consumer interest, the consumer affairs unit must take an active part in marketing decision making. Since the unit can acquire information on consumer opinions and problems that might otherwise be ignored, it can contribute to basic goals, such as increased sales and the attraction of new customers.[11] Most of these units, however, have been poorly integrated into the corporate structure.[12] Only when top management appreciates the benefits of involving such units in corporate planning can they bring their special perspective to marketing decisions.

LEARNING FROM CONSUMER EXPERTS.   A growing breed of outside advisors is stepping from the ranks of consumer advocates, government officials, and media figures. These *consumer-oriented consultants* translate their own experience and sensitivity into recommendations that business can act upon. They bring managers into contact with activist consumers and help firms shape strategies to head off public criticism and government regulation.

For Bristol-Myers, Bess Myerson (former New York City commissioner

---

[10] E. Patrick McGuire, *The Consumer Affairs Department: Organization and Functions* (New York: The Conference Board, Inc., 1973), p. 5.

[11] Esther Peterson, "Consumerism as a Retailer's Asset," *Harvard Business Review* 52 (May-June 1974): 91.

[12] Claes Fornell, *Consumer Input for Marketing Decisions: A Study of Corporate Departments for Consumer Affairs* (New York: Praeger Publishers, 1976), pp. 146–48.

of consumer affairs) edited the *Guide to Consumer Product Information*, which covers the buying, using, and storing of forty-six household products. Advertisements offering the book free brought in a huge response. Ellen Zawel (former president of the National Consumer Congress) advised a supermarket client that its obligation in the nutrition area consisted of providing information only, and contended that nutrition education belonged in the schools.

Building the Consumer Information Network

Companies need not choose between the traditional and the new generation sources of consumer information. Greater sensitivity to consumers can be gained by combining the approaches into what we call the *consumer information network*. For firms with an all-encompassing marketing information system, the network would comprise a major subsystem. For others, it would provide a way to upgrade consumer intelligence capability. Although few companies can point to a full-fledged network, many are taking steps in this direction.

For companies seeking more consumer insights, here is how to launch a consumer information network.

SETTING NETWORK OBJECTIVES. System objectives must be established. When they are clearly defined and measurable, they permit monitoring of the network and future corrective actions.

Some objectives include:

- timeliness—the minimum time needed to react to consumer input;
- accuracy—the minimum acceptable level of valid information; (This depends on confidence in the consumer information, as well as on the cost involved to deliver it.)
- sensitivity—how close the information is to consumer realities;
- outreach—how extensive the data are. (Do they include consumers and their intermediaries—consumer advocates, media executives, and government officials?)

ANALYZING EXISTING INFORMATION. Each of the consumer sources should be rated according to its success in generating information. The effectiveness of conventional consumer sources depends on how the firm uses them. For example, Philadelphia's Strawbridge and Clothier department store regards its many part-time sales people as an early and reliable gauge of customer sentiment. Because part-timers respond more as customers than as regular employees, management listens carefully to their comments on merchandise, service, and community relations.

Many companies rely on focus group research to create hypotheses about consumer behavior, while ignoring other potential applications. In contrast, New Jersey-based Supermarkets General considers focus groups a key source of information, running about ten groups annually on specific issues, such as meat, automated check-outs, and the universal product code.

Next, the company should determine whether existing consumer sources actually influence the organization. For example, do sales representatives' reports that customers are misusing a new product trigger a market research study? Is a consumer survey automatically initiated after a 3 percent slide in market share? Raising such questions can indicate whether the information is being integrated into a system for actual use.

Management should then assess the weaknesses within the familiar consumer sources. Because some companies depend largely on lagging indicators of consumer opinions, there is inadequate lead time to prevent problems. Also, various sources show insufficient sensitivity to what consumers actually experience and feel.

IMPROVING NETWORK EFFECTIVENESS.   Evaluating traditional sources of consumer information should reveal gaps in the system. Now many can be filled by the new generation of consumer sources. In predicting the consumer of the future, Pillsbury's marketing research staff expressed confidence in its demographic projections but enriched its fuzzy estimates of consumer attitudes with the impressions of consumer affairs professionals.

A closely related issue is determining how extensive a network the firm requires. This involves specifying the number of sources and initial investment and operating expenses. Intense competitive pressure compels consumer goods producers and large retail chains to maintain close contact. . . . Clearly, the more competition and government impinge on a given company, the more it must understand consumers.

Linking together as many of the network's components as possible increases its effectiveness. For example, a consumer consultant arrives to give advice on setting up or reviewing a consumer affairs department. In turn that unit takes on responsibility for analyzing voluntary consumer communication, studying sales force feedback, and organizing consumer advisory boards.

In this network context, management can create hybrid approaches— such as Colorado-based Apollo Supers' "Buyers' Participation Days." Weekly, in one of its stores, a buyer sets up shop to interview wholesale food representatives. Through store handouts and newspaper ads, shoppers are informed that they may sit in on the sessions to ask questions and to make complaints or suggestions. Goodwill is generated, and buyers and store managers became more attuned to customer preferences for services, prices, and assortments.

RALLYING ROUND THE NETWORK.   Prospective home bases for the consumer information network include marketing intelligence, consumer affairs, or even a separate unit. The specific location of a well-functioning network matters less than centralization and identifiability. In any case, a coordinator and staff should be appointed to ensure the network's integrity and accountability. At Pillsbury, a consumer information system was forged when the marketing research and consumer affairs staffs were reorganized under the vice-president of marketing services, who reports to the head of the group of consumer product divisions.

The company's chief executive officer should get involved in committing the organization to the network concept. When the CEO assumes an active role, impressive results can occur. Complaint letters read by RCA's president led to some pointed remarks about the long time between receipt of a letter and final action by the service branches. Subsequently, the consumer affairs unit directly notified the service people, thus slashing response time and the complaint rate.

Companies can benefit by forming a task force of representatives from those units gathering consumer information and those units using it. This can increase consumer influence on decisions in functional areas and overall corporate strategy. Such committees throughout the Bell System studied policies affecting telephone customers and put their recommendations into action.

MONITORING NETWORK PERFORMANCE.   An annual audit makes possible an evaluation of the consumer information network's performance. The auditors may come from an internal staff or from the outside. A systematic review would cover network objectives, policies, operating costs, and results. If performance should fall below the planned level, modification of the network could follow.

One food manufacturer audits certain corporate operations every six months to ensure responsiveness to its consumer information system. It checks, for instance, on whether quality control remedied consumer complaints in less than two weeks, whether complaint letters got answered within hours of receipt, and whether products achieved a predetermined ratio of compliments to complaints.

Network users should state periodically how the consumer information has been incorporated into their decision making. Senior management should monitor these reports to encourage greater use of the network. In addition, the reports provide a basis on which to adjust the network.

Conclusion

Many companies gather extensive information about their marketplace, and some operate elaborate marketing information systems. Yet, executive understanding of the consumer viewpoint—at the heart of progressive marketing—all too often is inadequate. The consumer information network within an organization can help solve this dilemma. Conventional sources and new generation sources are used to increase executive sensitivity to the changing consumer world. For a company to be consumer-oriented today, it must take steps to develop an effective network. The network concept promises to narrow the gap between what consumers need and what a company thinks they need.

QUESTIONS

1. What types of techniques or procedures are included in the traditional marketing "information mix"?
2. What are some of the suggested alternatives for firms to use to obtain additional insights and information about their consumers?
3. How do consumer advisory boards differ from systems using face-to-face customer interactions as an information source? In general, when would advisory boards be more appropriate?
4. What are the steps involved in establishing a consumer-information network?
5. Should the research procedures suggested in this article replace the traditional marketing research techniques or supplement them? Give reasons for your answer.

2

THE ATM-PRONE CONSUMER: A PROFILE AND IMPLICATIONS

Thomas J. Stanley
George P. Moschis

This selection provides details of a consumer study on the acceptance of automatic teller machines. It also uses demographic and psychographic profiles to develop a strategy for the delivery of financial services.

The introduction of Automated Teller Machines (ATMs) by banks promised financial institutions significant increases in productivity by reducing the need to retain more costly live tellers and expensive branches, thus lowering the costs associated with retail banking. The success of this strategy, implemented by an increasing number of banks, depends on the consumer's propensity to use ATMs and substitute them for live tellers.

A recent consumer study, however, revealed a low ATM-usage rate, with highest usage volumes generated by the younger, better-educated, higher-income, upscale-employed, financially active respondents.[1] The same study found that the perceived importance of ATMs varied by similar characteristics. However, low usage of the ATMs and different consumer characteristics associated with it may simply reflect the lack of ATM availability or low availability in areas populated by consumers of different characteristics. The present study was undertaken to answer questions regarding consumer

---

[1] Thomas J. Stanley, Murphy A. Sewell, George P. Moschis, "Consumer Profiles by Payment Types," Strategic Research and Planning Paper, Working Paper Number Five, Georgia State University 1982.

acceptance of the ATM innovation in retail banking by identifying consumer life-style and demographic characteristics associated with ATM usage. The article also presents several important implications for those interested in developing strategies for productively marketing ATMs.

Methodology

The data used in this study were collected by mail questionnaire during the fall of 1981. Fifteen hundred households were randomly selected from households listed in the city directory of a major city located in the eastern United States. The sample included only those households that were located within census tracts where the average household income was in excess of $25,000. It was the intent of the study to sample households located in neighborhoods in the top quartile of income distribution for the entire Standard Metropolitan Statistical Area, since such households were relatively more likely to be potential users of ATMs than were lower-income households.

From a double first-class mailing, 662 completed questionnaires were returned (a 44.0 percent response rate). Comparisons were made with regard to the age, income, and housing values of those responding, and census figures for those areas selected for study. Those responding were statistically similar as a group to those heads of households within the census tracts used as a sampling base.

A letter was sent with the questionnaire requesting that the individual responsible for making the financial decisions for the household complete the survey instrument. To overcome the issue of ATM availability, respondents were asked to indicate *intention* to use, rather than actual use, assuming that those already using ATMs would respond affirmatively.

Forty-five percent of the 662 respondents surveyed indicated that they would use an ATM if one were placed near their home or place of work. These respondents were categorized as ATM-prone. Approximately the same percentage of respondents indicated that they would not be likely to use an ATM. These 296 respondents were classified as non-ATM-prone. Seventy-two respondents, or 10.9 percent of the sample, had no preference or no opinion.

Respondents were also asked to respond to several financial life-style statements. Some of these items were used in previous studies.[2] Others were developed specifically for this study. Finally, respondents were asked to

---

[2] Thomas J. Stanley, William D. Danko, and Elizabeth C. Hirschman, "Life Style Correlates of Bank Patronage Decisions," *Journal of Retail Banking* (December 1980), pp. 10–20. Also see Thomas J. Stanley, Leonard L. Berry, and William D. Danko, "Personal Service Versus Convenience," *Journal of Retail Banking* (June 1979), pp. 54–61.

indicate the desirability of selected financial services, and to provide demographic information.

Because the sample was generated from one section of the country and focused on high-income households, the results must be interpreted in light of these limitations. In addition, because the main purpose of the study was to identify consumer characteristics associated with ATM usage, the emphasis is on examining relationships, rather than on describing response distributions.

Results

FINANCIAL LIFE STYLES.   The responses to the financial life-style statements by the ATM-prone and non-ATM-prone groups are given in Table 1.

CONVENIENCE ORIENTED.   The ATM-prone respondents were found to be significantly more convenience-oriented than those who were unlikely to use ATMs. More than sixty percent of the ATM-prone respondents agreed with the statement, "If I drive to a bank, I generally use the drive-in window rather than go into the lobby." Only 49.5 percent of the non-prone group agreed with this statement.

A significantly larger percentage of the ATM-prone group as opposed to the non-ATM-prone group (56.0 vs. 42.2 percent) agreed with the statement, "If a bank near me were open on Saturdays, and my bank remained closed on Saturdays, then I would consider switching my account to the bank open on Saturday." In addition, 53.3 percent of the ATM-prone respondents agreed with the statement, "It would be very helpful to me if banks stayed open at night like department stores and supermarkets." Only 43.4 percent of the non-prone group agreed with this statement. However, only 27.8 percent of the ATM-prone group agreed with the statement, "I would be very hesitant to use a bank in a department store or supermarket even if it were more convenient to do so." More than half of the non-prone group (55.7 percent) agreed with this statement. Interestingly, no significant difference separated the groups in terms of convenience of location (70.3 vs. 68.7 percent). Thus, the groups differ more along the time-convenience factor than they do along the location-convenience factor.

TRANSACTION-INNOVATIVENESS ORIENTED.   The ATM-prone group, when compared with the non-prone respondents, is more likely to be innovative in terms of financial transactions. For example, 49.9 percent of the ATM-prone group agreed with the statement that "I would prefer to pay bills by telephone if I had the opportunity." Only 33.5 percent of the non-prone group agreed with this statement. Also, seventy-five percent of the ATM-prone respon-

Table 1

FINANCIAL LIFE-STYLE CORRELATES OF ATM-PRONE CONSUMERS

Financial Life-Style Statements	Percent of Respondents Agreeing with Financial Life-style Statements ATM-Prone		Significance Level
	Yes (n=294)	No (n=296)	
Convenience Oriented			
If I drive to a bank, I generally use the drive-in window rather than go to the lobby.	60.4	49.5	.05
If a bank near me was open on Saturdays, and my bank remained closed on Saturdays, then I would consider switching my account to the bank open on Saturdays.	56.0	42.2	.05
It would be very helpful to me if banks stayed open at night like department stores and supermarkets.	53.3	43.4	.05
I would be very hesitant to use a bank in a department store or supermarket even if it were more convenient to do so.	27.8	55.7	.05
The convenience of a bank's location is the most important factor in my selection of a bank.	70.3	68.7	.77 [sic]
Transaction-Innovativeness Oriented			
I would prefer to pay bills by telephone if I had the opportunity.	49.9	33.5	.05
I would like to be able to make financial transactions from my own home-based teller terminal.	75.0	54.6	.05

Table 1 (continued)

| Financial Life-Style Statements | Percent of Respondents Agreeing with Financial Life-style Statements ATM-Prone | | Significance Level |
	Yes (n = 294)	No (n = 296)	
Financial-Service, Bargain-Shopping Oriented			
I would switch banks if I could earn 1 or 2 percent more interest on my checking account balance.	73.6	57.3	.05
I would change banks if I had to keep $300 in my checking account to avoid a service charge.	77.0	64.0	.05
Economic Aspirations			
In terms of wealth accumulation, my greatest achievements are ahead of me.	78.9	64.6	.05
Credit Union Oriented			
A credit union is an excellent place to have a savings account.	80.0	71.4	.05
I would rather borrow money from a bank than a credit union even if the interest rate was 2 or 3 percentage points higher.	16.2	28.9	.05
Credit unions are really for working class people—people who don't make a lot of money.	17.7	24.2	.05
Personal Service Oriented			
It makes me feel better if the tellers at my bank know my name.	76.2	78.9	n.s.

Table 1 (continued)

Financial Life-Style Statements	Percent of Respondents Agreeing with Financial Life-style Statements ATM-Prone		Significance Level
	Yes (n = 294)	No (n = 296)	
I think it is important to personally know the officers of the financial institution with which I deal.	64.0	67.0	n.s.
It doesn't matter to me whether tellers are friendly as long as they are fast and efficient.	43.8	46.4	n.s.

dents, compared with only 54.6 percent of the non-prone respondents, indicated that they would like to be able to make financial transactions from their own home-based teller terminals.

FINANCIAL-SERVICE, BARGAIN-SHOPPING ORIENTED.   The ATM-prone group is more price sensitive than is the non-ATM-prone group. Nearly three-fourths (73.6 percent) of the ATM-prone respondents indicated that they would switch banks if they could earn one or two percent more interest on their checking account balances. Only 57.3 percent of the other group responded in a similar manner. In addition, seventy-seven percent of the respondents classified as ATM-prone, compared with sixty-four percent of the non-prone group, agreed with the statement, "I would change banks if I had to keep a minimum balance of $300 in my checking account to avoid a service charge."

ECONOMIC ASPIRATIONS.   The ATM-prone consumers are more likely to have stronger economic aspirations than are their non-ATM-prone counterparts. Nearly eighty percent of the ATM-prone consumers agreed with the statement, "In terms of wealth accumulation, my greatest achievements are ahead of me," compared with only 64.6 percent of the non-prone group agreeing with this statement.

CREDIT UNION ORIENTED.   The ATM-prone group was found to be more credit union oriented than was the other category of consumers. Eighty percent of the former agreed with the statement, "A credit union is an excellent place to have a savings account." Approximately seventy-one percent of the non-ATM-prone group also agreed with this statement. Similarly, only 16.2 percent of the ATM-prone respondents indicated that they would rather borrow money from a bank than from a credit union, even if the interest rate were two or three percentage points higher, compared with 28.9 percent of the non-ATM-prone group. Also, a relatively smaller percentage (17.7 percent) of the ATM-prone group agreed with the statement, "Credit unions are really for working class people—people who don't make a lot of money," compared with 24.2 percent of their non-ATM-prone counterparts.

PERSONAL SERVICE ORIENTED.   Table 1 also shows some interesting similarities between the ATM-prone and non-prone groups. No significant statistical difference separates the two groups in terms of attitudes toward personal service. Nearly equal percentages of the ATM-prone (76.2 percent) and the non-ATM-prone respondents (78.9 percent) agreed with the statement, "It makes me feel better if the tellers at my bank know my name." Also, no significant difference was found in terms of the percentage of both groups agreeing with the statement, "It is important to personally know the officers of the financial institution with which I deal" (64.0 percent vs. 67.0 percent). Approximately forty-five percent of both groups agreed with the statement, "It doesn't matter to me whether tellers are friendly as long as they are fast and efficient."

SPECIAL SERVICE ORIENTED.   Respondents to the study were asked to rate the desirability of several special financial-service offerings (see Table 2). The ATM-prone segment was more likely than the other group to indicate

Table 2
DESIRABILITY OF SPECIAL SERVICE OFFERINGS OF ATM-PRONE CONSUMERS

Financial Service	Percent of Respondents Evaluating Services as "Desirable" ATM-Prone Yes	No	Significance Level
Personal Line of Credit/Overdraft	81.8	68.4	.00
Transactions by Phone	64.7	43.4	.00
Bill Paying	63.0	52.4	.02
Investment Advice	72.2	62.9	.03
Estate Planning/Advice	65.1	57.1	.08

preference for the following upscale financial-service features: personal line of credit/overdraft (81.8 vs. 68.4 percent); transactions by phone (64.7 vs. 43.4 percent); preauthorized bill paying (63.0 vs. 52.4 percent); investment advice (72.2 vs. 62.9 percent); and estate planning/advice (65.1 vs. 57.1 percent).

DEMOGRAPHIC CHARACTERISTICS.   Compared with the non-prone consumer, the ATM-prone respondent is more likely to be younger and have more years of formal education (see Table 3). More than forty percent of the ATM-prone group was found to be under thirty-six years of age. Only 20.4 percent of the other group was under thirty-six years of age.

The ATM-prone group as a whole is well-educated, with 62.8 percent being college graduates. Less than one-half (47.2 percent) of the other group graduated from college. Educational differences did not translate into significant income differences between the two groups, however. Nearly forty-four percent of the respondents who favored ATMs and 40.7 percent of the other group had annual incomes in excess of $30,000. Thus, although both groups generate similar incomes, the ATM-prone group is significantly younger and better-educated than is the non-prone segment. This ATM-prone segment is significant because it represents a major population-growth cohort that is the product of the baby boom of the 1940s and 1950s.

Discussion

These results indicate that ATM-prone consumers may be more sensitive than non-ATM-prone consumers to variations in time convenience when making financial-service patronage decisions. For example, a significantly greater percentage of the ATM-prone respondents indicated preferences for banks that stayed open on Saturdays or at night. These results would suggest that ATM users are very time-sensitive, and consequently seek innovations that

Table 3	**DEMOGRAPHIC CHARACTERISTICS OF ATM-PRONE CONSUMERS**		
	ATM-Prone		Significance
Characteristics	*Yes (%)*	*No (%)*	*Level*
Age (under 36 years of age)	41.3	20.4	.00
Education (college graduates)	62.8	47.2	.00
Annual Income (more than $30,000)	43.7	40.7	.78

will help them increase the productive use of this resource. However, both the ATM-prone and non-prone groups almost equally rated location convenience as important when making such decisions.

Most financial institutions within the study area that offer ATMs placed them in or directly adjacent to traditional offices and branches. Thus, these institutions have overlooked a potentially major advantage that ATMs have over traditional branch offices. ATMs are most productive when they are not directly competing in the same physical space with alternative facilities.[3] "ATMs can provide high volume services . . . while a hub office dispenses a full range of services within a reasonable distance."[4]

Why should the consumer use an ATM instead of a live teller if both are equally conveniently located? It is highly plausible that ATMs will be significantly more attractive to consumers when these innovations have the advantage of location convenience. Thus, marketers of financial services should consider placing ATMs in viable market areas where alternative distribution systems are not present.

Location advantage may be the most important factor that will encourage consumers from both groups to trade off live-teller transactions in favor of ATM transactions. Live tellers and ATMs are likely to be complementary where they are located near each other. Thus, the ATM may not necessarily be displacing live-teller transactions. When ATMs and live tellers are located outside each other's "trade areas," they are more likely to be viewed as substitutes and less likely to be used as complements. Distribution systems that are complements may be redundant, and therefore unproductive.[5]

Implications

The results of transaction-innovativeness orientation have several important implications for financial-service organizations. Consumers who have a propensity to adopt one transaction innovation are likely to adopt related innovations. Thus, a consumer with experience in using ATMs or even the intention to use an ATM would be more likely than others to adopt a home terminal. Financial institutions that successfully market ATMs will likely gain long-run strategic advantages in the marketing of home terminals and related innovations. The results of this study suggest that ATM users will be more easily cross-sold on adopting home terminals than will consumers who have

[3]David A. Brooks, "Automated Teller Machines Only EFT Promising Profits Over the Near Term," *American Banker* (May 19, 1980), pp. 14–15.

[4]*Ibid.*, p. 14.

[5]"Can You Afford Not to Offer ATM Services?" *Savings and Loan News* (August 1981), p. 110.

had no experience with these types of innovations. Therefore, financial institutions should recognize the importance of long-term investments in transaction innovations.

Since the ATM-prone consumer is price sensitive, it is important that financial-service organizations wanting to attract and retain these customers provide perceived value in their offerings. It is likely that this group would be willing to trade off some traditional service features for a lower price on services and/or higher returns on savings and investments. Financial institutions able to productively substitute ATMs for expensive brick-and-mortar facilities and live tellers may want to pass on some of those cost benefits to their patrons. They should reward customers who adopt cost-saving innovations with such benefits as rebates or reduced service charges for conducting financial transactions via ATMs instead of through live tellers. Alternatively, financial institutions wishing to reduce consumer demand for live tellers may find a service charge per live-teller transaction to be an effective demarketing tactic. Those consumers who genuinely need to use live tellers will likely be willing to pay for this service. Financial institutions must begin to realize that free services are often abused services.

These results on personal-service orientation indicate that many members of the ATM-prone group perceive personalized service as being important. One plausible interpretation of this finding would be that ATM-prone consumers are not alienated from bank personnel or personal service. These individuals are as strong in a statistical sense in their personal orientations as are the non-ATM-prone consumers. Although it is possible for a financial institution to successfully replace some live tellers with ATMs, personalized service is still important, even to the ATM-prone consumer. A substantial number of respondents from both groups indicated that they would like tellers to know their names, while a minority believed that teller speed and efficiency are more important than friendliness. Even the ATM-prone consumer desires high-quality personal service from financial institutions. Financial institutions are making a serious miscalculation if they attempt to increase productivity by reducing the quality of the personnel that deal with their clients. Many of those persons who prefer personal transactions demand fast, friendly, and efficient service, and will pay a premium for it. Others will use those services only if they are free.

Conclusion

This study indicates that many ATM-oriented consumers are likely to purchase upscale-service offerings such as those previously outlined. Financial institutions should recongize that these types of consumers have multiple financial-service needs. These needs extend beyond a transaction vehicle such as the ATM.

ATMs and related financial innovations have significant potential for increasing the productivity of financial institutions. To date, electronic technology has advanced faster than has the ability of marketers to change consumer habits. Producers of ATMs as well as financial service marketers must place greater priority on the marketing of ATMs and related technological innovations. Without this commitment, innovations will continue to be developed before the majority of consumers are willing to adopt them.

QUESTIONS

1. Table one shows a statistical difference between the life-styles of ATM-prone customers and non-ATM-prone customers. Do these results provide differences that you feel are managerially useful? That is, do the data suggest strategic alternatives that could be used to attract more customers in either segment? Give reasons for your answer.

2. Do you agree with the strategy implications suggested at the end of the article? Do the data provided support these suggestions? Give reasons for your answer.

3

A MODEL OF INDUSTRIAL BUYER BEHAVIOR

Jagdish N. Sheth

This article introduces a model that presents in an understandable and systematic form the complex variables and relationships involved in an industrial buying decision.

The purpose of this article is to describe a model of industrial (organizational) buyer behavior. Considerable knowledge on organizational buyer behavior already exists[1] and can be classified into three categories. The first category includes a considerable amount of systematic empirical research on the buying policies and practices of purchasing agents and other organizational buyers.[2] The second includes industry reports and observations of

[1] For a comprehensive list of references, see Thomas A. Staudt and W. Lazer, *A Basic Bibliography on Industrial Marketing* (Chicago: American Marketing Assn., 1963); and Donald E. Vinson, "Bibliography of Industrial Marketing" (unpublished listing of references, University of Colorado, 1972).

[2] Richard M. Cyert, et al., "Observation of a Business Decision," *Journal of Business*, Vol. 29 (October 1956), pp. 237–248; John A. Howard and C. G. Moore, Jr., "A Descriptive Model of the Purchasing Agent" (unpublished monograph, University of Pittsburgh, 1964); George Strauss, "Work Study of Purchasing Agents," *Human Organization*, Vol. 33 (September 1964), pp. 137–149; Theodore A. Levitt, *Industrial Purchasing Behavior* (Boston: Division of Research, Graduate School of Business, Harvard University, 1965); Ozanne B. Urban and Gilbert A. Churchill, "Adoption Research: Information Sources in the Industrial Purchasing Decision," and Richard N. Cardozo, "Segmenting the Industrial Market," in *Marketing and the New Science of Planning*, R. L. King, ed. (Chicago: American Marketing Assn., 1968), pp. 352–359 and 433–440, respectively. Richard N. Cardozo and J. W. Cagley, "Experimental Study of Industrial Buyer Behavior," *Journal of Marketing Research*, Vol. 8 (August 1971), pp. 329–334; Thomas P. Copley and F. L. Callom, "Industrial Search Behavior and Perceived Risk," in *Proceedings of the Second Annual Conference, the Association for Consumer Research*, D. M. Gardner, ed. (College Park, Md.: Association for Consumer Research, 1971), pp. 208–231; and James R. McMillan, "Industrial Buying Behavior as Group Decision Making," (paper presented at the Nineteenth International Meeting of the Institute of Management Sciences, April 1972).

industrial buyers.[3] Finally, the third category consists of books, monographs, and articles which analyze, theorize, model, and sometimes report on industrial buying activities.[4] What is now needed is a reconciliation and integration of existing knowledge into a realistic and comprehensive model of organizational buyer behavior.

It is hoped that the model described in this article will be useful in the following ways: first, to broaden the vision of research on organizational buyer behavior so that it includes the most salient elements and their interactions; second, to act as a catalyst for building marketing information systems from the viewpoint of the industrial buyer; and, third, to generate new hypotheses for future research on fundamental processes underlying organizational buyer behavior.

A Description of Industrial Buyer Behavior

The model of industrial buyer behavior is summarized in Figure 1. Although this illustrative presentation looks complex due to the large number of variables and complicated relationships among them, this is because it is a generic model which attempts to describe and explain all types of industrial buying decisions. One can, however, simplify the actual application of the model in a specific study in at least two ways. First, several variables are included as conditions to hold constant differences among types of products to be purchased (product-specific factors) and differences among types of purchasing organizations. These exogenous factors will not be necessary if the objective of a study is to describe the process of buying behavior for a

---

[3] Robert F. Shoaf, ed., *Emotional Factors Underlying Industrial Purchasing* (Cleveland, Ohio: Penton Publishing Co., 1959); G. H. Haas, B. March, and E. M. Krech, *Purchasing Department Organization and Authority*, American Management Assn. Research Study No. 45 (New York: 1960); *Evaluation of Supplier Performance* (New York: National Association of Purchasing Agents, 1963); F. A. Hays and G. A. Renard, *Evaluating Purchasing Performance*, American Management Assn. Research Study No. 66 (New York: 1964); Hugh Buckner, *How British Industry Buys* (London: Hutchison and Company, Ltd., 1967); *How Industry Buys/1970* (New York: Scientific American, 1970). In addition, numerous articles published in trade journals such as *Purchasing and Industrial Marketing* are cited in Vinson, same reference as footnote 1, and Strauss, same reference as footnote 2.

[4] Ralph S. Alexander, J. S. Cross, and R. M. Hill, *Industrial Marketing*, 3rd ed. (Homewood, Ill.: Richard D. Irwin, 1967); John H. Westing, I. V. Fine, and G. J. Zenz, *Purchasing Management* (New York: John Wiley & Sons, 1969); Patrick J. Robinson, C. W. Farris, and Y. Wind, *Industrial Buying and Creative Marketing* (Boston: Allyn & Bacon, 1967); Frederick E. Webster, Jr., "Modeling the Industrial Buying Process," *Journal of Marketing Research*, Vol. 2 (November 1965), pp. 370–376; and Frederick E. Webster, Jr., "Industrial Buying Behavior: A State-of-the-Art Appraisal," in *Marketing in a Changing World*, B. A. Morin, ed. (Chicago: American Marketing Assn., 1969), p. 256.

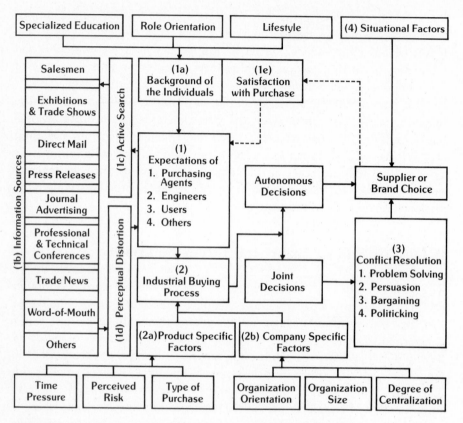

FIGURE 1   *An integrative model of industrial buyer behavior*

specific product or service. Second, some of the decision-process variables can also be ignored if the interest is strictly to conduct a survey of static measurement of the psychology of the organizational buyers. For example, perceptual bias and active search variables may be eliminated if the interest is not in the process of communication to the organizational buyers.

This model is similar to the Howard-Sheth model of buyer behavior in format and classification of variables.[5] However, there are several significant differences. First, while the Howard-Sheth model is more general and probably more useful in consumer behavior, the model described in this article is limited to organizational buying alone. Second, the Howard-Sheth model is limited to the individual decision-making process, whereas this model explicitly describes the joint decision-making process. Finally, there

---

[5] John A. Howard and J. N. Sheth, *The Theory of Buyer Behavior* (New York: John Wiley & Sons, 1969).

are fewer variables in this model than in the Howard-Sheth model of buyer behavior.

Organizational buyer behavior consists of three distinct aspects. The first aspect is the psychological world of the individuals involved in organizational buying decisions. The second aspect relates to the conditions which precipitate joint decisions among these individuals. The final aspect is the process of joint decision making with the inevitable conflict among the decision makers and its resolution by resorting to a variety of tactics.

Psychological World of the Decision Makers

Contrary to popular belief, many industrial buying decisions are not solely in the hands of purchasing agents.[6] Typically in an industrial setting, one finds that there are at least three departments whose members are continuously involved in different phases of the buying process. The most common are the personnel from the purchasing, quality control, and manufacturing departments. These individuals are identified in the model as purchasing agents, engineers, and users, respectively. Several other individuals in the organization may be, but are typically not, involved in the buying process (for example, the president of the firm or the comptroller). There is considerable interaction among the individuals in the three departments continuously involved in the buying process and often they are asked to decide jointly. It is, therefore, critical to examine the similarities and differences in the psychological worlds of these individuals.

Based on research in consumer and social psychology, several different aspects of the psychology of the decision makers are included in the model. Primary among these are the *expectations* of the decision makers about suppliers and brands [(1) in Figure 1]. The present model specifies five different processes which create differential expectations among the individuals involved in the purchasing process: (1a) the *background of the individuals*, (1b) *information sources*, (1c) *active search*, (1d) *perceptual distortion*, and (1e) *satisfaction with past purchases*. These variables must be explained and operationally defined if they are to fully represent the psychological world of the organizational buyers.

Expectations

Expectations refer to the *perceived* potential of alternative suppliers and brands to satisfy a number of explicit and implicit objectives in any particular buying

---

[6]Howard and Moore, same reference as footnote 2; Strauss, same reference as footnote 2; McMillan, same reference as footnote 2; *How Industry Buys/1970*, same reference as footnote 3.

decision. The most common explicit objectives include, in order of relative importance, product quality, delivery time, quantity of supply, after-sale service where appropriate, and price.[7] However, a number of studies have pointed out the critical role of several implicit criteria such as reputation, size, location, and reciprocity relationship with the supplier; and personality, technical expertise, salesmanship, and even life style of the sales representative.[8] In fact, with the standardized marketing mix among the suppliers in oligopolistic markets, the implicit criteria are becoming marginally more and more significant in the industrial buyer's decisions.

Expectations can be measured by obtaining a profile of each supplier or brand as to how satisfactory it is perceived to be in enabling the decision maker to achieve his explicit and implicit objectives. Almost all studies from past research indicate that expectations will substantially differ among the purchasing agents, engineers, and product users because each considers different criteria to be salient in judging the supplier or the brand. In general, it is found that product users look for prompt delivery, proper installation, and efficient serviceability; purchasing agents look for maximum price advantage and economy in shipping and forwarding; and engineers look for excellence in quality, standardization of the product, and engineering pretesting of the product. These differences in objectives and, consequently, expectations are often the root causes for constant conflict among these three types of individuals.[9]

Why are there substantial differences in expectations? While there is considerable speculation among researchers and observers of industrial buyer behavior on the number and nature of explanations, there is relatively little consensus. The five most salient processes which determine differential expectations, as specified in the model, are discussed below.

BACKGROUND OF INDIVIDUALS.   The first, and probably most significant, factor is the background and task orientation of each of the individuals involved in the buying process. The different educational backgrounds of the purchasing agents, engineers, and plant managers often generate substantially different professional goals and values. In addition, the task expectations also generate conflicting perceptions of one another's role in the organization. Finally, the personal life styles of individual decision makers play an important role in developing differential expectations.[10]

---

[7] Howard and Moore, same reference as footnote 2; *How Industry Buys/1970*, same reference as footnote 3; Hays and Renard, same reference as footnote 3.

[8] Howard and Moore, same reference as footnote 2; Levitt, same reference as footnote 2; Westing, Fine, and Zenz, same reference as footnote 4; Shoaf, same reference as footnote 4.

[9] Strauss, same reference as footnote 2.

[10] For a general reading, see Robert T. Golembiewski, "Small Groups and Large Organizations," in *Handbook of Organizations*, J. G. March, ed. (Chicago: Rand McNally & Company, 1965),

It is relatively easy to gather information on this background factor. The educational and task differences are comparable to demographics in consumer behavior, and life style differences can be assessed by psychographic scales on the individual's interests, activities, and values as a professional.

INFORMATION SOURCES AND ACTIVE SEARCH.   The second and third factors in creating differential expectations are the source and type of information each of the decision makers is exposed to and his participation in the active search. Purchasing agents receive disproportionately greater exposure to commercial sources, and the information is often partial and biased toward the supplier or the brand. In some companies, it is even a common practice to discourage sales representatives from talking directly to the engineering or production personnel. The engineering and production personnel, therefore, typically have less information and what they have is obtained primarily from professional meetings, trade reports, and even word-of-mouth. In addition, the active search for information is often relegated to the purchasing agents because it is presumed to be their job responsibility.

It is not too difficult to assess differences among the three types of individuals in their exposure to various sources and types of information by standard survey research methods.

PERCEPTUAL DISTORTION.   A fourth factor is the selective distortion and retention of available information. Each individual strives to make the objective information consistent with his own prior knowledge and expectations by systematically distorting it. For example, since there are substantial differences in the goals and values of purchasing agents, engineers, and production personnel, one should expect different interpretations of the same information among them. Although no specific research has been done on this tendency to perceptually distort information in the area of industrial buyer behavior, a large body of research does exist on cognitive consistency to explain its presence as a natural human tendency.[11]

Perceptual distortion is probably the most difficult variable to quantify by standard survey research methods. One possible approach is experimentation, but this is costly. A more realistic alternative is to utilize perceptual mapping techniques such as multidimensional scaling or factor analysis and compare differences in the judgments of the purchasing agents, engineers, and production personnel to a common list of suppliers or brands.

---

chapter 3. For field studies related to this area, see Donald E. Porter, P. B. Applewhite, and M. J. Misshauk, eds., *Studies in Organizational Behavior and Management*, 2nd ed. (Scranton, Pa.: Intext Educational Publishers, 1971).

[11] Robert P. Abelson, et al., *Theories of Cognitive Consistency: A Source Book* (Chicago: Rand McNally & Company, 1968).

SATISFACTION WITH PAST PURCHASES. The fifth factor which creates differential expectations among the various individuals involved in the purchasing process is the satisfaction with past buying experiences with a supplier or brand. Often it is not possible for a supplier or brand to provide equal satisfaction to the three parties because each one has different goals or criteria. For example, a supplier may be lower in price but his delivery schedule may not be satisfactory. Similarly, a product's quality may be excellent but its price may be higher than others. The organization typically rewards each individual for excellent performance in his specialized skills, so the purchasing agent is rewarded for economy, the engineer for quality control, and the production personnel for efficient scheduling. This often results in a different level of satisfaction for each of the parties involved even though the chosen supplier or brand may be the best feasible alternative in terms of overall corporate goals.

Past experiences with a supplier or brand, summarized in the satisfaction variable, directly influence the person's expectations toward that supplier or brand. It is relatively easy to measure the satisfaction variable by obtaining information on how the supplier or brand is perceived by each of the three parties.

Determinants of Joint vs. Autonomous Decisions

Not all industrial buying decisions are made jointly by the various individuals involved in the purchasing process. Sometimes the buying decisions are delegated to one party, which is not necessarily the purchasing agent. It is, therefore, important for the supplier to know whether a buying decision is joint or autonomous and, if it is the latter, to which party it is delegated. There are six primary factors which determine whether a specific buying decision will be joint or autonomous. Three of these factors are related to the characteristics of the product or service (2a) and the other three are related to the characteristics of the buyer company (2b).

Product-Specific Factors

The first product-specific variable is what Bauer calls *perceived risk* in buying decisions.[12] Perceived risk refers to the magnitude of adverse consequences felt by the decision maker if he makes a wrong choice, and the uncertainty

---

[12] Raymond A. Bauer, "Consumer Behavior as Risk Taking," in *Dynamic Marketing for a Changing World*, R. L. Hancock, ed. (Chicago: American Marketing Assn., 1960), pp. 389–400. Applications of perceived risk in industrial buying can be found in Levitt, same reference as footnote 2; Copley and Callom, same reference as footnote 2; McMillan, same reference as footnote 2.

under which he must decide. The greater the uncertainty in a buying situation, the greater the perceived risk. Although there is very little direct evidence, it is logical to hypothesize that the greater the perceived risk in a specific buying decision, the more likely it is that the purchase will be decided jointly by all parties concerned. The second product-specific factor is *type of purchase*. If it is the first purchase or a once-in-a-lifetime capital expenditure, one would expect greater joint decision making. On the other hand, if the purchase decision is repetitive and routine or is limited to maintenance products or services, the buying decision is likely to be delegated to one party. The third factor is *time pressure*. If the buying decision has to be made under a great deal of time pressure or on an emergency basis, it is likely to be delegated to one party rather than decided jointly.

Company-Specific Factors

The three organization-specific factors are *company orientation*, *company size*, and *degree of centralization*. If the company is technology oriented, it is likely to be dominated by the engineering people and the buying decisions will, in essence, be made by them. Similarly, if the company is production oriented, the buying decisions will be made by the production personnel.[13] Second, if the company is a large corporation, decision making will tend to be joint. Finally, the greater the degree of centralization, the less likely it is that the decisions will be joint. Thus, a privately-owned small company with technology or production orientation will tend toward autonomous decision making and a large-scale public corporation with considerable decentralization will tend to have greater joint decision making.

Even though there is considerable research evidence in organization behavior in general to support these six factors, empirical evidence in industrial buying decisions in particular is sketchy on them. Perhaps with more research it will be possible to verify the generalizations and deductive logic utilized in this aspect of the model.

Process of Joint Decision Making

The major thrust of the present model of industrial buying decisions is to investigate the process of joint decision making. This includes initiation of the

---

[13] For some indirect evidence, see Strauss, same reference as footnote 2. For a more general study, see Victor A. Thompson, "Hierarchy, Specialization and Organizational Conflict," *Administrative Science Quarterly*, Vol. 5 (March 1961), p. 513; and Henry A. Landsberger, "The Horizontal Dimension in Bureaucracy," *Administration Science Quarterly*, Vol. 6 (December 1961), pp. 299–332, for a thorough review of numerous theories.

decision to buy, gathering of information, evaluating alternative suppliers, and resolving conflict among the parties who must jointly decide.

The decision to buy is usually initiated by a continued need of supply or is the outcome of long-range planning. The formal initiation in the first case is typically from the production personnel by way of a requisition slip. The latter usually is a formal recommendation from the planning unit to an ad hoc committee consisting of the purchasing agent, the engineer, and the plant manager. The information-gathering function is typically relegated to the purchasing agent. If the purchase is a repetitive decision for standard items, there is very little information gathering. Usually the purchasing agent contacts the preferred supplier and orders the items on the requisition slip. However, considerable active search effort is manifested for capital expenditure items, especially those which are entirely new purchase experiences for the organization.[14]

The most important aspect of the joint decision-making process, however, is the assimilation of information, deliberations on it, and the consequent conflict which most joint decisions entail. According to March and Simon, conflict is present when there is a need to decide jointly among a group of people who have, at the same time, different goals and perceptions.[15] In view of the fact that the latter is invariably present among the various parties to industrial buying decisions, conflict becomes a common consequences of the joint decision-making process; the buying motives and expectations about brands and suppliers are considerably different for the engineer, the user, and the purchasing agent, partly due to company policy of reward for specialized skills and viewpoints.

Interdepartmental conflict in itself is not necessarily bad. What matters most from the organization's viewpoint is *how* the conflict is resolved (3). If it is resolved in a rational manner, one very much hopes that the final joint decision will also tend to be rational. If, on the other hand, conflict resolution degenerates to what Strauss calls "tactics of lateral relationship,"[16] the organization will suffer from inefficiency and the joint decisions may be reduced to bargaining and politicking among the parties involved. Not only will the decision be based on irrational criteria, but the choice of a supplier may be to the detriment of the buying organization.

What types of conflict can be expected in industrial buying decisions? How are they likely to be resolved? These are some of the key questions in an

---

[14] Strauss, same reference as footnote 2.

[15] James G. March and H. A. Simon, *Organizations* (New York: John Wiley & Sons, 1958), chapter 5; and Landsberger, same reference as footnote 13.

[16] George Strauss, "Tactics of Lateral Relationship: The Purchasing Agent," *Administrative Science Quarterly*, Vol. 7 (September 1962), pp. 161–186.

understanding of industrial buyer behavior. If the inter-party conflict is largely due to disagreements on expectations about the suppliers or their brands, it is likely that the conflict will be resolved in the *problem-solving* manner. The immediate consequence of this type of conflict is to actively search for more information, deliberate more on available information, and often to seek out other suppliers not seriously considered before. The additional information is then presented in a problem-solving fashion so that conflict tends to be minimized.

If the conflict among the parties is primarily due to disagreement on some specific criteria with which to evaluate suppliers—although there is an agreement on the buying goals or objectives at a more fundamental level—it is likely to be resolved by *persuasion*. An attempt is made, under this type of resolution, to persuade the dissenting member by pointing out the importance of overall corporate objectives and how his criterion is not likely to attain these objectives. There is no attempt to gather more information. However, there results greater interaction and communication among the parties, and sometimes an outsider is brought in to reconcile the differences.

Both problem solving and persuasion are useful and rational methods of conflict resolution. The resulting joint decisions, therefore, also tend to be more rational. Thus, conflicts produced due to disagreements on expectations about the suppliers or on a specific criterion are healthy from the organization's viewpoint even though they may be time consuming. One is likely to find, however, that a more typical situation in which conflict arises is due to fundamental differences in buying goals or objectives among the various parties. This is especially true with respect to unique or new buying decisions related to capital expenditure items. The conflict is resolved not by changing the differences in relative importance of the buying goals or objectives of the individuals involved, but by the process of *bargaining*. The fundamental differences among the parties are implicitly conceded by all the members and the concept of distributive justice (tit for tat) is invoked as a part of bargaining. The most common outcome is to allow a single party to decide autonomously in this specific stituation in return for some favor or promise of reciprocity in future decisions.

Finally, if the disagreement is not simply with respect to buying goals or objectives but also with respect to *style of decision making*, the conflict tends to be grave and borders on the mutual dislike of personalities among the individual decision makers. The resolution of this type of conflict is usually by *politicking* and back-stabbing tactics. Such methods of conflict resolution are common in industrial buying decisions. The reader is referred to the sobering research of Strauss for further discussion.[17]

---

[17] Same reference as footnote 16.

Both bargaining and politicking are nonrational and inefficient methods of conflict resolution; the buying organization suffers from these conflicts. Furthermore, the decision makers find themselves sinking below their professional, managerial role. The decisions are not only delayed but tend to be governed by factors other than achievement of corporate objectives.

Critical Role of Situational Factors

The model described so far presumes that the choice of a supplier or brand is the outcome of a systematic decision-making process in the organizational setting. However, there is ample empirical evidence in the literature to suggest that at least some of the industrial buying decisions are determined by ad hoc *situational factors* (4) and not by any systematic decision-making process. In other words, similar to consumer behavior, the industrial buyers often decide on factors other than rational or realistic criteria.

It is difficult to prepare a list of ad hoc conditions which determine industrial buyer behavior without decision making. However, a number of situational factors which often intervene between the actual choice and any prior decision-making process can be isolated. These include: temporary economic conditions such as price controls, recession, or foreign trade; internal strikes, walkouts, machine breakdowns, and other production-related events; organizational changes such as merger or acquisition; and ad hoc changes in the market place, such as promotional efforts, new product introduction, price changes, and so on, in the supplier industries.

Implications for Industrial Marketing Research

The model of industrial buyer behavior described above suggests the following implications for marketing research.

First, in order to explain and predict supplier or brand choice in industrial buyer behavior, it is necessary to conduct research on the psychology of other individuals in the organization in addition to the purchasing agents. It is, perhaps, the unique nature of organizational structure and behavior which leads to a distinct separation of the consumer, the buyer, and the procurement agent, as well as others possibly involved in the decision-making process. In fact, it may not be an exaggeration to suggest that the purchasing agent is often a less critical member of the decision-making process in industrial buyer behavior.

Second, it is possible to operationalize and quantify most of the variables included as part of the model. While some are more difficult and indirect, sufficient psychometric skill in marketing research is currently available to quantify the psychology of the individuals.

Third, although considerable research has been done on the demographics of organizations in industrial market research—for example, on the turnover and size of the company, workflows, standard industrial classification, and profit ratios—demographic and life-style information on the individuals involved in industrial buying decisions is also needed.

Fourth, a systematic examination of the power positions of various individuals involved in industrial buying decisions is a necessary condition of the model. The sufficient condition is to examine trade-offs among various objectives, both explicit and implicit, in order to create a satisfied customer.

Fifth, it is essential in building any market research information system for industrial goods and services that the process of conflict resolution among the parties and its impact on supplier or brand choice behavior is carefully included and simulated.

Finally, it is important to realize that not all industrial decisions are the outcomes of a systematic decision-making process. There are some industrial buying decisions which are based strictly on a set of situational factors for which theorizing or model building will not be relevant or useful. What is needed in these cases is a checklist of empirical observations of the ad hoc events which vitiate the neat relationship between the theory or the model and a specific buying decision.

QUESTIONS

1. How can the model of industrial buyer behavior be used by marketing managers to develop and implement selling strategies?
2. What factors affect the expectations of potential buyers?
3. What is the key aspect of the joint decision-making process in industrial buying?
4. Do you agree with the statement that industrial buying decisions are the result of a completely rational process? Why?
5. What are the three distinct aspects of the industrial buyer behavior model? How does this model differ from that for consumers?
6. What variables in the model are conditional on the product and organization being analyzed?

4

MARKET SEGMENTATION AS A COMPETITIVE STRATEGY

Nelson N. Foote

According to this article, simply identifying the subgroups or segments in the market with unique needs or demands should not be the major focus of the segmentation process. The main purpose of segmentation is the development of competitive strategy. Guidelines on how segmentation can be used in this way are provided.

Let us assume we have made the discovery that consumers of ice cream differ significantly in their preferences for chocolate, strawberry, and vanilla. And let us assume that these flavor preferences are not distributed randomly among all kinds of people, but are differentially associated with some other characteristic of customers for ice cream, such as hair color, and that these associations are substantial in degree and practical to ascertain. For example, let us say that brunettes tend strongly to like chocolate, redheads to favor strawberry, and blondes, vanilla. Finally, let us imagine that this pattern is just that simple and orderly—product differences nicely match customer differences.

Then what?

What is the businessman who wants to sell ice cream in this market to do about our findings? Is he to conclude that he should offer all three flavors, the same as the rest of the industry, lest he forego any important source of sales? Or should he try to serve only blondes and brunettes, since there are not enough redheads to make serving them profitable? Or should he seek to establish a reputation as the producer of the finest Dutch chocolate ice cream, so that he captures nearly all that segment of the market? Or should he go after the great mass of vanilla fans, by upgrading this lowly flavor with a French accent? Or should he take account of his newness or smallness in the industry and challenge the incumbent giants of the trade by introducing pistachio or frozen custard? Or should he offer the normal product line of his industry, but allow some major chain of retail outlets to apply its store brand to his product? Should he go after the door-to-door trade with a very short line—like Neapolitan only—or open his own chain of soda fountains with 28 flavors? Or should he be creative and try to think up some utterly new way to exploit his knowledge of differing customer preferences, since all these strategies—and more besides—are already in use today in the ice cream business?

Plainly, even if one knew far more than is known already about patterns of correlation between product and customer differences in any particular market, it takes a lot of thinking and doing before this knowledge can be turned into a calculated competitive strategy. Meanwhile we find examples of marketing managers who have very successfully employed a strategy of market segmentation, quite without the resources of detailed information that as professional marketers we like to think are indispensable to decision-making in matters of such complexity and risk.

It seems important throughout discussion of market segmentation to recognize that the main source of interest in the concept is its potential value as a competitive strategy. There may be quite a number of people whose interest is in promoting the sale or purchase of data regarding the "strati-graphics" of consumer choice. But unless these data can be put to practical use in improving or defending the market position or profits of their user, only the data seller will benefit, and he not for long. So my self-chosen assignment here is to bear down on the task of thinking out the use of such data in actual marketing management. Although I make my living as a marketing researcher, I think that we need more thinking on this matter as much as we need more research.

Immediately, however, the question arises of who is going to discuss competitive strategy in public—especially in the presence of competitors of his own firm—save in empty generalities. A salesman of research data, or representatives of advertising agencies or media, might set forth some hypothetical tactics of market segmentation as a means of soliciting business. But other than personal vanity or the desire to solicit another job, what would induce someone connected with a manufacturer or a retailer to disclose his thinking about competitive strategy? The incentives of professional exchange of technique or the teaching of younger members of the fraternity are not sufficient justification. Many kinds of professional know-how are properly kept proprietary by the firm which paid for their development. If market segmentation is to be analyzed publicly and candidly from the standpoint of an actual competitor in a market, it has to be justified by some benefit that it will bring to this competitor. If it were not my conviction that in fact it is to the benefit of every competing firm that market segmentation be discussed publicly in terms of its implications for competitive strategy, you would not be listening to these words at this moment.

Moreover, we can go one step further and declare that market segmentation as a competitive strategy is also in the interests of customers. If it were not—if it did not offer customers a firmer base for choice among competing offerings and a wider array of genuine choices—it would not work as a competitive strategy. Like any deal, market segmentation is good business only when both parties to the transaction benefit. Market segmentation is thus in effect a logical extension of the basic principles of marketing.

The process of market segmentation, however, when approached as a task of formulating and executing a marketing strategy, involves matching not merely customer characteristics and product characteristics, but a tripartite matching of customers and offerings *and* the array of competitors in the market, as seen from the standpoint of any one competitor within this constellation. If we think of offerings by competitors as expressions of their differing *capabilities*, it will not only be easy to remember the three C's— *customers*, *competitors*, and *capabilities*—but the full task of developing a strategy is more clearly pushed into view.

Let me illustrate concretely by referring to one of our most respected competitors in the Chicago area, the Zenith Radio Corporation. Zenith won a pre-eminent position in the television receiver market some ten years ago by becoming established in the minds of consumers as the leading exemplar of product reliability. Its policy of manufacturing products of good workmanship goes back many years, but during the middle fifties many consumers became quite concerned to identify the set that would, they hoped, give them the least trouble from breakdown. That was when Zenith's market share soared, until it surpassed the erstwhile industry leader. Servicemen and the radio-TV specialty stores with which they are associated lent vigorous aid. Zenith's management and its advertising agency pressed the opportunity that had widened for them. But Zenith had not adopted product reliability as a self-consciously opportunistic, short-term tactic. As far as known, Zenith's strategy was not derived through marketing research, although marketing research by competitors soon verified its efficacy. After some delay, other competitors raised their quality control standards, but none has been able, coming in later on a me-too basis, to emulate Zenith's success. One could quibble about some details of Zenith's reputation—whether hand-wiring is in fact more or less reliable than printed circuits, whether reliability has not been confused to some extent with repairability, whether Zenith sets any longer enjoy the lowest breakdown rate—but from the marketing standpoint, Zenith remains king among that segment of the set market which emphasizes reliability above other virtues when buying sets. The quality standards of the whole industry were forced up by Zenith's success, an outcome of obvious benefit to the consumer, but of at least equal benefit to all the other competitors in the industry, whose personnel devote their whole lives to their industry and much prefer feeling proud of their occupation to feeling ashamed of it.

The meaning of the Zenith example would be very incomplete, however, if we paid attention only to the success story and failed to note that there are many other virtues in television sets which consumers prize besides reliability. If there were not, it would be hard to explain why the Zenith brand share at its zenith rose barely above a fifth of the market. To be sure, Zenith may have preferred its profitability to the greater volume it may have deliberately foregone by upholding a price premium. On the other hand, maybe not; a price premium is just about the loudest advertisement for quality there is.

Meanwhile Zenith's major rival did not simply decide it had to emulate Zenith, but staunchly pursued its strategy of industry statesmanship through the introduction of color, achieving handsome victory and reward from matching its offering with the rising wants of all those customers who were reaching for color in magazines, movies, photography, and other visual media. Alongside these two industry leaders were certain other manufacturers, one of whom has done well by stressing portability and personalization, another by treating the television set as a major piece of furniture, and so on. What is important here is that several competitors held their own or improved their position, even during the period of greatest success by Zenith and RCA, not by seeking to manufacture some hypothetically optimum television set, but by addressing themselves to some substantial segment of the market which *they saw themselves as peculiarly fitted to serve.* The firms which got shaken out during the past dozen years—among which some were big for a time—or which severely lost position can best be described as undistinguishable in their capabilities and offerings, hence undistinguished by consumers.

Now what has been added to the understanding of market segmentation by the example of television receivers? What has been added that is indispensable is the element of competitive capability—a virtue that one particular competitor preeminently possesses—which matches a substantial or rising consumer want. In colloquial terms, what have I got that the other guy hasn't, and which the customer wants badly enough to walk a mile for it?

A few years back, we looked at some commonplace demographic characteristics of television customers arrayed by the brands they tended to favor. When we looked at these demographic characteristics simultaneously, certain results were far more revealing in combination than singly. Only a limited example—because here we are indeed verging on the disclosure of competitive intelligence: we found that one highly meaningful segment of the market—meaningful in terms of sensitivity of discrimination among brands—consisted of households below the median in years of schooling but above the median in income. For convenient reference we called them merely the new-rich, obviously an inexact term. One particular brand seemed to be designed and advertised and priced—properly over-priced, as it were—specifically for this segment, and in fact it enjoyed at that time an inordinate share of their set-buying. Now that company has not noticeably changed its offerings during recent years; they still seem pointed toward the new-rich segment; but its brand share has dwindled substantially. It appears that people with more money than schooling nonetheless are able to learn from experience and do upgrade their taste, given a little time.

The moral of this example is that market segmentation has to be viewed as a continuous process, and marketing strategy has to keep in step with the changing structure of the market. While this implication is probably obvious, perhaps less obvious is the corollary that, just as consumers learn, it is necessary for competitors to learn to exercise differing capabilities from those which may have won them success in the past. And here we come to a matter which lies beyond not only research but also ordinary logic and in the realm of managerial will. Who is to tell a manufacturer that he is capable of doing something he has not done before, and of doing it better than any of his other competitors? By definition, the ordinary kinds of evidence are lacking, because there is no past experience to be projected forward.

In the course of interpersonal relations among individuals, a teacher or a parent may tell a child that he possesses talents he did not previously recognize; the child may then adopt this observation as a conviction about himself which empowers him to demonstrate that it is true. All of us are familiar enough with instances of this outcome not to need to debate whether they occur. The faith of a coach in an athlete, of a critic in a writer, of an employer in an employee, of a wife in a husband, is often the ingredient which brings out a latent capability. Because so little is understood about the process, we cannot make it happen on demand. We are fortunate to recognize it when it does happen, even more so when we spy the opportunity beforehand and do not waste it, for ourselves or for others. Even further beyond present understanding is the possibility of specifying here a reliable formula whereby the management of a company can truly discern those latent talents in its own organization which can be mobilized more effectively by itself than by any of its competitors to satisfy some important emerging customer want.

I do know this, however: recognition of such a talent feeds on itself; it is a cumulative process, a benevolent spiral. I am positive that when the management of Zenith found itself being recognized by consumers for its virtues of good workmanship, it was immensely stimulated to push further in that direction. Thus one of the most valuable functions of marketing research in implementing a strategy of market segmentation is to listen to what is being said about a company by its customers in terms of recognizing its special talents. Developing something that is already there—watering a plant that is already growing, to mix a metaphor—is surely much easier and more likely to succeed than trying to create new capabilities out of whole cloth or, for that matter, borrowing the garments of others, in the sense of imitating or acquiring another company and offering that as an expression of one's own capability.

Part of the growing sophistication of consumers is their increasing interest in the character of the organization they are dealing with. At General Electric we are acutely conscious that certain of our competitors, whose products are no better and sometimes not as good as ours by any measure of product quality, nonetheless enjoy the preference of certain customers. This problem repeatedly confronts the manufacturer who finds himself in competition with retailers who handle only store brands. The whole fascinating issue of what is going to emerge as private branding widens its sway is too vast to open up here. Yet it deserves mention here as constituting market segmentation on an utterly different axis from market segmentation on the axis of product features and brand images.

Segmentation varies in degree as well as in kind. The famous case of the ordinary salt which "rains when it pours" [sic] illustrates a valued product feature which has maintained for a particular brand a large and stable market share for many years, while conferring on consumers a valued satisfaction for which they are quite willing to pay a price premium and a rewarding degree of brand loyalty. Many such product features are easily imitated, however, and the reputation for distinctiveness originally achieved may dissolve in the minds of consumers despite advertising. The impermanence of minor product features as a source of competitive distinctiveness and effective market segmentation is a conspicuous failing of the current picture in package goods competition. Like rock-and-roll music, there is too little difference between the new ones and the old ones to make much difference. The proliferation of trivial product differences which appeal to trivial differences among consumers and represent trivial differences among the capabilities of their makers is in effect a mockery of the theory of market segmentation. This proliferation of trivial differences provokes denunciation by producers, retailers, and consumers alike as market fragmentation rather than segmentation and makes an industry vulnerable to the outsider who commences to segment on a different axis. The effective response to the trivialization of market segmentation, however, is not to abandon it as a strategy. To do that would be to abdicate all initiative to competitors. The way out of the expensive waste of trivial segmentation is to engage in serious segmentation, which means segmentation on a larger scale or even on another axis.

Serious, large-scale innovation seems often to come from outside an industry rather than inside. Examples like General Motors in locomotives, Volkswagen in autos, IBM in typewriters, Corning in housewares, Lestoil in detergents, come to mind. Rivalry within a going constellation of competitors seems often to lead to implicit imitation, even when everyone involved is convinced that he is trying to be different from everyone else. How this result occurs is not hard to discern. Close rivals tend very easily to magnify the importance of small differences, whether initiated by themselves or others. If created by another, a close competitor often feels he must come up with a rival innovation but only of corresponding scale.

One detects nothing very distinctive about Silvertone television sets, to mention another respected Chicago competitor. Viewed as manufactured products, they are close to the industry's average line. But where Zenith stresses the reliability built into the product, Sears stresses the services offered by the stores in which Silvertone sets are bought—the promptness of repair service, the easy credit, the ample parking, the special sales well advertised in local newspapers or by direct mail. That is, Sears segments the market on another axis than Zenith. But thus far, Silvertone has encroached far less upon Zenith's clientele than upon the portions of the market occupied by companies whose offerings are less distinctive.

We shall come back to this intriguing question of how far the competition of store brands with manufacturer brands may go before some equilibrium is reached. Some companies as yet have a less urgent private-brand problem anyway, like the auto and gasoline firms and the sellers of services—insurance, banking, air travel, lodging, dry cleaning—which distribute through their own exclusive retail outlets. So for some moments longer, let us stay within the sphere of competition among manufactured products and nationally advertised brands.

Assuming this sphere, we can now state our main hypothesis in further detail: Market segmentation works best as a competitive strategy, i.e., contributes most to the success of competitors and the satisfaction of customers, when product and brand and maker are closely identified in the minds of all concerned.

If we were to assume that one by one more competitors in a market choose to attract particular segments of customers on the basis of correct appraisal of their own special capabilities to satisfy these segments, then the competitors who do not make such deliberate choices will find themselves increasingly confined to the miscellaneous and dwindling residue. As alluded to in our first example, such a development is to some extent a description of what has already happened in some markets, so we may be prophesying simply an intensification of current tendencies rather than anything new under the sun. In other words, self-conscious segmentation may become not only a means of success but the price of survival in a market.

Beyond the ordinary criteria of survival or success as measured in profitability and market share, however, are some other benefits of segmentation to an industry and the various competitors in it. We have mentioned the feeling of pride in their occupation and the quality of its products which most people desire in their life work. Some other benefits of belonging to an industry which steadily adds to the values it offers its customers also deserve explicit recognition. They include the fact that being bested by a competitor whom one respects is easier than being bested by a competitor whom one does not respect. There is a good deal of satisfaction to the producer as well as the consumer in seeing an industry progress over time through advanced applications of science and technology. In an industry plagued with cut-throat price competition instead of value competition, imitation is almost inevitable, because no one can afford the research and development required for innovation. In the vicious downward spiral which obtains in such an industry, jobs are insecure because companies are insecure; and morale and morality seem to decline together. Enough examples spring to mind. An industry trapped in such a spiral, worst of all, has rarely been able to reverse it without outside help, as from major suppliers. DuPont, for example, has struggled quite nobly to raise the plastics molding industry from its swamp. Customers themselves, especially in recent years, have sometimes under these conditions willingly paid substantial premiums for quality and reliability, and this has brought a turnabout, but not before the damage became painful to all concerned.

Both competitors and customers share the benefits of stabilized markets wherein strong degrees of mutual loyalty exist between particular companies and particular segments of customers. Distribution and advertising costs are significantly lower under conditions in which repeat sales make up a high proportion of total sales. The model line of any competitor can be shorter, yet his volume nowadays may be higher, than when he tries to carry everything everyone else in the industry offers. All phases of marketing are much more intelligently, effectively, and efficiently conducted when companies and customers, having chosen each other with care and sophistication, can rely on each other's growing discrimination and sympathetically anticipate the orderly, developmental unfolding and matching of their future wants and capabilities. Some marketing researchers even envision a paradise in which companies will spend as much money in listening as in talking and will make more money doing so.

Let us commence to summarize while injecting a few additional elements into this consideration of market segmentation as a competitive strategy. Our first proposition was that any approach to market segmentation which dealt only with matching customer characteristics with product features was seriously incomplete. The very incentive for exploring market segmentation is to gain advantage—to seek some basis for customer preference—against the array of other competitors and their offerings in a particular market. If one plays only with customer characteristics and product features, he may arrive at the notion of some optimum product for an average customer, in effect, a recipe for reducing his product to commodity status, hence the very opposite of market segmentation, which implies product differentiation. But if he goes to the opposite extreme and tries to equal or surpass the total array of differing products offered by all competitors to all segments of his market, he courts the usual fate of me-too-ism, while suffering impossibly mounting marketing costs. Hence he must seek to identify those offerings which most appeal to some desirable segment of the total market and simultaneously express those capabilities in which he is strongest. The problem of choice here is analogous with that of the boy who must seek distinction from a brother who excels him athletically and another who excels him academically: what talent can he develop which, though different, will seem equivalent in the eyes of those whose approval he seeks? To be all things to all people, to excel in every virtue, is impossible: to be average in all means indistinguishability. Achieving only trivial distinctiveness is a barely-veiled form of imitation, although it can immensely add to promotional expense in an industry. Hence the evolution of a criterion for selecting which customer segments and matching product distinctions to pursue must come from and be disciplined by correct identification of the real strengths and weaknesses of the company itself, as compared with other competitors in its market.

Companies, like individuals, sometimes involuntarily suffer crises of identity, as when merged with other companies. A company embarking upon market segmentation as a competitive strategy is deliberately precipitating a crisis of identity. In place of identity, however, which seems to apply only to the maker of a product rather than to a triple set of interrelations, I believe the concept of theme is more applicable and explanatory of the common element which has to be discovered or invented to match customer characteristic with product feature with company capability. The so-called total marketing approach in its sophisticated form seems finally to come forth with such recognizable themes. The theme of *ease of use* of essentially highly-technical equipment has served Kodak for generations and recurs in numerous notable expressions—from the Brownie to the Instamatic, from the ubiquitous yellow box to the universally recognizable name itself. It illustrates how versatile in its manifestations a theme can be.

But just as product innovation can be trivialized through pointless small variations which make no real contribution to anyone, the concept of theme can be trivialized also, and in fact is, whenever some advertising agency tries to adorn an advertiser with a superficial image that has no real structural relationship to customer segments, competitive constellation, or company capabilities.

The concept of theme is useful in teaching marketing and market segmentation to managers whose experience has been in more exact fields. It helps to avoid the mental blocks that arise when segmentation is grasped as a series of pigeonholes in which various kinds of customers are filed for separate treatment, whereas the manager is eager for all the sales he can get from any source whatever, and finds it hard enough to devise one marketing strategy without having to devise many. To return to our main example, the television receiver market, the theme of reliability can be applied by one manufacturer to all the models in his line and throughout all the functions of marketing in his total marketing program. But the same manufacturer could hardly pursue simultaneously with equal thoroughness and equal success such contrasting themes as modern and traditional cabinetry, portability, technical innovation and retail convenience, although he may keep pace with the industry average in these respects. Market segmentation does not deal with water-tight compartments, but with emphases sufficiently simple and distinctive to win notice and preference among customers to whom they are important, without alienating customers by being deficient in the other virtues which they more or less take for granted.

In terms of demographic and other statistical dimensions by which customers and products may be differentiated, the possibilities for market segmentation are troublesomely infinite. But when the problem of choosing a theme to emphasize is disciplined by attempting to match customers, competitors, and capabilites, these troubles are usually reduced to very few choices that are actually open to a particular firm—though hopefully at least one. The real difficulties of choice are not statistical but spiritual—the anguish of facing up to the fact that if a company is going to move in one direction, it must forego moving in all the others. Such a decision comes especially hard in diversified companies, yet some diversified companies have achieved real synergy through this discipline.

Once this clarifying commitment has been made, its effect on everyone in the organization is to release spontaneous ingenuity in its implementation. A good theme stimulates numberless applications and suggestions, furnishes a guide in numberless subordinate decisions, and eases numberless chores of communication, both inside and outside.

Not only does a positive theme help to mobilize an organization in pursuit of its marketing objectives and heighten their satisfaction, but it wins respect from competitors, even while strengthening and securing its position against them. Spirit is harder to imitate than matter; hardware is easy to copy, but the spirit of a whole organization is not. The competitor who wishes to emulate the success of a competitor's dominant theme must, instead of echoing it, come up with an equivalent theme that uniquely fits himself to his situation, that matches his own three C's.

When my wife was forced to listen to the draft of this paper, her first reaction was that there is much more to marketing than she had previously realized. But there is bound to be more than she or we realize even now. Imagine, for example, how much thicker the atmosphere would get if we tried to push onward into the problems of market segmentation faced by such diversified companies as General Electric which sells many products under mainly a single brand, General Motors which sells mainly one product under several brands, and General Foods which sells many products under many brands, but now seems bent on making the customer aware of the identity of the maker. To add General Mills to this list might also be instructive, if we recall its brief effort to diversify by getting into the electric iron market. There are limits to diversification, at least in consumer markets which are set not only by internal considerations of manageability but externally by the market itself.

We did promise to come back before closing to that matter of competition between the retail sphere and the manufacturing sphere, as an example of market segmentation along radically different axes. It was partly a matter of convenience to set this question aside and partly a matter of conviction. One observes that retailers, regardless of size, seem to want to sell what their customers want to buy. If these customers show no very pronounced preferences among the offerings of various manufacturers, it is probably because there is no very pronounced basis for preference among the competing products. And when this is so, the manufacturers of these more or less indistinguishable commodities are most vulnerable to the substitution of store brands for manufacturer brands. Retailers can compete with retailers in the sale of commodities, by offering store values instead of product values; manufacturers cannot. But when a real basis for product preference exists, the preferred brands either show up on the retailer's shelves, or the retailer is forced to forego substantial business to his competitors who will stock the preferred products. A&P is not about to discontinue Campbell's soup or Heinz ketchup or Jello or other items of this character.

Competition is far from dead among retailers. And as long as competition among retailers exist, manufacturer brands which offer distinctive values to customers will find their way to those customers, if not through one channel, then through another. In a competitive society, the customer will not be denied his choice between less satisfaction and more.

Hence the problem of the manufacturer in confronting the rise of private branding is only in part a task of confronting changes in his environment. The other half of the task is to confront himself and his need for continuous learning and development of his own distinctive capabilities. It is the birthright of the manufacturer to determine the character of his product.

Nowadays we have the phenomenon of the publisher who dreams up an idea for a book and then hires someone to write it. Such offerings by publishers, however, are so poorly received by critics and readers that they have become known as non-books. In the same sense, we might speak of products which no longer portray the identity of their makers as non-products. But the consuming public will always remain more responsive to the author than to the publisher—to the manufacturer than to the middleman—if only the maker will put himself into his product.

QUESTIONS

1. What is the difference between a market segment and a demographic or psychographic profile group?

2. What are the social benefits resulting from market segmentation that are outlined by the author? What additional social benefits can you think of?

3. When does market segmentation tend to be more effective as a competitive strategy?

4. According to this article, what are the disadvantages of basing the development of market segments only on the match-up between customer needs and product benefits?

5. Define "concept of theme" as used in this article. Discuss its role in the market-segmentation process.

5

HOW RESEARCH RELATES TO MARKETING PROCESS

Jack J. Honomichl

Market research is often seen as a related area, but not as being totally involved in the marketing strategy process. This article describes how research can be integrated into the decision-making process for marketing.

The marketing and advertising research industry has an identity problem; it appears more confusing and forbidding than need be.

Most outsiders—and, in fact, many insiders—are boggled by a seemingly endless list of trade abbreviations and personalized company/service names, most of which are familiar but vague.

NFO, AIM, ASI, MSA, TGI, NPD, NFI, ORC, MIC, HTI, MOR, Yankelovich, Simmons, Nelson, *et al*—who are they? What are they? How does the research work they do relate to the marketing process? How does it all hang together?

What follows is an attempt to put things into perspective—to relate research companies, activities and research expenditures to the marketing process. If it appears to have a new-product orientation, that's because a majority of products and services available today were "new" at some point within the past ten years, and a disproportionate amount of marketing energy and research money have gone into their development.

If it appears to have a packaged goods orientation, that's because high-powered packaged goods marketers have been the heaviest and most sophisticated users of marketing and advertising research. That's changing, of course, especially as service industries with mass consumer thrusts adapt packaged goods research techniques to their own needs.

For every research company, or syndicated service, that is mentioned here, there are probably eight to ten more that go unmentioned. But take the ones I specify, total them up, and they account for something in excess of 75% of all marketing and advertising research expenditures in the U.S.

13 Stages of Marketing Strategy

The work of these organizations has been related to a marketing pipeline, a sequential course of actions that most products go through—however informally—from conceptualization to use-up, 13 convenient stages that have become total pivotal points for marketing information activity.

1. Market Segmentation

A major trend toward spending market research monies "up front" started in late 1969. The idea was to do a basic piece of survey research—a market segmentation study—to determine what consumers were looking for (needs) from a product class, how existing products satisfied those needs, and how new product development could be geared to filling "voids" in the market place.

If this worked, management concluded, much risk could be eliminated from new product marketing—and research expenditures could be saved further down the line.

Four research organizations quickly became prominent in market segmentation work: Market Facts Inc.; the research department of Grey Advertising Inc.; MPI Marketing Research; and the company that was Grudin/Appel/Haley. During 1970 and 1971, it is estimated, about $3,000,000 a year was spent for market segmentation studies, and the desire to have one reached near-fad proportions. In 1972, this tapered off, and today it's a declining market—partly because of a limited number of product class areas to study, and partly because the great promise of market segmentation studies often was not realized, either because management didn't know how, or was unable, to act on the information.

2. Product Concept Testing

The refinement of new product concepts stimulates a considerable amount of custom research activity.

Much of this takes the form of focused group interviews, where small groups of prospective consumers are brought together for lengthy, in-depth discussions of the concept idea—or reaction to some sort of stimulus, such as a product mock-up or a dummy advertisement.

Literally hundreds of such group sessions go on in the U.S. each year—and they range in sophistication from Ph.D.'s in psychology serving as moderators with all proceedings tape recorded and videotaped for further analysis, to informal bull sessions where a brand manager gets "a feel" for the viability of his pet idea.

Much of this type of work is done by the manufacturer directly, or by his advertising agency. In addition, numerous small research firms specialize in focused group interviews.

Controlled mail panels—such as are operated by National Family Opinion Inc., Market Facts Inc., and Home Testing Institute—are often used for a large-scale evaluation of concepts. Households participating in these mail panels agree to respond to queries about products, services and their usage and/or attitudes toward them. So, through the mail panels, a manufacturer can expose his product idea to thousands of households and evaluate how different segments of the population react.

3. Development of Product Components

This phase of product development can be likened to pulling petals from a rose, and it can involve a multitude of small-scale, but important, *ad hoc* research projects.

Coming up for minute, and separate, evaluation would be all elements that make up the product gestalt—name, odor, taste, color, package design, texture, etc.

Most of these type studies are funneled through Central Location Testing Facilities, which are either fixed in or near high-traffic areas (like a shopping center), or mobile trailers that can be moved from one area to another.

Many of these Central Location facilities—of which there are hundreds in the U.S.—are elaborately equipped with such accouterments of the trade as kitchens, one-way mirrors, tape recorders and, in some cases, videotape equipment. Most are set up for focused group interviews and the fast, relatively inexpensive exposure of a large number of respondents to some simple stimulus, such as a taste or package design.

It is almost impossible to document the money spent for this phase of consumer research, but something more than $3,000,000 a year seems likely. The sum continues to grow as manufacturers try to perfect their product prior to test market exposure.

4. Prototype Evaluation

An idea becomes a physical product when small-scale production of prototypes starts; now it is possible to expose prospective consumers to the product as it will appear for sale. And this is commonly done.

In-home placement tests are often used; a relatively small number of households are sent the prototype to use in actual day-to-day practice—then, at a later date, queried as to product qualities, faults, comparisons with existing products, etc. Many manufacturers prefer to do this consumer research directly, but others elect to work through research firms that specialize in this work.

5. Development of Advertising Theme

Closely allied to points 2, 3 and 4 (the development of the product) is the development of a product's consumer sales campaign which, in many cases, is synonymous with advertising strategy or tv commerical (pre)testing.

About 25,000 tv commercials are produced in the U.S. each year, it is estimated—10,000 of which are "finished." The balance are "roughs" done in stages of producing the "finished." Nearly $20,000,000 is spent testing these commercials (not counting air time costs), with about 75% being "pre-test"— evaluating the commercials prior to refinement and selection for actual campaign use.

The larger share—about $12,500,000—of the testing money goes into "off-air," or laboratory testing systems, with Audience Studies Inc. leading the field in dollar volume and number of projects. Other leaders are Tele-Research Inc.; McCollum/Spielman & Co.; Walker Research Inc., plus a number of major advertising agencies which have their own proprietary systems.

The remainder—about $7,500,000—goes into "on-air," or live television exposure tests, with Burke Marketing Research being the leading practitioner. Other important factors are Gallup & Robinson and various CATV cable services, such as ASI's In-Home Test Service and Television Testing Co., a joint venture between Audits & Surveys and TelePrompTer Corp. In addition, some major advertisers have their own on-air testing facilities, with the Tv II system of Gillette being an example.

It is estimated that of all tv commercial testing, about 35% is associated with new products; the remainder, of course, pertains to new campaigns for existing products.

6. Pre-Test Market

In recent years, there has been increased interest in research techniques that develop a measure of how consumers will react to a new product in an actual sales context—before committing the large production and advertising money required for full-scale test market operations.

Two research firms have been prominent specialists in this sort of work. One is Homarket Inc., a firm which offers a fixed panel of household products for sale through a catalog—the new product being salted in among existing brands. Respondents can purchase and repurchase the items through the mail.

The second company is Communications Research Clinic, a subsidiary of Daniel Yankelovich Inc. CRC operates a small-scale replica of a supermarket where respondents are allowed to shop under controlled conditions. New products—under test—are stocked on the shelves alongside existing products. Actual sales, plus post interviews regarding motivations for purchase, are claimed to predict the test product's ultimate success in real-world sales conditions.

Both these systems—as well as comparable systems run by individual manufacturers such as General Foods and General Mills—enable the testing of sales at different price levels.

7. Complete Test Market

Easily $30,000,000—and probably considerably more—is spent in the U.S. each year to do customized marketing research related to the test marketing of new products.

The "average" test market program is based on actual sales experience in three "typical" marketing areas, lasts for ten months, and measures two or more variables, most commonly advertising weights and consumer promotional devices.

In practically all test markets there is a custom store audit program to develop volume and share-of-market measures. An estimated $13,000,000 is spent annually toward this end, with the lion's share being divided among seven firms: The Retail Index Division of A. C. Nielsen Co.; the Test Audit Division of Audits & Surveys; Ehrhart-Babic Associates Inc.; Market Facts Inc.; Store Audits Inc.; Lloyd H. Hall Co., and Burgoyne Index Inc.

On top of store audits, almost all test markets include one or more waves of consumer interviews (usually via telephone) to measure levels of consumer awareness of the test product, attitudes toward it (and the advertising), and incidence of purchase. This sort of work is often done by the manufacturer directly, or by the manufacturer through a local field supervisor, or through a marketing research firm—and there are literally dozens involved in this sort of work.

In major test market efforts it is common to create a custom, diary-type consumer panel to measure, among other things, continuous new-and-repeat patterns, *i.e.*, how many households have bought the product to date, how many have bought a second, third, fourth time, etc. Given this input, it is often possible to predict the ultimate level a product will obtain in the market place.

Several firms specialize in the fielding and/or interpretation of diary panel results. These are Market Research Corp. of America; Sum of Squares Inc.; Home Testing Institute; National Family Opinion Inc.; the Marketing

DEVELOPMENT OF PRODUCT CONCEPT

(Marketing Strategy)
1. Market segmentation
2. Product concept testing
3. Development of product components
4. Prototype evaluation
5. Development of advertising theme

CONCEPT REFINEMENT

(Marketing Tactics)
6. Pre-test market
7. Complete test market
8. Regional distribution

PIPELINE

(Market Tracking)
9. Factory shipment
10. Warehouse inventory movement
11. Retail on-shelf availability
12. Consumer purchasing dynamics
13. End usage

Information Center (a division of Reuben H. Donnelly Corp.); and Market Science Associates.

A major trend in recent years has been to by-pass "real-life" test markets and go into test markets where on-going research facilities ensure immediate product distribution and measures of consumer acceptance. Leading this field is the Marketest Division of Market Facts Inc., which has permanent operations in seven test market cities, including warehousing facilities and arrangements with local grocery retailers that permit controlled in-store stocking of test products.

The A. C. Nielsen Co. recently announced that it is setting up a comparable system—Data Markets—in four cities.

8. Regional Distribution

In some cases, new products are expanded out of test markets into regional distribution—then held, either because more extended sales experience is desired before going national, or because of extenuating circumstances, such as limited production capacity. In addition, are the regional manufacturers who limit marketing to a specific region.

In such cases, the market tracking needs are similar to these discussed later in points 10, 11, and 12. So, most of the national tracking services offer regional reports—some of which are very flexible (in terms of geography), and others quite rigid.

9. Factory Shipment

In many industries, a gross—but workable—measure of product moving to market is achieved by voluntary pooling of factory shipment information.

Naturally, such a system depends on the complete cooperation of major manufacturers, plus, in many instances, some knowing estimates for non-cooperators. When a total is developed, of course, any given manufacturer can take his shipment data and compute his own share-of-market.

10. Warehouse Withdrawals/Inventory

The most important innovation in marketing measures in recent years started in 1965 when an organization called Pipeline Research Inc. delivered its first reports.

Pipeline, using actual product withdrawal records from wholesale and chain drug warehouses, produced amalgamated reports of item movement on a variety of over-the-counter drug and sundry products.

A comparable, but more ambitious, service for the grocery trade started in 1965 with the advent of SPEEData (now defunct) and, one year later, Selling Areas-Marketing Inc. (SAMI), a subsidiary of Time Inc. SAMI now does an annual volume close to $15,000,000, and Pipeline does over $1,000,000, it is estimated.

A combination of factors made these services desirable—and feasible. One was the installation of EDP inventory control systems at the warehouse level. Another was the desire of chains to recoup some of the EDP investment—*i.e.*, turn internal records into a revenue source. A third was—assuming the cooperation of most warehousing operations in a given marketing area—the ability to produce a total measure of product movement, which was deemed more useful than projections from audits done in a sample of stores.

This became more desirable as inventory levels in individual stores were reduced, making for a closer "pull-through" relationship between warehouse withdrawals and actual consumer purchases at retail.

After considerable start-up frustrations and capital investment, warehouse withdrawal reports have become an established part of the marketing scene, with numerous manufacturers using them for share-of-market and tonnage movement evaluations in major markets.

One step back on the marketing pipeline is warehouse inventory levels, as chains—in an effort to reduce their own warehousing costs—cut back inventory in their warehouses. This increases the possibility of lost sales for the manufacturer and, hence, the need to monitor warehouse inventory levels. SAMI is now contemplating a separate reporting service to fill this need.

11. On-Shelf Availability

This is the pipeline point where most marketing research money has been spent traditionally—between $36,000,000 and $40,000,000 a year—mostly due to the development of the "share-of-market" concept by Arthur C. Nielsen Sr., back in the 1920s, which turned marketing success into a continuous horse race.

Retail sales volume data have, generally, been obtained by means of auditing product movement through a projectable sample of retail stores within a specific time period. Most of this activity has been concentrated in retail food and drug outlets where invoices are, relatively, complete and accessible compared to other classes of trade. In recent years, there has been increased emphasis on including mass merchandisers, mostly because of the volume they represent in the health and beauty aids product class.

The major syndicated services are the A. C. Nielsen Co.'s National Food Index and Retail Drug Index, plus the National Total Market Audit run by Audits & Surveys. In the health care field, various continuous audit programs have been run in hospitals and retail drug outlets by such research organizations as Armbruster, Moore & MacKerell; IMS/Davee, Koehnlein & Keating; and Lea Inc. Another organization—Drug Distribution Data—was started by the National Wholesale Drug Assn. in 1967, and was bought by Cambridge Computer Corp.

These services are continuous and syndicated, measuring—by product class—volume of sales, share of market, distribution levels, and related measures. Changes and developments in these services have been rare through the years, with a couple of exceptions: Nielsen's streamlining of its NFI and RDI services and their attempt to start a continuing audit of gasoline service stations.

Correlative services are syndicated measures of on-shelf availability of specific products, by chain, within major markets. These services usually report number of food stores stocking, posted shelf prices, number of product facings, and a variety of other observational measures. Major services: National Retail Tracking Index (a service of Ehrhart-Babic Associates); the

Metropolitan Supermarket Audit (a service of Market Research Corp. of America); Market Check (a service of the Lloyd H. Hall Co.), and the 65-City Supermarket Audit (a service of Ferguson Enterprises).

All told, about $1,700,000 is spent for syndicated distribution check measures a year.

12. Consumer Purchase Dynamics

Many sophisticated marketers, especially in the packaged goods industry, feel the need to know on a continuous basis the consumer purchasing dynamics underlying their product class.

For instance: What percent of U.S. households are buying the product class, or major brands? How often do they buy (purchase cycle)? What are the brand switching patterns? How does brand loyalty differ from brand to brand? And so on through a variety of related questions that can best be answered from sequential purchase records obtained at the household level.

The need for these data is answered by national, diary-type mail panel systems, of which there are four in operation today. Two general-purpose, syndicated panels are operated by the Market Research Corp. of America (National Consumer Panel) and National Purchase Diary Panels Inc. (National Purchase Diary). Another panel, which is devoted to pet food and supplies, is operated by the Marketing Information Center, a division of the Reuben H. Donnelley Corp. A fourth system, devoted to wearing apparel and software, is operated by National Family Opinion Inc., for a group of textile manufacturers.

In total, these national panel operations do about $4,000,000 annually.

In recent years, there have been two major attempts to gather sequential purchase data with non-mail techniques. One was Dial-Diary Panel, a telephone panel supported by Listfax, and the second was National Consumer Audit, an in-home pantry audit system developed by Appel Haley Fouriezos Inc. Both have since terminated.

13. End Usage

Starting in 1958, a syndicated study conducted by the Market Research Corp. of America—the Menu Census Study—educated marketers to the importance of knowing how consumers prepare and consume food stuffs in the home.

This led to measurements of "homemade" markets that were ripe for commercial exploitation, such as casseroles (who makes them, and what are the ingredients?) and cakes and cookies, etc.; the use of foods in tandem (what vegetable is most commonly served with ham at a main meal?); and basic information on changing eating habits—*i.e.,* breakfast and between-meal snacking.

There have been three such Menu Census Studies, and the fourth is in preparation now. The last one had about $2,000,000 of manufacturer support.

Away from food—especially in health and beauty aid classifications—several manufacturers have done custom research to learn about in-home consumption habits—for instance, hair shampooing habits of family members.

QUESTIONS

1. What are the three categories of market information for implementing a marketing strategy?
2. Which of the thirteen stages of a marketing strategy fall in the information category entitled "product concept development"?
3. What are the informational requirements of the regional distribution stage of a marketing strategy?
4. Describe the characteristics of the average test market program.

PART THREE

Products

After analyzing the needs and characteristics of its market, a firm must focus its efforts on providing the benefits and services that best satisfy those needs. Thus, the foundation of an effective strategy will be the product decisions resulting from analyses of customers, competitors, and the environment. Part Three reviews major decision-making tools for making product decisions. These decisions range from the strategic concerns of long-term resource allocation and the development of new products to the management of existing products over their lifetime.

Specifically, the tools that will be discussed are product-portfolio analysis, new product development, and the product life cycle. Although all of these procedures are generally regarded as useful tools for making product decisions, none are without limitations or pitfalls. The selected articles provide a balanced review of these techniques, pointing out both the promise and the pitfalls. They also provide guidelines on how to benefit from the former and avoid the latter.

The first article, "Diagnosing the Product Portfolio," focuses on portfolio analysis that views the firm and its competitors as a collection of interrelated products, each having a different position in the marketplace and each having a different role within its respective firm. The article also describes situations in which portfolio analysis provides useful information for strategic planning and situations in which the analysis can be misleading.

The next article focuses on new product development. Marketers face a dynamic world where customer tastes and preferences, technology, and competitive capabilities are constantly changing. To remain vital and growing, the firm must change as its markets and environments change; it must regularly introduce successful new products. The failure rate of new products remains high in most industries, and some basic rules for reducing failures are provided in "Developing and Managing New Products."

The product life cycle is a conceptual model that helps guide management strategy from the initial commercialization of a new product through its ultimate removal from the market. "Resource Allocation within the Product Life Cycle" describes how a major firm successfully integrated the life-cycle concept into its budgeting process.

1

DIAGNOSING THE PRODUCT PORTFOLIO

George S. Day

Although generally accepted as a useful tool for strategy formulation, product portfolio analysis is sensitive to violations of assumptions, measurement error, and the possibility of infeasible results. This selection discusses these sensitivites and suggests ways they can be avoided.

The product portfolio approach to marketing strategy formulation has gained wide acceptance among managers of diversified companies. They are first attracted by the intuitively appealing concept that long-run corporate performance is more than the sum of the contributions of individual profit centers or product strategies. Secondly a product portfolio analysis suggests specific marketing strategies to achieve a balanced mix of products that will produce the maximum long-run effects from scarce cash and managerial resources. Lastly the concept employs a simple matrix representation which is easy to communicate and comprehend. Thus it is a useful tool in a head-quarters campaign to demonstrate that the strategic issues facing the firm justify more centralized control over the planning and resource allocation process.

With the growing acceptance of the basic approach has come an increasing sensitivity to the limitations of the present methods of portraying the product portfolio, and a recognition that the approach is not equally useful in all corporate circumstances. Indeed, the implications can sometimes be grossly misleading. Inappropriate and misleading applications will result when:

- The basic **assumptions** (especially those concerned with the value of market share dominance and the product life cycle) are violated.

- The **measurements** are wrong, or
- The **strategies** are not feasible.

This article identifies the critical assumptions and the measurement and application issues that may distort the strategic insights. A series of questions are posed that will aid planners and decision-makers to better understand this aid to strategic thinking, and thereby make better decisions.

What Is the Product Portfolio?

Common to all portrayals of the product portfolio is the recognition that the competitive value of market share depends on the structure of competition and the stage of the product life cycle. Two examples of this approach have recently appeared in this journal.[1] However, the earliest, and most widely implemented is the cash quadrant or share/growth matrix developed by the Boston Consulting Group.[2] Each product is classified jointly by rate of present or forecast **market growth** (a proxy for stage in the product life cycle) and a measure of **market share dominance**.

The arguments for the use of market share are familiar and well documented.[3] Their basis is the cumulation of evidence that market share is strongly and positively correlated with product profitability. This theme is varied somewhat in the BCG approach by the emphasis on relative share— measured by the ratio of the company's share of the market to the share of the largest competitor. This is reasonable since the strategic implications of a 20% share are quite different if the largest competitor's is 40% or if it is 5%. Profitability will also vary, since according to the experience curve concept the largest competitor will be the most profitable at the prevailing price level.[4]

---

[1] Bernard Catry and Michel Chevalier, "Market Share Strategy and the Product Life Cycle," **Journal of Marketing**, Vol. 38 No. 4 (October 1974), pp. 29–34; and Yoram Wind and Henry J. Claycamp, "Planning Product Line Strategy: A Matrix Approach," **Journal of Marketing**, Vol. 40 No. 1 (January 1976), pp. 2–9.

[2] Described in the following pamphlets in the *Perspectives* series, authored by Bruce D. Henderson, "The Product Portfolio" (1970), "Cash Traps" (1972) and "The Experience Curve Reviewed: The Growth-Share Matrix or the Product Portfolio". (Boston Consulting Group, 1973). By 1972 the approach had been employed in more than 100 companies. See "Mead's Technique to Sort Out the Losers," *Business Week* (March 11, 1972), pp. 124–30.

[3] Sidney Schoeffler, Robert D. Buzzell and Donald F. Heany, "Impact of Strategic Planning on Profit Performance," *Harvard Business Review* Vol. 52 (March-April 1974), pp. 137–45; and Robert D. Buzzell, Bradley T. Gale and Ralph G. M. Sultan, "Market Share—A Key to Profitability," *Harvard Business Review*, Vol. 53 (January-February 1975), pp. 97–106.

[4] Boston Consulting Group, *Perspectives on Experience* (Boston: 1968 and 1970), and "Selling Business a Theory of Economics," *Business Week*, September 8, 1974, pg. 43–44.

The product life cycle is employed because it highlights the desirability of a variety of products or services with different present and prospective growth rates. More important, the concept has some direct implications for the cost of gaining and/or holding market share:

- During the **rapid growth stage**, purchase patterns and distribution channels are fluid. Market shares can be increased at "relatively" low cost by capturing a disproportionate share of incremental sales (especially where these sales come from new users of applications rather than heavier usage by existing users).

- By contrast, the key-note during the **maturity stage** swings to stability and inertia in distribution and purchasing relationships. A substantial growth in share by one competitor will come at the expense of another competitor's capacity utilization, and will be resisted vigorously. As a result, gains in share are both time-consuming and costly (unless accompanied by a breakthrough in product value or performance that cannot be easily matched by competition).

Product Portfolio Strategies

When the share and growth rate of each of the products sold by a firm are jointly considered, a new basis for strategy evaluation emerges. While there are many possible combinations, an arbitrary classification of products into four share/growth categories (as shown in Exhibit [i.e., Figure] 1) is sufficient to illustrate the strategy implications.

Low Growth/Dominant Share (Cash Cows)

These profitable products usually generate more cash than is required to maintain share. All strategies should be directed toward maintaining market dominance—including investments in technological leadership. Pricing decisions should be made cautiously with an eye to maintaining price leadership. Pressure to over-invest through product proliferation and market expansion should be resisted unless prospects for expanding primary demand are unusually attractive. Instead, excess cash should be used to support research activities and growth areas elsewhere in the company.

High Growth/Dominant Share (Stars)

Products that are market leaders, but also growing fast, will have substantial reported profits but need a lot of cash to finance the rate of growth. The appropriate strategies are designed primarily to protect the existing share level by reinvesting earnings in the form of price reductions, product improvement, better market coverage, production efficiency increases, etc. Particular

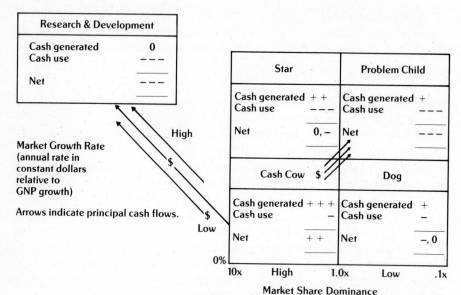

FIGURE 1   *The Cash Quadrant Approach to Describing the Product Portfolio*

attention must be given to obtaining a large share of the new users or new applications that are the source of growth in the market.

Low Growth/Subordinate Share (Dogs)

Since there usually can be only one market leader and because most markets are mature, the greatest number of products fall in this category. Such products are usually at a cost disadvantage and have few opportunities for growth at a reasonable cost. Their markets are not growing, so there is little new business to compete for, and market share gains will be resisted strenuously by the dominant competition.

The slower the growth (present or prospective) and the smaller the relative share, the greater the need for positive action. The possibilities include:

1. Focusing on a specialized segment of the market that can be dominated, and protected from competitive inroads.
2. Harvesting, which is a conscious cutback of all support costs to some minimum level which will maximize the cash flow over a foreseeable lifetime—which is usually short.
3. Divestment, usually involving a sale as a going concern.
4. Abandonment or deletion from the product line.

High Growth/Subordinate Share (Problem Children)

The combination of rapid growth and poor profit margins creates an enormous demand for cash. If the cash is not forthcoming, the product will become a "Dog" as growth inevitably slows. The basic strategy options are fairly clear-cut; either invest heavily to get a disproportionate share of the new sales or buy existing shares by acquiring competitors and thus move the product toward the "Star" category or get out of the business using some of the methods just described.

Consideration also should be given to a market segmentation strategy, but only if a defensible niche can be identified and resources are available to gain dominance. This strategy is even more attractive if the segment can provide an entrée and experience based from which to push for dominance of the whole market.

Overall Strategy

The long-run health of the corporation depends on having some products that *generate* cash (and provide acceptable reported profits), and others that *use* cash to support growth. Among the indicators of overall health are the size and vulnerability of the "Cash Cows" (and the prospects for the "Stars," if any), and the number of "Problem Children" and "Dogs." Particular attention must be paid to those products with large cash appetites. Unless the company has abundant cash flow, it cannot afford to sponsor many such products at one time. If resources (including debt capacity) are spread too thin, the company simply will wind up with too many marginal products and suffer a reduced capacity to finance promising new product entries or acquisitions in the future.

The share/growth matrix displayed in Exhibit 2 shows how one company (actually a composite of a number of situations) might follow the strategic implications of the product portfolio to achieve a better balance of sources and uses of cash. The *present* position of each product is defined by the relative share and market growth rate during a representative time *period*. Since business results normally fluctuate, it is important to use a time period that is not distorted by rare events. The *future* position may be either (a) a momentum forecast or the results of continuing the present strategy, or (b) a forecast of the consequences of a change in strategy. It is desirable to do both, and compare the results. The specific display of Exhibit [Figure] 2 is a summary of the following strategic decisions.

- Aggressively **support** the newly introduced product A, to ensure dominance (but anticipate share declines due to new competitive entries).

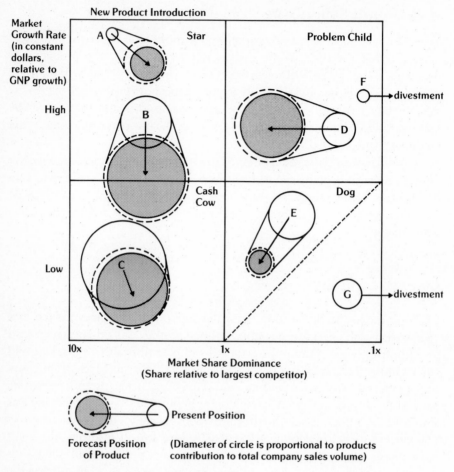

FIGURE 2 *Balancing the Product Portfolio*

- Continue present strategies of products B and C to ensure **maintenance** of market share.
- Gain share of market for product D by investing in **acquistions**.
- Narrow and modify the range of models of product E to **focus** on one segment.
- Divest products F and G.

Pitfalls in the Assumptions

The starting point in the decision to follow the implications of a product portfolio analysis is to ask whether the underlying assumptions make sense.

The most fundamental assumptions relate to the role of market share in the businesses being portrayed in the portfolio. Even if the answers here are affirmative one may choose to not follow the implications if other objectives than balancing cash flows take priority, or there are barriers to implementing the indicated strategies.

What Is the Role of Market Share?

All the competitors are assumed to have the same overhead structures and experience curves, with their position on the experience curve corresponding to their market share position. Hence market share dominance is a proxy for the *relative* profit performance (e.g., GM vs. Chrysler). Other factors beyond market share may be influential in dictating *absolute, profit performance (e.g., calculators versus cosmetics)*.

The influence of market share is most apparent with high value-added products, where there are significant barriers to entry and the competition consists of a few, large, diversified corporations with the attendant large overheads (e.g., plastics, major appliances, automobiles, and semiconductors). But even in these industrial environments there are distortions under conditions such as:

- One competitor has a significant technological advantage which can be protected and used to establish a steeper cost reduction/experience curve.

- The principal component of the product is produced by a supplier who has an inherent cost advantage because of an integrated process. Thus Dupont was at a cost disadvantage with Cyclohexane vis-à-vis the oil companies because the manufacture of the product was so highly integrated with the operations of an oil refinery.[5]

- Competitors can economically gain large amounts of experience through acquisitions or licensing, or shift to a lower (but parallel) cost curve by resorting to off-shore production or component sourcing.

- Profitability is highly sensitive to the rate of capacity utilization, regardless of size of plant.

There are many situations where the positive profitability and share relationship becomes very tenuous, and perhaps unattainable. A recent illustration is the building industry where large corporations—CNA with Larwin and ITT with Levitt—have suffered because of their inability to adequately offset

---

[5]Robert B. Stobaugh and Philip L. Towsend, "Price Forecasting and Strategic Planning: The Case of Petrochemicals," *Journal of Marketing Research*, Vol. XII (February 1975), pp. 19–29.

their high overhead charges with a corresponding reduction in total costs.[6] Similar problems are also encountered in the service sector, and contribute to the many reasons why services which are highly labor-intensive and involve personal relationships must be approached with extreme caution in a product portfolio analysis.[7]

There is specific evidence from the Profit Impact of Market Strategies (PIMS) study[8] that the value of market share is not as significant for consumer goods as for industrial products. The reasons are not well understood, but probably reflect differences in buying behavior, the importance of product differentiation and the tendency for proliferation of marginally different brands in these categories. The strategy of protecting a market position by introducing line extensions, flankers, and spin-offs from a successful core brand means that product class boundaries are very unclear. Hence shares are harder to estimate. The individual brand in a category like deodorants or powdered drinks may not be the proper basis for evaluation. A related consequence is that joint costing problems multiply. For example, Unilever in the U.K. has 20 detergent brands all sharing production facilities and marketing resources to some degree.

When Do Market Shares Stabilize?

The operating assumption is that shares tend toward stability during the maturity stage, as the dominant competitors concentrate on defending their existing position. An important corollary is that gains in share are easier and cheaper to achieve during the growth stage.

There is scattered empirical evidence, including the results of the PIMS project, which supports these assumptions. Several qualifications must be made before the implications can be pursued in depth:

- While market share *gains* may be costly, it is possible to mismanage a dominant position. The examples of A&P in food retailing, and British Leyland in the U.K. automobile market provide new benchmarks on the extent to which strong positions can erode unless vigorously defended.
- When the two largest competitors are of roughly equal size, the share positions may continue to be fluid until one is finally dominant.

---

[6] Carol J. Loomis, "The Further Misadventures of Harold Geneen," *Fortune*, June 1975.

[7] There is incomplete but provocative evidence of significant share-profit relationships in the markets for auto rental, consumer finance, and retail securities brokerage.

[8] Same as reference 3 above.

- There are certain product categories, frequently high technology oriented, where a dominant full line/full service competitor is vulnerable if there are customer segments which do not require all the services, technical assistance, etc., that are provided. As markets mature this "sophisticated" segment usually grows. Thus, Digital Equipment Corp. has prospered in competition with IBM by simply selling basic hardware and depending on others to do the applications programming.[9] By contrast, IBM provides, for a price, a great deal of service backup and software for customers who are not self-sufficient. The dilemma for the dominant producer lies in the difficulty of serving both segments simultaneously.[10]

What Is the Objective of a Product Portfolio Strategy?

The strategies emerging from a product portfolio analysis emphasize the balance of cash flows, by ensuring that there are products that use cash to sustain growth and others that supply cash.

Yet corporate objectives have many more dimensions that require consideration. This point was recognized by Seymour Tilles in one of the earliest discussions of the portfolio approach.[11] It is worth repeating to avoid a possible myopic focus on cash flow considerations. Tilles' point was that an investor pursues a balanced combination of risk, income, and growth when acquiring a portfolio of securities. He further argued that "the same basic concepts apply equally well to product planning." The problem with concentrating on cash flow to maximize income and growth is that strategies to balance risks are not explicitly considered.

What must be avoided is excessive exposure to a specific threat from one of the following areas of vulnerability:

- The economy (e.g., business downturns).
- Social, political, environmental pressures.
- Supply continuity.
- Technological change.
- Unions and related human factors.

---

[9] "A Minicomputer Tempest," *Business Week* January 27, 1975, pp. 79–80.

[10] Some argue that the dilemma is very general, confronting all pioneering companies in mature markets. See Seymour Tilles, "Segmentation and Strategy," *Perspectives* (Boston: Boston Consulting Group, 1974).

[11] Seymour Tilles, "Strategies for Allocating Funds," *Harvard Business Review*, Vol. 44 (January-February 1966), pp. 72–80.

It also follows that a firm should direct its new product search activities into several different opportunity areas, to avoid intensifying the degree of vulnerability. Thus, many companies in the power equipment market, such as Brown Boveri, are in a quandry over whether to meet the enormous resource demands of the nuclear power equipment market, because of the degree of vulnerability of this business compared to other possibilities such as household appliances.

The desire to reduce vulnerability is a possible reason for keeping, or even acquiring, a "Dog." Thus, firms may integrate backward to assure supply of highly leveraged materials.[12] If a "Dog" has a high percentage of captive business, it may not even belong as a separate entity in a portfolio analysis.

A similar argument could be used for products which have been acquired for intelligence reasons. For example, a large Italian knitwear manufacturer owns a high-fashion dress company selling only to boutiques to help follow and interpret fashion trends. Similarly, because of the complex nature of the distribution of lumber products, some suppliers have acquired lumber retailers to help learn about patterns of demand and changing end-user requirements. In both these cases the products/businesses were acquired for reasons outside the logic of the product portfolio, and should properly be excluded from the analysis.

Can the Strategies Be Implemented?

Not only does a product portfolio analysis provide insights into the long-run health of a company; it also implies the basic strategies that will strengthen the portfolio. Unfortunately, there are many situations where the risks of failure of these strategies are unacceptably high. Several of these risks were identified in a recent analysis of the dangers in the pursuit of market share.[13]

One danger is that the company's financial resources will not be adequate. The resulting problems are enormously compounded should the company find itself in a vulnerable financial position if the fight were stopped short for some reason. The fundamental question underlying such dangers is the likelihood that competitors will pursue the same strategy, because they follow the same logic in identifying and pursuing opportunities. As a result, there is a growing premium on the understanding of competitive responses, and especially the degree to which they will be discouraged by aggressive action.

An increasingly important question is whether government regulations will permit the corporation to follow the strategy it has chosen. Antitrust

---

[12] This argument is compelling when $20,000 of Styrene Monomer can affect the production of $10,000,000 worth of formed polyester fiberglass parts.

[13] William E. Fruhan, "Pyrrhic Victories in Fights for Market Share," *Harvard Business Review*, Vol. 50 (September-October 1972), pp. 100–107.

regulations—especially in the U.S.—now virtually preclude acquisitions undertaken by large companies in related areas. Thus the effort by ITT to acquire a "Cash Cow" in Hartford Fire and Indemnity Insurance was nearly aborted by a consent decree, and other moves by ITT into Avis, Canteen Corp., and Levitt have been divested by court order at enormous cost. Recent governmental actions—notably the *ReaLemon* case—may even make it desirable for companies with very large absolute market share to consider reducing that share.[14]

There is less recognition as yet that government involvement can cut both ways; making it difficult to get in *or out of* a business. Thus, because of national security considerations large defense contractors would have a difficult time exiting from the aerospace or defense businesses. The problems are most acute in countries like Britain and Italy where intervention policies include price controls, regional development directives and employment maintenance which may prevent the replacement of out-moded plants. Unions in these two countries are sometimes so dedicated to protecting the employment status quo that a manager may not even move employees from one product line to another without risking strike activity.

The last implementation question concerns the viability of a niche strategy, which appears at the outset to be an attractive way of coping with both "Dogs" and "Problem Children." The fundamental problem, of course, is whether a product or market niche can be isolated and protected against competitive inroads. But even if this can be achieved in the long-run, the strategy may not be attractive. The difficulties are most often encountered when a full or extensive product line is needed to support sales, service and distribution facilities. One specialized product may simply not generate sufficient volume and gross margin to cover the minimum costs of participation in the market. This is very clearly an issue in the construction equipment business because of the importance of assured service.

Pitfalls in the Measures

The "Achilles' Heel" of a product portfolio analysis is the units of measure; for if the share of market and growth estimates are dubious, so are the interpretations. Skeptics recognize this quickly, and can rapidly confuse the analysis by attacking the meaningfulness and accuracy of these measures and offering alternative definitions. With the present state of the measurements there is often no adequate defense.

---

[14] See Paul N. Bloom and Philip Kotler, "Strategies for High Market-Share Companies," *Harvard Business Review*, Vol. 53 (November-December 1975), pp. 63–72.

What Share of What Market?

This is not one, but several questions. Each is controversial because they influence the bases for resource allocation and evaluation within the firm:

- Should the definition of the product-market be broad (reflecting the generic need) or narrow?
- How much market segmentation?
- Should the focus be on the total product-market or a portion served by the company?
- Which level of geography: local versus national versus regio-centric markets?

The answers to these questions are complicated by the lack of defensible procedures for identifying product-market boundaries. For example, four-digit SIC categories are convenient and geographically available but may have little relevance to consumer perceptions of substitutability which will influence the long-run performance of the product. Furthermore, there is the pace of product development activity which is dedicated to combining, extending, or otherwise obscuring the boundaries.

BREADTH OF PRODUCT-MARKET DEFINITION?   This is a pivotal question. Consider the following extremes in definitions:

- Intermediate builder chemicals for the detergent industry *or* Sodium Tri-polyphosphate.
- Time/information display devices *or* medium-priced digital-display alarm clocks.
- Main meal accompaniments *or* jellied cranberry.

Narrow definitions satisfy the short-run, tactical concerns of sales and product managers. Broader views, reflecting longer-run, strategic planning concerns, invariably reveal a larger market to account for (a) sales to untapped but potential markets, (b) changes in technology, price relationships, and supply which broaden the array of potential substitute products, and (c) the time required by present and prospective buyers to react to these changes.

EXTENT OF SEGMENTATION?   In other words, when does it become meaningful to divide the total market into sub-groups for the purpose of estimating shares? In the tire industry it is evident that the OEM and replacement markets are so dissimilar in behavior as to dictate totally different marketing mixes. But how much further should segmentation be pushed? The fact that a company has a large share of the high-income buyers of replacement tires is probably not strategically relevant.

In general the degree of segmentation for a portfolio analysis should be limited to grouping those buyers that share situational or behavioral characteristics that are strategically relevant. This means that different marketing mixes must be used to serve the segments that have been identified, which will be reflected in different cost and price structures. Other manifestations of a strategically important segment boundary would be a discontinuity in growth rates, share patterns, distribution patterns and so forth when going from one segment to another.

These judgments are particularly hard to make for geographic boundaries. For example, what is meaningful for a manufacturer of industrial equipment facing dominant local competition in each of the national markets in the European Economic Community? Because the company is in each market, it has a 5% share of the total EEC market, while the largest regional competitor has 9%. In this case the choice of a regional rather than national market definition was dictated by the *trend* to similarity of product requirements throughout the EEC and the consequent feasibility of a single manufacturing facility to serve several countries.

The tendency for trade barriers to decline for countries within significant economic groupings will increasingly dictate regio-centric rather than nationally oriented boundaries. This, of course, will not happen where transportation costs or government efforts to protect sensitive industry categories (such as electric power generation equipment), by requiring local vendors, creates other kinds of barriers.

Market Served versus Total Market?

Firms may elect to serve only just a part of the available market, such as retailers with central buying offices or utilities of a certain size. The share of the market served is an appropriate basis for tactical decisions. This share estimate may also be relevant for strategic decisions, especially if the market served corresponds to a distinct segment boundary. There is a risk that focusing only on the market served may mean overlooking a significant opportunity or competitive threat emerging from the unserved portion of the market. For example, a company serving the blank cassette tape market only through specialty audio outlets is vulnerable if buyers perceive that similar quality cassettes can be bought in general merchandise and discount outlets.

Another facet of the served market issue is the treatment of customers who have integrated backward and now satisfy their own needs from their own resources. Whether or not the captive volume is included in the estimate of total market size depends on how readily this captive volume can be displaced by outside suppliers. Recent analysis suggests that captive production—or infeeding—is "remarkably resilient to attack by outside suppliers."[15]

---

[15]Aubrey Wilson and Bryan Atkin, "Exorcising the Ghosts in Marketing," *Harvard Business Review*, Vol. 54 (September-October 1976), pp. 117-27. See also, Ralph D. Kerkendall, "Customers as Competitors," *Perspectives* (Boston: Boston Consulting Group, 1975).

What Can Be Done?

The value of a strategically relevant product-market definition lies in "stretching" the company's perceptions appropriately—far enough so that significant threats and opportunities are not missed, but not so far as to dissipate information gathering and analysis efforts on "long shots." This is a difficult balance to achieve, given the myriads of possibilities. The best procedure for coping is to employ several alternative definitions, varying specificity of product and market segments. There will inevitably be both points of contradiction and consistency in the insights gained from portfolios constructed at one level versus another. The process of resolution can be very revealing, both in terms of understanding the competitive position and suggesting strategy alternatives.[16]

Market Growth Rate

The product life cycle is justifiably regarded as one of the most difficult marketing concepts to measure—or forecast.

There is a strong tendency in a portfolio analysis to judge that a product is maturing when there is a forecast of a decline in growth rate below some specified cut-off. One difficulty is that the same cut-off level does not apply equally to all products or economic climates. As slow growth or level GNP becomes the reality, high absolute growth rates become harder to achieve for all products, mature or otherwise. Products with lengthy introductory periods, facing substantial barriers to adoption, may never exhibit high growth rates, but may have an extended maturity stage. Other products may exhibit precisely the opposite life cycle pattern.

The focus in the product portfolio analysis should be on the long-run growth rate forecast. This becomes especially important with products which are sensitive to the business cycle, such as machine tools, or have potential substitutes with fluctuating prices. Thus the future growth of engineered plastics is entwined with the price of zinc, aluminum, copper and steel; the sales of powdered breakfast beverages depends on the relative price of frozen orange juice concentrate.

These two examples also illustrate the problem of the self-fulfilling prophecy. A premature classification as a mature product may lead to the reduction of marketing resources to the level necessary to defend the share in order to maximize net cash flow. But if the product class sales are sensitive to market development activity (as in the case of engineered plastics) or advertising expenditures (as is the case with powdered breakfast drinks) and

[16]George S. Day and Allan D. Shocker, *Identifying Competitive Product-Market Boundaries: Strategic and Analytical Issues* (Boston: Marketing Science Institute, 1976).

these budgets are reduced by the dominant firms then, indeed, the product growth rate will slow down.

The growth rate is strongly influenced by the choice of product-market boundaries. A broad product type (cigarettes) will usually have a longer maturity stage than a more specific product form (plain filter cigarettes). In theory, the growth of the individual brand is irrelevant. Yet, it cannot be ignored that the attractiveness of a growth market, however defined, will be diminished by the entry of new competitors with the typical depressing effect on the sales, prices and profits of the established firms. The extent of the reappraisal of the market will depend on the number, resources, and commitment of the new entrants. Are they likely to become what is known in the audio electronics industry as "rabbits," which come racing into the market, litter it up, and die off quickly?

Pitfalls from Unanticipated Consequences

Managers are very effective at tailoring their behavior to the evaluation system, *as they perceive it*. Whenever market share is used to evaluate performance, there is a tendency for managers to manipulate the product-market boundaries to show a static or increasing share. The greater the degree of ambiguity or compromise in the definition of the boundaries the more tempting these adjustments become. The risk is that the resulting narrow view of the market may mean overlooking threats from substitutes or the opportunities within emerging market segments.

These problems are compounded when share dominance is also perceived to be an important determinant of the allocation of resources and top management interest. The manager who doesn't like the implications of being associated with a "Dog," may try to redefine the market so he can point to a larger market share or a higher than average growth rate. Regardless of his success with the attempted redefinition, his awareness of how the business is regarded in the overall portfolio will ultimately affect his morale. Then his energies may turn to seeking a transfer or looking for another job, and perhaps another prophecy has been fulfilled.

The forecast of market growth rate is also likely to be manipulated, especially if the preferred route to advancement and needed additional resources is perceived to depend on association with a product that is classified as "Star." This may lead to wishful thinking about the future growth prospects of the product. Unfortunately the quality of the review procedures in most planning processes is not robust enough to challenge such distortions. Further dysfunctional consequences will result if ambitious managers of "Cash Cows" actually attempt to expand their products through unnecessary product proliferation and market segmentation without regard to the impact on profits.

The potential for dysfunctional consequences does not mean that profit center managers and their employees should not be aware of the basis for resource allocation decisions within the firm. A strong argument can be made to the effect that it is worse for managers to observe those decisions and suspect the worst. What will surely create problems is to have an inappropriate reward system. A formula-based system, relying on achievement of a target for return on investment or an index of profit measures, that does not recognize the differences in potential among business, will lead to short-run actions that conflict with the basic strategies that should be pursued.

Alternative Views of the Portfolio

This analysis of the share/growth matrix portrayal of the product portfolio supports Bowman's contention that much of what now exists in the field of corporate or marketing strategy can be thought of as contingency theories. "The ideas, recommendations, or generalizations are rather dependent (contingent) for their truth and their relevance on the specific situational factors."[17] This means that in any specific analysis of the product portfolio there may be a number of factors beyond share and market growth with a much greater bearing on the attractiveness of a product-market or business; including:

- The contribution rate.
- Barriers to entry.
- Cyclicality of sales.
- The rate of capacity utilization.
- Sensitivity of sales to change in prices, promotional activities, service levels, etc.
- The extent of "captive" business.
- The nature of technology (maturity, volatility, and complexity).
- Availability of production and process opportunities.
- Social, legal, governmental, and union pressures and opportunities.

Since these factors are situational, each company (or division) must develop its own ranking of their importance in determining attractiveness.[18] In practice

---

[17] Edward H. Bowman, "Epistemology, Corporate Strategy, and Academe," *Sloan Management Review* (Winter 1974), pp. 35–50.

[18] The choice of factors and assessment of ranks is an important aspect of the design of a planning system. These issues are described in Peter Lorange, "Divisional Planning: Setting Effective Direction," *Sloan Management Review* (Fall 1975), pp. 77–91.

these factors tend to be qualitatively combined into overall judgments of the attractiveness of the industry or market, and the company's position in that market. The resulting matrix for displaying the positions of each product is called a "nine-block" diagram or decision matrix. [19]

Although the implications of this version of the product portfolio are not as clear-cut, it does overcome many of the shortcomings of the share/growth matrix approach. Indeed the two approaches will likely yield different insights. But as the main purpose of the product portfolio analysis is to help guide—but not subsitute for—strategic thinking, the process of reconciliation is useful in itself. Thus it is desirable to employ both approaches and compare results.

Summary

The product portfolio concept provides a useful synthesis of the analyses and judgments during the preliminary steps of the planning process, and is a provocative source of strategy alternatives. If nothing else, it demonstrates the fallacy of treating all businesses or profit centers as alike, and all capital investment decisions as independent and additive events.

There are a number of pitfalls to be avoided to ensure the implications are not misleading. This is especially true for the cash quadrant or share/growth matrix approach to portraying the portfolio. In many situations the basic assumptions are not satisfied. Further complications stem from uncertainties in the definitions of product-markets and the extent and timing of competitive actions. One final pitfall is the unanticipated consequences of adopting a portfolio approach. These may or may not be undesirable depending on whether they are recognized at the outset.

Despite the potential pitfalls it is important to not lose sight of the concept; that is, to base strategies on the perception of a company as an interdependent group of products and services, each playing a distinctive and supportive role.

QUESTIONS

1. Under what conditions would the product portfolio provide misleading conclusions?

2. What assumptions underlie the product portfolio? When do these assumptions tend not to hold?

---

[19] William E. Rothschild, *Putting It All Together: A Guide to Strategic Thinking* (New York: AMACOM, 1976).

3. What are the advantages of the product portfolio theory?

4. What are the problems associated with determining market share?

5. What other considerations should be evaluated together with the product portfolio?

2

DEVELOPING AND MANAGING NEW PRODUCTS

Eugene F. Finkin

Despite its importance to the long-run survival of the firm and the large base of experience possessed by a number of firms, new product failure rates remain high. This article presents rules of thumb for effective and efficient new product introduction.

Today we know enough about the process of new-product development and commercialization to manage it properly. We have learned, over time, from much repeated experience, important rules of thumb concerning what works and doesn't work, what not to do, and what requires attention. Yet company after company has trouble managing this area, and can be seen making the same mistakes—needlessly.

This article pulls together some of the less well-known, but important, elements of this body of knowledge, either discovered or confirmed from actual experience. It will assist those who wish to avoid repeating some of the common pitfalls and mistakes, and thereby raise their likelihood of success in the new products area.

The chief executive of an industrial business, whether a corporation's CEO or a division's general manager, often feels ill-equipped to pass judgment on the new product management decisions brought to him for approval. He or she usually has little background in this area, having risen from finance or marketing. This article will help the chief executive make the right decisions by showing the right questions to ask.

Types of New-Product Approaches

Most new product development efforts follow, and can be classified as belonging to, one of two approaches. These are frequently referred to as:

- Technology push.
- Market need/market pull/demand pull.

Technology Push

Technology push results when the driving force of the effort is the perceived potential of the technology itself. Marketing's role is secondary, becoming important only after the product or process has been developed. Most of the truly great inventions of the period 1830–1915 fall into this category (e.g., steam turbine, triode, telephone). For great inventions, it is truly impossible to estimate the ultimate size of the market. Who, at the outset, could have estimated the market for computers or xerography? In fact, Sperry Univac is purported to have initially estimated that the size of the total computer market by the year 2000 would be 1,000 or 2,000 machines. This type of product, in effect, follows Says Law in economics, "supply creates demand." It is this kind of success that inspires all technology push efforts, whether warranted or not.

Most new products, however, do not fall into the category of man's greatest 500 inventions. The problem arises when minor innovations are treated as if they did. Most corporate and division R&D groups have one or more inspired new-product-idea generators. These people often become obsessed with the cleverness of an idea and will push its development with little market information, in the simple belief that a market will automatically develop later. This might be termed an answer looking for a question. The frequent result is a technical success and a commercial failure. In this category we can put some of the highly publicized technical innovations of the last twenty years—the heat pipe, rolamite, and laser (most firms developing lasers in the 1960s lost large sums of money without discovering a real market for the products).

One test of the appropriateness of the technology push approach for a specific product effort is its level of innovativeness. Does the product perform a new function and employ a substantially different technology? If not, are we actually faced with a substitution of new technology in existing products (e.g., changing from electromechanical to solid state electronic technology), or a materials substitution, or a size change, or the addition of new features? Technology push is then an inappropriate management approach. Exhibit [Table] 1 lists the basic criteria for a truly new product. Only such products may warrant development in the absence of solid market information (which

Table 1

TECHNOLOGY PUSH APPROPRIATENESS FOR NEW PRODUCT		
Criteria	Yes	No
1. Uses new technology.		
2. Performs new function.		
3. Isn't a technology substitute for any existing product.		
4. Isn't a material substitution.		
5. Isn't a size or capacity change in an existing product.		
6. Isn't a new model with added minor features.		

would not exist). If the prospective new product warrants a check in the "no" column for any of the listed criteria, it should not be managed as a technology push effort.

By and large, technology push is an unproductive corporate approach to new products. However, it usually proves difficult to kill such an effort in the typical industrial corporation when it is of long standing because such efforts develop a constituency. It may also be hard for the chief executive to admit that he was wrong and should have ended the effort long ago.

Market Need/Demand Pull

Most successful new products, say 80 percent, were developed as solutions to perceived market needs. This is the most reliable way to succeed in new products, for it means lessened business risk—lessened because there is less chance that the fully developed product cannot be successfully sold. This approach is much more difficult to manage than technology push, because it requires significant input and coordination with elements outside the new products organization. It also requires skillful handling of the temperamental egos of inventive engineers and technical managers, who must be prevented from doing what is personally technically interesting but of little potential commercial merit.

Expenditure Escalation Points

The increase in cost associated with going from stage to stage in product development and commercialization is often unappreciated when the initiation of a product-development effort is approved. This may be the single greatest reason why new-product ideas do not eventually become successfully commercialized. Amazingly, this fact seems little known.

The cost of conception is little, say under $5,000. The cost of feasibility studies are often modest, say under $50,000 (depending, of course, on the industry). The cost of product development and process development may not be straining, say typically twenty times the cost of establishing feasibility. The costs of pilot production and sales, including outlays for fixed assets, will probably be substantially greater than those of development, say by a factor of twenty. This is an economic critical point in the process for it requires financial commitments far beyond the scope of the typical R&D organization. Full commercialization will raise the tab still higher. This is shown in Exhibit [Table] 2.

Many managements do not appreciate the major escalation in expense required in going from step to step. New-product efforts usually fail, in my observation, in going from the development stage to the pilot production and sales stage, because of lack of understanding of the increases required in funds, people, equipment, and time—many managements expect this stage to be accomplished solely with good intentions.

In mature industries, most family-owned firms or industrial firms with under $100 million in sales spend somewhere around 1 percent of sales, year after year, on new-product development. These firms almost never have a new-product success. The reason lies in the stillbirth, due to an unwillingness to provide the required funds at the expenditure escalating points of the new-product process, of what may actually be viable new products.

Testing Economic Feasibility

It is surprising how far new-product programs can go before someone asks the questions, "What can happen if we succeed? Is the potential market large enough to warrant an effort?"

Two actual examples from my own experience will illustrate the importance of asking this last question:

- *Example 1.* A government aerospace facility said it needed a substitute for a special grease containing Japan wax. When I looked into how much was used per year, I learned it was fifty pounds. End of interest.
- *Example 2.* When I learned it might be possible to manufacture small, single-cylinder engine crankshafts by new, proprietary, lower-cost methods, I wanted to know how many such crankshafts were used in the United States in a year. According to some data obtained from the Outdoor Power Equipment Institute, it was about 11.5 million crankshafts. This was worth exploring further.

Another major aspect of economic feasibility is the probable willingness of the intended customer to buy. This subject is far too often neglected,

Table 2

EXPENDITURE	
Point	**Cost**
Conception	$5,000
Feasibility	$50,000 (depending on industry)
Product/process development	20 × cost of feasibility
Pilot production critical point sales	20 × cost of development
Full commercialization critical point	Much more

particularly when firms wish to develop an industrial product for sale outside their usual product area. For example, many firms have developed automotive components for sale to major automobile companies only to learn the hard way that Detroit has a very strong "not-invented-here" attitude. It is foolish to develop technology for automotive original equipment manufacture (OEM) use on speculation, and for other industries that are also disinclined to accept either outside suppliers or new suppliers.

The willingness of a supplier to supply a proprietary component essential to the new product is an aspect that is sometimes overlooked. For example, a chemical mixture may require a compound made only by Monsanto; Monsanto, however, may have other preferred uses for their output. Beside chemicals, this type of problem may also occur in electronics, materials, and a great many other areas. Availability of critical-purchase items should be estimated as part of the economic feasibility examination.

For nonconsumer goods another important question to answer is whether or not the new product would perform the function of what it replaces at a lower cost. If not, be wary. All human needs are already met, in some way or another. The question is, at what cost? Even unique new products can be examined from this viewpoint. In the days before copying machines, when a Japanese businessman wanted a copy of an article or a book chapter, a secretary was sent to the library with a portable typewriter to type the material. We now know that xerography is clearly a less expensive alternative.

Technical Feasibility Study

Before embarking on full technical development, it is important to know how likely it is that the product can be developed to do what is intended. Spending $5,000 to $50,000 trying to show that it can be done, even crudely, by the people who will have to do the actual development will save many times that cost if an unexpected but fundamental problem is uncovered.

Most organizations that have a pattern of technical development failure can be found to have neglected the feasibility study phase in order to rush prematurely into full technical development. The establishment of technical feasibility before embarking on full-scale product development should be a requirement in all firms.

A good example of a fiasco resulting from lack of technical feasibility study is the Cheyenne helicopter. Developed by Lockheed for the U. S. Army at a cost of many millions of dollars, the design of the Cheyenne helicopter uniquely combined the power and control systems. Several crashes and near crashes later, the U. S. Army insisted that Lockheed call in outside consultants to examine the feasibility of this technical approach. As part of the consulting team, I found analytically that the control system was inherently mechanically unstable—the basic concept was not feasible!

Financial Evaluation

When should a complete financial and business evaluation take place? Obviously, at a decision point. Two such natural points exist. The first is whether or not to go from product development to pilot production and sales, and the second is whether or not to proceed on to full-scale production and commercialization. Of course, a preliminary financial evaluation is needed to enter upon product development in the first place. At the point of entering pilot production, market potential can be reassessed using additional market research, direct product and overhead costs estimated, and capital investment requirements established for fixed assets and working capital. If the probable return on investment is attractive and other company criteria are met, then going forward is permissible.

However, this is not the same as a commitment to full-scale production and commercialization. This step requires much higher capital expenditures and market development costs and need not automatically follow from a decision to enter into pilot production.

Having once started down a road, one need not feel compelled to go to its end. Pilot production and sales will be educationally important. They will allow for a much more accurate assessment of the probable level of sales that can be ultimately achieved, and a better ability to estimate production and overhead costs. If costs creep up, as they often do, so that significant further investment is no longer attractive, a complete financial and business analysis before committing to full production should reveal this. If this is so, then a decision should be made to either liquidate or sell off the specific new product effort.

An often neglected, but critical, question that needs to be addressed during the financial evaluation is whether or not the firm can afford to have the new product succeed. A successful new product makes significant demands on working capital; as sales mount the resulting requirements for inventory and accounts receivable surge. Does the firm have the resources for this? A significant new-product success may also present major demands for new plant and equipment needed to handle the additional sales volume. Can this be handled? If a firm doesn't have the resources needed for the new product if it succeeds, it should realize this as early as possible. A good example of a product whose requirements were too big for its innovators is the Weed-Eater lawn tool—they were forced to sell out while nearing insolvency.

Organizational Relationship of Manufacturing Process Development and New-Product Development

The organizational relationship of manufacturing process development and product development in a company is a key element in new-product development and commercial success. The importance of this structural relationship is never written about and is generally misunderstood.

Essentially, one of three possible organizational relationships may exist. Product development may report to or be a part of engineering, while manufacturing process development is a part of manufacturing or operations. In this scheme of organization, manufacturing process development usually enters the scene when engineering is nearing completion of the product's development. Another type of organization may exist in which elements of the engineering and manufacturing process development groups are brought together to form a project team for this one product and their work occurs at the same time. A third and rather unusual organizational arrangement has both product development and manufacturing process development as parts of the same technology organization with a single functional head. Schematically, this is shown in Exhibit 3 [Figure 1].

Of the three organizational approaches, the first is the most common and least effective. It requires a great deal of additional time in the total product development cycle because the actions occur in series rather than in parallel. The resulting final product often dissatisfies the product developers due to manufacturing-induced changes, and an increased likelihood exists that the final product cannot be made at a competitive cost.

The adoption by companies of CAD/CAM systems forces better coordination of product and manufacturing development activities. This is an important, but frequently misunderstood, benefit of using such systems.

A significant percentage of failed new-product efforts, in my view, arise from this poorly understood organizational problem. Product development

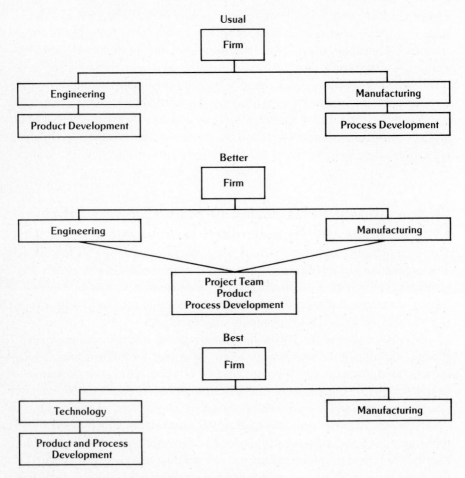

FIGURE 1   *Three Organizational Approaches to New-Product/Process Development*

and manufacturing process development function best when integrated. Optimum product development that is optimum in respect to:

- Development time;
- Development cost;
- Product utility; and
- Product manufacturing cost,

can only arise when combining product development and product manufacturing development functions. The same people must be concerned about what the product is intended to do and how to accomplish this cheaply.

The third organizational approach, combining new-product development and manufacturing process development, has been found to be the best of the three approaches by those few corporations which have tried it. It has the additional advantage of allowing management to easily shift resources between the two activities to better fit transitory changes in program needs, as the engineers and technicans involved are members of the same organization.

Physical Location and Isolation

New-product efforts are often placed in a central R&D center physically separated from the rest of the company (often in an attractive building whose picture may appear in an annual report). The frequent result is few, if any, commercial successes. Why?

In most companies, particularly those in industrial products, new-product identification is usually the province of the R&D organization. It is often almost exclusively relied upon to perform this task. A company's R&D organization, however, is poorly positioned to see market needs for new products.

New-product R&D organizations have an inherent tendency to be too removed from the marketplace and input from the company marketing and sales function. It normally takes considerable perceptiveness and effort to overcome this. Geographically removing the organization compounds this problem. The physical apartness degrades the "business sense" of the organization.

A good example of what can happen when a new-product/R&D organization is not too removed from market information was Amsted Industries entry into the OEM diesel-engine valve-guide business. The sales organization and R&D organization were geographically together and had easy, informal communication. The sales manager of Amsted's machine-foundry products operation visited the purchasing agent of Detroit Diesel Allison Division of General Motors, a major diesel engine manufacturer, in order to try to obtain an order for rocker arms. The purchasing agent told him that he didn't need a new supplier of rocker arms. As the conversation progressed the purchasing agent mentioned that he did need a new source of valve guides and if the price and quality were right, he might go for an initial order of 10 million pieces. This information was informally carried back to R&D, which acted on it and, in time, a new, more cost-effective manufacturing technology was developed, a sales agreement negotiated, a plant built, and a successful new product line introduced.

Usually, the new product will ultimately have to be made by the company's existing manufacturing organization, possibly in an existing plant. Technology transfer is largely a matter of human relations. The operating people will have to want the new product to succeed and will need help with a myriad of minor, but critical, details that will continue to arise over a considerable period of time. Being there helps. It cements personal relationships and allows answers to be informally and instantly obtained from the R&D organization by operating organization staffers. All this is inhibited, if not frustrated, by a geographical separation of R&D and operations.

Geographic separation also lessens the direct knowledge of new-products staffers of the manufacturing capabilities in existing plants that can be utilized in commercializing new products. Seeing the machinery every day creates a certain awareness that would otherwise be lacking.

Putting the new-products organization in the same location as the manufacturing plant intended to receive its creative output has a strong logic. Yet example after example can be found which show that this too doesn't work. Why?

Here we frequently have insufficient organizational isolation. An operating organization always has immediate and important problems hindering it in accomplishing its mission of "getting the stuff out the door." An attached R&D organization, possessing manufacturing technology know-how, will be called on for immediate help with these problems. In time, the natural consequence is for this "fire fighting" to overwhelm the resources of the new-product effort, which cannot be continually interrupted by short-range tasks if it is to effectively execute long-time horizon programs.

The best solution, in my experience, is to locate the new-product/R&D organization at the manufacturing site intended to exploit the bulk of its creative output, while keeping it organizationally apart. It should not be placed under the operating organization at this site. It should have its own budget and resources, and a firm understanding must exist about the level of technical support that it will provide the plant with its problems. Having the new-product/R&D organization provide some support, say up to 20 percent of its total effort, will teach the new-products organizational staff realism about what can be accomplished on the manufacturing floor, as well as about the actual capabilities of machines and processes.

A schematic of these three approaches is shown in Exhibit 4 [Figure 2].

Positioning New Products in the Company Structure

New products either have some fit with the firm's existing resources, including:

- Manufacturing,
- Selling,
- Engineering and technical service, and
- Purchasing and raw materials,

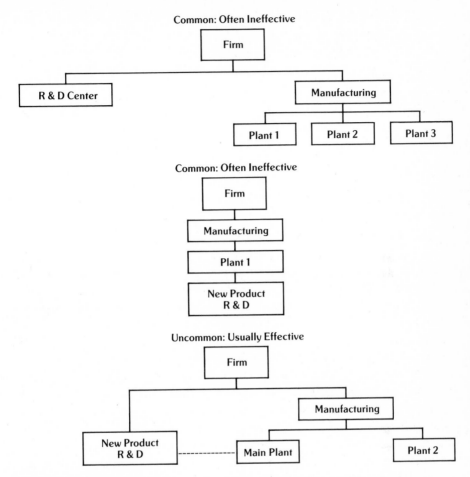

FIGURE 2   *Alternative Physical Locations for New-Product Development*

or no fit at all. If there is no fit then the new product is really a new business investment and logic dictates that it be run as a separate business, as a division, subsidiary, or venture. Management problems arise in what to do with a product that does fit, which is the usual case. The best way to kill a new product, particularly in its early commercialization stage, is to put it under normal functional control. Let's examine why.

Manufacturing

Manufacturing likes the longest possible runs, and hates to stop for setup changes, particularly where they have not had the benefit of significant prior experience in making the same item. A new product violates all the established norms. As a result, the manufacturing organization inevitably creates a production schedule with huge lead times for the new product—lead times that make selling the new product impractical.

Sales

Salespeople would much rather visit an old customer and exchange a few pleasantries knowing they will most likely walk away with a good-sized order than visit a new customer and have to battle to possibly, just possibly, receive a small order. In fact, among themselves, salespeople refer to this as "missionary" sales activity. Consequently, salespeople for ongoing products are usually a poor resource to use to sell new products. The exception is when the new product is a natural adjunct to an existing product and would be sold to the same purchasing agents.

R&D

Engineers frequently don't know when enough is enough. They will forever propose and test modifications of the product and process. A point of diminishing returns is frequently passed by a substantial margin. Consequently, the decision of when to go on from development to commercialization must often be made by someone other than those directly doing the development.

For a new product to be successfully commercialized, manufacturing must not be controlled by normal manufacturing management, and sales responsibility cannot be entrusted to the usual sales organization. A new product in the pilot production and early commercialization stage requires full control to be vested in a single project team. In time, this project management team will either be disbanded or made the nucleus of a new division. The key responsibilities of this team are in development, manufacturing, and sales. In order to get the product made in a timely manner, the team will often have technicians doing some of the manufacturing, assembly, and testing. They will argue with and push conventional manufacturing in order to get what they need made in an acceptable time frame. They will overcome bottlenecks by going to outside vendors and job shops. As a result, the product will be available as needed. Similarly, they will visit key potential customers, often accompanied by regular salespeople, for introduction purposes and carry out themselves the "missionary" sales activity.

The commercialization of the new product, its sales and manufacture, must be a specific responsibility. Divided authority here often leads to stillbirth. The question of sponsorship—who's in charge—must not be left unresolved.

Market Share Consideration

Except in a few high-technology industries, the results of most new-product development efforts are without meaningful patent protection. A firm usually has to rely on the know-how it developed through the development process and the marketing advantage of being the first to offer a product, in order to inhibit the entry of competitors (if it is the innovator).

When a new product falls within the scope of a firm's existing product lines (and those of its existing competitors), current market share becomes an important consideration in assessing the long-range prospects for the new product. If the product-innovating company has a small market share relative to those of its competitors, these larger competitors can copy the product (i.e., reverse engineering) and, by dint of their greater marketing power, shoulder the innovator aside. This has happened countless times.

Product R&D, in general, does not benefit holders of small market share and they would often improve their financial performance by limiting these expenditures.

Timing Considerations

It is a common belief of general management that a new-product R&D effort that is succeeding will provide meaningful additional profits in another two or three years. This is usually a false notion. When you think of the difficulty of getting customers to accept a new product—any new product—and the need to pass from the development stage to a pilot production stage to full commercialization, it is no wonder that the time needed to achieve meaningful profits from the inception of a specific R&D program is, in my observation, usually in the range of six to seventeen years, with seven to eleven years being typical. Edwin Mansfield[1] has made similar findings. This is never stated at the outset because it would cause most product R&D to be terminated. Nevertheless, this is a fact of life.

An implication of the long time frame required for new industrial products to capture significant market share is that business for present products will rarely decline precipitously due to the commercialization of competitive new products. An automobile piston engine parts company, for example, concerned about the Wankel engine at the time General Motors announced its adoption, concluded that it would be years, if ever, before they would be seriously affected. History proved them right.

Portfolio Considerations

Those responsible for new-product management usually feel that all their major new-product efforts should be expected to succeed. They feel defensive

---

[1] Mansfield, Edwin, *The Economics of Technological Change* (New York: W. W. Norton & Company, 1968).

about their failures. This is an obsolescent as well as self-destructive view. Modern concepts of portfolio management should be applied to our new-products expectations.

Portfolio management tells us that a large number of ambitious new products, each started with excellent prospects for success, will result in a large number of products that achieve only modest or normal success, a few that are total fiascos, and a few that are tremendous successes. It is the few that become tremendous successes that make the whole process worthwhile.

This means that a company must have a large number of new-product efforts if it is to grow and succeed by introducing new products. Limiting the scope to only a few efforts, and those selected to insure against risk of failure (and consequently against upside gain), will over time probably result in virtually no benefit to the company.

If we look at the success record of venture capital company investments, each investment representing a new-product development and commercialization effort, a typical tally for twenty-five new products would be three major successes, five total failures, and seventeen that are either modest successes or modest failures. The twenty-two that aren't major successes may be thought of as costs needed to achieve the three major successes.

Conclusions

New-product development, evaluation, and management can be made to follow good management practices. Effectiveness, efficiency, and a reasonable likelihood of success can be achieved. The rules of thumb and analyses of causes and effects presented in this discussion will help firms to improve their performance in this area.

QUESTIONS

1. Identify the two types of new product approaches discussed in the article and describe the distinguishing characteristics of each.

2. In most situations, which of the two new product approaches would be preferable? Why?

3. What are the advantages and disadvantages of an organizational structure that integrates product development and manufacturing development?

4. Where in the organization should new product development be placed for greatest effectiveness?

5. What can a firm do to ensure that it is introducing the new products it needs for long-term growth and profitability?

3

RESOURCE ALLOCATION WITHIN THE PRODUCT LIFE CYCLE

Richard S. Savich
Laurence A. Thompson

*This article describes how Lear Siegler
successfully integrated the product life
cycle concept into its budgeting process.*

The product life cycle has been used by marketing researchers for years to forecast sales revenues. Their work has been documented by many articles and books.[1] Little attention, however, has been directed toward using life cycle concepts to allocate resources within the budgetary process. If the ideas

---

[1] C. L. Bachtel, "What a Supervisor Should Know about Product Life Cycle Management," *Supervisory Management* 18 (October 1973): 35–40; Frank Bass, "A New Product Growth Model for Consumer Durables," *Management Science* 15 (January 1969): 215–27; Bernard Catry and Michel Chevalier, "Market Share Strategy and the Product Life Cycle," *Journal of Marketing* 38 (October 1974): 29–34; William E. Cox, Jr., "Product Life Cycles as Marketing Models," *Journal of Business* 40 (October 1967): 375–84; W. R. Davidson, Albert D. Bates, and Stephen J. Bass, "Retail Life Cycle," *Harvard Business Review* 54 (Nov-Dec 1976): 89–96; George A. Field, "Do Products Really Have Life Cycles?" *California Management Review* 14 (Fall 1971): 92–95; Robert Fildes and Stephen Lofthouse, "Market Share Strategy and the Product Life Cycle: A Comment," *Journal of Marketing* 39 (October 1975): 57–59; Jay W. Forrester, "Industrial Dynamics," *Harvard Business Review* 36 (July-August 1958): 37–66; James B. Kobak, "A Magazine's Life Cycle and Its Profits," *Folio* 5 (October 1976): 48–55; F. J. Kovac and J. R. Dague, "Forecasting by Product Life Cycles Analysis," *Research Management* 15 (July 1972): 66–72; C. M. Lillis, Chem L. Narayana, and John L. Gelman, "Competitive Advantage Variation over the Life Cycle of a Franchise," *Journal of Marketing* 40 (October 1976): 77–80; George F. MacKenzie, "On Marketing's 'Missing Link'—The Product Life Cycle Concept," *Industrial Marketing* 56 (April 1971): 42–43; Rolando Polli and Victor Cook, "Validity of the Product Life Cycle," *Journal of Business* 42 (October 1969): 385–400; John Smallwood, "Product Life Cycle: A Key to Strategic Marketing Planning," *MSU Business Topics* 21 (Winter 1973): 29–35; Thomas A. Staudt and Donald A. Taylor, *A Managerial Introduction to Marketing* (Englewood Cliffs, N.J.: Prentice-Hall, 1970); Raymond Vernon, "International Investment and International Trade in the Product Cycle," *Quarterly Journal of Economics* 80 (May 1966): 190–207; and Louis T. Wells, Jr., "Test of Product Cycle Model of International Trade: U. S. Exports of Consumer Durables," *Quarterly Journal of Economics* 83 (February 1969): 152–62.

of PLC are used not only for sales forecasting, but also for incorporating cost and expense characteristics, a more integrated and comprehensive profit plan can be developed resulting in more efficient resource allocation.[2]

A PLC Budgeting System has been introduced into Lear Siegler, Inc., a large diversified company with multiproduct divisions, to meet the objectives of budgeting. These objectives include the facilitation of planning, assistance in control of operations, and provision for evaluation of performance.[3] A lack of understanding of these main purposes in preparing and adhering to an operating budget often leads to dysfunctional consequences.

The traditional budget process usually does not provide for recognition of the phase a product is occupying in the PLC. In many instances the traditional budgeting process also fails to achieve planning, control, and evaluation objectives. The PLC Budgeting System does not exhibit these shortcomings because its underlying assumptions depend on a product's phase—start-up, growth, maturity, or harvest. Each phase has specific characteristics making it distinct from other phases. Revenues, capital expenditures, departmental expenses, cash flow, and pertinent financial statements are distinctive at each stage of a product's life cycle.

The classic product life cycle is illustrated in Figure 1.[4] The horizontal axis represents time; the vertical axis, sales. The various phases of a product's life are evident. Because purchasing patterns and competitive pressures change over the life cycle, progressive companies are likely to manifest different organizational philosophies, goals, and structures.

The risks and returns associated with a new product might be compared to buying a lottery ticket; the potential returns are phenomenal, but one stands to lose all one's initial investment.[5] Many new products never leave phase I. They die before the market even knows they are being developed (Exhibit [Table] 1).

Organizational Characteristics

The stock market provides two means of earning a profit. One is through capital appreciation, the second through dividends. If a product does make it

---

[2]John C. Chambers, Satinder K. Mullick, and Donald D. Smith, *An Executive's Guide to Forecasting* (New York: John Wiley & Sons, 1974).

[3]Donald K. Clifford, Jr., "Leverage in the Product Life Cycle," *Dun's Review and Modern Industry* 85 (May 1965): 62–70; and George F. MacKenzie, "Product Life Cycle Makes ROI Analysis Relevant," *Industrial Marketing* 56 (June 1971): 100–104.

[4]Robert B. Young, *Product Growth Cycles—A Key to Growth Planning* (Palo Alto: Stanford Research Institute, 1962).

[5]Robert V. L. Wright, *Strategy Centers—A Contemporary Managing System* (Cambridge, Mass.: Arthur D. Little, Inc., 1971).

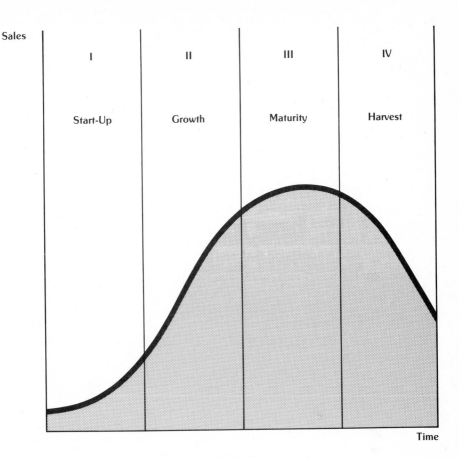

FIGURE 1 *The Classic Product Life Cycle Curve*

to the growth phase, potential risk is lessened, and some recoupment of investment is possible through increasing sales.

In the mature phase, a product's acceptance is realized, and the sales rise flattens. Bonds are a good example of the risk-return ratio similarity. Interest is paid semiannually, and principal is returned at the maturity date. Both principal and interest are "guaranteed" by the bond issuer. In the case of stocks, neither investments nor dividends are guaranteed.

The mortgage market is indicative of the harvest phase. Both principal and interest are certain; but if problems arise, chattel is available for foreclosure. A product that reaches this phase after proceeding through the first three should be a cash cow. Sales of the product have provided substantial returns over the years, and now the dismantling of production assets should provide additional funds.

The style of management as well as measuring and reporting, corporate departments, and structure are also different in each phase. In the start-up of a product, entrepreneurial types who deal with free-form organizations using

Table 1

PRODUCT LIFE CYCLE CONCEPTS

Phase	I	II	III	IV
Market	Start up	Growth	Maturity	Harvest
Risk-return comparisons	Lottery	Stock	Bond	Mortgage
Management style	Entrepreneur	Sophisticated manager	Critical administrator	Opportunistic milker
Measuring and reporting	Qualitative, Marketing oriented, Unwritten	Qualitative and quantitative, Early warning system	Quantitative, Production oriented, Written	Numerical, Balance sheet oriented, Written
Corporate departments	Market research, Product development	Operations research Organization development	Value analysis, Data processing, Taxes and insurance	Purchasing
Structure	Free form or task force	Semipermanent task force, Product or market divisions	Business divisions plus task force for renewal	Pared-down divisions
Planning time frame	Long enough to draw tentative life cycle (7–10 years)	Long-range investment payout (5–7 years)	Intermediate (3–5 years)	Short-range (1–3 years)

qualitative measurements take precedence. Market research and product development are predominant. No one has a past history of the product, and all prognostications are based on studies done on a what-if basis. Sometimes data from similar products can be used, but invariably each new product must stand on its own merit.

Later, a managerial style must take over to institute a more formal system of marketing, production, and accounting. Divisions are established to assign responsibilities and begin the task of forming the company into a uniform set of operating units. If these systems are not established, there may be problems in the third phase of not knowing the results compared to the business plan and budget.

By the time phase III is reached, most of the management tasks have evolved to those of an administrative type. All systems are in existence, and monitoring becomes of primary importance. Most companies, when budgeting, view themselves in this phase. However, as can be seen from the other phases, a different style is necessary in each for better planning, control, and evaluation. Of corollary importance is the establishment of a group to search for expansion of the mature phase. The search should look for new uses for the product, new consumers, greater differentiation, or adaptations which will allow the product to realize continued sales.

As product sales start to decline, someone who can face the hard facts of disposition needs to take command. This person must tie purchases and production directly to sales and begin paring the business down to a shell of its former operations. While this phase is the least desirable, it can provide much-needed funds to finance other evolving products. The spare parts business is a good example of a harvest market. If a product has been successful in prior phases, spare parts for that equipment can provide a lucrative profit without the risks associated with trying to market an entirely new product.

Figure 1 showed the PLC with time represented on the horizontal axis. In PLC budgeting, thought should be given to planning a complete PLC from inception. The time frame of seven to ten years referred to in Exhibit 1 is only relative to the other numbers. This is not to say that life cycles only last this long, or that a product will be in phase I for that many years. It simply means that these years, or five to seven for phase II, should be used as the time period for which a product is planned. In other words, if the entire life cycle is thought to be only five years, one should be looking five years into the future in phase I, three and a half years in phase II, two and a half in phase III, and so forth. In the harvest market, very short-term planning is done because the potential market is declining, and any planning for longer than a one-year period is self-defeating. Even though these figures are relative, note that the time frame of three to five years in the mature market is similar to the long-range planning model of most organizations. Long-range plans are drawn up for five years, while operating budgets are for one year.

These organizational characteristics describe what type of corporate management is predominant in each phase. Of equal importance are the financial characteristics of each phase. Exhibits [Tables] 2, 3, and 4 illustrate the three major financial statements used in budgeting operations—the income statement, the balance sheet, and funds flow analysis. Each of these can be considered from a phase-by-phase perspective to see how to manage revenues, costs, expenses, assets, and liabilities.

Financial Characteristics

START-UP.   In phase I, sales are low or nonexistent, and costs are expended.[6] Budgeting during this phase will reflect allocation or resources to marketing

---

[6] Margaret A. Kilgore, "Lear Siegler Devices Provide Life Saving Whiff of Fresh Air," *Los Angeles Times*, 12 April 1976, p. 16; and G. E. White and P. F. Ostwald, "Life Cycle Costing," *Management Accounting* 54 (January 1976): 39–40.

Table 2

	INCOME STATEMENT			
	Start-up	**Growth**	**Maturity**	**Harvest**
Sales	Low but rising	Rising fast	Level	Declining
Cost of Goods Sold				
Direct material	Lots of scrap	Rising	Search for efficiencies	Tied to sales
Direct labor	High per unit	Learning curve benefit	Dependent on union negotiations	Reduced considerably
Overhead				
Depreciation	High due to accelerated depreciation	Rising due to acquisitions	Stable	Low
Indirect labor	Minimal	Growing with labor force	Stable	Redirected
Taxes, property	Minimal	Growing with equipment	Depend on mill levy	Down
Utilities	Related to R&D	Growing with equipment	Stable	Reduced
Gross Profit	Fluctuating	% established	Smooth	Market bearing
Expenses				
Sales				
Compensation	Variable	Individual rewards	Group rewards	Fixed
Advertising	High	Rising	Stable	None
Travel and entertainment	Very high	Grows with sales force	Reduced	None
Market research	Very high	Leveling	Seek new markets	Accept defeat
General and administrative				
Salaries	Division management	Expanding with work force	Administrative	Reduced
Depreciation	Minimal	Growing with furniture	Stable	None

Table 2 (continued)

	Start-up	Growth	Maturity	Harvest
Research and development	Very high	Production oriented	Cost-reduction oriented	Look for new products
Income taxes	Negative	Rising	Stable	Declining
Distribution costs	Looking	Rising	Stable	Cut back
Accounting and information	Start-up costs	Formalizing	Stable	Looking for benefits
Insurance	Minimal	High	Constant and business interruption	Unnecessary
Earnings	Lowest	Good	Highest	Below average
Earnings per Share	Lowest	Average	Highest	Average

research and product development and for capital expenditures to provide technical development capabilities.[7] The property, plant, and equipment requirements grow at an increasing rate to meet expected long-range projections of market demand. In relation to other products in other product life cycle phases, long-lived asset balances are low compared to net worth.

When budgeting for expenses, the plans are for high market research and engineering expenses for the development of acceptable prototypes and the testing of consumer acceptance. Also, large amounts should be budgeted for promotional and sales expenses. Compensation is tied directly to sales as a high variable expense. The company pays for sales ability, not just the existence of a sales force.

During this phase the manager should be aware of some of the pitfalls in moving to phase II, growth. These include a negative cash position, low working capital, and high inventory turnover (due to low inventory balances).

[7]Dik Twedt, "How Long Does It Take to Introduce New Products?" *Journal of Marketing* 29 (January 1965): 71–72.

Table 3

BALANCE SHEET

	Start-up	Growth	Maturity	Harvest
Current Assets				
Cash	Starved	Hungry	Rich	Fair
Marketable securities	None	None	Use for idle cash	High
Accounts receivable	None	Factored-assigned	Stable	Collected before
Inventory	Low	Rising	Average	Declining
Property, Plant, and Equipment	Starting	Rising	Stable	Declining
Intangibles	Building	Stable	Write off	Written off
Current Liabilities				
Accounts payable	High	Stretched	Constant	Supplies like cash
Taxes payable	None	None due to carry-forwards	Level	High
Long-Term Liabilities	High	Moderate	Available	Pay off
Deferred Liabilities				
Taxes	Receivables due to net operating loss	Offset by carry-forwards	Delayed by accelerated depreciation	High payoff
Compensation	Offered	Taken	Used	Refused
Stockholders' Equity				
Common Stock	Low	Public offering	Used for options	Only leverage
Retained earnings	Deficit	Reinvested	Stable	Paid out

Borrowings from the corporate office, or cash and working capital provided from other products, would help over the rough spots. The earnings picture is bleak because profits lag behind sales. The return on assets employed is at its lowest point, even though sales start to grow at an increasing rate. These indicators lead directly to the growth phase.

Table 4	FUNDS FLOW ANALYSIS			
	Start-up	**Growth**	**Maturity**	**Harvest**
Sources of Funds				
Net income	Low	Good	High	Declining
Long-term debt	High	Moderate	Capacity high but no new debt	None
Stock financing	Hesitant market	Lots of buyers	Looking for dividends	Sell out
Sale of property, plant, and equipment	None	None	Replacement	Extensive
Use of Funds				
Purchase of property, plant, and equipment	Mainly prototype	High	Replacement	None
Dividends	None	Little if any	Good	Extensive
Repayment of debt	None	None	High	Remainder
Treasury stock	None	None	For options	At deflated prices
Change in Cash	Negative	Not too bad	None	Very positive

GROWTH.   If a product considered marketable is developed, then phase II, growth, is entered.[8] In phase II, predictions would forecast a significant rise in sales at an extremely rapid pace, as shown in Figure 1. Budgeting during this phase should reflect rising revenues with related promotional costs as well as costs of production. Other costs relate to technical efficiencies and refinement of production. In single product companies, the expenses of accounting information systems and organizational development become necessary to allow for greater control during later stages and to provide early warning systems. Orders, it is hoped, exceed production capability, and major capital assets are purchased to pick up the slack. Overall earnings start to improve,

---

[8] Arch Patton, "Stretch Your Product's Earning Years—Top Management's Stake in the Product Life Cycle," *Management Review* 48 (June 1959): 9–14 and 67–79.

but there is little in the way of funds available due to reinvestment require-ments until the end of this phase. The financial statements shown explain some of the other accounts affected.

For example, with the production and marketing of computer terminals, a Lear Siegler product, two major strategies affected costs. During the develop-ment of prototypes, engineering costs were high, due to a search for cost reductions to aid continued production. As changes were made in production methods, an economical unit price was achieved. A marketing strategy also was developed and implemented. It consisted of three aspects. First, third party leasing was deemed desirable so no in-house leasing expenses would be incurred. Second, all sales would be made through distributors. Only highly qualified, well-recognized distributors in various geographical regions were used. Third, a small highly qualified marketing team was to be organized to deal with the distributors. These people would be experienced senior market-ing specialists. They would receive low base pay with high incentive compensation. One point worth noting is that commissions were received when sales were made, not when products were shipped. This caused expenses to be high initially for marketing in this growth stage.

MATURITY.   When budgeting costs and expenses, many managers view their products as being in the mature stage of the life cycle, and this was one of the major reasons for the installation of the system at Lear Siegler. The changes in complexion of the other stages were sufficient to cause costs and expenses to vary considerably when compared to the mature stage. As shown in the financial statement exhibits, most of the budgeted amounts are stable during this stage. In other words, historical data can be used to predict future cost budgets. By this stage of production, standards should have been established to aid the budget process, compensation is stable with the existing market being serviced by an established sales force, research is investigating cost cutting areas, and earnings are showing a long-run profit margin which recoups past losses and allows for payout to those who wisely invested earlier. [9]

Managers would like to stretch out the mature phase as long as pos-sible because it is profitable, easier to manage (that is, little variation from period to period), and, therefore, easier to plan for. However, as noted by the character of most product life cycles, the declining market will eventually be reached, and sales will diminish.

HARVEST.   The harvest stage is the least appealing to a single product firm because it signals that the company will soon be out of business unless it

[9] Harold W. Fox, "Product Life Cycle—An Aid to Financial Administration," *Financial Executive* 41 (April 1973): 28–34; Theodore Levitt, "Exploit the Product Life Cycle," *Harvard Business Review* 43 (November-December 1965): 81–93; and E. E. Scheuing, "The Product Life Cycle as an Aid in Strategy Decisions," *Management International Review* 9, No. 4–5 (1969): 111–24.

develops products to take the place of those no longer demanded. An example might be the spare parts business for radar systems. The initial production of complete systems took place more than seven years ago, but spare parts are continually needed. Decisions were made to disband the division which produced the original systems and transfer the spare parts support to another division. While the radar systems division wanted to stretch out the disbanding over three years, the management decision to redeploy the low-yielding assets to other more productive opportunities demanded a three-month shutdown.

The search for new products should be possible due to the account relationships inherent in phase IV. A cash-out position is assumed. Ideally, a long period of maturity will have allowed recapture of start-up costs, provided a return on the investment, and eliminated outstanding debt. The process of disbanding operations provides revenues through the sales of equipment, reduced costs of personnel, and lack of need for new facilities. These resources should be directed toward the start-up of other products to continue the company's existence.[10] At the same time, the organizational structure is that of pared-down operations using a command structure which is awaiting the inevitable. Investment ceases as overcapacity becomes common.

Concern should focus on the disposition of both equipment and inventory. An order which meets variable costs often is accepted, but the earnings picture is low and follows sales directly. There is a high return on assets, mainly because of the diminishing asset base. This phase is continued as long as it generates earnings and provides for the disposal of all related assets.

SUMMARY.　These organizational and financial statement characteristics are typical of the many products within Lear Siegler. While most of these characteristics appear to exist for most products, there are always some which are atypical. Management must be aware of those products which do not follow the classic PLC curve in sales or in financial statement characteristics. To help managers be cognizant of potential differences, a formal changeover plan should be instituted. Some ideas and recommendations on converting to a PLC Budgeting System follow.

Changing to PLC Budgeting

The above examples show some general thought processes which took place as Lear Siegler viewed its various products. The financial exhibits provide some ideas as to what to expect from certain financial statements about life

---

[10] Philip Kotler, "Phasing Out Weak Products," *Harvard Business Review* 43 (March-April 1965): 107–18; and George C. Michael, "Product Petrification: A New Stage in the Life Cycle," *California Management Review* 14 (Fall 1971): 88–91.

cycle phases. Of more importance are suggestions about how to adopt a PLC Budgeting System and make it work. Basically, there are four separate and distinct steps which lead to the realization of the benefits: identification, education, implementation, and evaluation.

IDENTIFICATION.   The first step involves identification of the phase of the life cycle the products are occupying. This step may consist of simple guesswork, trend analysis, or elaborate computer simulation. The search here is for products in phases II, III, or IV. One already should be aware of new products being developed in phase I. Another technique is to discuss each of the products with the sales force. Their ideas on where the product stands relative to competition of similar and substitutable goods could provide insight into future revenue patterns. Finally, the age of the product itself might provide ideas as to where in the PLC the product is. If a firm is selling a product that has been around for many years, someone may soon be developing a newer, more efficient product to replace it. The firm's own research and development department may even be thinking about such a replacement.

All of these are ideas about how to identify the position of an individual product in relation to the classic PLC curve. Slight errors in judgment at first are acceptable. As resources are allocated by phase, people who believe the product to be in a phase different from the one specified will fine-tune their decision and possibly reassess their opinion. However, this is a starting point for subsequent planning and budgeting.

EDUCATION.   The second step requires education of personnel concerning the most sensitive costs and expenses to be controlled in each of the phases. As can be seen from the financial exhibits, engineering yields to marketing, which in turn is replaced by a production orientation, and, eventually, administration. Recognition of this information is important if the personnel involved are to budget adequately and control the various operations. At a number of the management meetings which Lear Siegler conducts during the year, discussions regarding the PLC Budgeting System are included. Planning meetings, annual evaluation reviews, and visits to division group headquarters by corporate staff all provide avenues for mentioning, discussing, and stressing PLC budgeting, its methods, and its advantages for the benefit of those who are primarily responsible for its success, divisional management.

Lear Siegler instituted, as part of the management development function, seminars on finance and accounting for nonfinancial managers which empha-sized the PLC Budgeting System. These seminars were conducted over the years and included a basic type, which introduced accounting control concepts to managers, and an advanced type, which provided working capital management techniques to graduates of the first seminar. At both of the sessions, discussions on PLC planning and budgeting were included. These seminars and discussions were necessary to allow managers at all levels who prepare budget requests to understand what PLC budgeting is and how it will affect their resource allocations.

Also needed is a complete set of planning and budgeting instructions. This documentation is necessary so each person involved in preparing PLC budgets will know what is expected and how to complete all forms needed for budget requests. Lear Siegler produced a corporate planning guide composed of the following sections:

1. Introduction
2. Plan outline
3. Definitions and flow of information
4. Instructions for plan preparation
    a. Introduction and summary
    b. Basic factors
    c. Market/business audit
    d. Divisional goals
    e. Product line(s), goals, strategies, and tactics
    f. Tactical actions
    g. Resource plans

In addition, appendices outlining Lear Siegler's corporate objectives and criteria for classifying products by life cycle phase were included. The Corporate Planning Department works on-site with each division to assist in the analysis of the division's PLC position and the determination of its strategies. All these educational tools have led to better and faster acceptance of the new system.

IMPLEMENTATION.   The third step is implementation. Through actual experience, managers did realize benefits from the PLC Budgeting System. Lear Siegler has implemented this system in its divisions, and it is used extensively by the long-range planning group in considering all products, groups, and divisions as well as the future of the company as a whole. The process consists of plotting all future cash flows for current and proposed products to determine by how much, and when, cash will pass the break-even point. In this manner, cash requirements can be forecast and adjusted as plans are altered.

This step also provides the fine-tuning mentioned in the identification step. Managers will rarely misidentify a product by two phases, that is, put a growth product in a harvest market. However, continuing to call a product mature when indications are that sales are declining could lead to the misdirection of resources needed elsewhere in the company. Once implemented, the PLC Budgeting System involves so many people in the ultimate allocation process that correct identification will be realized within one pass through the budgeting process.

Another point of fine-tuning involves the passing of a product from one phase to another. This idea has often caused individuals to doubt the viability of the PLC.[11] What should always be remembered is that the PLC is a continuous curve, not one in which a product miraculously moves from start-up to growth overnight. A product evolves from one phase to another; it rarely jumps. Costs and expenses are not stopped immediately; they are reduced over a few periods, while others begin to rise. In other words, market research is not cut off when a product enters phase II; it is reduced as market acceptance rises and as extensive surveys, such as those used in start-up, are no longer necessary. At the same time, production line research expenses begin to rise as operating efficiences are sought. As labor costs come down with the learning curve, and as engineering expenses begin to decline, accounting controls start to take over. These are just some examples of costs and expenses which follow their own life cycle within the classic PLC. All of these cost and expense characteristics become evident during the implementation step.

EVALUATION.   The final step is evaluation. By comparing costs predicted through the PLC Budgeting System to the actual costs incurred, Lear Siegler has been able to identify changes in products as they move from one phase of the life cycle to another. In the past, this has been a major drawback to application of life cycle concepts. Through careful monitoring of actual costs, some transition between phases can be discerned. The process is being constantly refined, and patterns are developing. This step also makes various levels of management cognizant of the commitment of Lear Siegler's top management to the PLC Budgeting System. It also provides rationale and logic to the resource allocation process and makes managers aware that their actions involving both planning and control are taken into account in their total evaluation for promotion and salary.

For example, the Lear Siegler calendar of planning, budgeting, and evaluation stems from a June 30 fiscal year. In March a long-range plan is submitted and approved. During May the fiscal forecast for divisions is approved, and in July the fiscal year begins. A management appraisal form prepared in November evaluates the performance and personal characteristics

---

[11] Nariman K. Dhalla and Sonia Yuspeh, "Forget the Product Life Cycle Concept!" *Harvard Business Review* 54 (January-February 1976): 102–12.

of each divisional president. Finally, bonuses are decided upon during July, based on year-end results. This sequence allows for PLC budgeting to be considered in all aspects of management evaluation.

Overall, the concepts of the PLC Budgeting System can improve the management of the planning and allocation process. It provides guidelines not only for revenues, as the classic life cycle has provided for years, but also for expenses, related capital expenditures, and the sources and uses of funds. Applications and the degree of sophistication of implementation are still developing. While these changes take time, the concepts are proving well worth the effort.

QUESTIONS

1. What advantages does the Lear Siegler budgeting system have over more traditional budgeting procedures?
2. What are some of the budgetary problems that should be considered when a firm moves from the introduction to the growth stage?
3. What are the most sensitive cost areas for a product in the maturity stage of the life cycle?
4. What steps are involved in implementing a product life cycle budget system for a particular firm?

PART FOUR

Distribution

In its early years of development, marketing was defined as consisting of those activities required to get products and services from producers to consumers. The focus was clearly on the function of distribution. Although the definition and domain of marketing have broadened considerably, distribution is still tremendously important for any marketing process. Clearly those activities most involved in a firm's day-to-day competitive posture and marketing costs are distribution activities. Specifically, distribution activities consist of those involved with the design and management of marketing channels and the physical handling, storage, and movement of products.

The breadth and complexity of issues in distribution are immense, far beyond the scope of this book. Consequently, the articles in Part Four were selected to provide the reader with:

1. An understanding and appreciation of the critical role that distribution plays in the implementation of marketing strategies;
2. A description of the decisions required by the major distribution activities, such as channel management, wholesaling, retailing, and physical distribution; and
3. Insights on the changes in distribution that are expected to occur through the end of the decade.

The first of these objectives is addressed by the article, "A Look at Channel Management," which explains what a distribution channel is and what problems and responsibilities are associated with channel management. This article suggests ways that firms should view the channel management function, and an example substantiating the importance of having an effective distribution system is provided in "Don't Sell Food, Sell Peace of Mind."

Two important components of any distribution channel, the wholesaler and the retailer, are examined in the next two articles. "Dollars from Doodads" points out that because of changes in the structure of the work force, productivity gains needed to foster economic growth will have to come from areas other than manufacturing. The two most promising areas are wholesaling and retailing. The role in and contributions to a distribution system of the retailing function is described in "The Retailer's Changing Role in The Marketing Channel."

The final article in Part Four discusses the elements involved in the logistical aspects of a distribution system. "Logistics: Essential to Strategy" emphasizes the importance of recognizing cost trade-offs of logistical activities and balancing them against customer service.

1

A LOOK AT CHANNEL MANAGEMENT

Reavis Cox
Thomas F. Schutte

The authors note that managers often attempt to solve distribution problems with nondistribution solutions. This situation occurs because of a lack of a clear definition of what distribution involves and because the responsibilities for distribution functions are scattered throughout the firm. This article develops guidelines to correct these types of problems.

A Look at Channel Management

A strange anomaly in marketing today is the extent to which both managers and students who accept the idea that marketing efforts should be customer-oriented, overlook the fact that, if efforts so oriented are to be successful, managers must use effective marketing channels. Conventional textbooks speak of the four P's as constituting the variables which management has under its control in working with marketing problems—a product, place, price, and promotion. They discuss in great detail some of the things managers can do under these headings, but they offer little more than vague descriptions of the numbers and kinds of agencies through which these things must be done. Only a small number of specialized students—and most of these only in very recent years—have come to grips with what is involved if these agencies are to be organized into combinations and sequences that will do well the whole job of connecting production and consumption. This is a major but largely neglected problem in management. Some of the managers themselves are beginning to see dimly what is required, but they have made little progress in formalizing their ideas into rules or procedures.

The purpose of this paper and of the panel discussion that will follow is to stimulate a rethinking of the role of management as applied to the channel. Emphasis will be placed upon the problems of the firm rather than the academic discipline of marketing in general. What we hope to do is to help managers, as well as students, develop new perspectives in channel management by providing:

1. Some examples of managerial problems raised by channels.
2. An operational definition of channel management.
3. A look at some characteristics of managerial thinking about channels.
4. Some suggestions for rethinking the channel concept and its application to management.

Examples of Distribution Problems

The scope and magnitude of channel problems may be obscured both by the way marketing or distribution is defined and by the ways in which distribution programs are developed and carried into effect. It is interesting to note how often firms visualize their problems, not as problems in distribution, but as problems in selling, advertising, sales promotion, pricing, product management, or even manufacturing. A good way to see what we mean is to look at some examples of confusion which were selected by the authors without any attempt to be systematic or thorough.

1. A well-known pharmaceutical manufacturer assigns the responsibility for what it calls customer trade relations to its public relations department. The management of finished goods, inventories, warehouses, and physical distribution is a responsibility of the manufacturing department. Customer requests, servicing, returns, and allowances are divided between marketing and finance without a clear assignment to either group. No one is formally responsible for seeing to it that these scattered activities add up to a coordinated overall program. Can one be surprised that the central management is beginning to wonder whether its organization does not automatically produce under-achievement in distribution?

2. A leading manufacturer of toiletry products distributes exclusively through drug wholesalers and drug chains. In response to spending heavily for promotion, advertising, and personal selling, it built up a strong consumer demand for one of its lines. Nearly two-thirds of the potential market for the sorts of goods constituting this line is bought by consumers through non-drug trades, and this proportion is increasing. Members of these trades wanted the product, but the

company, dominated by principles derived from other products, would not change its distribution policy. Consequently, sales of the line have been falling for two years as the company refuses to see that products must be sold where consumers expect to find them not where sellers like to put them.

3. A large trucking company receives as many as 300,000 garments in one day from local manufacturers. Through a program of prompt efficient handling and shipping, the firm can put garments on hangers in the receiving room of retailers, over a large geographic area, within 24 hours of receipt. The chairman of the board of the trucking company laments, "We get the garment quickly to the stores, on hangers, and ready to move to the sales floors. Then we discover that they sit around for days or even weeks waiting for someone to attach price tags." One part of a marketing system was done well, but the system, as a whole, faltered.

4. The idea that the economy offers an opportunity for someone to set up a gigantic distributor of automotive parts for competing manufacturers, is relatively new. Until the creation of such a firm, the thousands of manufacturers, producing even more thousands of products, marketed them through a multitude of selling organizations. Customers for these parts, primarily garages and service stations, were constantly badgered by a plethora of salesmen representing manufacturers. Not only was the selling costly, but the complexity of the enormous number of automobiles, the number of parts needed for one vehicle, and the models to be served were all such that parts service centers required an intelligence system, effective inventory control, and sharp reductions in selling costs. But the need was not visualized until the new distributing firm recognized the need for analyzing the entire distribution system, brought it to the consciousness of parts users, and provided a service to meet it.

5. A furniture retailer currently receives many goods from manufacturers that require repair and refinishing. It employs two full-time men to do this work. The president of the retail operation justifies the presence of the two workers because they cost less than he would have to pay for the work involved and the loss of sales incurred in shipping the damaged goods back to the supplier. This retailer is looking for a manufacturer who will help him eliminate the need for having two full-time men. He believes a less costly system is possible. Some supplier that does its homework in looking at the entire channel may find this retailer to be a good, profitable account.

6. A well-known manufacturer of consumer paper products introduced a "giant economy box" of one product. Thanks to heavy promotion, consumers wanted it. So the retailers stocked it, but many supermarkets did so reluctantly because they had to stock it on the floor. They lacked shelf space for it. Thus, the manufacturer was vulnerable to competition from others who could satisfy the consumers' demand without penalizing the retailers. The extensive marketing research done by the producer during product development found a consumer need but failed to recognize that the retailer also had needs to be satisfied.

One could go on and on with such illustrations of the failure of businessmen to recognize the true nature of the channel problems, but these examples are sufficient for our purposes.

What the Channel of Distribution Is

For present purposes, a channel of distribution may be defined as an organized network of agencies and institutions which, in combination, perform all the activities required to link producers with users, and users with producers in order to accomplish the marketing task. From the point of view of the seller, the channel permits him to find and supply users of his goods. From the point of view of the buyer, the channel finds and delivers to him the want-satisfying goods he seeks. Some intangible services, also require the use of channels to connect suppliers with users.

Contrary to many textbooks, a channel of distribution is not a static network. Not only are new channels created for new products as they appear, but also, new channels often are developed for existing products. For example, a manufacturer of proprietary drugs may restrict his distribution of a sun-tan lotion to drug stores and the agencies that serve them until his penetration of the drug store market is optimized, at which time he may revise his distribution system to include variety chains and supermarkets. Likewise, the same proprietary drug manufacturer may decide to modify his policy of distributing exclusively through wholesalers because chain stores that will not buy through wholesalers now hold more of the market than do independent drug stores.

It should be noted that a new channel of distribution normally is created because both buyers and sellers need it in order to fulfill their joint marketing task as effectively as possible. For example, Smith, Kline and French Laboratories relies on over 400 drug wholesalers and over 35,000 drug stores to perform the services required if products such as Contac, Sea and Ski, and Love are to reach and satisfy consumers. On the other hand, the Drug House, Inc., one of the country's largest drug wholesalers of proprietary and ethical products expects SKF to perform a number of services that will facilitate its servicing of individual drug stores; for example, putting inner-packs of six units each in the shipping cases.

Hartz Mountain, Inc., a producer of proprietary health care products for small animals, distributes through numerous rack jobbers to many thousands of pet shops and supermarkets. It does so because these jobbers provide, more cheaply than anyone else, the services of weekly stocking, dusting, and rehabilitation of goods on the shelves. Furthermore, the rack jobber provides the financial service of reimbursing the central offices with their due net profits without any previous billing to the chain and with subsequent dollar pay-out by the chain.

Conventional Thinking About Channels

Although the management of marketing channels has not received the formal attention it deserves from businessmen, a number of ways in which managements tend to view the problem may be discerned. Some of these are not really conscious formulations but rather, what we may call "*as if* propositions". That is, the managers behave *as if* the channel is a certain kind of structure without spelling out their assumptions in detail. At least six such propositions can be stated.

1. *Channels are determined by the characteristics of the product.* A seller of goods following this rule holds that the shape and design of the channel that distributes his products are determined by their characteristics. Thus, goods of high unit-value can absorb high costs but require protection against loss or theft; perishability imposes a need for refrigeration and quick handling; large size or heavy weight calls for special materials handling equipment; and so on. The best channel in this view is the one that minimizes the cost imposed by the products' characteristics. This orientation may cause a seller to become so preoccupied with his product that he loses sight of other needs felt by intermediate traders and ultimate users.

2. *The channel stops at the loading platform.* Some businessmen seem to see distribution as ending (rather than beginning) when the goods have been shipped. In essence, this notion sees distribution as an activity consisting of loading the product onto a common or contract carrier at the shipper's dock. What happens thereafter is the buyer's responsibility. The concept, thus badly stated, may be oversimplified in many cases; but it would be interesting to know how many firms see marketing in effect as a process of getting customers to take goods physically as near to the manufacturing plant as possible and to assume responsibilities for them from that point on.

3. *The channel is primarily, if not exclusively, an agency for the physical distribution of goods.* The literature and traditions of marketing are such that one can easily come to view distribution as physical distribution alone and thus overlook all the other tasks that must be performed by channels. Such a view is really an extension of the loading-platform thesis; but it opens the way to a consideration of choices as to where the seller's loading platform shall be located. Physical distribution is an important component part of the distribution process but viewing it as the distribution process is still a very narrow concept. Too often, sellers who overemphasize physical distribution tend to look upon their channel problem as being that of locating warehouses or selecting a viable form of transportation system for their products.

4. *There is no provision within firms for the management of channels.* This may be called the vacant-chair thesis. Of the many possible conventions followed in channel management, this is one of the most important. It can be stated simply: Nobody serves or is expected to serve as manager of the firm's channels because the firm has no manager of marketing. If the company is well organized functionally, the various aspects of marketing will be handled by a number of officers—the purchasing agent, the customer relations manager, the traffic manager, the sales manager, the warehouse manager, and so on. But there will be no one man who coordinates the relations of the firm with all the agencies that form its marketing channel.

This view carries some significant consequences with it. In the absence of a channel manager one must ask: Who designs the distribution system for new products? Who reviews the needs and resources for existing products in order to make certain that required adjustments are made in the channel system? Who speaks for the company in dialogues with members of the channel?

Somehow or other management gets questions answered; but the officers who answer them remain unidentified, and the chair of the distribution manager seems to remain vacant.

5. *The manufacturer constructs and manages the channel.* This concept can be called the dominant force thesis. It sees the manufacturer as both the architect and the captain of the channel. His is the dominant force. Textbooks commonly look at the distribution function almost as if the manufacturer presents all the stimuli and the distributive agencies (whether wholesalers, agents, or retailers) merely respond to what he does.

The fact that some manufacturers seem to act according to the dominant force theory may cause strain and conflict within the channel. The chairman of the board of the Rawlings Corporation says of the relationship between manufacturers and retailers, "I have been surprised and appalled at the *bad feelings, complete misunderstanding, and even distrust that exist between the manufacturers and the retailer,*"[1] He explains his concept of the relationships between the two by offering an analogy:

> The situation reminds us a little of the climax of a "Western". Two cowboys silently face each other in the middle of a hushed Front Street, each waiting for the other to draw.
> Each of our "heroes" feels that the other has done him dirt. The manufacturer is telling himself that the dealer hasn't been loyal, while the

---

[1] P. D. Brown, "Selling Through—Not to—Retailers," in Malcolm P. McNair and M. Berman, Eds., *Marketing Through Retailers* (New York: American Management Association, 1967), p. 59.

dealer firmly believes that the manufacturer has gotten just what he deserves.

So they stand there and stand there—each waiting for the other to draw. Meanwhile back on the ranch, nobody is minding the cows and someone else is selling the beefsteak.[2]

6. *Nobody manages the channel.* Earlier in the paper we defined a channel as an organized network of agencies. But who organizes and manages the channel as a whole? One answer is that nobody does. The channel works as free competition is said to work in that the play of market forces attracts people to the performance of needed services and drives them to cooperate with one another in the absence of formal management. Somehow or other, the distribution task is accomplished even though no agency has any authority to command others.

Some students deplore this situation. They ask how a channel manager can be created, apparently assuming that formal management would improve the efficiency of the distribution system. A few writers seem to think that in practice, channel systems, even though they usually do not have formally recognized managers sometimes do have *de facto* managers or captains. They achieve their position by virtue of their firm's having market power and the will to lead.

Rethinking the Concept of Channel Management

We can now consider some suggestions as to how the marketing manager can develop a better understanding by his firm of the channel problems it faces. The central principle to be followed is that the firm must think not solely in terms of its own operation within the channel but rather in terms of relationships of its own operations to the operations of all other agencies within the channel. It also must keep in mind the fact that effectiveness in its own activities is not enough.

Somehow, matters must be worked out so that everything done by everybody in the channel adds up to effectiveness at the point where the final user chooses it over the offerings made to him by competing channels.

Thinking in Terms of Systems

Systems analysis is in danger of becoming a superficial "buzz word" in the study of marketing today, but there is real merit in applying the concept to channel management. It must be admitted that very often, little rationale is

---

[2] *Ibid.,* p. 60.

apparent in a firm's distribution system. The utility of systems analysis may be demonstrated if we look upon it as being helpful in the following sorts of studies:

(a) A description of existing structure of a firm's channel or channels.
(b) An assessment of needs and responses of each agency in the actual or desired channel for each product.
(c) An evaluation of each specific channel and the flows it embodies from the joint or common viewpoint of *all* the agencies concerned.
(d) A consideration of modifications and adjustments that might be made in the channels for given products.

THE EXISTING STRUCTURE.   All too often, a seller of goods views his channel relationship as one between himself and his immediate customer or alternatively, as one between himself and the final user of his product, without regard to intermediate buyers. The first task in assessing a channel management system is to develop a critical-path description of the agencies performing the various channel services for given products. This assessment can often be made most effectively by considering the work done by the channel members as being that of conducting a number of "flows", i.e., the physical flow of the good, the flow of ownership, the flow of information, and so on.

The importance of this orientation has been stressed by one well known channel theorist, Professor Ralph Breyer. In an interview with one of the authors, he emphasized what he thought to be the most critical problems in distribution today. One of these was "the channel overview" problem. Here, he noted:

> One must examine the channel from a total-channel point of view—not just the manufacturer's, or the wholesaler's, or the retailer's. Without this commitment to the study and management of channels as a whole, little progress can be made toward the optimizing of distribution. It is entirely *wrong* to view a channel from the standpoint of the manufacturer only or to think that what is good for the manufacturer is good for the channel.

A simplistic version of a channel from the viewpoint of the manufacturer can be seen in Figure 1. A similar simplistic version from the viewpoint of the wholesaler can be seen in Figure 2. In Figure 1, the channel is for one product or line produced by one manufacturer. In Figure 2, the channel is for competing products made by several manufacturers but handled by one wholesaler. The charts are familiar enough but they ordinarily are used with little imagination. It takes little insight to see that the ideas of manufacturer

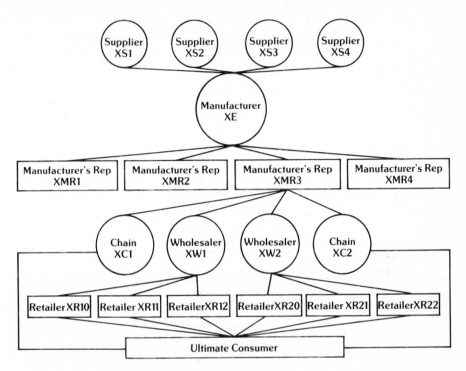

FIGURE 1   *A Simplistic Structure of a Trade Channel from the Viewpoint of a Manufacturer*

Due to the simplistic nature of the illustrated channel and the lack of space, the identification of the physical ownership, information and money flows was omitted.

and wholesaler as to what constitutes "effective" operation of a "good" channel can differ sharply. Anyone who sets himself up to be the channel leader or captain will need to keep this fact in mind.

Just recently, a Madison Avenue creative enthusiast has advocated that manufacturers take a more adventuresome approach to couponing ads.[3] He advocates the "wild" use of all shapes and sizes of the consumer "cents-off" tear-out coupons placed in print media. Uniformity of coupons in terms of the familiar rectangular approach would go by the wayside. Instead, a cents-off coupon for dog food would be shaped like a French Poodle or a cents-off coupon for wet soup would be shaped like a bowl of soup. While such new adventures may be eye catching and even appealing to consumers, we wonder if the Madison Avenue creative genius has ever appraised the consequences of

[3] Stephen Baker, "Wild Shapes, Sizes Are Today's Look in Coupons," *Advertising Age*, August 4, 1969.

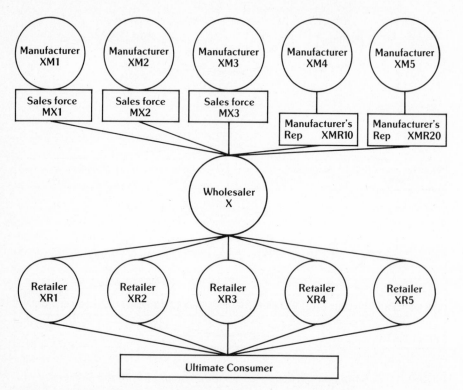

FIGURE 2   *A Simplistic Structure of a Trade Channel from the Viewpoint of a Wholesaler*
Due to the simplistic nature of the illustrated channel and the lack of space, the identification of the physical ownership, information and money flows was omitted.

the new shapes from the standpoint of the retailers who redeem the coupons. Imagine the stacking, sorting, cataloguing, and storing problems faced by retailers and redemption centers! Here is where some application of Figure 1 and Figure 2 might be helpful to manufacturers.

In trying to sort out the tasks performed by each agency in a channel, much less simplistic approaches are required. One of these is to use what has been called the "flow" approach. This elaborates the structures charted in Figure 1 and 2 by visualizing what happens in a channel not as one flow but as a group of several interrelated flows. In a book on channel management being prepared by the present authors, channels are viewed as conducting four flows:

1. *The physical flow of the goods*, i. e., a sequence of agencies or (more precisely) facilities through which the goods move for transportation, storage, sorting, and so on.

2. *The flow of ownership or control*, i. e., a sequence of agencies through which moves the authority to decide what shall be done with the goods.

3. *The flow of information*, i.e., a sequence of agencies through which users tell producers and distributors what they want, while producers and distributors simultaneously tell users what they have to sell and try to persuade users to buy it.

4. *The flow of money*, i.e., a sequence of agencies through which capital is assembled and brought into the marketing process and an overlapping sequence of agencies through which buyers pay sellers for what they buy.

Application of the flow concept to channel management makes it possible to determine the precise role of each agency or facility in the channel of distribution. Discrepancies in the effectiveness with which agencies perform specific activities may be observed. For example, one firm has developed a critical-path appraisal of its physical distribution system. In doing so it has found that its three public warehouses are handling in a dissimilar manner customers' original orders, the shipping orders, bills of lading, and the informational feedback to the sales (carbons of various order papers). As a result, customers were receiving inconsistent and often poor service.

ASSESSING THE NEEDS AND RESPONSES OF EACH FIRM WITHIN THE CHANNEL.   One of the saddest shortcomings in channel management is the seller's frequent failure to consider the marketing needs and responses of his customers. How often does a seller objectively determine what his customers need in each of the flows? The manufacturer, if he makes any guess at all, is likely to decide intuitively what the customers want to do, or even can do, relative to each of the flows. There is nothing unusual about a firm that thinks one or two reports by salesmen will tell us what its wholesalers are thinking.

Very unusual is a carefully designed, thorough, and systematic effort to find out the facts. An example is what one company calls its "Dealer Forum":

> I write from some experience. In the Office Machines Division we created a Dealer Forum, and this proved very effective. We rotated our members on this Dealer Forum every two years. The meetings were held with the top management of the Division, including the manufacturing, engineering, financial, and marketing heads, as well as the general manager. Many fine programs came out of the Dealer Forum, and it was so successful . . . We . . . are going to adopt the same type of program with our sporting goods retailers. [4]

In a recent informal study, a drug manufacturer found that one of its advertising agencies not only failed to understand the nature of the management system for the total channel but did not really understand the role of its detail men. The agency was aiming its promotional pieces at the doctors without realizing that these pieces must also meet the needs and wishes of the

---

[4] Brown, *op. cit.*, p. 60.

detail men. For many of the pieces, there was no opportunity to test their effectiveness with doctors because the detail men never used them. The moral to be drawn from this simple illustration is that knowing the needs and responses of channel members is just as important as knowing the needs and responses of ultimate consumers.

EVALUATION OF THE CHANNELS AS A WHOLE.   As Professor Breyer's comments suggested earlier, what is good for the manufacturer or any other seller is not necessarily good for all other sellers and buyers within the channel. Once the needs and responses of all the components within the trade channel have been assessed, it becomes possible to evaluate the viability of the present channel system. Here, numerous questions might serve as a guideline in evaluation. Such questions as the following might be raised: Are there discrepancies in the performance of the flows among members of the channel? Are there alternative firms or agencies that might be more effective than those now used in carrying the product through the channel and to the ultimate consumer? What will be the impact on the channel structure and the requisite channel flows if new agencies or firms are added to the channel? Are there conventional ways of acting that inhibit the marketing effectiveness of sellers and buyers within the channel?

POSSIBLE MODIFICATIONS AND ADJUSTMENTS OF THE CHANNEL.   After evaluation of a channel system comes the problem of making whatever modifications or adjustments seem to be needed. The appropriate guideline should be: "Observe the consequences of any change upon all agencies in the entire structure." Also, it should be emphasized that modifications or adjustments ought to occur *only after* the preceding three steps in the systems procedure have been taken.

The Managerial Responsibility for Channels

Despite the fact that every businessman and every consumer needs effectiveness in the operations of every complete channel of which he is a member, formal management of the system can rarely be established by any method other than vertical integration. However, one tremendous service can be performed by each member of a non-integrated channel. This is to make someone in its corporate hierarchy responsible for doing what can be done to achieve full channel efficiency. Thus, the channel function would become just as distinct an operating assignment as sales, advertising, or promotion.

The responsibilities of the channels manager should be stated broadly as opposed to, say, the narrow view of those who want to make physical distribution a managerial task.

The responsibilities should include at least the following:

1. *Systems management.*
   (a) Reviewing the existing structure of specific flows (ownership, physical movement, information, and money).
   (b) Developing an inventory of the needs of each agency within the channel.
   (c) Modifying and adjusting the channel to meet the needs for change.
2. *Channel relations.*
   (a) Informing channel members of marketing programs and changes in any facet of marketing and non-marketing programs.
   (b) Receiving information and questions from trade customers relative to any facet of marketing and non-marketing programs.
3. *Internal coordination of distribution, as affected by:*
   (a) Manufacturing.
   (b) Finance.
   (c) Marketing.

The above list of responsibilities is not definitive. It nevertheless provides a start toward the development of a well-organized channel management function within the firm. It thus offers business management an opportunity to make a significant contribution to the strengthening of what is unquestionably one of the least managed areas of marketing today.

Questions [by Author of Article]

1. Offer reasons why channel management "is unquestionably one of the least managed areas of marketing today." In other words, how is it that deficiencies in channel management persist in companies?

2. What four flows, according to the authors, comprise the activities within a distribution channel?

3. When "channels are viewed as conducting four flows," what agencies besides manufacturer, wholesaler, retailer, and consumer would be involved in distribution channel activities?

4. Should there actually be a Channels Manager *per se* within a medium-to-large manufacturing firm or should the channels management responsibilities be assigned to some other person? If you favor having a Channels Manager, explain why, If not, who (by title) should be responsible for channel management?

QUESTIONS

1. What are some of the problems created when the management responsibility for channel decisions is spread throughout the firm?

2. Comment on the following statement: Most channel decisions involve physical distribution decisions and management of channel members (not selection and development decisions) because once a firm has an established channel structure, it rarely changes.

3. Identify the four flows in a channel system.

4. Do the different flows in a channel occur at the same time? Do they move at the same rate within a channel? Give reasons for your answers.

5. What is the key principle or concept that should guide channel management?

6. What type of organization structure would you recommend for managing channels? Why?

2

DON'T SELL FOOD, SELL PEACE OF MIND

Anne Bagamery

The Sysco Corporation's $1.7 billion annual sales leads the wholesale restaurant and institutional food industry, which is composed of over 2000 firms, even though it is usually the highest priced distributor. One of the key factors for this success is the customer service it can guarantee through its extensive distribution system.

Why is $1.7 BILLION (sales) Sysco Corp. more profitable than almost any of the other 2,000-odd firms in the $55 billion-a-year business of wholesaling food to restaurants and other institutional servers? A favorite company anecdote tells this story:

Preparations for a lobster roast at Houston's toney Inn on the Park were going smoothly until the chef noticed unexpected guests and found he was ten lobsters short. At 5 p.m. on a Saturday, where was he going to find fresh lobsters? Panic-stricken, the chef called his Sysco representative at home. The salesman jumped into his car, drove to a gourmet store that he knew would be open until 6 p.m., bought the lobsters and delivered them to the hotel. He even slapped them on the grill himself.

Chairman John Baugh, who has worked 35 years in food distribution, drives home the point: "The typical food service company picks a case of frozen french fries out of the warehouse and dumps it on the restaurant's back porch. Where's the skill in that? Where's the creativity? Our people don't just sell food—they sell peace of mind."

If Baugh sounds a little like an IBM salesman promising worry-free computing, well, the parallel is apt. Houston-based Sysco maintains an army of some 2,200 "marketing associates" (Baugh's words). Two-thirds of that army are salesmen whose job is to assure Sysco's 90,000 nationwide customers that 98% of the items they order will be delivered on time. The rest are product specialists, preparation specialists and customer-service representatives who do everything from preparing restricted-diet menus for hospitals to explaining how to hold stuffed peppers through a two-hour luncheon buffet.

Naturally, this handholding isn't free: Sysco is usually the highest-priced distributor in the market. And it isn't for everyone: A burger joint that needs only a handful of items and no advice will tend to go elsewhere. But the willingness of Sysco's customers to pay for convenience means that Sysco can post a net margin of 2%, well ahead of its top competitors' average of 1.5%. Sysco's revenues—the industry's largest—have been growing 18% a year for a decade, largely because of acquisitions of local food distributors. But its earnings for the same period have increased 22% a year. Earnings per share have grown at a compound annual rate of 18%, to $1.71 in the fiscal year ended July 3. Return on equity has averaged 16.5% with moderate leverage—debt hovers around 25% of total capital.

Achieving that kind of growth means walking a fine line in a business where slow food-price escalation and stiff competition chip away at potential profits and labor costs eat up 10% of sales. But Baugh, 66, has President John Woodhouse, 51, handling the finances for Sysco—the name is a contraction of Systems & Services Co.—which today has 69 distribution centers in 45 states serving 116 of the top 150 metropolitan areas. Woodhouse, a onetime financial man at Ford Motor, keeps receivables down to 24 days' sales—where the industry norm is around 35. Sysco headquarters must approve all subsidiaries' presidents' salaries, major expenditures and borrowings. Salesmen work on commissions that are set locally, based on the profitability of each order, which may be based on dollar size and frequency of delivery as well as gross profit.

Sysco started life in 1970 when Baugh—then president of a Houston company called Zero Foods—and eight other regional distributors decided to centralize finances, the better to expand and modernize. Their timing couldn't have been better, as eating away from home became a growth industry in the 1970s.

Now, however, with Americans spending less to eat out, Baugh and Woodhouse are looking for other ways to keep Sysco growing. In February 1981 they set up Compton Foods in Kansas City to purchase meat and move the Sysco 15,000-item product line into the so-called center of the plate—the meat and prepared entrées that constitute 50 cents of every food-service dollar. Sysco had shied away from meat previously because Baugh and Woodhouse thought the subsidiaries could not control quality or get good prices from meatpackers accustomed to selling huge lots to supermarket chains.

But with Sysco's current size, Compton can buy in truckload and boxcar lots from Iowa Beef or Swift & Co. and therefore is able to negotiate on price. Also, as a good customer, Compton gets the right to send its own inspector into the meatpackers' plant to check quality. Compton contracts with the big processors for prepared frozen entrées—where the watch on quality must be exacting. "One person decides he can shave a few pennies by putting cheaper meat in the beef stew," explains Woodhouse. "Another decides he can put in more potatoes, and before you know it, a perfectly acceptable dish has become garbage." Baugh and Woodhouse think sales of Compton-purchased foods just to existing customers could add as much as $800 million to sales.

Limits to growth? Baugh and Woodhouse want to move into the 34 metropolitan areas where Sysco doesn't have a presence—but they are as careful with their expansion plans as with the frozen beef stew. "We've had to walk away from acquisitions because we didn't have the people to keep track of them," admits Woodhouse. Sysco's secret? Simple: paying attention—to costs, to resources, and to a customer needing lobsters at 5 o'clock on Saturday.

QUESTIONS

1. How has Sysco differentiated its product?
2. What is the "total product" that is being marketed by Sysco?
3. Describe the impact that Sysco's customer service has on sales volume and profits.

3

DOLLARS
FROM DOODADS

William Baldwin

*Because of recent developments in the
economy, manufacturing employs only
one out of five workers. The author
points out that although historically gains
in productivity have been considered the
responsibility of the manufacturing
sector, the economy's future productivity
gains must come from other areas; in
particular, wholesaling and retailing.*

Most wholesalers are faceless, unimaginative ordertakers eking out
1% profit margins. The right entrepreneur, however, can turn distribution
into a glamour business with growth rates and returns on equity reaching
20%. Look at Lawson Products Inc., which has found a way to clear 9% net
profit margins on spare parts, by sparing customers valuable time. Or W. W.
Grainger Inc., which has become a Sears, Roebuck of industrial supply,
marketing everything from grommets to hot-tub pump motors. Then there's
Vallen Corp., a seller of safety equipment, which is finding ways to save its
customers the cost of maintaining stockrooms.

What these companies and others like them [see Table 1] . . . know is
that the cost of industrial supplies just begins with the price tag on the item.
"The dollar you spend on the invoice is the tip of the iceberg," says William
O'Connell, president of Vallen. Beyond this, there are the salaries in the
purchasing department, the paperwork in accounts payable and the cost of
discarding obsolete stock. Helping customers minimize expenses like these is
how good distributors can earn their keep.

In fact, smart suppliers and other service-sector firms must provide most
of the economy's future productivity gains. The reason is simple arithmetic:
Manufacturing is already so automated that it employs only one out of five
workers. A year ago wholesale and retail trade overtook the manufacturing

Table 1

MIDDLEMEN MAKE MONEY, TOO

These companies make wholesaling look easy. Leonard Bruce started his Vallen Corp. at the age of 27 with $5,000 in savings and $2,000 in consigned goggles. G. B. Van Dusen, now 68 and chairman of the company bearing his name, was 26 when he borrowed $300 for some parts and opened shop in a Minneapolis airport terminal. But the nice returns vanish if management does not rapidly add new product lines and accounts and kill slow ones. NCH's return on equity is half what it was a few years ago. Thanks to the recession, Van Dusen's earnings per share have tumbled from $1.76 in fiscal 1980.

Company/products	Revenues (millions)	1981 Net profit margin	Return on equity	Earnings per share latest 12 months	Earnings per share 10-year growth rate	Recent price	Price/ earnings
Aceto Chemical/*chemicals*[1]	$ 91	3.4%	13%	$2.67	24%	15⅞	5.9
American Hospital Supply/*medical*	2,870	5.1	15	2.22	14	38	17.0
WW Grainger/*motors, misc*	867	6.5	18	3.91	17	44	11.3
Lawson Products/*fasteners*	110	9.2	22	1.94	21	24¼	12.5
NCH/*bldg maint supplies*[2]	348	4.3	9	1.25	14	15	12.0
Premier Industrial/*fasteners, electronics*[3]	340	10.2	23	1.66	19	24½	14.8
Vallen/*safety equipment*[3]	37	6.4	19	1.58	30[4]	15	9.5
Van Dusen Air/*aircraft parts*[5]	143	2.2	9	0.91	18	9¾	10.7

[1] Year ended 6/30/82.
[2] Year ended 4/30/82.
[3] Year ended 5/31/82.
[4] Five-year growth rate.
[5] Year ended 3/31/82.

sector in total employment, and the lead is widening. That leaves plenty of room for efficient distributors to supply themselves with handsome profits.

Lawson Products: "A Fastener Program"

The 1,100 Lawson salesmen on the road pushing 17,000 different replacement parts don't talk price, they talk quality and convenience. Customers don't buy nuts and bolts, but a "fastener program." That means hardware of a higher grade than usual, kept in Lawson parts bins, each neatly labeled and periodically restocked by a Lawson man.

"We don't claim to be the cheapest," says Sidney Port, 71, founder (in 1952) and executive committee chairman of the Des Plaines, Ill. company. "Our products go into big pieces of equipment. Whether they pay a few cents more for a tiny part doesn't make a bit of difference." Except to Lawson, which earned just over $10 million last year on $110 million in revenues.

This labor-intensive selling scheme yields savings for Lawson customers like Steve Stevens, head of maintenance for a school district stretched over 186 square miles northwest of Houston. He seems to be paying a stiff price: $12.64 a box for one style of wood screw, for example, quoted at $4.53 at a screw wholesaler in the city. Trouble is, this wholesaler is 20 miles away and happened to be out of that particular style when a reporter called.

Lawson, by contrast, ships from five regional warehouses, each well enough stocked to boast 99% order fulfillment. For Stevens, the arrival of the Lawson salesman has meant more time for his carpenters to fix broken school windows. "Before, they were buying a few screws here and a few there and leaving them around in bags," he says. "It would take them an hour to get to the hardware store and back."

Lawson knows about conventional productivity gains, too. Automated parts counters gobble screws from kegs and feed them into prim Lawson-yellow boxes, at which point they're marked up an average 240% and sent by UPS to customers. Although a majority of its parts carry the Lawson brand, none are manufactured in-house.

Will Lawson try that soon? Not likely, since that may be why earnings per share have climbed 620% over the past decade. Manufacturing is always vulnerable to foreign inroads. First-class service is not.

Vallen Corp.: Vendor Stocking

Back in 1947, Leonard Bruce, then a 27-year-old Chicago goggles salesman, set off in search of a new territory. He landed in Houston and prospered mightily. The Vallen Corp. he founded and still presides over netted $2.4 million on $37 million (sales) in its fiscal year ended in May.

Bruce owes some thanks to growth in the postwar petrochemical industry and to ever-tighter job-safety regulations. But his would probably still be just another small, family-run industrial supplier if not for a special emphasis on making things convenient for customers. Vallen broadened its product line as fast as finances permitted, so that plant safety directors could do all their ordering from one salesman. Today the company handles 6,000 items, from acid hoods to vapor sniffers.

Vallen has found other ways to streamline distribution. In 1974 it won an account at Dow Chemical's Freeport, Tex. complex under what Dow calls its "vendor-stocking program." This lets Dow dodge most of the costs of keeping a stockroom, shopping by phone and scrambling for out-of-stock items. Instead, when a plant manager needs 12 hardhats he keys that request into a computer system with a terminal at Vallen's Freeport branch. Vallen agrees to maintain enough inventory on 250 items to answer 95% of requisitions immediately, and Vallen trucks deliver to Dow every two hours. Vallen also accepts slightly lower than usual prices under the Dow contract. In return, it gets a large account and payment within ten days.

Vendor stocking can work only at large plants—the Freeport chemical complex is the western hemisphere's largest—so Vallen is working on smaller variations. It is negotiating to set up safety equipment stores inside customers' plants, staffed by part-time workers who have retired from jobs at those same plants. What Vallen is really selling, then, is a way for its customers to cut stockroom staff. With ever-rising labor costs, that's a strategy that can't miss.

W. W. Grainger: Fast Turnover

Grainger calls its 1,092-page catalog the "motorbook" because of a heavy dose of electric motors, fans and blowers, some of which it manufactures. But for this $867-million-a-year company, making motors has proved far less lucrative than distributing them—along with a lot of other things. That's why Chairman David Grainger, 54, son of the man who founded the firm in 1927, describes his business this way: "Having the right thing in the right place at the right time."

And what a collection of things. The motorbook advertises bits, bolts, sheaves, shelves, pillow blocks, posthole diggers, solar hotwater heaters, self-extinguishing garbage cans and mop wringers. Why does a motor distributor sell mop wringers? Why not, if that saves a maintenance worker a side trip? Signs at Grainger's 165 stores warn WHOLESALE ONLY, but this is really a retail business, with a $111 average sales ticket. The typical customer is a hurried repairman who comes for a replacement motor—and who may, while he's at it, pick up a $9.65 pound of solder that he could have gotten for $6.20 at a plumbing shop. Time is money.

There's another side to this mass-merchandise approach. Grainger's line of 9,800 products and 24,000 parts has reached a critical mass that keeps shipping costs down. All merchandise is gathered through 1.6 million square feet of warehouses near its Skokie, Ill. headquarters. (This hub will be duplicated with a 1.4-million-square-foot building to open in Kansas City this winter.) There it is arranged into assortments shipped at least weekly, in full truckloads, to the stores. With less volume, Grainger would have to settle for half-filled trucks or less-frequent deliveries. The weekly deliveries in turn enable branches to satisfy buyers without holding huge inventories of their own.

Altogether, the company turns over its distribution inventory 3 times a year. That doesn't sound like much, but remember that Grainger is straddling two levels in the distribution system. The alternative is hardware jobbers gathering merchandise from the manufacturers and dispersing it to local industrial-supply houses. If jobber and supplier both turn inventories 4 times a year, their combined turnover rate is only 2. That's why the competition seems to be losing ground: Grainger has quadrupled sales over the past decade, while getting long-term debt down to 4% of total capital and rarely letting return on equity dip below 17%. Many a high-productivity manufacturer would be lucky to do so well.

QUESTIONS

1. What key operating factors must be changed in the traditional management practices in wholesaling in order for profit margins to increase?
2. What is involved in wholesaling productivity?
3. Why would vendor stocking be inefficient for small firms?
4. How can a total-product concept aid in increasing wholesaling productivity?

4

THE RETAILER'S CHANGING ROLE IN THE MARKETING CHANNEL

Bert Rosenbloom

The problem of poor market responsiveness on the part of retailers is examined in this article. The author identifies five factors that have created this problem and lists suggestions that may help correct it. The article raises some questions about the appropriateness of having retailers as captains in a channel structure.

Abstract

The retailer's role in the marketing channel is changing to a more powerful and independent one. As a result, retailers are in a position to demand more from their suppliers in the way of strategic marketing support in the major areas of the marketing mix.

Introduction

About two decades ago, McVey raised the issue of the retailer's role in the marketing channel. He argued that the retailer tends to view himself more as the buying agent for his customers than as the selling agent for his suppliers (McVey 1960).

Developments in the retail sector over the last twenty years as well as current developments and those which will occur in the future (Mason and

Mayer 1978), suggest the McVey's observation is increasingly accurate. Retailers in many lines of trade are becoming a more dominant and independent force in the marketing channel.

The fundamental reasons for this are the growing size and concentration of retailers, especially the continued growth of chain store systems and affiliated groups, technological developments such as POS and computerized management information systems that have helped retailers to increase their level of management sophistication, and an overall upgrading of the quality of retail management personnel.

This more powerful and independent role for the retailer in the distribution channel has important implications in terms of the retailer's needs and expectations with respect to his suppliers. Specifically the retailer's needs and expectations are likely to be greater than they were and his increased size and power means that he will be in a strong position to see that his demands are met.

This paper explores some of the changing needs and expectations of retailers as their role in the distribution channel continues to grow stronger. The discussion is structured around retailer needs and expectations in the four areas of the marketing mix: product, pricing, physical distribution, and promotion.

Product Management and Retailer Expectations

Retailers will want to play an increasing role in product planning, development and management. This is likely to hold not only in terms of retailers developing more of their own products but also in their exerting a greater influence over what products the manufacturer produces and how they are sold over the course of the product life cycle (Little 1970). Several key issues illustrative of the growing retailer role in product planning, development, and management are discussed below.

More Retailer Input into New Product Planning

Retailers in many lines of trade are no longer content to let the manufacturer dominate in the development of new products. More retailers now have the marketing expertise to help determine what kinds of new products are right for the market segments they serve (Czepiel 1977). One case in point involved the development of a highly successful no-wax tile for the do-it-yourselfer by a major floor covering manufacturer. Prior to the introduction of the tile, the no-wax vinyl flooring was available only in large six or twelve foot sheets cut from a large roll. Retailers of these products soon learned that the home handyman was not buying the product because he was not capable of installing it in this form. Several of the retailers requested that the manufacturer develop the product in a 12 × 12 inch tile form for the home handyman. The manufacturer complied and the product was highly successful.

Failure on the part of manufacturers and suppliers to take more note of the retailer's potential contributions for new product ideas is likely to lead to increased development by retailers of their own products. The introduction of the so-called "no frills" products by a number of supermarket chains is a good example of the retailer's capacity to respond with a new product offering aimed at a growing segment of the market which national brand manufacturers were apparently overlooking.

Product Acceptance by Retailers

It is not enough for a new product to be acceptable only to consumers. More than ever, the product must also be acceptable to the retailers through whom it passes (Gearing 1978). Gaining such retailers acceptance, however, is going to be increasingly difficult in the future because retailer standards and requirements for product acceptance are becoming more stringent and sophisticated.

In supermarket retailing, for example, the battle for shelf space has become fiercer than ever. A poll of supermarket executives taken by *Progressive Grocer* magazine showed that supermarkets have increasingly more sophisticated and uniform ideas about what kinds of products they are willing to accept (Categories 1978). They want products that have either a *demonstrated history* or show *obviously strong potential* for high margins, high turnover, good impulse buying potential, stapleness, and that takes up relatively little space. Suppliers will have to do an especially effective job of making a case for their products meeting these criteria if they hope to gain supermarket acceptance in the future.

Drug retailers especially the large chain, voluntary, and cooperative organizations which now dominate drug retailing have equally stringent criteria for accepting new products in their stores. But they now also take note of more subtle criteria such as a product's ability to attract customers into their stores.

General merchandise chains and department stores have also become more demanding in their acceptance of new products. For example, some are taking a conservative "wait and see" attitude in stocking expensive personal computers which their manufacturers believe will be a hot, even booming item in the near future (Personal 1978). But to an increasing extent, these retailers are more inclined to rely on their own analysis of the market for these products than on manufacture hype.

To sum up, larger and more sophisticated retailers with their more stringent product acceptance criteria will play a larger role in determining which products move through the distribution channel to the final consumer. Suppliers will thus have to develop their channel strategies for gaining retailer acceptance of new products to a much higher level if they expect to reach consumers effectively through major retail outlets.

More Innovative Assortment Planning by Retailers

Scrambled merchandising will continue to play a major role in fostering wider and more unusual merchandise assortments among retailers. But rather than let the scrambled merchandise assortments evolve on a haphazard basis, more retailers are taking a conscious and active part in the broadening or scrambling of their merchandise assortments. That is, retailers are taking more of a leadership role in initiating changes in the kinds of merchandise they will add to their assortments. For instance, several major drug chains recently added a broad line of auto parts and supplies. According to executives in one of these drug retailers, the decision to carry the new line of auto parts and supplies was based on an analysis of the market by the drug chain (Gearing 1978). The research showed that the potential buyers for auto parts and supplies were coming not only from the ranks of blue-collar workers but from the mainstream of the drug chains' customers including many professional and upper income customers. Hence, the decision to add the new line of products was based on an analysis by the retailer of his markets rather than cajoling from suppliers. This is likely to become a common pattern in the future as retailers become more sophisticated in using the tools of market research and more adept at making merchandise assortment decisions on *research* rather than a trial and error basis. Astute suppliers seeking to sell merchandise through unusual types of retail outlets, will improve their chances of gaining retailer acceptance if they recognize that retailers will be expecting more research based facts about the potential of a new line of merchandise and less glib talk about great potential that is unsubstantiated.

Retailers and the Product Life Cycle

The retailer plays a critical role in a product's success as it moves through the product life cycle. In the introductory stage, strong retailer acceptance can make the difference between the product dying or moving into the growth stage. As the product enters the growth stage, continued support and the maintenance of adequate inventories by the retailer help to nurture the growth of the product. In the maturity stage, further support by the retailer can help to prolong the life of the product by keeping it available to the consumer.

Retailers, however, are becoming increasingly sensitive to the strategic merchandising implications of the product life cycle. Greater inventory management sophistication and vastly improved computer based inventory monitoring and control systems have made this possible. Retailers are now able to monitor the success or failure of products much more closely than was feasible just a few short years ago. If a newly introduced product in their stores is not catching on they know about it—and very quickly. When the rate of sales growth of a successful product begins to slow down they are able to spot this pattern at a very early stage. And products whose sales are stagnant are hardly likely to go unnoticed. On the other hand, hot selling products are also spotted more quickly by retailers and reorders are equally rapid. A case in point involved a buyer for Penney's who had bought a new toy product called Slime (Slom 1977). With the electronic scanner device and sophisticated inventory management system used by Penney's, the buyer knew in days the exact sales for the product in various Penney's store units. A large reorder was placed immediately. According to the buyer, this reorder was placed weeks earlier than would have been the case under the previous less sophisticated inventory management system.

Thus, better inventory management made possible through sophisticated computer based hardware in use by retailers is a two edged sword for suppliers. On one edge, quicker responses by retailers to fast-selling products can allow suppliers more time to plan ahead to increase production. But on the other edge, the retailer's faster response to slow sellers can mean a sudden, widespread halt in orders instead of a gradual phase-out.

Pricing and Retailer Expectations

The retailer's role in the manufacturer's (supplier's) pricing strategy has been given comparatively little attention. The manufacturer's pricing strategies tend to focus mainly on consumer demand, competitive, and cost considerations. Little attention has been paid to the retailer's viewpoint when pricing decisions are made. With the growing size and sophistication of retailers this situation is now changing. Retailers are taking a more critical look at their suppliers' pricing policies in terms of how they affect retailers. In short, retailers increasingly want pricing strategies that are consistent with their particular needs and that help them to achieve their own objectives. They are less likely to acquiesce to supplier pricing policies which they feel are not in their best interests. Several issues discussed below are illustrative of the kinds of needs and expectations that retailers have with regard to supplier pricing policies.

Adequate Margins

While provision for adequate margins has always been a key demand for retailers, their expectations have increased and they have become more stringent in evaluating suppliers' offerings in terms of margin potential. Retailers are in a stronger position to make suppliers "buy distribution" in a competitive market environment. As Warshaw states:

> The concept of buying distribution emphasizes the fact that the price paid to gain channel support must reflect not only the marketing job performed by the channel, but also the competitive environment in which the channel operates (Warshaw 1962, p. 51)

Thus, if supplier margins are not equal to the "prices" sought by the retailers for their services, suppliers will not be able to buy their services in a competitive environment. With this in mind, suppliers will have to give far more attention to the implications of their pricing policies on retailers, and continuous reviews of trade discount structures will have to be made to determine their adequacy. Particular attention will also have to be paid to changes in the competitive environment that are likely to influence retailers' perceptions of existing discount structures.

Pricing to Different Kinds of Retailers

In an ideal world, trade discounts available to different kinds of retailers would vary in direct proportion to the level of service provided to the supplier by each type of retailer. In reality, few distribution channels operate in this manner. Trade discount structures at both the wholesale and retail levels are typically governed by strong traditions and conventions that permeate the trade and have little to do with service rendered.

Larger and more sophisticated retailers, however, have become much more attuned to the discrepancies and inequities existing in traditional trade discount structures. They have become much more astute and aggressive in challenging these conventions. For example, chain and affiliated drug retailers, who now dominate in drug retailing are demanding and getting direct purchases from the manufacturers for general merchandise items at prices just as favorable as those offered to mass merchandise chain and discount department store retailers. Many department stores who have traditionally offered a full range of services have cut back or stopped carrying altogether, major appliances which are also sold to discount store retailers who often provide considerably less services. Independent hardware stores, many of whom are now affiliated in cooperative groups, have been more astute in seeing that they obtain equivalent prices and the special deals offered by manufacturers to the large chain building supply, home centers, and discount department store retailers.

In sum, across a wide range of retail trade, retailers are more aware of and are better able to bargain with suppliers for discount structures which they feel reflect fair payment for their services.

Margin Potentials of Rival Brands

Improved information systems have enabled retailers to become better aware of which of the particular brands they carry are profitable and which are not (Czepiel 1977). If a particular manufacturer's brand is at a clear disadvantage compared to the margins a retailer can obtain from it relative to another brand (and this cannot be offset by higher turnover), he will not devote much effort to promoting it. Only when the margin differentials among rival brands carried by the retailer are justified on the basis of differing levels of supplier support will major margin variations be acceptable to retailers. A manufacturer such as RCA, for example, that is well entrenched in many consumer electronic products can depend on its mass advertising and sales promotion to establish strong consumer preference to pull its products through the channel. Promotion by the retailer in the form of local advertising, and strong personal selling are relatively minor factors in achieving high sales for RCA products. Accordingly, the relatively low margins granted to the retailer are feasible. On the other hand, a smaller, specialized manufacturer such as Magnavox has to concentrate its distribution through fewer, more carefully selected and aggressive retailers who can draw customers to themselves with strong local advertising and personal selling. A manufacturer in this position will have to grant larger margins to its retailers to cover the higher costs associated with the more aggressive selling effort expected. Thus, the manufacturer must attempt to weigh any margin differentials between his own and competitive brands in terms of what kind of support he offers and what level of support he expects from retailers.

Physical Distribution and Retailer Expectations

Retailers who are now almost routinely using POS, computerized inventory control systems and other technological marvels, have high expectations for their suppliers to use equally sophisticated technology. Suppliers are expected to provide the kind of physical distribution service that meets retailers' needs in a flexible and efficient manner. In particular they expect their suppliers to understand and meet their changing and more demanding physical distribution services standards and to help them reduce their inventories without sacrificing sales volume.

Meeting Retailer PD Service Standards

Physical distribution service standards refer to what kinds and levels of service retailers expect from their suppliers (Hutchinson and Stolle 1968). Several types of service standards that are frequently important to retailers are the following:

1. time from order receipt to order shipment
2. order size and assortment constraints
3. percentage of items out of stock
4. percentage of orders filled accurately
5. percentage of orders filled within a given number of days from receipt of order
6. percentage of orders filled
7. percentage of orders that arrive in good condition
8. order cycle time (time from order placement to order delivery)
9. ease and flexibility of order placement

Because retailer needs for these service standards differ, suppliers will have to pay careful attention to the particular needs of retailers if they expect to develop physical distribution systems that will satisfy the more demanding retailers. A physical distribution program no matter how sophisticated and technologically advanced, will not be welcomed by the modern retailer unless it actually fulfills the service standards as defined by the retailer. This may require suppliers to use formal and systematic methods such as survey research to find out about retailer service requirements.

Reduction of Retailer Inventories

The high costs associated with carrying inventories have always plagued retailers. But over the last five years high inflation and the 1974 recession which left many retailers holding large inventories which they could not move, have made retailers extremely sensitive to the need to minimize their inventories.

A well designed and responsive physical distribution system developed by the supplier can mean shortened order cycles which in turn can mean lower inventories carried by retailers. Retailers are looking to their suppliers to develop physical distribution systems that will enable the retailer to reduce his inventories but still provide a high level of customer services. Those suppliers who are able to meet this challenge will be sought after by progressive retailers while those suppliers who cannot will not escape the notice of the growing ranks of astute retailers.

Promotion and Retailer Expectations

Retailers are frequently called upon to play an important role in supplier's promotional programs. Retailers are asked to participate in cooperative advertising, use of displays and selling aids, in-store promotions, contests and incentives and a variety of other forms of suppliers initiated promotions. Retailers, however, are becoming much more discriminating in their decisions to participate in these promotional programs. They are asking more penetrating questions about how various supplier promotional efforts which require retailer cooperation are benefitting the retailer. And they are becoming increasingly reluctant to participate in promotional programs whose benefits are not clearly perceived or which appear to offer benefits almost exclusively to the supplier. In short, retailers have become far more choosey about what kinds of supplier promotions they will support (Harmonious 1978). In particular, retailers want promotional programs that are consistent with their objectives, and that will actually be useful to the retailer.

Supplier Promotional Programs and Retailer Objectives

Retailers have become more sophisticated in terms of projecting a carefully developed image and position for their stores (Fenwick 1978). They recognize that the whole gammut of their marketing and merchandising strategies contributes to their image and positions. All of these strategies must fit together into a coherent and consistent whole to maintain and strengthen their marketing efforts.

Supplier initiated promotional programs must therefore fit in with the retailer's own promotional strategies if the retailer's enthusiastic support is sought. Consider, for example, the case of in-store promotions which suppliers often use to create added interest and excitement for their products. Too often these promotions are ill-conceived gimmicky or overblown and most importantly can detract from the image that the retailer is trying to build. When this happens, retailers in increasing numbers will be reluctant to participate in these promotional programs.

Contests and incentives are another area where growing retailer resistance may be encountered if they are inconsistent with the retailer's policies. For example, a supplier may offer push money (PM's) directly to the retailer's salespeople for pushing some of his products. From the standpoint of the retailer, however, this may be seen as conflicting with his objectives.

Specifically the retailer attempting to build an image of high service in meeting customer demands may not want his salespeople to pressure customers into buying products which may not serve their needs merely to get the PM's.

Useful Promotional Programs

Despite the enormous expenditures by suppliers on promotional programs requiring retailer support, many of these programs fall far short of expectations because they do not meet the needs and requirements of retailers (Hinkle 1965). Failure to recognize retailer needs and requirements are particularly common with respect to understanding the retailer's promotional schedule, recognizing the retailers perception of the profitability of promotional offers, and inventory problems created by special promotions.

Understanding the retailer's promotional schedule is necessary because retailers often plan their advertising several weeks in advance, and display space is allocated sometimes as much as three to four months ahead and four to five weeks in advance at a minimum. Consequently, retailers may be unable to cooperate in a special promotion due to conflicting prior commitments of space and effort. If this is the case, even the enticement of a large price allowance may be inadequate to force a change in the retailer's plans.

Suppliers often do not think of the profitability of their offers from the retailer's perspective. Instead they tend to think in terms of how good the offer is from their own vantage point. They forget that when the retailer allocates extra effort to a particular supplier's products, other suppliers' products will receive less selling space and attention. Thus, in deciding whether to accept or reject a particular promotional program, the retailer asks himself if the profit associated with the promotion is likely to offset possible profit losses from competitive product which he carries. When this is done, many seemingly terrific supplier initiated promotional offers do not appear so terrific from the retailer's point of view.

Finally, given the high carrying costs and risks attendent to holding inventories, retailers more than ever are attempting to minimize their inventories. Merchandise involved in special promotional deals, however, often *increase* the amount of inventory the retailer must carry leading in turn to higher carrying costs. This added inventory burden will cause many retailers to be reluctant to cooperate in promotions which load them up with higher inventories.

Summary and Conclusion

The retailer's role in the marketing channel is changing to a more powerful and independent one. As a result, retailers are in a position to demand more from their suppliers in the way of strategic marketing support in the major areas of the marketing mix.

In product planning and management, retailers will expect to play a greater role in new product development. Product acceptance by retailers is also becoming more stringent and they are taking a more active role in the scrambled merchandising phenomenon. Finally, retailers are gaining an increased understanding of their part in shaping the product life cycle.

With respect to pricing, retailers have become more stringent than ever, in demanding adequate trade discounts for their services and are increasingly sensitive to the fairness of margin variations for different kinds of retailers. Further, they will be keeping a close watch on the varying margin potentials of rival brands which they carry.

In the area of physical distribution, retailers expect more supplier attention to meeting their increasingly sophisticated service standards, and to the problems of reducing retailer inventories.

Finally, in the promotional area, retailers are looking for promotional programs which are more consistent with their objectives and that are of demonstrated usefulness to the retailer.

References

"Categories on Parade," (1978), *Progressive Grocer* (January), 70-75.

Cohen, Arthur I. and Ana Loud Jones. (1978), "Brand Marketing in the New Retail Environment," *Harvard Business Review*, 56 (September-October), 141–48.

Czepiel, John A. (1976–1977), "Management Science in Major Merchandising Firms," *Journal of Retailing*, 52 (Winter), 3.

Fenwick, Ian. (1978), "Advertising Experiments by Retailers," *Journal of Advertising Research*, 18 (August), 35–40.

"Gearing Up for Big Auto Supply Business," (1978), *American Druggist*, 177 (April), 45–46.

"Harmonious Marketing: Balance Push-Pull," (1978), *Advertising Age*, 49 (May 22), 66.

Hinkle, Charles L. (1965), "The Strategy of Price Deals," *Harvard Business Review*, (July-August), 75–85.

Hutchinson, William M. and John F. Stolle. (1968), "How to Manage Customer Service," *Harvard Business Review*, 46 (November-December), 85–96.

Little, Robert W. (1970), "The Marketing Channel: Who Should Lead This Extra-Corporate Organization," *Journal of Marketing* (January), Vol. 34, 31.

Mason, J. Barry and Morris L. Mayer. (1978), "Retailing Executives View the 1980's," *Atlanta Economic Review*, (May-June), 4–10.

McVey, Philip. (1960), "Are Channels of Distribution What the Textbooks Say?" *Journal of Marketing*, 24 (January), 61–65.

"Personal Computers Score for Committed Retailers," (1978), *Merchandising*, 3 (September), 93.

Slom, Stanley H. (1977), "Scanners in Stores are Making Waves in Retail Trade," *Wall Street Journal* (August 30), 11.

Warshaw, Martin R. (1962), "Pricing to Gain Wholesalers Selling Support," *Journal of Marketing*, 26 (July), 50–51.

Weigand, Robert E. (1977), "Fit Products and Channels To Your Markets," *Harvard Business Review*, 55 (January-February), 95–105.

QUESTIONS

1. What contributions could a retailer make to a manufacturer in terms of product planning?
2. What role does a retailer play in the successful introduction of a new consumer product?
3. What changes have occurred in the management capabilties of retailers? How have these changes affected manufacturers?
4. What expectations do retailers generally have regarding distribution service?
5. Would consumers be better served if retailers became more influential in channel structures? Give reasons for your answer.

5

LOGISTICS: ESSENTIAL TO STRATEGY

James L. Heskett

The ways a firm can use the logistical areas of transportation, warehousing, and inventory to more effectively implement marketing strategies are outlined in this article, which also provides an overview of the physical distribution concept.

Logistics can spell the difference between success and failure in business. For example, a few years ago a young engineer-entrepreneur began to build a company from scratch. His first product was liquid bleach. Actually, he didn't know much about the business at the time. He knew that liquid bleach is nearly all water and that the U.S. market is divided among two large manufacturers, Clorox and Purex, and a number of smaller producers that sell branded and private-label bleach on a regional basis. He also knew that the market for private-label bleach in New England, where he wanted to be, was dominated by a manufacturer located in New Jersey.

So the entrepreneur decided to found a private-label bleach manufacturing company near Boston. This location provided his company with a distinct transport cost advantage over its chief competitor. But he didn't stop there. He located his plant near a concentration of grocery chain retail outlets. This enabled him to sell his bleach under an arrangement in which retailers' trucks were loaded with his bleach after making their retail deliveries and before returning to their respective distribution centers. Given this double cost advantage, he was able to go one step further. By adding other items to his product line, he was able to obtain efficient truckload orders from his retail chain customers.

Another new venture in which logistics plays a major role was set up by two honor students. On their graduation from business school, they devised an innovative, low-cost way to distribute a high volume of milk and other products. Building a retail "store" that consisted of a convenience-oriented self-service front end and a large truck dock in the rear, they have raw milk delivered by tank trucks and put into vats in the rear of the store. Milk and cream is then separated, homogenized, and bottled on site for sale direct to consumers at significantly lower prices than through traditional channels. Having expanded its line to include other food items often purchased in large quantities, this retailer now enjoys one of the highest sales-per-square-foot ratios of any retailer in the United States and does a volume of sales through its relatively small outlet that many supermarket operators would be pleased to achieve.

Logistics-oriented strategies are also important in large companies. As an example, one of the world's largest chemical manufacturers recently had to replace its ships. The ships carried materials in bulk from plants in the Caribbean to Gulf and East Coast ports for subsequent transfer to barges and rail cars for delivery to terminals at which customers' orders were packed into containers for final delivery by rail and truck. Instead of merely replacing its ships with more modern versions of the same design, the company instead is converting its entire distribution system to one using containers.

This system requires that orders processed in Puerto Rico be shipped in containers that will be delivered direct to customers in the eastern United States by a combination of river barge, rail, and truck. As a result (1) repackaging at all inland terminals eventually will be eliminated, (2) material handling costs and capacities at Gulf and East Coast port facilities will be greatly reduced, and (3) because of the increased frequency of departures of ocean-going container barges from plants, orders will be delivered to customers with little or no increase in order response time and only a small increase in total inventory in the the system. Because of the company's sales volume, it is unlikely that competitors will be able to emulate the program even though their geographic production and transport patterns are similar.

What do these examples have in common? They all involve decisions that are long-term in their implications. All involve actions that are big-dollar in relation to the overall size of the companies in which they are implemented. All provide a competitive advantage that, unlike pricing or other actions, is hard for competitors to duplicate. And they all are based on nontraditional approaches to logistics, encompassing those activities that facilitate product movement and the coordination of supply and demand in accomplishing specified cost and service objectives, as suggested in *Exhibit 1* [Table 1].

These are but three of a growing number of companies that place major reliance on logistics in their business strategies. In this article I shall explore reasons behind the rebirth of interest in this method of developing competitive advantages, the common elements of successful logistics-oriented strategies, the questions to be asked in auditing the extent to which your

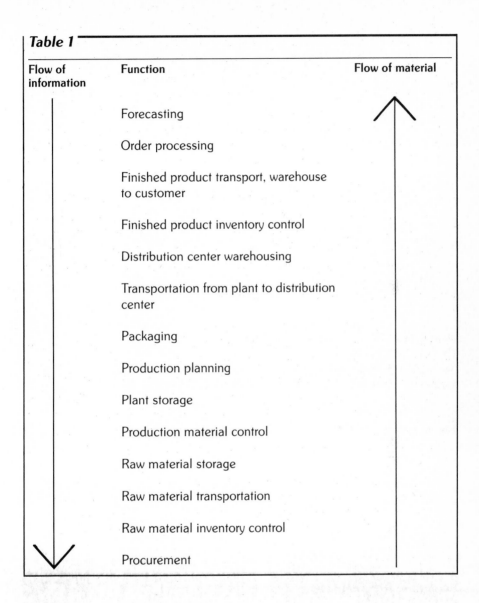

Table 1

Flow of information	Function	Flow of material
	Forecasting	
	Order processing	
	Finished product transport, warehouse to customer	
	Finished product inventory control	
	Distribution center warehousing	
	Transportation from plant to distribution center	
	Packaging	
	Production planning	
	Plant storage	
	Production material control	
	Raw material storage	
	Raw material transportation	
	Raw material inventory control	
	Procurement	

management has taken advantage of opportunities for making logistics an integral part of its strategy, and the ways of factoring logistics into strategy formulation.

Growing Influence of Logistics

There are a number of reasons for the growing influence of logistics in business strategy. Included among these are:

1. An increasing number of alternatives for meeting cost and service standards— containerization, minicomputers, air freight, and worldwide satellite communications systems.

2. The threat of energy shortages. During periods of energy shortages, transport costs may figure more heavily in plant and warehouse location decisions. And the locations of retail facilities from resorts to department stores may be influenced more strongly by their proximity to major markets.

3. Closer scrutiny of the long-standing trend toward complex product lines. To a greater extent, the threat of material shortages is injecting logistics as opposed to marketing considerations into product-line decisions.

4. The recent emphasis on effective inventory management through wide swings in business cycles characterized by varying rates of increase in labor costs, fluctuating interest costs, and changing rates of sales. This pressure has been accompanied by the assumption on the part of management that developments in computer-oriented inventory control methods have more than kept pace with user needs— an assumption not always borne out in practice.

5. The increasing involvement of federal and state agencies in issues ranging from the seminationalization of a portion of the transportation network to the availability of advertised sale merchandise on the shelves of retail establishments.

All these pressures are leading many companies to reexamine their view of logistics. What types of responses have these pressures elicited?

Patterns in Uncommon Responses

The increased size and complexity of business operations combined with the application of problem-solving techniques and computer technology have made it possible for many companies to consider less common logistical responses to perceived competitive cost or service disadvantages. Among these are strategies that involve postponement and speculation, standardization, consolidation, and differentiation.

Postpone & Speculate

Although they have done it intuitively for years, many companies are more systematically reviewing ways of postponing their commitment of resources to specific end products as long as possible in channels of distribution in order to reduce the risks of accumulating obsolete or unusable stocks. Others are willingly incurring the risks of speculation, involving the preparation of stocks in advance of need, in order to achieve economies of scale and lower the costs of production. Automobile manufacturers, for example, have pursued strategies of both postponement and speculation at different production and distribution stages.

Automakers practice postponement by operating market-oriented distribution centers at which relatively light manufacturing takes place. Although these facilities commonly are called assembly plants, they really are distribution centers equipped to receive orders, assemble automobiles to the individual desires of millions of prospective auto owners from stocks of standard components, and deliver individually designed autos to dealers and customers in a reasonable period of time.

Similarly, steel service (distribution) centers have become important distribution links for fabricated steel by bending, cutting, shaping, and even welding basic steel products to order. The wave of decentralized packaging of standard products shipped in bulk to distribution centers suggests that postponement will continue to be an effective means of providing a wide array of desired items from a smaller number of mass-produced and bulk-shipped finished components or ingredients.

In fact, postponement at one level in the distribution channel with an attendant decoupling of functions from those performed "upstream" has enabled automakers to enjoy the benefits of speculation from the mass production of a relatively small number of standard engines, bodies, and other major components, often at locations some distance from end markets. Steel manufacturers have been able to concentrate on mass production because of the growth of steel service centers. And canners of private-label food products process and pack their wares in "bright," unlabeled forms for labeling-to-order in response to later orders from hundreds of retailers.

Standardize Products

It stands to reason that standardization within product lines can reduce production costs, cut inventories, and increase field stock coverage while nevertheless providing the basis for differentiating end products. For example, General Motors is able to produce an endless number of lines, brands, and models of automobiles from its standard A, B, and C auto bodies.

Manufacturers of both consumer and industrial electronic products have created a standardized response to a variety of potential product failures by designing products around modules composed of several components. Given the failure of one or another of these components, the module composed of both operative and defective components can be replaced quickly and with little expertise.

In purchasing, a technique called value analysis has led on occasion to decisions to purchase fewer items and in larger quantities. This has resulted in price discounts and logistical savings that more than compensate for the application of standard components to tasks for which smaller, less-expensive components might be suited under programs not emphasizing standardization.

The potential for product standardization represents an important element of "slack" in the productive capacity of many companies. As an illustration, after it had cut its product line in half late in 1973 in response to soaring demand and restricted capacity, one manufacturer of white papers found that it could achieve 116% of the theoretical capacity of its mills through reduced machine setups. This discovery has led to more stringent guidelines in this company for the evaluation of new-product proposals.

Consolidate Services

For the most part, consolidation involves practices that encourage the simultaneous storage, long-haul transportation, or delivery of two or more products or orders to achieve economies of scale. It does not have to be achieved at the cost of reduced customer service. An example is that during the most recent recession many companies began to schedule orders for delivery on a once- or twice-per-week basis rather than whenever they were received. Suppliers could maintain speed of service for many customers under these programs by advising them of scheduled shipping dates so that those located in particular areas to which consolidated shipments were destined could time their orders to coincide with the schedules. This practice provided an acceptable level of service while maximizing use of limited fuel and lowering delivery costs significantly.

The use of shared or pooled services such as common carrier transport, shippers' cooperatives, and public warehouses is another form of consolidation.[1] Potential savings from the use of shared services have led many manufacturers to consider joint efforts with makers of complementary products requiring similar logistical efforts. In one case, a large manufacturer of grocery products recently sought out other companies selling products to identical kinds of customers to explore joint approaches to distribution for one of its product line's "problem children," a limited-volume item with somewhat distinctive distribution needs.

In another case, a pasta manufacturing company distributed its product daily in Manhattan by using trucks that could only be loaded partially because of the small number of deliveries possible in a given day in the city. Thus, it sought to find another grocery-product manufacturer desiring frequent deliveries in Manhattan for a joint distribution venture. And beer manufacturers in Canada have for some years maintained a joint venture for the retail delivery of their products. Many of these efforts have resulted from the

---

[1] Walter F. Friedman has described many of these services in *Physical Distribution: The Concept of Shared Services* (Thinking Ahead), HBR March-April 1975, p. 24; for a discussion of other examples, see my article, "Sweeping Changes in Distribution," HBR March-April 1973, p. 123.

realization that once a delivery vehicle stops, the costs of delivery are relatively insensitive to the size of the delivery.

Consolidation programs require products with homogeneous characteristics or logistics needs. Thus it is no surprise that the most successful consolidation programs undertaken with other manufacturers have been achieved in the distribution of product groupings such as frozen foods, drug products, and dry grocery products. Many of these programs have been able to reduce the actual costs of distribution beyond the field warehouse by as much as 40%.

Differentiate Distribution

For some years, many managers intuitively have recognized potential economies from the differentiated treatment of various product-line items in their distribution. For example, using ABC inventory methods managers establish more restrictive inventory rules for high-value , low-sales-volume items than for others in a product line. This effort reduces inventory holding costs in relation to a given sales volume. . . .

Given the increasing number of logistical choices available to competing companies, opportunities for the development of more extensive programs for differentiated product distribution present themselves. As an illustration, several years ago a major farm equipment manufacturer, confronted with a growing line of replacement parts and with deteriorating service to its dealers and customers, revamped its parts distribution strategy.

Up to that time, its logistics system for parts consisted of a mail and phone order program in which a dealer would contact the manufacturer's nearest regional parts depot of 12 located throughout the United States. Regional depots would either fill all or part of an order and refer the remainder to a sister depot, which might or might not have those items that were found to be out of stock at the first location.

The weekly update of regional depot inventories often produced inaccurate knowledge of inventory availability on the part of order takers. So-called "standard" orders were shipped to dealers by surface methods. Dealers could designate emergency orders, which were then shipped by the fastest method with transportation costs billed to the dealer. One indicator of the ineffectiveness of the system was that a growing proportion of orders were emergencies.

As a result of its review, the company decided to reduce the number of items stocked in its regional depots and to create a complete stock of all items at a master depot located near Chicago. A real-time method of inventory accounting was created. Electronic terminals were provided for many dealers. On receipt of an order, a regional depot would ship those high-sales-volume items in its stock by surface methods to its dealer. Items not in stock were ordered from Chicago. These items were packed immediately for next-morning shipment by air in containers destined for each regional depot.

As a result of this program, dealers were assured of nearly complete order availability in a short period of time; reductions in inventory holding costs more than compensated the company for increased transportation costs; and customer goodwill improved significantly. In fact, the manufacturer gained a reputation throughout the industry for having an outstanding parts supply program achieved by means of a differentiated distribution system.

While postponement and speculation, standardization, consolidation, and differentiation are all means of achieving strategic competitive advantage, a conscious program of review must be maintained to ensure that they are not overlooked in formulating strategy.

Factoring Logistics into Strategy

To employ logistics as an effective competitive lever and as a significant component of strategy, management must take two actions. First, it must adapt logistics programs to support ongoing corporate strategies in the short term. Second, it must factor logistics into the design of business operating strategies on a continuing long-term basis. Steps necessary to ensure this include the performance of a logistics strategy audit, possible logistics system redesign, and the maintenance of procedures to ensure continued attention to logistics as an integral element of corporate strategy.

Strategy Audit

A first step in achieving this objective can begin immediately in the form of an audit to explore strategic questions such as the following:

1. *What levels of service (a) do our customers expect? (b) do our competitors provide?*

Factors influencing answers to these questions include the degree of loyalty that customers exhibit in the purchase of the company's products and of its competitors', the criticality of the company's products to customers, the influence of its service on sales, and the costs of supplying varying levels of service. As I mentioned in the ruled insert, customer expectations and competitive levels of service may vary from product to product and from one geographic area to another.

It is not surprising that perhaps the highest levels of product support services are provided by manufacturers who maintain ownership of products they distribute. Revenues of the Xerox Corporation, largely derived from royalties assessed on each page of copy produced by its machines, immediately reflect machine downtime. As a result, Xerox's army of service personnel has reached division size (about 12,000) and its parts distribution system has received a great deal of scrutiny in its effort to maintain a service program that can put a disabled machine anywhere in the continental United States back into operation within three hours after it ceases production.

At a time when their technological leadership is being threatened by expiring patents and eager competitors, companies like Xerox and IBM may well have to rely on their service programs to maintain the strategic advantage that they have enjoyed in their respective industries for years.

Wholesalers and retailers must ask themselves the same questions. Answers may lead to alterations in buying and stocking policies as well as in warehouse and store location. For traders and manufacturers alike, service goals will influence inventory levels and locations as well as transport and customer order processing methods employed.

2. *How do competitors achieve the service levels that we think they achieve?*

Answers to this question require the preparation of a competitive product flow plan, based on information about competitors' plant locations, production strategies, warehouse locations, and methods of transportation. Most if not all of this information exists in the collective, unrecorded knowledge of members of the organization who spend a great deal of their time in the field in contact with customers and others. It need only be collected and organized in a systematic fashion.

There is little reason today why a competitor's logistical product flows and attendant costs cannot be simulated in the same manner as those of in-house logistics operations. In an informal poll of logistics managers in attendance at a professional seminar, I found that managers from about 15% of the companies with representatives at the meeting already collect these data on an informal basis. Information of this type is important in responding to the next two questions.

3. *Through how many outlets should we distribute our products? Of what type? Where?*

Retailers have long since identified location as a major element of service and sales in their businesses. The area from which a retail outlet draws its business depends on the type of goods sold, the size of the store, the degree to which competing stores sell identical or comparable merchandise, and the importance associated with the purchase of its products by consumers. These factors determine the density of retail locations and the geographic intensity with which various types of retail goods are offered for sale.

The number and type of wholesale outlets for a product are determined by customer service needs ranging from those associated with sales assistance to product availability. Some wholesalers may concentrate on promotional effort while performing no logistical (product stocking) function, leaving it to retailers or manufacturers to supply the latter.

Among manufacturers, there has been a general reduction in the number of warehouses through which products of any one company are distributed. This probably has resulted from a combination of factors, including increased attention to costs of distributing through too many warehouses, improved methods of order processing and transportation, and a vastly improved highway system, which has extended the territory that can be served from a given warehouse location.

4. Are our plants located and focused properly to support corporate strategy?

By definition, a plant location becomes outdated before the paint is dry on the facility. This question of location becomes important only when an existing location is at such odds with the company's logistical needs that economic savings from a move are more than enough to compensate for the economic and psychic costs of the move.

Of greatest interest in the logistics study audit, however, is the extent to which the location of producing facilities can provide the very core of a corporate strategy, as in the case of the private-label bleach manufacturing business cited earlier. Production processes that rely heavily on ubiquitous raw materials such as water will require market-oriented facilities. Those involving large weight reductions (as in the production of metal from ore) will logically be located near sources of raw materials. Those requiring large sources of inexpensive power (such as the smelting of aluminum from alumina) may obtain competitive advantage by locating producing facilities near such power sources.

The degree to which plants are focused on the production of one or a limited number of products in a larger product line may be influenced by the economies of scale in production, the extent to which production can be concentrated in a small number of product modules or components for subsequent assembly to order, and the overall volume of demand for the output of one plant from a given customer. An examination of the benefits of a focused production strategy may require an analysis of the logistical costs of mixing (assorting) required by focused plant operations as opposed to the costs of small shipment and mixed shipment transportation and handling required by an unfocused plant production strategy. This leads naturally to the next question in the audit.

5. Where is our company on the logistics life cycle for all or a portion of its business?

A manufacturing company may begin its life cycle by scheduling small quantities of production at a single facility for local or regional distribution.

As sales volumes increase, more efficient production and shipment quantities are achieved, reducing costs of logistics in the cost profile of the company. At this point, additional plants may be established, each of which may be focused on a portion of the product line. Sales territories are extended. Logistics networks become more complicated, often involving the operation of large numbers of market-oriented warehouses to minimize the cost of delivering small orders. Product-line extensions and customer orders of increasing size may, at some point, permit the mixing of carload and truckload orders at locations intermediate to plants and markets through the use of distribution centers, such as those established by General Foods.

With the continued growth of individual customer orders, it may once again become possible to ship directly from plants to customers, as in the initial stage of the company's life cycle. But this time the shipments may comprise single products moving in vehicle-load quantities.

Each stage of the logistics life cycle may require different manufacturing policies, plant and warehouse locations, and transportation and order processing methods. Awareness of the logistics life cycle can reduce the lag between needs produced by changes in corporate strategy and appropriate logistical responses.

6. *Have we taken advantage of the full potential for postponement and speculation, standardization, consolidation, and differentiation in our logistics programs?*

Opportunities associated with these strategies were discussed earlier.

7. *To what extent have we assured ourselves that our strategy meets desired levels of costs and services where it counts most, to the end-user?*

Earlier I described a logistics program that improved one farm equipment manufacturer's ability to respond to its dealers' needs for replacement parts and that enabled the company to establish a reputation for logistics leadership. Recently a competing manufacturer decided to measure the level of service delivered by its own much-maligned system and that provided by the well-publicized system of its competitor.

Its survey revealed that end-users perceived no significant differences in the levels of service delivered by the two systems. Puzzled by these results, the study team decided to investigate comparative dealer practices as well. This investigation revealed that its competitors' dealers had come to rely on the company's excellent system so heavily that they had reduced their inventories of spare parts below the levels required to maintain a high level of service to customers. The concerned manufacturer's dealers, on the other hand, had experienced such poor support from their supplier that they maintained a much larger stock of parts on their premises, thus taking up the slack in the system.

This suggests the need to ask the next question as part of the audit.

8. *To what extent have we employed "channel vision" in determining who should do what, when, where, and how in our channels of distribution? Have we taken steps to ensure that all parties carry out their functions as planned?*

A good example of "channel vision" is provided by Theodore Levitt's description of the Honeywell Tradeline program, implemented several years ago.[2] At that time the company was distributing its 18,000 separate catalog parts and pieces through 100 company warehouses to some 5,000 distributors, few of whom carried adequate replacement parts stock. Distributors instead were relying on Honeywell to maintain their inventory. As a result, the manufacturer was losing a lot of business and so it devised the Tradeline program.

In essence, the program transformed the inventory maintenance function to distributors through (1) redesigning original equipment with standard, interchangeable parts, some of which were compatible with competitors' products, (2) closing all Honeywell field parts warehouses, and (3) requiring distributors to maintain full stocks of all Honeywell replacement modules. Although Honeywell lost most of its distributors in implementing the Tradeline program, the stronger ones who remained formed the nucleus of a group that helped Honeywell achieve rapidly increasing sales in the years following initiation of the program.

9. *What implications do technological trends have for our company?*

In my previous article, which I referred to earlier, I suggested that the rate of technological change in logistics may not keep pace in the intermediate-term future with that of the recent past. However, logistics is a technology-prone activity. Investments in technology often yield handsome returns, suggesting continued efforts of significant magnitude.

Research expenditures today may be reasonably good predictors of the direction of technological development. Because the government plays such an active role in funding research into logistics technology, government budget allocations may provide clues for strategic planning. For example, it is a pretty good bet that a larger proportion of attention will be devoted to the development of methods and energy sources providing for the uninterrupted flow of goods *at any cost* rather than to the most cost-effective technologies. As environmental constraints close in on us, larger shares of effort will be redirected in this manner. To the extent that they favor one method of transportation over another, technological developments may raise logical

---

[2]Theodore Levitt, "Production-Line Approach to Service," HBR September-October 1972, p. 41.

questions about the proper orientation of a company's facilities in relation to those of its competitors.

10. *What implications do regulatory trends have for us?*

In the past, much regulatory activity in the field of logistics has been of an economic nature, particularly associated with transportation rates and operating rights. The recent ground swell of support for economic deregulation of various aspects of logistics has been accompanied by more laws stipulating noneconomic restrictions concerning matters as diverse as housekeeping procedures in the maintenance of sanitation standards in warehouses (with at least one chief executive indicted under this law) to restrictions on the movement of hazardous materials.

The future may bring even more attention to matters of a more strategic nature, including the legality of certain geographic practices that discourage freight-on-board (as opposed to destination- or market-oriented) pricing. In several instances, the Federal Trade Commission has even become interested in the quantities of advertised merchandise maintained in stock in support of special promotional efforts.

11. *Does our logistics strategy support our corporate strategy? To what extent should our strategy be logistics-oriented?*

On what markets and market segments does the corporate strategy rely most heavily? Is this reflected in the program of differentiation (if one exists) practiced in the corporation's logistics efforts?

Does the corporate strategy envision important compromises in, for example, the decoupling of manufacturing processes to achieve lower costs through the creation of larger in-process or finished product inventories? Will the logistics system accommodate this strategy?

What does the financial plan imply for the ownership of transport equipment, warehouses, inventories, and order-processing and other communication facilities?

Does the relative importance of logistics cost or service levels in the total "package" offered to customers suggest an important means for differentiating the company from its competitors? To what extent can the ideas suggested earlier be applied to accomplish this in formulating corporate strategy?

System Redesign

A strategic audit may reveal so much conflict between corporate strategy and logistics methods that a logistics system redesign is called for. While the audit may provide some of the data necessary for the preparation of a systems analysis effort dealing with specific customer service standards, product flows, and the like, other questions will have to be answered to supply the information needed for system redesign. Such questions, along with techniques for system redesign, have been described extensively in these pages and elsewhere.[3]

This is not to suggest that the impact of a strategy audit will be only on the design of the logistics system. It should also lead to the establishment of a vehicle to ensure continued attention to the potential for achieving strategic advantages through logistics when corporate strategy is being formulated or altered.

Longer-Term Actions

The strategy audit and any resulting logistics system redesign or corporate strategy adjustment will serve to bring logistics efforts into alignment with corporate needs in the short term. Unless some formalization of the process takes place, however, there is little guarantee that logistical considerations will continue to be taken into account in the strategy formulation process. The examples that I cited at the outset of this article serve to suggest ways by which this may be accomplished.

First, top management holds nearly all of the cards in the process. Managers responsible for various logistics functions have not, in the course of their work, had access to the goals and strategies formulated by top management. Quite appropriately, their goals and views have been relatively short-range and nonstrategic in nature. Ironically, they have participated least in decisions that have had the greatest long-run impact on their performance, as suggested in *Exhibit II* [Table 2]. All of this indicates that if a vehicle is to be found to raise logistical considerations to an appropriate level of awareness in the strategy formulation process, top management will have to take the initiative.

Second, entrepreneurs have formulated some of the most remarkable logistics-oriented business strategies. The entrepreneur wears so many hats that he or she embodies the wedding between top management and logistical considerations in the strategy formulation process. But what of the large corporation in which organizational differentiation necessarily has created both specialized responsibility and a widening gulf between top functional logistics management?

Here the experience of the large chemical manufacturer may be enlightening. This producer carefully maintains a liaison between functional and long-range planning personnel. Members of logistics groups in operating divisions that are responsible for shorter-range planning and for maintaining

---

[3] See, for example, John F. Magee, "The Logistics of Distribution," HBR July-August 1960, p. 89.

Table 2	**PARTICIPATION IN STRATEGIC DECISION MAKING**	
Degree of participation by logistics management	**Nature of decision**	**Degree and length of impact of decision on operations**

Least   *Most*

Locating a new plant

Setting customer service standards

Changing geographic pricing policies

Recombining products to be produced at various plants

Changing marketing territories

Establishing long-term purchase contracts with major suppliers

Introducing a new product line

Redesigning inventory control procedures

Redesigning order-processing procedures

Selecting a method of transportation

Locating a warehouse

Changing the allocation of business to carriers, public warehousers, or other suppliers

Most   *Least*

an awareness of current problems are kept informed of those elements of corporate strategy that might influence their thinking. Conversely, a member of the corporate long-range planning group purposely maintains both an acquaintance with trends in the logistics "environment" and a line of communication with members of the logistics planning groups found in the operating divisions of the company as well as at the corporate level.

By this means, a member of the logistics planning group was able to sense the need and appropriate timing for the proposed system that required a major revision in the business strategy employed by one of the corporation's divisions. Because of the open lines of communication between long-range planning, logistics planning, and operating managers within the division, it was possible to "sell" the concept both to the division management and to top management.

Given the focus of attention among larger companies on the reorganization of management for logistics activities in recent years, a growing number of companies have staffed their logistics-oriented departments with managers capable of being included in the process of formulating strategy in this manner.

Finally, those companies that have achieved some success in structuring some part of their strategies around logistical considerations have, in many cases, been the same ones that have (1) staffed senior positions in logistics with individuals capable of being promoted to general management positions, (2) viewed logistics as an important step in a program to produce well-rounded general managers, and (3) looked to logistics to provide its share of general managers along with marketing, finance, production, engineering, control, and other major functions.

It is no surprise that members of general management at companies such as PPG, Eastman Kodak, Xerox, General Foods, and Johnson & Johnson have consistently maintained a high level of awareness of the potential for developing competitive strategies based to a substantial degree on logistical considerations.

Corporate Strategy of the Future

If the arguments for the systematic consideration of logistics in formulating corporate strategy in a healthy company primarily serving domestic markets are not sufficiently appealing, there are compelling reasons for considering them more seriously in the future. The reasons include a decline in the growth rate of domestic markets, large incremental costs of energy, and an increasing emphasis on multinational markets in corporate strategies.

Rapid corporate growth conceals many blemishes of poor decision making and operating inefficiencies. And while individual organizations will continue to wax and wane in the future, in general there will be fewer growth opportunities on which to rely in a stable population increasingly concerned about its consumption rates. This will lead to a shift from emphasis on growth per se to what might be called the quality of earnings, obtained through the prudent control of costs required to serve relatively slow-growing markets and sales bases. Logistical considerations will weigh heavily in programs designed to improve the quality of earnings.

There is little doubt now that the most rapidly growing cost to doing business in the foreseeable future will be that of energy. Inevitable energy allocation and conservation programs will involve significantly higher costs of one sort or another. Energy-intensive activities of transportation and materials handling will represent increasingly important methods of gaining competitive advantage in costs and of improving the quality of earnings. The most effective means for obtaining such results will not be through tactical decisions such as a shift from one method of transportation to another. Rather, strategic facility locations, for example, will be primary determinants of the quality of earnings produced from logistics cost advantages.

With the inevitable slowing of certain domestic markets, U.S. producers will look abroad to a growing involvement in multinational business. To the extent that this will involve importation and exportation of goods, whether as part of an export program or as a truly multinational production and distribution strategy, multinational business can be much more logistics-intensive than can domestic business.

Attention to logistics can support expanded product lines in good times or provide a basis for gaining a competitive profit edge during periods of slow growth. Whether the goal is increased market shares or increased profits from existing or smaller market shares, logistics considerations can be basic to these accomplishments. If, as many have predicted, general management inevitably will have to spend an increasing proportion of its time dealing with low or no growth situations, it is not too early to put in place a process to ensure that logistical considerations will not be overlooked in formulating strategy.

QUESTIONS

1. Describe some of the ways that logistics can have an impact on the profits of a firm.

2. Why has logistics become so important in recent times? Do you expect its importance to remain high in the future? Why?

3. Describe the logistical responses discussed in the article. What are the unique characteristics of each response?

4. What basic steps should be taken to effectively include logistics into a firm's marketing strategy?

5. What is channel vision? How can a manager acquire this perspective?

PART FIVE

Promotion

Promotional decisions involve a number of activities that enable a firm to communicate its marketing strategy to its markets. In general, these activities are grouped into the areas of advertising, personal selling, sales promotion, and publicity. Communication, though, takes place through every aspect of the firm's strategy and cannot be completely restricted to the promotional areas listed above.

The objective of promotion is to develop in the market segments positive attitudes and behavior toward the firm and its products. The decisions that must be made to achieve this objective involve determining what message is to be communicated to whom; which promotional tools should be used to deliver this message; how to implement the promotional tools selected; and how to fund and coordinate the various promotional areas. The articles selected for Part Five focus on the last two types of decisions. They describe how advertising, personal selling, and sales promotion decisions should be made and how these areas should be coordinated to achieve an overall communication objective.

As implied earlier, the essence of promotion is communication. "A Decision Sequence Analysis of Developments in Marketing Communications," the lead article in Part Five, examines the role of communications in a marketing plan and shows how the various promotional activities should be coordinated within this plan. The remaining articles discuss the factors involved in making decisions in specific promotional areas.

Advertising is a major area of concern, both because of the level of advertising expenditures allocated by firms and because of the presumed powerful impact it has on society and the economy. "A New Look at 'Old' Advertising Strategy" describes techniques involved in implementing an advertising plan. Next, the communication objectives that underlie one of the most successful advertising campaigns ever launched are described in "Confession of a Creative Chief: 'I Squeezed the Charmin.'"

Sales promotion involves activities such as contests, coupons, premiums, free samples, and other incentives to stimulate sales. Although the use of sale promotion has been growing, the extent to which it is managed has often not kept pace. "Sales Promotion—Fast Growth, Faulty Management" provides guidelines for more effective management of this area of promotion.

The final article, "Manage Your Sales Force as a System," focuses on the area of personal selling, and develops guidelines for an effective sales management program.

1

A DECISION SEQUENCE ANALYSIS OF DEVELOPMENTS IN MARKETING COMMUNICATION

Michael L. Ray

This article describes a marketing communication mix and outlines the informational and decisional requirements for developing a specific mix. In addition to identifying the decisions that have to be made, the article provides the procedures to make those decisions.

Marketing communication is an area of marketing that provides a unique perspective for looking at the entire field of marketing. This subfield, consisting of a group of functional activities that may be listed under promotion, has existed since modern marketing began. Yet, only within the last decade have serious attempts been made to consolidate personal selling, advertising, packaging, point-of-purchase, direct mail, product sampling, publicity, and public relations under "marketing communication." Marketers have only recently begun to view the area of communication in the sophisticated way possible with today's advanced behavioral and quantitative tools. [1]

These developments have produced the normal amount of failures and false starts typical when new techniques are employed. It now appears,

[1] For example, Edward L. Brink and William T. Kelley, *The Management of Promotion* (Englewood Cliffs, N.J.: Prentice Hall, 1963); Edgar Crane, *Marketing Communication* (New York: John Wiley and Sons, 1965); James F. Engel, Hugh G. Wales and Martin Warshaw, *Promotional Strategy*, Revised Edition (Homewood, Illinois: Richard D. Irwin, 1971); and Frederick E. Webster, Jr., *Marketing Communication: Modern Promotional Strategy* (New York: The Ronald Press Company, 1971).

however, that marketing communication is beginning to produce some tangible contributions. The promise of a synergistic effect and more profitable performance in promotional activities due to the application of scientific tools is finally being realized.

This article documents the progress made in the implementation of marketing communication. First, marketing communication is defined in terms of an information gathering and decision sequence which links all elements of the communication mix. Second, the decision sequence and each of its steps is described in terms of the tools now available to decision makers. Finally, the impending developments in the field are discussed.

A Decision Sequence

The focal point of the development of marketing communication is the series of decisions that have to be made to carry it out. These decisions have both caused and have been influenced by the developments and applications of modern scientific tools. The general decision sequence commonly used to develop corporate marketing communication has not changed dramatically. Generally, this sequence consists of the following steps:

1. A situation analysis must be performed in order to determine the company's strengths, weaknesses, and general objectives; analyze the product, the consumer, and the trade.
2. Marketing sales objectives can be set.
3. The kinds of communication activities can be considered that are necessary to accomplish the objectives. The manager must formulate a coordinated plan, with each component carrying its proper share of the burden.
4. A series of specific decisions must be made for each communication element. These will include the communication goals for each element, the communication positioning, message factors, and the message distribution plan.
5. Budgets are set and control procedures are instituted in order to evaluate the communication program.

This general decision process for marketing communication has evolved over the years into the specific and sophisticated sequence illustrated in Figure 1. The decision sequence indicates (1) the relationship between communication functions and other elements of the mix; (2) the links between the various components of the communication mix; (3) the common decisions involved in each of the components of the mix; (4) the common utilization of both communication and sales goals; and (5) the possibilities for adaptation in the decision process based on new information and ongoing decisions.

These five major issues are seldom stated clearly in descriptions of the marketing communication process. Therefore, this lack of attention has greatly retarded the development of marketing communication. The issues are discussed more fully below.

The Communication Mix and Other Marketing Functions

The communication functions in Figure 1 are primarily promotional. They relate to other aspects of the mix through the situation analysis and marketing objectives stages. The situation analysis is explained in communication terms. Although product, price, and channels are not part of the communication mix, they and other parts of the situation are considered because of their communication implications. For example, if products are developed through perceptual mapping procedures,[2] some researchers suggest that the nature of the communication message is predetermined; i.e., all messages should only communicate those product characteristics which are salient to consumers.[3]

How Communication Functions are Linked Together

Marketing communication has not worked very efficiently in the past because little apparent commonality existed among the communication functions. How can a manager simultaneously deal with such disparate activities as sales territory assignment, advertising copy writing, and liaison with publications for publicity purposes? The answer is found in Figure 1. The manager allocates financial resources to the functions on the basis of expected response. This tentative budget mix is altered only if decisions and research within each function indicate a need for more or less support. The manager's ability to establish accurate budgets is increased greatly if an information system is used to provide data for evaluation and control. Present and future models for this purpose are discussed in the following sections.

Similar Decisions Across Components

Marketers could not effectively implement marketing communication unless decisions were somewhat similar across communication functions. In fact, communication activities can be efficiently integrated only because they consist of similar, yet different, decisions. As shown in Figure 1, there are essentially five decision areas common to all communication types—com-

---

[2] Edgar A. Pessemier and H. Paul Root, "The Dimensions of New Product Planning," JOURNAL OF MARKETING, Vol. 37 (January, 1973), pp. 10–18.

[3] Volney Stefflre, "Market Structure Studies: New Products for Old Markets and New Markets (Foreign) for Old Products," in *Application of the Sciences in Marketing Management*, Frank Bass, Edgar A. Pessemier, and Charles King, eds. (New York: John Wiley and Sons, 1968).

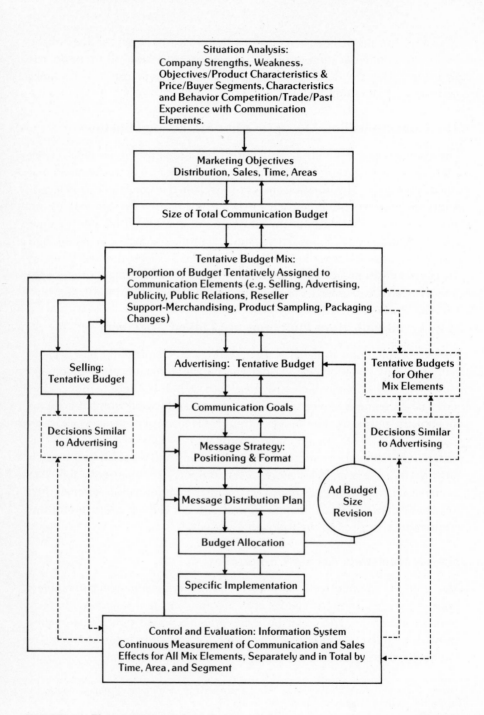

FIGURE 1   *The sequence of marketing communication information gathering and decisions.*

munication goals, message strategy, message distribution plan, budget allocation, and implementation. Since these exist for all communication functions, decision making and research information can be applied to all functions. For example, a message strategy designed and tested for advertising may have a clear application in selling, publicity, or direct-mail promotion. For communication goal decisions, comparisons across functions are made to determine which function can best accomplish each type of communication goal.

Sales and Communication Goals Reconciled

At one time some marketers viewed these two types of goals as being incompatible. They are reconciled in Figure 1. Sales are the most important goal for the marketing communication program, making sales response the key variable to consider in allocating the tentative budget across elements of the communication mix. Communication goals, such as awareness and attitude change, are still quite important to decision making because they are the focal point for decisions on the use of funds for advertising, selling, and so forth. Thus, both sales and communication goals must be coordinated for the marketing communication decision process to work properly.

Adaptive Decisions

A process is "adaptive" if it includes procedures for gathering information and adapting on the basis of that information. The decision sequence shown in Figure 1 is adaptive in that a number of feedback points are used to change the system in accordance with new information and decisions. For instance, the original budget mix is only tentative, and an analysis of the communication elements may lead to a budget-size revision. This feedback loop is shown for only the advertising decisions in Figure 1, but the same reanalysis and feedback would be done for every communication element.

Another series of adaptive loops comes out of the bottom "control and evaluation: information system" box of Figure 1. The results of past campaigns may indicate changes in communications goals, message strategy, and message distribution plan. These loops are shown in the center of the figure for the advertising decision sequence. A final important adaptive feedback loop is shown on the left side of the figure. It indicates that campaign results as measured by the information system would be accounted for in the tentative budget allocation in the next planning period.

Most of the applications of quantitative and behavioral tools discussed in the next section relate to this adaptive characteristic of the decision sequence in Figure 1. These developments involve new ways to collect information, new forms of decisions, and new adaptive models.

Present and Prospective Applications of Behavioral and Quantitative Techniques

The sequence in Figure 1 is both normative and descriptive. Marketing communication *should be* integrated in this way if it is to realize its full potential. Parts of this sequence *are operative* today with available behavioral and quantitative tools. These tools are reviewed below in the order of the steps in the Figure 1 decision sequence.

Methods for Determining Tentative Budgets

In order to allocate the budget among the communication elements, the manager must have knowledge of their sales responsiveness or elasticity. In other words, he needs an estimate of how his communication dollars work.

Two general methods have been developed to provide these critical estimates. A computer planning model is used to show the manager the implications of his estimates of responsiveness, while the other involves research and analysis to determine what the responsiveness actually is. Computer planning models have been successful devices for dealing with the tentative budget problem.[4] Because the budget is only tentative, any aid the manager can get makes very good use of his knowledge of the market.

These models typically have a data base which indicates past sales, expenditures, and some representation of how the communication and marketing mix elements work together. For each run of the model, the manager supplies a budget allocation and his estimate of the budget change-sales response for each mix element. The model then supplies a profit and loss statement for each time period. The manager continues to make runs of the model, changing budget and response coefficients, until he achieves an acceptable run in terms of reality and profitability.

The marketing communication decision process can then continue. The subsequent goals, message, and distribution decisions for each communication element are attempts to improve the response coefficient estimates. The budget size revision is actually a more sophisticated estimate of response for each element than the budget estimate.

If the manager wishes to go beyond his own sales response estimates, he can utilize one of several research methods which give empirical estimates of actual market response. Some researchers have developed models which

---

[4] Gerald Eskin, "Concorn Kitchens," unpublished paper, Graduate School of Business, Stanford University, 1970.

utilize both subjective judgments and empirical response data.[5] From a scientific standpoint, controlled experimentation is the best approach to gathering empirical response data. Test markets are assigned various weights of promotional expenditure, and sales measures are taken. A market group comparison indicates sales responsiveness which then can be used in establishing the budget.

Marketing is one of the few disciplines where services have been set up for field experimentation. In the 1960s, the Milwaukee Advertising Laboratory facilitated field experimentation within that city, and split cable television experimentation facilities are now available.[6] Several books on experimentation in marketing and communication are available, and success in long-term field experimentation has been reported by Budweiser and others.[7]

On the other hand, experimentation presents certain shortcomings. It is expensive; it cannot be done on a continuous basis; and it is only valid for the particular set of circumstances in which the experiment occurred. The practical alternative to experimentation is continuous campaign monitoring.

With campaign monitoring, measurements of sales and other market response are made on a periodic basis, ideally monthly. This is shown as the evaluation and control information system in Figure 1. These response measures can be related to expenditures during the time periods; therefore, responsiveness can be inferred. The response estimates can then be used to set tentative budgets.

Such information systems are becoming quite common.[8] Several researchers have concentrated on marketing communication effects. Maloney developed a system which made it possible to look at the relationship between

[5] Jean-Jacques Lambin, "A Computer On-line Marketing Model," *Journal of Marketing Research*, Vol. 9 (May, 1972), pp. 119–126; and John D. C. Little, "BRANDAID: An On-line Marketing Mix Model," Working Paper 586–72, Sloan School of Management, Massachusetts Institute of Technology, February, 1972.

[6] John Adler, "Adtel: A New Product Case History," *Journal of Advertising Research*, Vol. 12 (April, 1972), inside front cover advertisement; G. Maxwell Ule, "The Milwaukee Advertising Laboratory—Its Second Year," in *Proceedings of the 12th Annual Meeting of the Advertising Research Foundation*, 1966; and Edward Wallerstein, "Measuring Commercials on CATV," *Journal of Advertising Research*, Vol. 7 (June, 1967), pp. 15–19.

[7] Seymour Banks, *Experimentation in Marketing* (New York: McGraw-Hill, 1965); Jack B. Haskins, *How to Evaluate Mass Communications* (New York: Advertising Research Foundation, 1968); and Ambar G. Rao, *Quantitative Theories in Advertising* (New York: John Wiley and Sons, 1970).

[8] Alvin A. Achenbaum, *How Advertising Works: A Study of the Relationship Between Advertising, Consumer Attitudes and Purchase Behavior* (New York: Grey Advertising, 1968); and Henry Assael and George S. Day, "Attitudes and Awareness as Predictors of Market Share," *Journal of Advertising Research*, Vol. 8 (December, 1968), pp. 3–12.

media exposure and point-of-purchase deals in affecting purchase.[9] As the data bank of such a system becomes larger and more detailed, it becomes more and more valuable in determining response.

The problem with the information systems approach is in analysis. Lack of control means that causation (sales response) must be determined from correlation. In order to get around this problem, a number of econometric techniques have been applied to continuous market data. These have produced adequate indications of market response for planning purposes.

One econometric study on communication expenditures and response indicates that marketing communication is not often planned and evaluated consistently as Figure 1 indicates.[10] The primary output from the study was the response coefficient or elasticity for each of three pharmaceutical communication elements: journal advertising, samples and literature (distributed by detail men), and direct mail. The estimated elasticities for these three variables are shown in Table 1. Since these numbers relate changes in expenditure to changes in market share, the larger the number in the table, the greater the market response to that communication element. Although the elasticities in the table are only a sample of those developed in the study, their direction across communication elements is clear. The results show a substantial response to journal advertising, less to samples and literature, and much less to direct mail. Yet, the company's resource allocations are inversely related: most for direct mail, followed by samples and advertising. These results must be related to sales and profitability; however, a close examination and revision of the budget are needed.

Aside from illustrating the value of such research and the decision sequence, this study shows that it is difficult to consolidate communication elements without being biased toward a particular communication mix. In the pharmaceutical industry, the bias is toward direct mail and detail work. In consumer fields, there is a bias toward advertising. Without continuous information on market response, possibly in combination with the use of planning models, a particular communication mix is used continually without reevaluation. Each component of the mix is given a share of the budget, and planning continues without the consolidation and cross-comparison suggested in Figure 1. This situation will continue unless management science techniques are utilized more consistently.

---

[9] John C. Maloney, "Attitude Measurement and Formation," paper read at the AMA Test Marketing Workshop, Chicago, 1966, mimeo.

[10] David B. Montgomery and Alvin J. Silk, "Estimating Dynamic Effects of Marketing Communication Expenditures," *Management Science*, Vol. 18 (June, 1972), pp. 485–501.

Communication Goals

While the budget decision can be aided by management science tools, the key developments in setting communication goals have recently come from behavioral science.

The "hierarchy of effects" controversy blossomed in advertising and marketing in the early 1960s, but it is now a dead issue. One part of the controversy concerned whether the goals of marketing communication should be sales or some level on hierarchy of communication goals, such as awareness, comprehension, conviction, intention, or action. A series of studies make it clear that *both* sales and the hierarchy are necessary. They are not competitors. Sales provide a measure which can be used to test the market responsiveness of mix elements and thus set tentative budgets. Communication goals provide measures which are different for each of the mix elements. For example, advertising can achieve awareness and comprehension while personal selling aims may be conviction and action. While a sales goal does not in itself indicate what communicators must do, a goal of awareness or attitude change can indicate specific steps that must be taken in selling, advertising, or publicity to achieve the general sales goal.

Another aspect of the hierarchy controversy dealt with the relationship among and existence of the hierarchy stages. It was erroneously assumed within marketing that the hierarchy viewpoint presupposed a rigid set of stages, each linked together in a stair-step fashion; e. g., awareness must occur before comprehension, before conviction, before action.

Several interesting studies were done on this hypothesis; some found the stair-step relationship, and others found important deviations from it.[11] In fact, some suggestions for validation research have been made recently, so that the issue is not a closed one.[12]

But behavioral analysis and research indicates quite clearly that there are a number of alternative patterns of the communication effect which depend

---

[11] Alvin A. Achenbaum, "An Answer to One of the Unanswered Questions About Advertising Measurement," in *Proceedings of the 12th Annual Meeting of the Advertising Research Foundation*, 1966, pp. 24–32; Assael and Day, same reference as footnote 8; Henry J. Claycamp and Lucien E. Liddy, "Prediction of New Product Performance: An Analytical Approach," *Journal of Marketing Research*, Vol. 6 (November, 1969), pp. 414–420; Jack B. Haskins, "Factual Recall as a Measure of Advertising Effectiveness," *Journal of Advertising Research*, Vol. 4 (March, 1964), pp. 2–8; Herbert E. Krugman, "The Impact of Television Advertising: Learning Without Involvement," *Public Opinion Quarterly*, Vol. 29 (Autumn, 1965), pp. 349–356; and Kristian S. Palda, "The Hypothesis of a Hierarchy of Effects: A Partial Evaluation," *Journal of Marketing Research*, Vol. 3 (February, 1966), pp. 13–25.

[12] Leonard J. Parsons, "The Hierarchy of Effects Controversy: A Research Design," First Place Award, AMA Research Design Competition, 1971.

Table 1

LONG-RUN ELASTICITIES COMPARED TO RELATIVE EXPENDITURES FOR THREE COMMUNICATION ELEMENTS*

Communication Element	Long-run Elasticity	Relative Average Monthly Expenditures**
Journal Advertising	0.365	$1.209
Samples and Literature	0.108	$1.355
Direct Mail	0.018	$1.630

*Source: Montgomery and Silk, same reference as footnote 9.
**Not actual expenditures, but expressed so that relationships between expenditures for three components are preserved.

upon the buying situation. Thus, when the consumer is highly involved, it may be that the simple version of the hierarchy does hold. Under conditions of low involvement, the consumer may act before changing attitude.[13]

Some social psychologists assume that communication devices affecting one level of the hierarchy positively may quite consistently affect another level negatively.[14] Thus, humorous or sex-filled ads may attract attention and create awareness, but they may produce a negative effect on attitude toward the brand. The salesman who learns how his product relates to all aspects of his client's business may effectively apply this knowledge in generating conviction and action, but his emphasis on the client's business may draw attention away from his own product. Another example of this compensatory relationship between hierarchy levels occurs in publicity that generates comprehension of product features, but fails to generate name registration.

Several researchers have found that this "compensation" between levels of the hierarchy is not just speculation, but that it offers a possibility for better implementation of marketing communication.[15] If compensation between hierarchy levels is inevitable, or even frequent, then the elements of the

---

[13] Leo Bogart, *Strategy in Advertising* (New York: Harcourt, Brace and World, 1968); Krugman, same reference as footnote 11; and Michael L. Rothschild, "Two Types of Involvement: A Microtheoretical Notion," unpublished paper, Graduate School of Business, Stanford University, 1972.

[14] William J. McGuire, An Information Processing Approach to Advertising Effectiveness," in *The Behavioral and Management Sciences in Marketing*, Harry Davis and Alvin J. Silk, eds. (New York: Ronald Press, forthcoming); and Michael L. Ray and Alan G. Sawyer, "Behavioral Measurement for Marketing Models," *Management Science*, Vol. 18 (December, 1971), Part II, pp. 73–89.

[15] McGuire, same reference as footnote 14; Michael L. Ray and Alan G. Sawyer, "Repetition in Media Models: A Laboratory Technique," *Journal of Marketing Research*, Vol. 8 (February, 1971), pp. 20–30; and Michael L. Ray, Alan G. Sawyer and Edward C. Strong, "Frequency Effects Revisited," *Journal of Advertising Research*, Vol. 11 (February, 1971), pp. 14–20.

communication mix can be used to selectively deal with it. High awareness and negative attitude generated by advertising may be complemented by personal selling, product sampling, and point-of-purchase efforts with contrasting effects. In fact, "negative" byproducts of advertising, such as mild disbelief, may be converted to positive effects if other aspects of the mix are of high quality. [16]

Message Strategy: Positioning and Attitude Research

Message strategy consists of two parts: What is said, and how it is said. The "what" part has variously been called the copy platform, the unique selling proposition, the appeal, the brand image, the maker's mark, the message idea, and, most recently, the product positioning. [17] This most recent term is actually quite functional because it implies all the elements necessary at this stage of communication decision. The position consists of product appeals or characteristics to be communicated to target segments. The message can only be constructed with regard to the product's position in the market vis-à-vis buyers, competition, and trade. Each message should reflect this positioning whether it is transmitted through personal selling, packaging, samples, publicity, or advertising.

The positioning method is supported by recent advances in quantitative techniques. Attitude research has used nonmetric multidimensional scaling to position brands in a multidimensional space based on buyers' perceptions. [18] Managers use the perceptual map to decide how they might influence the position of their product. For instance, they can develop products to fill unsatisfied needs of the market, or they can attempt to change the positioning of their brand through communication. The positioning statement relates to both the dimensions of the map and the target market segment. Ambitious communication programs often attempt to switch dimensions or add completely new ones.

A related but different development that has influenced the positioning approach is the popularity of the Fishbein and Rosenberg attitude models. These models have generated a great deal of interest in marketing. They are based on the concept that a person's attitude toward a brand is due to the sum of the products of (a) that person's importance weights on each of the sa-

---

[16] John C. Maloney, "Is Advertising Believability Really Important?" JOURNAL OF MARKETING, Vol. 27 (October, 1963), pp. 1–8.

[17] Jack Trout and Al Ries, "The Positioning Era Cometh," *Advertising Age* (April 24, 1972), pp. 35 and 38.

[18] Alvin J. Silk, "The Use of Preference and Perception Measures in New Product Development: An Exposition and Review," *Industrial Management Review*, Vol. 11 (Fall, 1969), pp. 21–37; and Stefflre, same reference as footnote 3.

lient product characteristics, and (b) the rating of the brand on each characteristic.[19] The perceptual-map approach and the Fishbein-Rosenberg approach suggest several positioning alternatives, such as changing the importance weights or changing the brand's ratings on each of the characteristics.[20]

Several variants of the Fishbein-Rosenberg model have been used in certain purchasing situations. For instance, buyers sometimes use a lexicographic approach in which the salient product characteristics are ranked in terms of importance. The brands pass through a series of "gates" on the characteristics; e.g., if the brand meets the minimum quality criterion, it is judged on a price criterion, then convenience, and so forth. The brand remaining after this series of decisions is purchased. This lexicographic model has been used to describe cake mix purchasing and supermarket-buying committee decisions.[21]

Message Strategy: Format

Once the positioning statement is developed for each communication element, the manager has determined what appeals will be emphasized for each time period, geographic area, and market segment. The format question concerns how these appeals will be communicated. Should a one- or two-sided approach be used? A negative or positive approach? Emotional or rational? Hard or soft sell? What is the function of repetition and order within the message?

For advertising, the issues include: color versus black and white, types of media, ad size, and long versus short copy. For selling, the personality characteristics of salesmen vis-à-vis the customers have been found to be important. In general, however, the social psychological study of communication and persuasion has been found to have great value in planning the format of marketing messages.

Originally, the social psychological findings were adopted quite directly, but often with bad effect.[22] An example is the treatment of fear appeals. It had

---

[19] George S. Day, "Evaluating Models of Attitude Structure," *Journal of Marketing Research*, Vol. 9 (August, 1972), pp. 279–286.

[20] Harper W. Boyd, Jr., Michael L. Ray, and Edward C. Strong, "An Attitudinal Framework for Advertising Strategy," JOURNAL OF MARKETING, Vol. 36 (April, 1972), pp. 27–33.

[21] Gerald Eskin, "Hinesbury Mills (B)," unpublished paper, Graduate School of Business, Stanford University, 1972; and David B. Montgomery, "Initial Distribution: A Gate Keeping Analysis of Supermarket Buyer Decisions," paper presented at the Institute of Management Sciences fall meetings, Detroit, 1971.

[22] Donald Cox, "Clues for Advertising Strategists," *Harvard Business Review*, Vol. 39 (September-October, 1961), pp. 160–176; and Alan Greenberg, "Is Communication Research Really Worthwhile," JOURNAL OF MARKETING, Vol. 31 (January, 1967), pp. 48–50.

been assumed, on the basis of essentially one social psychological study, that fear or negative emotional approaches had no place in marketing communication strategy.[23]

Marketers now have developed their own analyses and research to examine not only fear appeals, but also issues such as the use of distraction, refutational approaches and immunization techniques, humor, sex, message size, source credibility, and distinctiveness.[24] Source credibility, diffusion of innovation, and opinion leadership studies have been conducted on personal selling effectiveness.[25]

While detailed communication research findings cannot be reviewed here, some examples give an idea of its wide range of application. Academic research has indicated that fear appeals are more effective with nonowners of insurance than with owners.[26] State Farm Insurance Company and others have been using fear appeals extensively in their home insurance ads. Avis, Hertz, Volkswagen, Philadelphia Electric Company, Renault, and Bayer have used refutational advertising. Some academic research has shown that the refutational approach is most effective among nonusers of the product and users of its competitive brands.[27] On the industrial front, source credibility of the firm (developed by advertising) was shown to significantly affect marketing

---

[23] Michael L. Ray and William L. Wilkie, "Fear: The Potential of an Appeal Neglected by Marketing," JOURNAL OF MARKETING, Vol. 34 (January, 1970), pp. 54–62.

[24] Stewart Bither, "Effects of Distraction and Commitment on the Persuasiveness of Television Advertising," *Journal of Marketing Research*, Vol. 9 (February, 1972), pp. 1–5; Leo Bogart, *Psychology in Media Strategy* (Chicago: American Marketing Association, 1966); McGuire, same reference as footnote 14; Bruce J. Morrison and Richard C. Sherman, "Who Responds to Sex in Advertising?" *Journal of Advertising Research*, Vol. 12 (April, 1972), pp. 15–19; Michael L. Ray, "The Present and Potential Linkages Between the Microtheoretical Notions of the Behavioral Sciences and the Problems of Advertising," in *The Behavioral and Management Sciences in Marketing*, Harry Davis and Alvin J. Silk (New York: The Ronald Press, forthcoming); and Alvin J. Silk and Frank P. Geiger, "Advertisement Size and the Relationship Between Product Usage and Advertising Exposure," *Journal of Marketing Research*, Vol. 9 (February, 1972), pp. 22–26.

[25] Donald Cox, ed., *Risk Taking and Information Handling in Consumer Behavior* (Boston: Division of Research, Harvard Business School, 1967); Theodore Levitt, *Industrial Purchasing Behavior* (Boston: Division of Research, Harvard Business School, 1965); and Thomas S. Robertson, *Innovative Behavior and Communication* (New York: Holt, Rinehart and Winston, 1971).

[26] John J. Wheatley, "Marketing and the Use of Fear- or Anxiety-arousing Appeals, JOURNAL OF MARKETING, Vol. 35 (April, 1971), pp. 62–64; Herbert Kay, "Do We Really Know the Effects of Using 'Fear' Appeals," JOURNAL OF MARKETING, Vol. 36 (April, 1972), pp. 55–57; and John J. Wheatley, "Research Methodology—How Much Emphasis?" JOURNAL OF MARKETING (forthcoming).

[27] Ray and Sawyer, same reference as footnote 14; and Alan G. Sawyer, "The Effects of Repetition of Refutational and Supportive Advertising Appeals," *Journal of Marketing Research* (forthcoming).

effectiveness.[28] For instance, when a salesman from a highly-regarded company (for instance, Monsanto) gave a relatively poor presentation, his evaluation by purchasing agents was much lower than was a comparable presentation by a salesman coming from a less well-regarded company.

One of the more intriguing questions in the message format area is to what extent computers can replace creative intuition. There is some indication that computers or management science models may assist the creative process. In brand and corporate naming, computers can be used to provide many alternatives to creative decision makers. In advertising, Diamond developed a regression model based on Starch readership scores.[29] The independent variables of the model were advertisement characteristics, such as size and proportion of illustration. Presumably, if a campaign goal was to maximize Starch scores, Diamond's model could be used to indicate the structural characteristics of the advertisement.

Gross developed an advertising model that can be used to determine how much should be spent on message development.[30] His model indicates that approximately three times more money should be spent on the creative process in advertising than is at present. Gross suggests that creativity in advertising should be managed by encouraging heterogeneity among alternatives and the development of valid testing methods.

Message Distribution Plan

The message distribution decisions provide the link between the creative message strategy input and the consolidating budget allocation and implementation steps. As such, the distribution decisions have generated new possibilities for the combination of behavioral input and management science models.

In advertising, media-scheduling models have forced managers to consider the interaction between various message strategies and distribution decisions.[31] Some media models allow managers to input different estimates of the response to repetitive exposures, for each media vehicle and market

---

[28] Levitt, same reference as footnote 25; and Theodore Levitt, "Communications and Industrial Selling," JOURNAL OF MARKETING, Vol. 31 (April, 1967), pp. 15–21.

[29] Daniel S. Diamond, "A Quantitative Approach to Magazine Advertisement Format Selection," *Journal of Marketing Research*, Vol. 5 (November, 1968), pp. 376–386.

[30] Irwin Gross, "An Analytical Approach to the Creative Aspects of Advertising Operations," *Sloan Management Review* (forthcoming).

[31] Dennis H. Gensch, "Media Factors: A Review Article," *Journal of Marketing Research*, Vol. 7 (May, 1970), pp. 216–225.

segment.[32] This kind of model puts new demands on behavioral research, thereby necessitating the development of pretesting techniques which will estimate the repetitive effects of various message alternatives. These estimates can then be used in the models to present a sophisticated picture of what the message alternatives might mean in market terms. This behavioral-model approach has already been applied with positive results.[33] Suggestions have been made for using this combination to validate both pretesting techniques and media models.[34]

In the personal selling area, models can be used to allocate sales force effort across products, salesmen calls across prospects, and salesmen over geographic areas.[35] As these models are developed, the same type of message strategy-distribution combination seen in advertising may apply to selling. In direct-mail promotion and sampling, computer use of data banks may also lead to this combination. The synergistic promise of marketing communication as originally conceived is finding potential realization in models and behavioral inputs at the message distribution decision point.

Budget Allocation

The first sequence of decisions for each communication element ends in a budget allocation for media, time, geography, and segments. This allocation is accomplished after the goals, message, and distribution decisions are made. The total process recycled for each element is the equivalent of what has been called the "objective and task" budgeting approach. In Figure 1, this budgeting approach takes on a new significance since it is used as a communication and planning check on the tentative budget. The revised budget for each element is based on much more information and planning than the tentative budget. These revised budgets are a statement of market responsiveness in communication terms rather than in sales terms only. The manager must decide whether to accept any or all of these revised budgets, adjust total budget size, or fall back on original budget statements. This may necessitate a new set of decision making through communication goals, message strategy, message

---

[32] David A. Aaker, "On Methods: A Probabilistic Approach to Industrial Media Selection," *Journal of Advertising Research*, Vol. 8 (September, 1968), pp. 46–55; and John D. C. Little and Leonard M. Lodish, "A Media Planning Calculus," *Operations Research*, Vol. 17 (January-February, 1969), pp. 1–35.

[33] Ray and Sawyer, same reference as footnote 14.

[34] Michael L. Ray, "A Behavioral-Laboratory-Model-Field Study of Alternate Message Strategies in Competitive Advertising Situations," Research Paper No. 83, Graduate School of Business, Stanford University, May, 1972.

[35] See "Special Issue on Marketing Management Models," David B. Montgomery, ed., *Management Science*, Vol. 18 (December, 1971), Part II.

distribution, and allocation. The cycling process for each communication element becomes part of what Little calls an "adaptive control" model. As in Figure 1, models of the communication process are built, they are tested in the market, and then adapted to specific market situations.[36]

The Key Role of Information Systems in Further Advances

Figure 1 represents the advances to date in the application of quantitative and behavioral tools to marketing communication. For further advances, managers must acquire data on communication response. The tentative budget allocation could be made on this information, as well as sales results information. Horizontal lines could be drawn across the "communication goals" boxes for the elements shown in Figure 1. Budgets could be allocated across elements by sales, communication goals, and positioning effects.

The type of control and evaluation system indicated in Figure 1, while often implemented partially, has not become the standard. One can only extrapolate from the few studies mentioned here to help understand the value of such information. If econometric response studies had specific information on which people were exposed to which messages, it would be possible to understand the response elasticities and to develop a very specific marketing communication plan.

Impending Developments

The decision sequence in Figure 1 could have been conceived ten years ago; however, it could not have been as properly implemented as it can be now. A decade ago, the only working media models were linear programming and simulation. The realistic on-line heuristic models and time sharing were not developed then as they are now. Comprehensive consumer behavior theories and models were not formulated ten years ago. The hierarchy of effects controversy was relatively new, as was the use of sales experimentation. Nonmetric, multidimensional scaling was not known, much less used as a tool for communication and product positioning. Marketing information systems were only discussed in general terms, and very few were in existence. Linking laboratory behavioral research findings to specific computer models was only a vague idea. Even the concept of the marketing communication process was just being introduced in marketing textbooks.

What is in store for marketing communication in the next ten years? The changes will primarily involve an increased use and development of tech-

---

[36] John D. C. Little, "A Model of Adaptive Control of Promotional Spending," *Operations Research*, Vol. 14 (November-December, 1966), pp. 1075–1097.

niques already available. As these techniques are applied in actual research situations, they will further be developed and refined.

But there are bound to be major breakthroughs in the future which will substantially change the very *nature* of marketing communication. Almost by definition a breakthrough cannot be predicted; however, the following trends are likely to influence many of these future developments:

TELECOMMUNICATIONS TECHNOLOGY.   Probably the clearest trend related to marketing communication is that the hardware is changing dramatically. Cable TV, satellite communications, videophones, computer-aided instruction, videotape, holography—all of these and more promise not only to change the media but also to change control of the media. With more channels and home and office information centers, the control of communication will shift from the sender side to the receiver side. Mass media communications will resemble personal selling, and "personal" selling will be conducted through the media to create a greater structural similarity among the elements of the communication mix than currently exists. Thus, a consolidation of marketing communication elements will be more feasible.

REGULATION RESULTS.   Coincident with the technological development of telecommunication, there has been a public concern about the effects of mass media, primarily advertising. Regulation will increase, and some of the regulatory action may produce changes in the nature of marketing communication. In particular, "corrective advertising," in which legally offending sponsors must advertise their previous errors, and "counter advertising," in which time and space would be provided for refutations of advertised positions, may lead to a greater diversity of viewpoints in commercial mass communication. At the same time, the regulation of personal, direct-mail, and telephone-selling activities could lessen the efficiency of these marketing communication tools.

ORGANIZATION CHANGES.   One of the major stumbling blocks in marketing communication is implementation, a decision stage discussed only briefly in this article. Some trends in business organization will alleviate these problems. Consolidation, multiple product companies and divisions, marketing communication directors, and organization by product rather than function—all will increase the likelihood of efficient marketing communication.

NEW APPLICATIONS.   Marketing communication has developed more from consumer marketing than from industrial or social marketing application. Now, there is more extensive use in both areas, leading to changes in marketing communication decisions. This is particularly true for social applications where objectives are seldom stated in financial terms. Marketing communication will increasingly be used for the social good and may develop into an entirely separate field.

QUESTIONS

1. What marketing areas and activities are a part of a firm's communication mix?

2. What steps are involved in developing a firm's marketing communication strategy?

3. What are some reasons for the general ineffectiveness of marketing communication strategies?

4. What are the communication contributions of physical distribution and price?

5. What parts of the decision sequence for marketing communications are operative, that is, capable of being fully measured and implemented?

6. What is involved in a message-distribution plan?

7. Describe what is meant by "compensation" between levels of the hierarchy of effects. What role does this compensation play in the coordination of the communication mix?

2

A NEW LOOK AT "OLD" ADVERTISING STRATEGY

Dodds I. Buchanan

This article provides rules of thumb for implementing advertising decisions. Specifically, the areas addressed involve selecting between primary and secondary demand, determining the nature of the desired response, selecting between brand awareness and brand insistence, and selecting between emphasizing the firm's advantages and emphasizing competitors' disadvantages.

In the attempt to justify advertising as a science, promising breakthroughs have been made in computerized techniques for media selection, and a constant though rather slow attack has been waged to close the information gap between actual purchasing behavior and media reach and frequency. Despite these irreversible advances, advertising remains essentially an art, rather than a systematizable set of equations gathered from the operations researcher's tool kit. The sophisticated agency whose "unscientific" copy calls its client's cars (Volkswagens) "lemons" is not in immediate danger of being displaced by wielders of Markov and stochastic processes.

Other unscientific approaches are not always so well thought out. Checklists of creative "do's" and "dont's" are legion. There are almost as many admonishments not to knock the corny approach of "They Laughed When I Sat Down at the Piano" as there are copy chiefs indoctrinating fledgling copywriters. And, as if in unison, advertising and copywriting texts stress the cardinal need for getting "YOU" into the copy while avoiding the passive voice and the verb "to be" like a modern-day plague.

The point is that, despite some worthwhile attempts to quantify the media selection process and to codify the creative process, media selection and the creative execution in an advertiser's campaign are processes that should come well after a resolution of campaign strategy. All too frequently they do not. In too many cases, little thought is given to the determination of campaign strategy at the appropriate time—at a stage well before the annual agency presentation, in advance of the budget thrashing and infighting that takes place among those with creative stakes in campaign themes. This article will analyze some of the elements that must be considered when setting strategy; it will pose some new approaches and qualify some more traditional points of departure.

The setting of campaign strategy for an advertiser of a mass, nationally distributed, packaged consumer good, such as Tide, Alka-Seltzer, or Viceroys should include a consideration of at least the following six areas:

1. Relative stimulation of primary versus selective demand
2. The immediacy and duration of the desired response
3. The intensity versus the ubiquity of the desired response
4. The relative emphasis targeted along the spectrum of brand awareness to brand insistence
5. Determination of issues or features to be made salient—ours or our competitors'
6. The quality of the desired response.

Primary or Selective Demand

The degree of emphasis an advertiser places on the stimulation of primary demand for his product category, relative to stimulation of demand for his particular brand, is primarily a function of his market share and the current stage in the life cycle of that particular product. At the introductory stage of a new product, the pioneering and educational task to be done necessarily entails strong emphasis on stimulating demand for the new product or idea in question. Then, as competitors enter the fray, more and more of our advertiser's emphasis will shift to stimulating demand for his particular brand in preference to the brands of competitors.

Yet this recognized transitional process is not as one-directional as is generally assumed. An advertiser of a brand in a competitive generic product category that has reached its market acceptance or even its mature stage cannot blithely ignore the balance between primary and selective demand stimulation in his over-all campaign strategy.

An example can be found in the steel industry—an industry that is hardly in the pioneering stage. With a plurality of approximately 27 per cent of the total market, United States Steel gains more than any other single competitor from any and all advertising stimulating steel's primary demand. It does not necessarily follow that United States Steel is therefore justified in going all out on a primary demand approach, since competitors in the aggregate will enjoy nearly 75 per cent of any increase in industry sales. Nevertheless, United States Steel is hurt less than any single competitor when it takes this approach, either directly in its own ads, or indirectly in ads placed by the trade association to which it contributes, the American Iron and Steel Institute.

While it may not make good strategy sense for any individual steel company to place ads that essentially stimulate primary demand at the cost of selective demand, it makes less sense for second-running Bethlehem, with approximately 14 per cent of the market, to do so than it would for United States Steel. And yet Bethlehem Steel is doing precisely this in one of its ads [which stressed the importance of using steel beams for basements but mentioned Bethlehem Steel only on the bottom line]. . . . This ad does more for steel in general than it does for Bethlehem Steel in particular, especially since the structural beam it features could be supplied by most steel companies and is not a proprietary product of Bethlehem.

The first rough rule of thumb in setting advertising strategy, then, could be expressed as follows: the smaller a firm's share of market, the less business it has sponsoring advertising that is more likely to stimulate primary demand than selective demand. Or, as a corollary, the smaller one's share of market, the more each ad should be beamed specifically at positioning the brand concerned.

The question of primary versus selective demand stimulation goes beyond an advertiser's posture in his own campaign, and raises serious signals concerning his relationship with and benefits expected from advertising sponsored by his trade association, advertising which usually focuses 100 per cent on primary demand for the industry involved. Chevrolet benefits more from last year's American Automobile Dealer's Association's outdoor campaign—"Drive a '65"—than does Plymouth, for instance. Even if the basis for contribution to such a trade association campaign is in linear relationship to sales volume, there is no reason to expect or suppose that the benefits from such a campaign will be received by contributing members of the industry in the same proportion.

Duration of Response Desired

An important step in defining an advertiser's strategy is to determine the balance in his campaign between immediacy of action sought and longer-range impact. Production costs form a large part of the consideration of how current one's ads are and, hence, how directly they tie into an urge for immediate action. The simple fact is that more separate ads are needed in order to keep abreast of seasonal changes; that is, a skier or Santa Claus enjoying a Coca-Cola doesn't ride too well in an August issue of *LOOK*. Although presentation of advertising sets in a seasonal backdrop is not necessary for ads for all products in all media when the advertiser desires immediate action, seasonal sets are frequently necessary for such ads in national consumer magazines and television. At an estimated $4,000 to $5,000 average cost of production, a plethora of such ads can make significant inroads into even the proudest of budgets.

The immediacy of advertising appeals has frequently been broken into three descending intervals:

1. Immediate action characterizes the majority of retail advertising. It is present whenever there is overt persuasion to clip a coupon, enter a contest, or write in for additional information. Some firms, of course, depend solely on inquiries from advertising to develop sales leads, and naturally their advertising strategy is a plea for immediate action.

2. Franchise building and brand name sustenance is characterized by most national advertising of packaged consumer goods. The continued campaigns of Morton salt provide a good example of advertising that seeks to build and sustain a share of mind for a particular brand.

3. Long-range image projection is characterized by most corporate institutional campaigns—for example, "General Motors is people making better things for you."

Many advertisers frequently blend any two or all three of these approaches in the same individual ad, and certainly in the same campaign. A typical sixty-second Coca-Cola television commerical, showing a room full of happy young people dancing or playing ping-pong, may tag out with "Try Coke, Right Now."

Naturally, a lot of advertising, particularly on the retail scene, screams out for immediate action. Fire sales, inventory sales, and going-out-of-business sales abound. But, just as a number of such establishments seem to be perpetually on fire, taking inventory, or going out of business, so are they vastly different from an advertiser with a nationally valuable brand image at stake. It would not be unusual for a loyal consumer to purchase and use well over 1,000 cans of Campbell's tomato soup alone in an adult life-span; this consumer franchise can hardly be built upon one-time distress appeals.

However, even a national advertiser can force the immediacy of any direct action that may accrue from his ads. Contests and couponed ads with deadlines provide ready examples, although the response frequently may well be to the contest or coupon per se, and not to the brand's longer-range goodwill. The same short range of possible effects probably applies to nondeadlined national ads that get too pushy on immediate action, although this clearly is a hypothesis at this stage.

Most national advertisers of packaged consumer goods, particularly in consumer magazines, do not slant most of their ads to the extreme of specific deadlines for action or of absence of sales pressure. Instead, and usually with copy that implies at least that it wouldn't hurt to try their brand soon, they rely on illustration and mood that enables readers to project themselves currently into a product-use situation.

An advertiser's precampaign strategy must determine the optimum trade-off between the following variables at least: timeliness of setting, number of separate insertions, size of insertions, and production costs. An advertiser with a fixed budget, whose main medium is national consumer magazines, must decide on one of two courses: sacrificing sharpness and clarity of seasonal setting by making up fewer separate ads to run over a campaign period, but with more insertions of a given size, or sacrificing size, and perhaps also color reproduction, in order to make up a sufficient number of separate ads to have sharp seasonal identification.

Intensity of Response Desired

Of strategic significance to a campaign planner is the need to decide whether to try to influence everyone a little bit, or to influence fewer people more intensely. Of course, the nature of the product and the likely number and characteristics of prospects answers this question in many cases, particularly for industrial goods. But the answer is not so simple for a mass-consumed product like cigarettes or beer, where consumers vary enormously in demographic and psychological characteristics, and no clear and precise profile of a prospect can be drawn.

Two current Schlitz ads provide examples. The "kiss" ad hopes, with a provocative headline, to induce readership of over 120 words of copy, in which the ad gets down to some real selling with real reasons why one might enjoy Schlitz. For those readers who do get lured into the ad, Schlitz has the opportunity for some intense persuasion. But for those who are scared off by the length of copy, Schlitz is lucky to get even a brand name impression— without any product attribute associations in the minds of glancers. The main variable under consideration here is apparent ease of readership, with total amount of copy the main subvariable. The "gusto" ad carries a quick and shallower message for all. The entire ad can be seen and comprehended by glancers, with at least some positive product attributes of Schlitz rubbing off. The first ad seeks an intense response, the second, a ubiquitous response.

Several other advertising decision areas involve related considerations. One is the question of whether an advertiser should concentrate his advertising efforts when and where his sales are or when and where his sales aren't—in short, is he going to advertise cyclically or countercyclically regarding both time and territory? Granted, it would be hard to convince someone that it is pretty clever to advertise sleds in Houston in August. But suppose he sells Dutch Boy house paint.

Cincinnati and Houston sustain about equal circulation of the *Saturday Evening Post*, which we will assume is an appropriate medium. Let us assume that Cincinnati sales of Dutch Boy house paint are about ten times greater than in Houston. One artificially simplified way of viewing the situation is that it costs ten times as much to sell a gallon of Dutch Boy via an *S.E.P.* ad in Houston as it does in Cincinnati. So the strategic question becomes where to place incremental effort—in Cincinnati, where the product is already well recieved, or in Houston, where the product is not well received. The artificial assumption here, incidentally, is that the potential is the same in both markets.

There are no quick or easy answers to problems such as these, but an advertiser's strategy must indicate his position within this general arena of intensity versus ubiquity of appeal.

Brand Awarness or Insistence

Naturally, every seller would like his product and brand to enjoy brand insistence. But many sellers should recognize that the best they can shoot for is brand preference or at least acceptance. Still others would be prudent to realize that merely to achieve brand awareness is a step ahead. These descending degrees of brand reception seem to parallel the level of interest that exists, or can be engendered, in a brand's product category: the higher the level of interest for a product in a given population or subgroup, the greater the possibility for a seller of this product to establish brand preference or insistence within this population. Conversely, the lower the level of interest, the more a producer may have to reconcile himself to brand awareness.

Brand insistence, the condition at the highest level of the spectrum, requires customers so loyal that they will accept no substitute brand and will buy at an alternative retail outlet in order to get that brand. An advertiser's ability to gain brand insistence for his product among some segment(s) of his prospect population depends on the product's advertisability. According to Neil H. Borden, a product's advertisability depends to a great extent on the presence of, among others, the following characteristics:

1. Physical differentiation from direct and indirect substitutes
2. Strong emotional buying motives
3. Hidden qualities not apparent or completely understood by the consumer.[1]

By these criteria, a Thunderbird convertible is highly advertisable whereas Acme clothespins are not. Many advertisers have recognized the limitations of their product from an advertising point of view and have correctly set their strategy at creating awareness and acceptance rather than striving for preference and insistence. Holly Sugar's campaign revolving around the simple, three-word copy theme of "Remember Holly Sugar" is a good example of this strategy.

The strategic point here is that an advertiser, however fascinated he may be with his product, must recognize and correctly assess its inherent interest and advertisability to consumers. It would be an erroneous strategy for the producer of a low interest product such as salt or sugar to assume that he can engender intense brand loyalty and brand insistence. His dollars are far better spent in gaining as wide a degree of brand awareness as possible, through short, simple, and ubiquitous ads. His goal is achieved when the consumer, at the moment of purchase, knows the brand name, although perhaps little else. The brand will then have at least a fighting chance among competing brands.

Issues to be Emphasized

Communication theory, particularly as applied to political situations, generally concludes that the argument for presenting both sides of an issue one has taken a position on becomes stronger the more educated and informed the audience is, and the more likely the audience is to hear the opposing side's arguments anyway from some other source.

What to do about the competing advertising is another resolution that must be made at the strategy-setting stage. Consider the second criterion first—how likely the audience is to hear the opposing side's arguments from some other source. This likelihood, in advertising, seems to be fairly well correlated with respective market shares within an industry, which in turn are usually associated with total dollar amount of advertising effort. In other words, the larger the market share one's individual competitor holds, the more likely his prospect group is to receive advertising, word-of-mouth, and point-of-purchase messages about this competitor's brand. A small or smaller member of an industry, then, has more to gain than a larger member in

[1] Neil H. Borden and Martin V. Marshall, *Advertising Management: Text and Cases* (rev. ed.; Homewood, Ill.: Richard D. Irwin, Inc., 1959), pp. 162–64.

comparing himself to that larger member or brand, directly or indirectly, since the opposing arguments are going to be heard anyway. A current well-known example of this is, of course, Avis' campaign theme: being only number two, they are forced to try harder.

Some interesting advertising battles that are now raging offer the opportunity to observe the relationship between market position and the degree to which industry members admit or combat the existence of competition. The first involves Bayer Aspirin, Bufferin, and Anacin. Bayer, with first market position and an edited quote from the A.M.A., makes not the slightest allusion to competition. Bufferin, in second place, shows the actual tablets—but not the package—of the front-running aspirin, and concentrates fairly directly on the alleged greater speed and strength of Bufferin. Third-running Anacin not only mentions and then cleverly X's out its two major and larger competitors, but feels it has nothing to lose by actually portraying the package shapes of Aspirin and Bufferin.

Currently both Alka-Seltzer and Bromo-Seltzer claim to have the fastest relief available anywhere, but whereas Alka-Seltzer makes no direct allusion to competition, second-running Bromo goes further to say, "There's no waiting for a tablet." Perhaps the best current example of this approach is Colgate's upward struggle against Crest in the battle of the fluorides, represented by Colgate's "Who really won?" campaign.

But it makes no difference whether the advertiser is Viceroy, asking us to compare all seven filter cigarettes but not mentioning any competing brand names, or Kent somewhat weakly saying, "First with the finest filter cigarette." An advertiser must assess his advertising position vis-à-vis competition under the sometimes uncomfortable realization that admitting "We're only number two" gives Hertz credit for being first, and asking "Who really won?" at least admits that Crest was strongly in the running.

To the extent that the first criterion of communication theory—how educated and informed the audience is—applies to advertising strategy, suffice it to say that one does not address the readers of the *Atlantic Monthly* in the same vein as he does the readers of *True Confessions* (although a check on duplication of readership can always be surprising). In general, one is more likely to get away with a one-sided argument in *True Confessions* than in *Atlantic Monthly*. That is, one can ignore competition in the former and countenance it one way or another in the latter. A stronger case can be made for the completely one-sided argument if one's audience is reached almost exclusively by a medium not used by one's competitors.

Quality of Response Desired

The quality of response to persuasive advertising messages may have just as much strategic significance for an advertiser as whether or not the desired response occurs. It makes some difference in over-all strategy why and through what process of influence a person buys a Thunderbird or a life insurance policy.

From a strategic point of view, it is very important how the one influenced views the influencer's source of power to induce the desired response. The source of power of the influencing agent, as perceived by the person being influenced, can be any one or more of the following:

> Means control, that is, his ability to reward or punish (this power may be perceived as legitimate or coercive, and frequently is presented by threats or appeals to guilt feelings)
> Attractiveness
> Knowledge and expertise in the particular subject area.

The perceived source of power determines why the induced action occurs—whether out of public conformity because of the influencer's ability to reward and punish, private acceptance because of the logic of his arguments, or some blend of the two.

Most advertising messages embrace some blend of these three types of influence, but the following examples are nearly pure.

American Tourister uses attractiveness . . . [by featuring Patrice Munsel in an ad]; Bayer Aspirin, expertise and logic[2]. . . and Great Books [in a 400-word ad], means control in the form of appeals to guilt feelings to influence the consumer . . . Of course, the individual who presents the message may have several sources of influence power. A movie actress may be both attractive and a known authority on fashion. A doctor is at once an

---

[2] The ad that illustrated the original article contained the following message: "For Colds and Flu . . . DOCTORS RECOMMEND: 1. Rest in bed. 2. Drink plenty of fluids. 3. Take Aspirin to reduce fever and relieve pain. Bayer Aspirin is pure aspirin . . . not just part aspirin."

Table 1 PATTERNS OF CONSONANT GROUPINGS		
Dimension	**Position Along Dimension**	
Quality of desired response	By rational arguments of an expert	By means control of influencer
Intensity vs ubiquity of response	Intensity	Ubiquity
Immediacy vs duration of response	Durable	Immediate action
Recognize competition or not	Recognize competition	Ignore competition
Brand awareness to brand insistence	Seek brand insistence	Seek brand acceptance

authority figure with ability to reward or punish and an expert in recommending cures. There's no reason why he has to be ugly in appearance, either.

Although Santa Claus is not quite as strong an authority figure in our culture as he is in Teutonic ones, his mythical power to know "when you've been bad or good" is valuable in this context. Perhaps a unique blend of the three types of influence might be present in a typical Coca-Cola ad around Christmas showing Santa relaxing from his labors of filling stockings to wipe his brow and take the pause that refreshes—it makes sense, he is attractive to identify with, and if he seems to recommend it, it must be socially sanctioned and OK.

An advertiser would do well to bear in mind some of the conditions for continued performance of the desired response. The more a campaign leans towards threats and means control, the more likely are responses to be short range, and quickly supplanted by the competing campaign. Persuasion by logical arguments will tend to create far more permanent effects, attitudes that will persevere until an even more convincing argument is made by a competitor.

It should by now be apparent that patterns of consonant positions can be taken along some of the other dimensions of strategy that have been considered. For instance, the groupings in [Table 1]. . . would be consonant.

These areas of strategy determination are neither exhaustive nor as clearly cut and definitive as this article may have appeared to make them. They are merely some ways of looking at precampaign strategy that might warrant a more conscious and more formal treatment than they are usually accorded in campaign planning. The fact that many campaigns and individual ads reflect disconsonant positions along each of these dimensions betrays not only the intrusion of chance and lack of conscious intent, but also fuzzy thinking along dimensions which are vitally important in the composite effectiveness of a campaign.

QUESTIONS

1. Do you feel advertising can ever completely be a science? Why?
2. What are the important decisional areas for a national advertising campaign?
3. When is primary demand a more appropriate advertising goal than selective demand?
4. What factors should be evaluated to determine how long the duration of response should be for advertising?
5. How can communication theory assist in making decisions concerning the structure of the advertising message?

3

CONFESSION OF A CREATIVE CHIEF: "I SQUEEZED THE CHARMIN"

John V. Chervokas

The objectives behind Procter & Gamble's famous advertising campaign are presented along with the factors that led to its success.

Jerry Della Femina, whose tasteful typewriter gave us "From the People Who Brought You Pearl Harbor," wrote in *Marketing/Communications* (December, '71): "I am not, by nature, a violent person. But if I ever get a chance to meet the man who did those God-awful terribly bad 'Don't Squeeze The Charmin' toilet tissue commercials—and he turns out to be small—I think I just may slug him."

Jerry, I'm just six foot, and depending on whether it's just before or after a holiday, I weigh anywhere between 180 and 195 lbs. The last time anyone slugged me was back in the third grade when Domenic Renzi (hey, why is it that Italians are always looking to belt me around?) knocked me for a loop behind the Callahan School in Norwood, Mass. Since then I've avoided violent confrontations by talking or walking.

This one I'm going to try to write my way out of.

Flashback to somewhere in the spring of '64. I'm 27 and a writer at Benton & Bowles. I'm reporting to a redheaded group head named Fi Fifield, who's reporting to a redheaded creative supervisor named Jim Haines, who's reporting to creative director Al Goldman. I forget if Al ever had hair.

Most Hated TV Spot—How It Happened

Now, with that kind of corporate layer cake it's very had to "own" a piece of work. I mean, it's tough to create a campaign, or a commercial for that matter, and be pointed out as the person solely responsible for its being. But I, me, besides Johnny Unitas, the only other defiant Lithuanian in America, in a cluttered little cubicle at 666 Fifth Ave. back in '64, gave the world the idea that there's a toilet paper worth squeezing. And the funny thing is that no one in eight years has tried to claim the concept as his very own. Strange? Not so strange when you listen to and read the things folks have said about the campaign's heretofore anonymous author.

It happened this way.

The Charmin Paper Co. was a Green Bay mill that Procter & Gamble bought back in 1957. The optimists at P&G (there's a redundancy for you—everyone's an optimist at P&G, and they have every right to be) saw an opportunity to do battle with Scott and Kimberly-Clark and other paper powers. At the time, the Green Bay mill was cranking out Charmin, a one-ply tissue, and White Cloud, a two-ply product.

When I got on the business, Charmin was being sold in a limited area of the Midwest, more or less. And that's all. Only there. My Massachusetts Mama never heard of Charmin, and until recently never saw the advertising her son had created. She kind of wishes she still hadn't.

The limited market of Charmin back in the mid-'60s is understandable. One mill just can't seem to produce enough rolls of toilet paper to service America, and competing with Scott Paper is like trying to go one on one on Kareem Jabbar. But even with those negatives when I began to work on Charmin, it wasn't doing too badly in its market.

Before my time at B&B, Bill Tyler was director of creative services. It was Bill who suggested to Procter that since everyone in TP land was saying their tissue was soft, Charmin would do well to say soft in a different way. Say it's . . . it's . . . "gentle," for instance. And so, faster than you can say, "Donde es el quarto para caballeros?" Charmin became the "gentle bathroom tissue." Gentle, animated characters skittered across your old DuMont telling the Charmin story. Gentle little kids, gentle jugglers, gentle dogcatchers, gentle fat ladies.

World Wasn't Begging for It

It just so happened that Charmin's animated shrimps recall-tested very well. Viewers even remembered that the cartoon kids said Charmin was gentle because "they fluff it and buff it and brush it." Okay, Della Femina, if you think squeezing toilet paper is obscene, imagine fluffing it and buffing it and brushing it.

But then, like every product everywhere, every so often Charmin went and "new and improved" itself. Charmin became even gentler. The boys back at the mill came up with something called the CPB process, which rearranged the fibers in every sheet that came onto the roller and spread the fibers out more evenly, and that, ladies and gentlemen of the viewing audience, makes Charmin gentler than ever. Now how do you go about advertising that not very significant improvement without sounding like Professor Irwin Corey? As I recall, at the time, the world was not begging, pleading, praying for a better toilet paper.

The agency tried to tell the Charmin-is-gentler story with the same cutesy-pie animated babes who had so much success in the commercials telling the Charmin-is-gentle story.

Bomb-o!

People who looked at the commercials made a snap judgment in the first five seconds that yes, it's a Charmin commercial, but tune out. They wouldn't pay any more attention to the rest of the commercial, which looked like every Charmin commerical they had ever seen. Had they listened, however, they would have heard the radically new message of how Charmin isn't merely gentle . . . it's *gentler* now. But no. They didn't listen. In fact, one commerical where a cartoon town crier was shouting the message was remembered by only 2% of the people watching—probably a couple of American history buffs aghast that a classic colonial figure was touting toilet paper.

Squeeze a Banana?

"Let's try something totally different. Let's even get away from animation." That was the direction given me by my redheaded superiors. And we did fool around with some serious stuff. Stuff like beautiful women of the world talking about Charmin's gentle fragrance. Have you noticed? The core of a roll of Charmin is scented. Really!

Scent may be too ephemeral—how about a funny demonstration of softness? Just what are the standards of softness?

Soft as a feather. No, it makes you think of tickling.

Soft as a baby's behind. Not bad, but too restrictive.

Soft as silk. Overpromise.

Now how do you go about measuring something like softness?

Fall on a pillow.

Hug a pillow.

Squeeze a . . .

Squeeze a what?

Shades of Louis Prima! Squeeze a banana?

No, not a banana.

But what does mom do in the supermarket?

She squeezes the melons. And the tomatoes. And the bread.
To see if they're soft.
Then . . . Then . . . Why not use the same test for Charmin?
Squeeze the Charmin.
Crazy advice? Supermarket managers will flip their corks.
Okay then, let's tell them *not* to squeeze the Charmin. Yes. Obsession.
Fad. It becomes the rage to squeeze the Charmin because it's irresistibly soft.
And the supermarket owner protests.

Breakthrough? No One Said So

It was that easy. In an hour and a half, America's most universally despised
advertising campaign was created.

Variety, Sept. 29, 1971: "Who and what kind of a ding-a-ling conceived
the boob notion that there's something about squeezing a roll of toilet paper
that turns people on?"

As I recall, the sale of the idea wasn't very, very tough to Procter. Maybe
they were humoring me. Ted Keller, the P&G guy more or less responsible for
its approval (there, Ted, I'm not going to take the rap myself!), might have
been figuring, "Let's try anything. A test can't hurt." Nobody at B&B seemed to
think "Wow, this is the breakthrough idea." They, too, figured, "Test it.
Maybe yes, maybe no."

The man cast as the bedeviled supermarket owner originally—and
still—is Dick Wilson, a face you look at and say, "Where have I seen him
before?" And you have—on tv shows, movies, even, gasp, in other commercials. A funny man, this Wilson, in the old silent film tradition, where a comic
had to rely on a curl of the lip or a raised eyebrow to express an attitude.

George Whipple Sells Name for $1

Video trivia: The original name I had selected for the supermarket owner was
Edgar Bartholomew, a name I thought bespoke fuddy-duddyness. But our
lawyers told us we had to find a real Edgar Bartholomew, and give him a buck
before we could use his name. Try as we might, we couldn't dig up a real Edgar
Bartholomew.

So we looked through the B&B employee list to see if any name there
tickled our fancy. And, it just so happened that the late George Whipple, then
head of Benton & Bowles' pr department, sold his name for a dollar.

I was home when account man Joe Burns called and said something like,
"Sit down, John. Your Charmin commercial scored a 55 recall."

And I stood, phone in hand, silly-grinning and saying something that will never get into Bartlett's like, "Say Joe, that's great . . . just great."

It's natural to get excited when a commercial you write scores well. But that period of elation lasts only so long, about as long as the client's Nielsen holds up. So I was happy, but rationally so. No one has a right to think that what he does in this business will last for eight years, and God knows how much longer. No one can every suspect that he'll create the world's most hated (and one of the most successful) campaigns. Especially for a toilet paper . . . er, bathroom tissue.

The commercial that scored so well was one titled "Digby," after the cop of the same name who was summoned by George Whipple to restrain the crazed Charmin-squeezing ladies. After Digby delivered his no-no to the ladies, he caught Whipple in mid-squeeze and gave him a shame-shame, "George Whipple . . . please don't squeeze the Charmin." Titter, titter, tittered the three ladies.

The incredible thing about this inanity was that "an unusually high 51% of the commercial audience," said the research report, recalled the story line of Digby. Previously-tested Charmin commercials ranged from 2% to 27% in this category.

Sure, there were some negative comments, says the shriven Lithuanian. But the researchers wrote, "However, the Information Management Department shares our view that the quality of these 'negative' comments is not of a sufficient degree for concern, and is generally similar [stupid, silly] to what we have experienced in the past."

What happened from '64 to the present? Have attitudes changed, or have people? Initially only a few vicious letters went through the Cincinnati Post Office. One I still have, and enjoy reading from time to time, was from a Valparaiso University professor who objected to folks squeezing the Charmin with such "vulgar vigor."

But now the Charmin commercials are honored—or rather, dishonored—by CROC, the Committee for Rejection of Obnoxious Commercials, which judged my effort to be one of the world's worst.

"Worst TV Series of 1971"

Time, reporting the dishonor, cited "Charmin toilet paper, which shows a group of half-crazed women pouncing on poor, effeminate store manager Mr. Whipple like the Erinyes attacking Orestes." June 19, 1972. Erinyes?

And Faith Popcorn pops off about the Charmin campaign: "My nomination of the worst tv series of 1971. It is a pity that such a potentially bountiful idea should have been executed in a form so banal, ineloquent, tasteless and boring. I cannot help but express my anguished criticism—since it is my belief that, had the execution been in any way equal in brilliance to the superlative concept itself, its sales effectiveness would have been infinitely greater." March, 1972.

Johnny Carson spoofs it, columnists columnize it, Nashville had a fair-to-middlin' hit based on it. Now what should I do? Crow? Hide? Lie, maybe? Or, perhaps, find succor in the fact that the Gallagher Report claims "Charmin climbs to 27% share of $400,000,000 market. Displaces Scott (Nov. 16, 1971) as number one brand. Charmin's patented softening process wins buyers despite irritating 'please don't squeeze the Charmin campaign'." Despite—or because?

"Insult to All Womanhood"

Pretty pastoral pictures have never sold a lot of TP. Gorgeous babies have never skyrocketed bathroom tissue sales.

Enough. I've made a clean breast of it. I'm able to face anyone now, Jerry. You, Faith, even Hank Seiden, who was unusually vicious when he wrote that my campaign is "an insulting campaign to all womanhood. I'd like to see some women's lib gal put the squeeze on the guy who thought it up."

Well, the women's lib gal I'm married to hasn't put the squeeze on me yet, and that's doubly reassuring. Maybe, just maybe, things are looking up, Jerry, because my wife's Italian, too!

QUESTIONS

1. What elements of communication theory explain the success of the Charmin campaign?
2. How can a commercial that is disliked be successful?
3. What was the sequence of decisions that led to the Charmin campaign?
4. What other factors in Procter & Gamble's marketing mix probably contributed to its communication success?

4

SALES PROMOTION— FAST GROWTH, FAULTY MANAGEMENT

Roger A. Strang

This article reviews the management practices of sales promotion firms and suggests ways to make these practices more effective.

Do you know how much your company spends on sales promotion activities? Do you know what returns it gets on its investment? For most companies, the answer to both questions is likely to be a resounding no.

Many companies do not keep records on couponing, premiums, trade allowances, bonus packs, sampling, sales incentives, and trade shows—the elements that make up promotion. Even where separate records are kept, it is unlikely that all expenses are recorded.

If you can manage to obtain promotion information for your company, then you are likely to find that in recent years your promotion expenditures have been increasing at a faster rate than advertising. In fact, at the present time you are probably spending more on promotion than on advertising in conventional media (television, radio, print, outdoor). It is also likely that no one in your organization knows what return you are getting for this substantial item of expenditure.

In this article I will report on my recent research into promotion activities over the past decade. It is based on a study that was undertaken for the Marketing Science Institute and includes interviews with 54 executives from 17 leading U.S. consumer goods manufacturers and advertising agencies.[1]

In reviewing promotion management practices, I found that while some companies have developed a sophisticated approach to managing this impor-

[1] Roger A. Strang, *The Relationship Between Advertising and Promotion in Brand Strategy* (Cambridge, Massachusetts: Marketing Science Institute, 1975). The American Association of Advertising Agencies provided financial support for this study through its Educational Foundation.

DEFINITIONS

Advertising—All nonpersonal communication in measured media under clear sponsorship. This includes T.V., radio, print, and outdoor media, but does not include direct mail.

Promotion—All other forms of sponsored communication apart from activities associated with personal selling. It thus includes trade shows and exhibits, couponing, sampling, premiums, trade allowances, sales and dealer incentives, cents-off packs, consumer education and demonstration activities, rebates, bonus packs, point-of-purchase material, and direct mail.

---

tant marketing area, most companies have a great deal of room for improvement. I will conclude by offering a guide for executive action.

Increasing Promotion Expenditures

No one has ever compiled a good estimate of what is spent on the various activities that make up sales promotion; indeed, *advertising* and *promotion* have been defined in a variety of ways. (The definitions I used for the purposes of my study are given in the [first boxed insert] . . . Still, my review of some major elements of promotion shows it to be more important than advertising and to be increasing rapidly.

For example, the figures in [Figure 1] . . . suggest that, on the average, promotion spending increased twice as fast as that of advertising between 1969 and 1975. Assuming this trend continues, 1976 expenditures on these selected promotion activities will total over $30 billion compared with just $20.5 billion for regular media advertising. (The media advertising total does not include public relations advertising while the total for promotion includes both direct mail and advertisement for promotion in print media.) [Figure 2] . . . gives an idea of the relative importance of some components of promotion.

From these data it appears that between 1968 and 1975 the proportion of total advertising and promotion spending devoted to promotion increased from 53% to 59%. Other studies have supported this trend and found it to be even more marked in certain categories. The market for consumer nondurables is one example. And among manufacturers selling these types of products to grocery stores, the proportion of advertising and promotion budgets allocated to promotion increased from 54% in 1968 to 65% in 1972, according to Leo Sheperd, vice president of General Foods.[2] The magnitude

---

[2] In an address before the Super Market Institute Convention, Chicago, 1973.

of this change is heightened when compared with a 1956 study of similar manufacturers, those producing toiletries and packaged goods. The manufacturers allocated less than 10% of their advertising and promotion budgets to promotion for toiletries and about 24% to promotion for packaged goods.

Even more dramatic figures can be reported from individual markets and by individual companies. In one market for a frequently purchased consumer product, the advertising/promotion mix of the three leading brands reversed from 63/67 in 1969 to 22/79 in 1972.[3]

Moreover, the growth in promotion spending is not simply a matter of increased expenditures by promotion-oriented companies, but rather of more widespread use of sales promotion techniques. The number of companies using coupons, for example, grew from 350 in 1962 to almost 1,000 in 1974, according to an estimate by the director of research for the Nielsen Clearing House.[4] The change has also involved service industries. A 1975 survey of insurance companies and banks found that the use of sales promotion had

[3] Richard J. Weber, "How Trade Allowances Are Making Mincemeat out of Profit Objectives" (New York: Association of National Advertisers Financial Management Workshop, 1973).

[4] Richard H. Aycrigg, "Coupon Usage and Redemption Patterns" (New York: A.N.A. Couponing Workshop, 1975), p. 1.

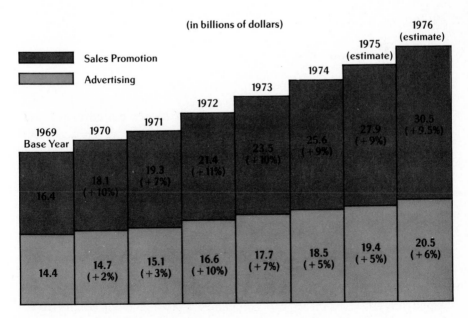

FIGURE 1 *Year to Year Growth of Advertising and Sales Promotion*
Source: Russell D. Bowman, John C. Young, and John Adler, "Improving the Payout of the Advertising/Promotion Mix" (New York: Association of National Advertisers, 1975).

risen sharply in recent years while the growth rate of investments in media advertising had steadily declined.[5]

Of course, these figures must be treated with some caution since there are a number of problems in accurately measuring promotion spending—differences in definitions, for instance. Nevertheless, they indicate a major change in the importance of a generally neglected area of marketing strategy.

This change may pass unnoticed in many companies because of a failure to record promotion expenditures separately. In some companies these expenditures are included with advertising; in others they may be considered as part of the sales force's expenses or perhaps go in a general marketing account. Even when companies do have separate promotion accounts, they may not record *all* promotion charges. For example, the extra product required for a bonus pack may be recorded as a manufacturing expense, or the costs of special labels or packs charged to packaging. The loss of revenue from a temporary price reduction may not be recorded at all.

Internal and External Reasons for Increase

Failure to analyze or effectively manage promotion spending will prove damaging because promotion is likely to remain an important element in marketing strategy. The executives I interviewed cited a number of reasons, reflecting both internal and external factors, for the growth in this area.

Internal Developments

First, there are three fundamental developments at work within companies that have enhanced the role of promotion:

Promotion has become more acceptable. Several executives reported an increased willingness by senior management to view promotion as an acceptable marketing activity. This acceptance is in contrast to a resistance to its use in the past by many executives, in some cases based on a feeling that promotion "cheapened" the brand. This attitude has been modified, and acceptance has been hastened, by apparent proofs of success. One example is the use of rebates by auto and appliance manufacturers in 1974 and 1975. General Electric found its rebate program so successful that it not only retained but expanded the program in 1976.

More executives are better qualified. The appointment of more executives with better qualification to positions of responsibility for promotion has also helped growth. Several of the companies I studied reported the recent

---

[5] Joseph M. Murtha in an address before the National Association of Life Companies, Palm Beach, Florida, December, 1975.

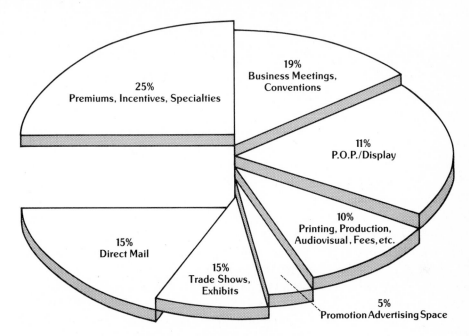

FIGURE 2   *Selected Elements of the Promotion Mix*

creation of new staff positions, usually at the corporate level. In other cases the established position of sales promotion manager has been upgraded from supervision of point-of-purchase production or premium purchases to activity involving broad responsibility for promotion planning.

The product manager looks for quick returns. Several respondents felt that the widespread adoption of the product manager system has also encouraged increases in promotion spending. This system frequently requires prompt demonstration of results for fast progress up the corporate ladder; promotion programs are usually implemented more quickly and produce results sooner than advertising. Also, in some companies the approval system for promotion programs may be easier and implemented at a lower level than the approval system for advertising campaigns. Promotions are also valuable in eliciting support from a frequently overloaded sales force.

External Changes

There have also been a number of changes in the business environment:

Brands have increased in number. Respondents noted an increasing number of new brands in recent years and suggested that, since most consumer goods rely heavily on promotion for introduction, this could increase the relative importance of the function. Support for this belief comes from one survey organization which reported that from 1968 to 1972 the number of brands in eight common food and personal care product categories increased by an average of 34%.[6]

This proliferation of brands makes the use of promotion more likely as companies seek their share of the limited retail shelf space. Respondents also felt that more brands mean less distinction among competitors and consequently less opportunity to effectively advertise product features. Others thought that an increased number of brands led to shorter life cycles and increased promotion in an effort to prevent decline.

Competitors are becoming promotion-minded. Many respondents described examples of promotion increases as a response to competitors who suddenly increased their promotion spending. The adoption of an aggressive strategy by one brand in 1970 led to a 450% increase in promotion expenditures by the three major competing brands in its market in three years. The [second boxed insert] . . . provides some details of this "promotion war."[7]

Economic conditions have been troubling. The economic recession of 1973-75 encouraged an expansion of promotion activities. The auto rebates of 1974-75 were a well-publicized example of the use of promotion to reduce inventory and improve liquidity.

Techniques such as rebates have also allowed a more flexible market posture in the face of rapid cost increases and material shortages. The recession apparently made consumers more responsive to promotion techniques, especially those which reduced prices. In 1975 coupons were used by almost two-thirds of the families in the United States as part of their regular shopping; this was the highest level of usage ever recorded.[8]

Trade pressure has grown. The increased size and sophistication of chain supermarkets, drugstores, discount houses, and other retailers has brought increased pressure on manufacturers for support and allowances. An extensive study by Booz, Allen, and Hamilton Inc. concluded that in 1973 manufacturers selling to grocery stores spent more on trade promotion than on advertising.[9] Retailers have been aided by the increased demand for shelf space I noted earlier.

While the executives I interviewed were divided as to whether promotion expenditures will increase further, there was general agreement that promotion will remain a substantial force calling for much more sophisticated management.

---

[6] Joseph A. Morein, "Shift From Brand to Product Line Marketing," HBR September-October 1975, p. 56.

[7] Documented by Weber in "Trade Allowances."

[8] Aycrigg, "Coupon Usage," p. 9.

[9] "The 1973 Study of Grocery Trade Dealing" (New York: Booz, Allen and Hamilton, 1974).

NO ONE WINS A PROMOTION WAR

Richard J. Weber, an experienced marketing executive, has documented the history of a trade promotion war that cut profits for the major competitors. He did not identify the market, but it appears to be that of a frequently purchased consumer good. In 1969 the market was growing at twice the population rate and three brands accounted for 55.5% of total sales. In the following year, a new brand manager for the smallest of these brands decided to try to increase sales by reducing advertising and offering higher trade allowances. This tactic led to an initial increase in sales, but it also led to a response from competitors.

Over the next two years, cycles of response and counter response saw promotion increase by 450% and advertising decrease by 38% (Figure [3]). The net result for all three brands together was: a 3% increase in total sales, a 1.4% drop in market share, and a 35% decline in profits.

Figure [4] . . . shows that all three leading brands were affected, although it appears that the greater reliance placed on advertising, the less severe the impact was.

Ineffective Management

We need a more sophisticated approach to promotion management not only because it is a financially and strategically important area, but also because it has been virtually ignored. The absence of basic information on how much companies are spending on promotion is only one indicator of the lack of attention.

Other problems lie in the planning process. Objectives for promotion programs are rarely established and, when they are established, are not likely to be in quantitative terms. This shortcoming applies both to the plan as a whole and to individual programs. Promotions may be scheduled simply because "there was one last year," or because competitors have them, or because of demands from the sales force for something to be done in their region.

Budgeting Procedures

The lack of direction for promotion activities is reflected in the budgeting procedure, which is not likely to involve extensive consideration of cost effectiveness. As one respondent described it, the usual approach may be: "How much did we have to spend last year? How much have we got to spend this year? How will we cut it up?"

One common approach has been to allocate a percentage of expected sales to be spent on promotion, but the figure often depends more on corporate financial requirements than on marketing strategy. This amount

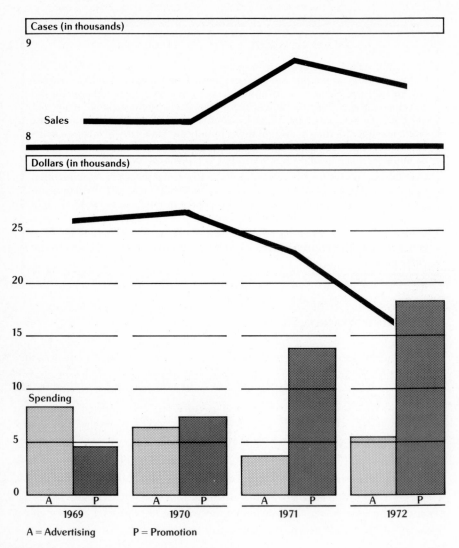

FIGURE 3 *Net results of promotion war*

may be related to advertising in some arbitrary way, perhaps by a desire to keep a fixed ratio of advertising to promotion. Another method has been the "left over" approach, in which a fixed percentage of sales is allocated to both advertising and promotion, with promotion getting what is left after advertising has been budgeted.

Several studies I encountered in my research demonstrated that advertising and promotion interact "synergistically" to produce higher sales than an

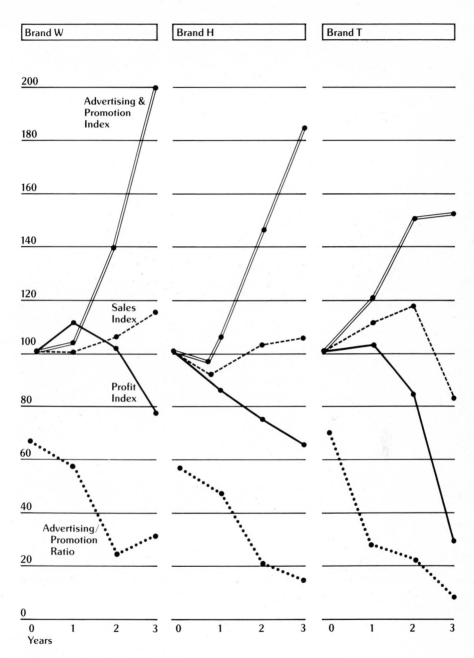

FIGURE 4   *Brand comparison*

equivalent investment in either alone. Yet in many companies the advertising and promotion budgets are prepared independently. The product manager system is theoretically ideal for coordinated planning, but this is often disregarded in practice.

Whatever promotion budget is established at the beginning of the planning period is likely to be upset by arbitrary changes during the year. Of course, a promotion is usually a short-term tactic and modifications are to be expected. However, there may be damaging changes in which advertising is cut back to improve brand contribution, with a small offsetting increase in the promotion budget. This was apparently a regular event at Purex during the 1960s in its unsuccessful battles with Clorox for the liquid bleach market.

A strategy such as this may maintain short-term sales, but these are likely to be at the expense of future ones and may impair the long-term future of the brand. Many of these advertising cuts made on a "once-only" basis turn out to be surprisingly permanent, as many executives know.

Planning Horizons

Earlier I mentioned the problem of the short-term horizon inherent in the product manager system. The promotion war described in the [second boxed insert] . . . is only one example of many cases where a new product manager is appointed, adopts an aggressive strategy, achieves some initial success, and takes another job before the effect of his strategy on long-term brand profitability can be determined.

High personnel turnover also creates a situation in which experience is ignored. This is especially true if records are not kept. Even where information on past promotion programs is available, lack of direction by senior executives often encourages newly appointed product managers to reject the information and set off again to "reinvent the wheel."

There is a general lack of research to guide managers in planning promotion activities. Despite the substantial sums involved, many companies do little or no pretesting. A survey in 1972 by the Premium Advertisers Association revealed that 42% of premium users rarely if ever tested their effectiveness, even though premiums can be reliably tested very quickly and at little cost. [10]

Evaluation of promotion programs receives equally little attention. This might be expected, given the infrequency with which quantitative objectives are established. Even where an attempt is made to evaluate a promotion, it is likely to be superficial; one company evaluated two types of coupon promotion as equally unsuccessful because both had low redemption rates. How-

---

[10] Russell D. Bowman, "Merchandising and Promotion Grow Big in Marketing World," *Advertising Age*, 30 December 1974, p. 21.

ever, a later examination of sales during the test period showed that one type of coupon had been significantly more successful than the other.

Evaluation in terms of profitability is even less common. One of the companies discussed in the [second boxed insert] . . . did not know how much money it had lost until the researcher began his study.

Indeed, if profitability were used as an evaluation criterion, few promotions would be approved a second time because an apparently small allowance or coupon can cut heavily into profits. A $1 per case allowance on a product that has a contribution rate of $3 per case has to increase sales by 50% to maintain the same level of contribution. Yet there are many brands on the market for which allowances have become so frequent that more than half their sales are made under some type of deal.

Trade allowances seem to be a particular problem, with many companies failing to check whether performance requirements are met. One study revealed that only 50% of 1,000 deals accepted by a major food chain received advertising or other promotional support.[11] Even when deals are accepted and promoted, probably less than half the merchandise is actually moved to consumers under those special terms agreed upon.

Role of Advertising Agencies

Before we turn our attention to the steps that companies can take to improve promotion management, I'd like to comment briefly on the role of advertising agencies.

Not only marketers have neglected promotion; agencies have continued to ignore opportunities to assist them with their promotional problems. In an address to the Association of National Advertisers in 1975, a vice president of Young & Rubicam commented that promotion programs were too often given to the youngest, least experienced person in an agency when they should be given to the veterans. This neglect has undoubtedly been a factor in the growth of in-house promotion departments and in the appearance of agencies specializing in sales promotion.

Actually, agencies have a number of advantages in handling promotion programs. They can ensure that advertising and promotion are effectively integrated; their existing research facilities can be readily adapted to pretesting promotions; and they have the creative staff to develop promotions that will stand out in the crowd.

Several leading agencies have exploited these advantages and established very successful promotion departments, but there is plenty of room for other agencies to follow suit.

---

[11] Michel Chevalier and Ronald Curhan, "Temporary Promotions as a Function of Trade Deals," Marketing Science Institute working paper, Cambridge, Mass., p. 15.

Improving Promotion Management

There are a number of steps management can take to improve the effectiveness of its promotion activities. Its first priority is to set up a system allowing identification of money spent.

Analyze Spending

Companies can come to grips with their promotion management problems only when they know how much they are spending and for what type of activities. This will probably require a modification of the management information system to identify promotion costs. As far as possible, identification should encompass *all* expenses associated with promotion, including items such as special packaging, consumer education programs, sales and dealer incentives, and the loss of revenue from temporary price reduction programs. Information such as this is the first step to more efficient planning and control.

Establish Objectives

Next, management needs to clearly define the role of promotion in achieving its marketing objectives. Is it tactical, strategic, or both? Will it be defensive or used for market expansion? What is its relationship to other elements of the marketing mix, especially advertising?

One bank, for example, broadly defines the role of promotion as increasing the use of its services by present customers, while advertising is aimed at attracting new customers. However, a manufacturer of consumer nondurable goods uses advertising to attract new customers and to maintain loyalty, and views promotion primarily as a defensive tactic. One advertising agency sees promotion as a short-term incentive to attract new customers who will be retained through the long-term benefits expressed in the advertising.

Unfortunately, many exeucutives exaggerate the effectiveness of promotion activities, and in setting objectives it is important that some of the limitations be realized. In general, promotion activities add to long-term sales only under certain conditions. When used in combination with advertising, promotion may be valuable in introducing new, or substantially modified, brands. Or it may help boost brands whose sales are already increasing. However, in mature or declining markets, it offers little more than temporary tactical support. As one executive commented, "In a mature market, sales promotion is really just tap dancing."

For example, two studies of the effects of coupons and in-store special offers were undertaken during the 1960s using Nielsen retail audit data.[12] They

---

[12] James O. Peckham, Sr., *The Wheel of Marketing* (Chicago: A.C. Nielsen, 1975).

Table 1

EFFECT OF COUPONS AND IN-STORE "SPECIALS" ON BRAND SALES

Brands with:	Before promotion	During promotion	After promotion
Declining trend	100	98	93
Stable sales	100	105	100
Increasing trend	100	110	107

Source: James O. Peckham, Sr., *The Wheel of Marketing* (Chicago: A.C. Nielsen, 1973).

found that these price promotions do not affect the basic sales trend. The results of the 84 promotions studied are summarized in [Table 1] . . .

Within this framework the specific objectives for each program can be developed. Promotions are usually directed to one or more of three audiences: salesmen, dealers, or consumers. The particular audience should be specified and the desired response quantified for later evaluation.

Select Appropriate Techniques

Once objectives have been established, the appropriate techniques for achieving them can be selected. Some techniques are decidedly better than others for achieving particular objectives; [Table 2] . . . gives a general guide for some consumer promotions. Many promotion techniques satisfy more than one objective of course, so this exhibit merely indicates the primary target of a particular technique.

Then, too, several different techniques can be used in combination to achieve a particular goal. For example, a 1975 campaign by Mobil Chemical Company to attract new users for its "Hefty" trash bags used a sweepstake, premiums, and point-of-purchase material, as well as dealer allowances.

Combined promotions will generally produce higher sales than single promotions but they may be less profitable. The Department of Agriculture has sponsored several experiments to test promotions on foodstuffs and found diminishing returns in many instances.

This use of a combination of techniques raises the issue of the relationship between consumer-oriented and trade-oriented promotion. I have already mentioned the growth of the latter; many executives apparently believe that trade promotions are as effective as consumer promotions. In fact, this is rarely the case; retailers often fail to use promotion funds that have been made available to them for price reductions or other sales incentives. In some categories, a certain level of trade promotion may be a "cost of doing business," but, where possible, as one experienced executive noted, "Trade promotion should only be used to make a good consumer promotion better."

Companies may find that programs have to be modified to suit the needs

Table 2

CONSUMER PROMOTION PLANNING GUIDE

Technique	Primary impact		
	Brand awareness	*Attract new customers*	*Increase sales to present customers*
Bonus packs			•
Cash refunds			
Single purchase		•	
Multiple purchase			•
Contests/sweepstakes	•		
Couponing			
Media/mail		•	
In/on pack			•
Multiple			•
Premiums			
Single purchase		•	
Multiple purchase			•
Price-off			•
Sampling		•	

of different markets. Marketing managers are aware that different types of promotions are more effective in certain areas of the country, and several respondents in my survey suggested the need for flexible programming rather than a blanket national approach.

One tactic has been to increase the involvement of field sales managers in promotion planning. Another has been the appointment of market managers to coordinate the marketing activities for all company products in their region. A promotion planning team at Kodak is made up of staff members who specialize in trade segments rather than products.

Pretest, Pretest, Pretest

Pretesting is important for verifying that the most suitable technique has been selected and that it is being presented in the most efficient manner. This is important because responses to promotions vary a great deal depending on the way they are presented. Redemption rates for a coupon promotion may range from 2% to 25% depending on the value of the coupon (relative to product price) and the way it is distributed. An inappropriate premium may actually reduce sales of the product. Pretesting also helps to set precise objectives and to avoid risks.

Promotions can usually be pretested quickly and inexpensively. One regular user of children's premiums I surveyed reported consistently valid results from testing new premiums with a small group. Coupons, samples, and refund offers can be tested against a small sample of households or in a limited media test. In-store tests with a few stores can be used for point-of-purchase material, bonus packs, and price-off packs.

Models can be useful in the pretest stage, and several companies are taking advantage of them. In some cases they may be nothing more than a review of data relating to past programs; in others they may involve sophisticated regression analysis or simulation models.

Testing does not end with selection and implementation of a promotion program. As a matter or policy, at least two of the companies I surveyed test alternative strategies in selected market areas with each of their national promotions.

Evaluate in Depth

Improved promotion management depends on understanding the effects of promotion programs, which means that they must be evaluated in depth. It is not sufficient merely to monitor sales during the course of a campaign and compare them with the preceding period or the same period a year ago. A great many outside factors—weather, competition, price changes—influence sales. Also, sales increases during a promotion might be achieved at the expense of future sales.

Several companies have recognized these problems and moved to improve their evaluation procedures. One company began with the simple comparisons noted here, but recognizing the effect of outside influences, decided to determine a long-term sales trend and make further comparisons on that basis. The company's final move to measure the "consumer dynamics" of a promotion came when a diary panel study showed that a joint promotion that seemed very successful in terms of sales was actually drawing customers away from one of the company's other brands. This company now relies extensively on diary panels for promotion evaluation.

This is only one example of the increasing amount of sophisticated information available for promotion evaluation. Several national research organizations provide information to help monitor the activities of competitors, and one recently formed organization audits trade shows and exhibits.

Focus on the Long Term

But all the information in the world will not improve promotion management unless that information is used properly. This means that planning must have a long-term perspective.

Already, some companies are moving to modify the product manager system in an attempt to encourage such a perspective. Measures include keeping product managers in the same job for longer periods, passing more decisions up the line to top management, and developing broader executive evaluation procedures.

In one company product managers are asked to submit three different advertising and promotion plans so the implications of alternative strategies can be considered. In general, corporate executives can help by avoiding arbitrary and uncoordinated revision of plans once they are approved.

A long-term focus also helps prevent hasty, ill-advised responses to a promotion-minded competitor. For example, one company reported that one of its long-established and heavily advertised brands had begun to lose its market share when a competitor suddenly eliminated his advertising and adopted a heavy promotion strategy. The company countered by dropping its advertising/promotion ratio from 70/30 to something less than 50/50, but to no avail. After two years the 70/30 strategy was restored and the brand is now regaining market share.

Encourage Research

Finally, there is a general need for more detailed information on promotions and their effects. Many companies are spending much more on promotion than on advertising, but it is unlikely that any are spending more money on promotion research than on advertising research.

Some companies, however, have begun using experimental designs to test the relation of promotion to advertising and other marketing variables. One company with which I am familiar has gone a step further by preparing a special promotion handbook that incorporates the results of its research to aid decision-making by its product managers. A leading advertising agency provides a similar service for its clients.

Any number of studies show how valuable such research can be:

- In one study, point-of-purchase displays related to current TV commercials were found to produce 15% more sales than similar displays not related to such advertising. [13]
- In another, a heavy sampling approach along with TV advertising proved more successful than either TV alone or TV with coupons in introducing a product. This was in a category where there was considerable consumer skepticism about product claims. [14]

---

[13] John P. Dickson, "Coordinating Images Between Media," *Journal of Advertising Research*, February 1972, p. 25.

[14] Strang, *Advertising and Promotion*, p. 131.

- A series of studies has shown that TV advertising plus promotion produces more sales than an equivalent investment in either TV or promotion for several consumer nondurables.[15]

These studies indicate what can be done and why companies should develop their own research programs. Of course, once these programs are established, the information must be made available to managers.

---

[15] Ibid., p. 132.

QUESTIONS

1. What distinguishes sales promotion from advertising and publicity?
2. In your opinion, have sales promotion expenditures grown at a rate faster than that of advertising over the last few years?
3. What are some of the areas of sales promotion that are generally mismanaged?
4. Describe the management activities that should be used for sales promotion.
5. When are contests, coupons, and samples most effective?

5

MANAGE YOUR SALES FORCE AS A SYSTEM

Porter Henry

This article encourages the application of the principles of "management by objectives" and "systems engineering" to sales management problems. It suggests that a "total systems" concept can be used to analyze the operating procedures of the selling system so that the controllable management variables can be manipulated to achieve the desired outcomes. This approach is supposed to result in more effective long-term selling strategies.

Sales managers, according to their critics, are not sufficiently "scientific" in their decision making. They pursue volume instead of profit, make piecemeal decisions instead of comprehensive plans, rely on instinct and hunch rather than on methodical decision-making processes.

Sales managers might well reply—and often do—that they are dealing with salesmen and customers who are capricious human beings, much more difficult to predict and control than a piece of production equipment.

It is true that the sales department is a complicated communications system, influenced by many variables that are difficult to quantify and that interact in unforeseen ways. For example, a sales training program designed to help salesmen sell more of a high-profit specialty product may fail because the company's compensation plan motivates salesmen to chase the volume dollars in easy-to-sell but low-profit items. Or an increase in the size of the sales force may result in a higher proportion of calls on marginal customers, creating an increase in the sales costs ratio and a decrease in profit per sales call instead of the intended higher profitability.

Because the function they are managing is so complex, sales managers can profitably use the basic principles, if not the mathematical trappings, of the most modern of all scientific methods. Known by such terms as "systems engineering," "systems analysis," "the total systems concept," and "the systems approach," this method has helped Americans produce energy from atoms and place men on the moon. It can also help increase the productivity of a sales department.

Essentially, a "system" consists of various inputs that go into a process or operation of some kind and result in a measurable output. The measurement is used to adjust the inputs or the process in order to produce desired results. To describe this procedure of measurement and adjustment, systems engineers have borrowed a term from electronics: *feedback*. The methodology of systems analysis can be described in six steps:

1. Define the system to be investigated. For example, it may be an entire city, just the transportation network, or perhaps only the subway system.
2. Define what the system ought to accomplish as well as the means to measure this. For the subway system: What quality and quantity of service are desired?
3. Define the elements that make up the system and quantify their relationships. In the case of the subway system: What is the effect on passengers moved per hour of such variables as the pattern of passenger arrival frequencies at stations, length of platforms, length of trains, headway between trains, and number of doors on a car?
4. For each element, or for each major subassembly of elements, determine the measurable performance desired. To achieve the objectives of the subway system, what is required of the signals, motors, brakes, and crew?
5. Consider the cost effectiveness of alternative methods to improve the performance of the system. For each dollar spent to improve the performance of one element of the system, how many dollars' worth of improvement will be obtained in the performance of the total system?
6. Implement the most desirable decisions and measure the results.

Although it may not be possible to quantify all the interacting variables that constitute the sales department of a typical company, nevertheless, "systems engineering" can be used by the sales manager to increase the overall production of his department. Let us examine the steps he takes and their potential value to him.

Defining the System

The system of concern to the sales manager is, of course, the sales department. It is a subsystem of the corporation's marketing program, which is in turn a subsystem of the corporation (see . . . [Figure] 1).

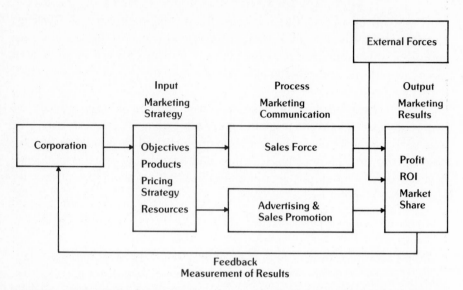

FIGURE 1   *The Sales Force as Part of the Corporation's Marketing System*

In the phraseology of systems engineering, the corporation's top management uses *feedback* from the marketplace and the results of previous marketing efforts to develop an *input* to the marketing system. This input includes the marketing objectives, the choice of products or services to be offered, the pricing strategy, and decisions about the resources to be committed to the attainment of marketing objectives.

Having developed products or services to meet identified customer needs, the corporation must then communicate their existence to potential customers. This communication is accomplished through two channels: (1) advertising and sales promotion, including every medium that reaches potential customers en masse, and (2) the sales force, which communicates to prospects primarily on a one-to-one basis.

Essential to the systems approach is the measurement of output. The output of the corporation is usually measured in terms of return on investment and/or corporate growth. Market share, profits as a percentage of sales volume, and cash flow are other measures of performance that may be stressed.

Measuring Efficiency

But the sales force is a subsystem of a larger subsystem, and return on investment, profit ratio, and market share, while good measures for the whole company, are greatly influenced by factors not completely controlled by the sales force. If these measures improve, everybody claims credit for the improvement.

Is there some way to show whether a sales force is operating at 60%, or 83.7%, or perhaps even 100% efficiency? If sales managers could agree upon two or three standard indices of sales force productivity, they could compare the effectiveness of their systems with that of other sales forces in the same industry. The following is a list of five possible yardsticks:

1. *Contribution to Profit.* The company's product can be turned over to the sales force at cost, or at cost plus some markup representing the production department's contribution to profit. The sales force in turn sells the products at a markup. This margin, minus *all* costs of the selling operation—salesmen's salaries, sales management and supervision costs, travel and entertainment expenses, credit losses, interest on accounts receivable—represents the contribution of the sales department to corporate net profits.

2. *Return on Assets Managed.* The sales force requires certain capital investments— goods in warehouses, branch offices, salesmen's automobiles, money tied up in accounts receivable. If current sales expenses such as salaries, travel, and entertainment are subtracted from gross profit on sales volume, the balance represents the return on these investments.[1]

   If a company uses this yardstick, some costs that are now absorbed in the current budget are logically capitalized and depreciated. A sales training program useful for five years, for example, would more logically be written off over five years than in just one year.

3. *Sales Cost Ratio.* A frequently used index is the ratio of sales expenses divided by dollar sales volume. This ratio should be used in conjunction with other yardsticks, because a sales force selling $10 million at a 5% expense/volume ratio may not be as profitable as a sales force selling $20 million with a 7% cost ratio.

4. *Market Share.* This output is influenced by variables other than sales department productivity. If, however, product quality, pricing, advertising effectiveness, and competitors' activity remain relatively constant, an increased market share could be considered an indication of increased sales force productivity.

5. *Achievement of Company Marketing Goals.* In addition to, or instead of, indices for comparing companies in an industry, measurements of *desired* performance may be used. An example might be "to increase our market share from 15% to 25%, provided net profits as a percent of sales do not go below 10%."

Every engineer agrees that the efficiency of an engine is its energy output divided by its energy input. Sales managers are not universally agreed upon any corresponding measurement, or even upon which activities should be

---

[1] A more detailed description of this accounting method is contained in J. S. Schiff and Michael Schiff, "New Sales Management Tool: ROAM" (HBR July-August 1967), p. 59.

considered as input and which as output. However, this state of affairs does not mean management must throw up its hands. It can and should decide what measurements best meet the needs of its company. The measurements chosen may not be perfect, but they can still be valuable, enabling management to apply the systems approach in a useful and productive way.

Improving the System

. . . [Figure] 2 is a flow chart of the sales force as a system. It employs four measurements of sales force output: contribution to profit, return on assets managed, sales costs ratio, and market share. If the sales manager discovers by these measurements or any others he chooses to adopt that sales force productivity is below its desired level, he then works his way *backward* through the flow chart, from right to left, to determine which control variables at the left need adjusting. As the chart indicates, no matter what improvement the sales manager seeks in output, there are only three ways in which the salesmen can achieve the change. These ways are labeled "Salesmen's output variables" because they are the result of every input salesmen can make. The output variables are:

- An increase in total sales volume, without any change in the product mix or sales cost ratio.
- A more profitable product mix, in which the products producing a higher profit represent a larger percentage of total sales volume.
- A reduction in the sales cost ratio, which can result from increasing sales without a corresponding increase in costs, or from decreasing sales costs. (This ratio refers to *all* sales costs, including such items as price concessions, service to the account, and adjustments of complaints.)

In most cases the desired profit goal will require some improvement in all three of the output variables. However, their relative importance is likely to vary from product to product and even from salesman to salesman. In using a systems approach, therefore, it is important to determine how much and what kind of emphasis should be placed on each variable.

Analyzing Sales Activity

If we now move one step to the left in the flow chart, we arrive at the "Salesmen's input variables." These are activities salesmen can change in order to alter the output variables. The arrows emerging from each input variable indicate which of the output variables is affected. Let us now consider the nature of the input variables.

1. THE NUMBER OF SALES CALLS.   Each salesman might be motivated to make more calls per week, or the company total could be increased by hiring more salesmen. An increased number of sales calls, . . . [Figure] 2 indicates, will probably affect total sales volume and can affect the sales cost ratio— adversely, if additional sales calls are made on unprofitable prospects.

2. THE QUALITY OF THE SALES CALLS.   This input is measured by such yardsticks as calls per order, dollar sales or profits per call, or percentage of calls that achieve specific objectives. In this context, a sales call refers to a salesman's conversation with one or more individuals. The "call" on a major plant might involve sales calls on many buying influences, but these calls should be considered separately in evaluating their quality and in establishing the frequency with which the buying influences should be contacted. As the flow chart indicates, call quality consists of these elements:

- The information content of the call. Is the salesman adequately informed about the customer's problems or plans, as well as about his own products and their applications?
- The effectiveness of the call as an act of communication. Does the salesman deliver the message in an understandable and convincing manner? (This is where visual sales aids may be useful.) Is the salesman effective while on the receiving end of the conversation? That is, is he a good questioner and listener?
- The interpersonal aspects of the call. Does the salesman rub the customer the wrong way without being aware of it? When the customer's "inner child" speaks, does the salesman's "inner child" respond?

Most companies do a reasonably good job of giving the salesman information on customer needs and product applications, or at least make it possible for the salesman to absorb it. Many companies try to upgrade salesmen's skills in communication and interaction by using some kind of standardized training program. (Too often, though, the program tends to concentrate on one element while ignoring the other.) Few companies take the trouble to investigate the basic question: If our sales calls are not good enough, what is the nature of their weakness?

Improvement in call quality can increase any of the three output variables—total volume, product mix, and sales costs. The content of the training will determine which of the three is most affected. Occasionally, a sales manager may ask himself which of these outputs most needs changing, but many of us never see this happen. Instead, before launching a training

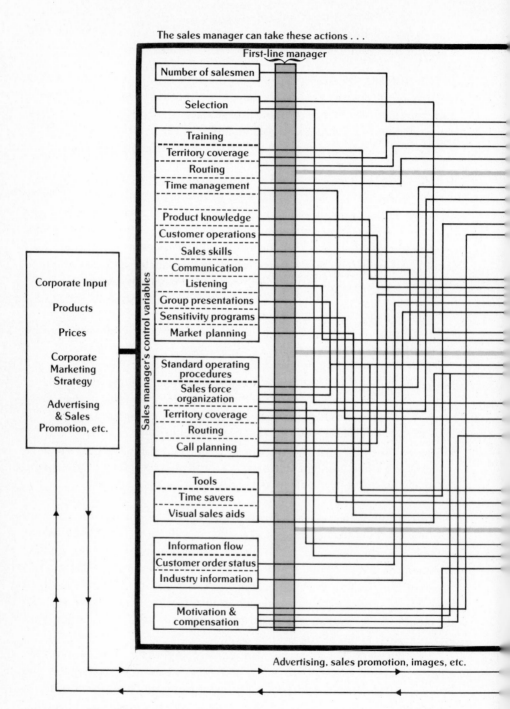

FIGURE 2 *The sales force as a system*

cause these behavioral changes . . . achieve these results.

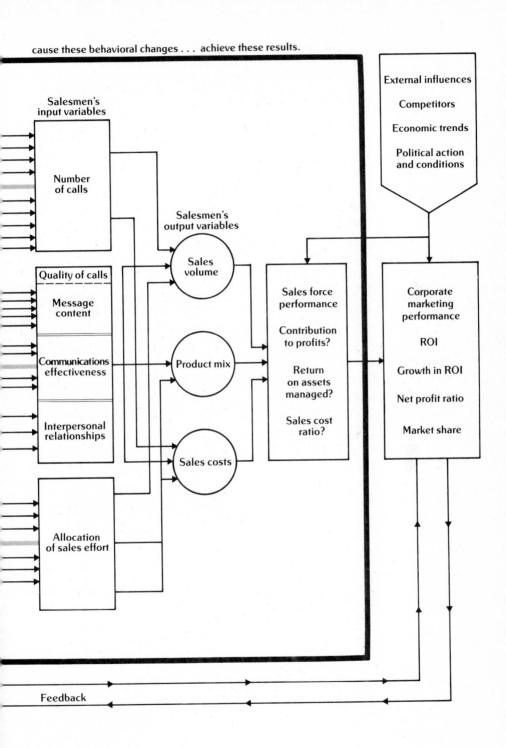

program or procedural change, sales managers opt for training that is mostly motivational, without first identifying desired behavioral changes.

3. THE ALLOCATION OF SALES EFFORT.   For each salesman and for the sales force as a whole, there is some optimum frequency of calls on large, medium, and small customers, and on large, medium, and small prospects, that will maximize the profit return per unit of sales effort expended. (Of course, customers may also be classified according to industry, geographical location, and other factors, but for the sake of simplicity let us assume here that volume and profit are the classifications used.)

Allocation of effort based on product profitability is related to allocation of calls by customer sizes or types: to sell more of the high-profit product, more time must be spent with customers who may buy it. If a salesman spends too much time with little customers, he will lose some of the additional potential volume from his key customers. On the other hand, if he calls too much on key customers, he will be trapped by the law of diminishing returns, for there comes a point at which additional calls could more profitably be made to smaller customers or prospective customers. If the salesman neglects prospect calls in favor of present customers, the inevitable attrition among those present customers will cost him future profits.

Except for those people following a rigid call schedule based on account classification and routing, most salesmen do not allocate their time for maximum returns. Selling is often a lonely and discouraging occupation, so it is only human to spend too much time with the friendly customers and easy buyers, while neglecting those psychologically chilling calls on hard-nosed buyers and nonbuying prospects.

Many companies attempt to solve this problem by establishing a standard procedure for classifying accounts into groups, such as A, B, and C, and assigning a call frequency to each group. The procedure itself, however, is usually based on seat-of-the-pants judgment rather than on objective methods of optimizing the allocation of sales effort.

An improvement in this salesmen's input variable usually has a marked effect on product mix, for the sales efforts are more heavily concentrated on prospective users of the more profitable products. Total sales volume and the sales cost ratio may go either up or down, but net profitability will go up.

Intermediate Measures

Many sales managers set up budgets for salesmen's output variables—sales volume by product, and sales costs—but few attempt to establish quantified goals for all of the input variables—number of calls, quality of calls, and allocation of sales effort. Since it is fairly easy to set targets for the number of calls a salesman should make, this is likely to be the only input goal established. Such a practice is extremely frustrating to the conscientious salesman, who rightfully insists that the quality of his calls is at least as important as the sheer number of calls.

Measurements of call quality can be established. They can consist of such indices as the ratio of calls to orders or to long-range purchases, the average order size, the number of different items purchased by each customer ("across-the-board" selling), the ratio of proposals to sales, and many others. And it is relatively easy to set targets for the allocation of sales effort.

Such measurements of the intermediate functions in selling can be highly important in providing prompt feedback to salesmen involved in lengthy or highly technical selling, where the sale itself usually takes place so long after the initial contact that it neither motivates the salesman nor helps him correct his weaknesses on a week-to-week basis.

Deciding on Changes

Once the sales manager can compare his salesmen's present performance with the desired level of input variables, he can determine which of the "Sales manager's control variables" should be adjusted. There are 22 of these. Listed at the left of the flow chart in . . . [Figure] 2, these control variables fall into seven categories:

1. The number of salesmen.
2. The selection of salesmen.
3. Training programs of various types.
4. Standard operating procedures.
5. Selling tools (visuals, demonstrators, films, and so on).
6. Information flow to and from salesmen.
7. Motivation, which also includes the practice of incentive compensation.

The arrows emerging from each control variable indicate which of the salesmen's input variables it primarily influences. For readers who do not like to trace arrows, Part A of [Table 1] . . . lists the controls and the variables each affects; Part B works in reverse, showing for each desired behavior change the necessary control changes.

Standard operating procedures divide as follows:

● *Sales Force Organization.* This category concerns such questions as: Should all salesmen sell all products, or should they be specialists in markets or products?

Table 1

MANAGERIAL CONTROL AND SALESMEN'S ACTION

A. Effect of Manager's Control Variables

The Manager Can Make the Following Decisions:	*These Actions of the Salesman Are Most Affected:*
Number of Salesmen	Number of calls
Selection of Salesmen	Call quality, primarily in communications effectiveness and interpersonal relationships
Training	
Territory coverage	Number of calls, allocation of sales effort
Routing	Number of calls
Time management	Number of calls, allocation of sales effort
Product knowledge	Call quality (message content)
Customer operations	Call quality (message content)
Sales skills, communications, listening, and group presentations	Call quality (communications effectiveness)
Sensitivity programs	Call quality (interpersonal relationships)
Market planning	Allocation of sales effort
Standard Operating Procedures	
Sales force organization	All three salesmen's input variables
Territory coverage	Number of calls, allocation of sales effort
Routing	Number of calls
Call planning	Call quality (message content and communications effectiveness)
Sales Tools	
Time savers (dictating equipment, calculators, etc.)	Number of sales calls
Visual sales aids	Call quality (communications effectiveness)
Information Flow	
Customer order status and industry conditions	Call quality (message content)

Table 1 *(continued)*

Motivation

Incentive pay, contests, recognition, opportunities for personal growth and promotion, etc.

All three salesmen's input variables

B. Salesmen's Input Variables Affected by Control Variables

The Salesman Can Take the Following Actions:	*These Actions of the Manager Influence the Salesman:*
Number of Sales Calls	Number of salesmen
	Training in territory coverage, routing, and time management
	Standard operating procedures for sales force organization, territory coverage, and routing
	Tools for time-saving
	Motivation and compensation
Quality of Sales Calls	
a. Message content	Training in product knowledge and customer operations
	Information flow on customer status, industry trends, and call planning
b. Communications effectiveness	Salesmen selection
	Training in sales skills, communications, listening, and group presentations
	Standard operating procedures for sales force organization and call planning
	Visual sales aids
c. Interpersonal relationships	Salesmen selection
	Sensitivity training
	Motivation and compensation
Allocation of Sales Effort	Training in territory coverage, time management, and market planning
	Standard operating procedures for sales force organization and territory coverage
	Motivation and compensation

How many salesmen should report to each first-line manager? Should the manager have account responsibilities of his own?

- *Development of Routines.* If some part of the salesman's job can be reduced to a standard operating procedure, it is easier and more effective to hand him the procedure than to train him in the skill of designing his own procedure. This approach to productivity is often overlooked.

    If, for example, salesmen are required to develop an annual territory marketing plan, it is easier to provide them with a form to fill out than to give them a course in territory planning. Again, it is easier and more effective to establish a standard method of classifying accounts into sales call frequencies than to train salesmen in time allocation.

    This approach does not mean that the company is trying to make robots of its salesmen or is ignoring the potential for job enrichment. It does mean that if some aspect of the salesman's function can be routinized, it makes sense to provide the routine and free more of the salesman's time for the creative aspects of his job that cannot be condensed into a procedure.

Power of the First-Line Manager

The sales manager has one other control variable at his command. It is unique in that it can either weaken or amplify the effects of changes in the other control variables.

As the flow chart indicates, this multiplier variable is the first-line sales manager. In larger companies this is the district, divisional, or branch manager; in smaller companies it may be the sales manager himself, or even the owner.

Any actions taken to improve call quantity, call quality, or time allocation will not be fully effective unless the first-line manager follows through on them. There are times, in fact, when his operations are the only control variable the sales manager needs in order to fine-tune—when any desired changes in the salesmen's actions can be achieved through the training, supervision, and motivation provided by the first-line sales manager.

A sales manager can upgrade the performance of the field managers by employing any of the variables listed for salesmen; that is, he can provide more managers, he can do a better job of selecting, training, and motivating them, or he can provide them with better procedures, tools, or information.

With some notable exceptions, primarily in the pharmaceutical and packaged consumer goods industries, the importance of first-line sales management tends to be underestimated. Many companies do not give their field managers the necessary training in how to observe, evaluate, and develop the individual salesman. Yet, second only to better sales time allocation, improved field supervision is usually the simplest and fastest way to improve sales force productivity.

Approaching Major Decisions

In using the systems approach to increase sales force productivity, the sales manager works backward through the flow chart, first setting his improvement objectives and then tracing back through the salesmen's output and input variables to determine which control variables should be changed.

His analysis will usually suggest the desirability of improving several of the control variables. To determine how much time or money should be invested in improving each control, the manager can ask himself these questions:

- *How Important Is This Variable in Affecting the Salesmen's Input Variable I Am Trying to Improve?* If its influence is small, it can be omitted from the productivity improvement plan. A good way to assess the relative importance of the control variables is to assign to each one a weight from 1 to 10. This weight will vary greatly from company to company. Information about previous orders and shipments, for example, would be highly valuable to a salesman making repeat calls to industrial purchasers, but of no value to a one-call, door-to-door sales operation.
- *How Well Am I Handling This Control Variable Now?* Percentage ratings are useful for this answer. For example, is our performance half of what it should be, or 90%? The industrial company mentioned in the previous paragraph might rate its flow of information to the salesman at only 50%, although its weight might be 9 or 10.

  The weight is a judgment of the importance of this function in a particular company; the rating is a judgment of how well it is being performed. Although these numbers are not an accurate, objective measurement, they do make it easier to consider a complex array of variables. Whether he realizes it or not, a sales manager goes through a similar mental process in deciding how much of his available funds to spend on sales training, contests, or salary increases.
- *What Would It Cost to Improve the Performance of a Function?* Here the manager needs to be mindful of the S-shaped curve, which indicates that the better a function is now being handled, the more difficult it is to produce an improvement in it. While it takes a certain amount of effort to raise the rating of a function from 50% to 55%, it might take three times as much effort to raise it from 90% to 95%.
- *How Would Sales Force Productivity Be Affected by the Projected Improvement in This Variable?* This question calls for an estimate of the increase in profit contribution, minus the immediate and continuing costs of the improvement in the control variable.

By using the systems engineer's approach, the sales manager can establish more useful long-term objectives. He can identify the most important changes that must be made to increase sales force productivity. And he can establish interim progress measurements for both himself and his salesmen.

QUESTIONS

1. In general, what are the basic components of a "systems approach" to management?
2. What should determine the sales-force objectives?
3. What are the controllable activities for the salesperson?
4. Which of the manager's controllable variables would have an impact on the number of sales calls by the sales force?
5. Do you feel this system approach is feasible for a first-level sales manager operating in the field? Why?
6. How should funds be allocated to the sales manager's controllable variables?

PART SIX

Pricing

Price is the amount paid for a particular product or service. In most cases, it is defined as the dollar amount needed to conclude a transaction. Often the concept is broadened to include transportation costs, financing costs, storage and maintenance costs, or other elements of costs or efforts involved in the consumer's securing a product. In either case, price represents the value consumers associate with the product. Along with promotion, it is the most visible element of a marketing strategy to the consumer.

However, price is a critical part of a marketing strategy for reasons beyond its high visibility. Price has an immediate impact on profits and cash flow through its creation of revenue; it plays an important role in the decision processes used by buyers; and pricing has a large number of legal considerations that must always be addressed. The articles in Part Six provide guidelines for determining the role of price in a particular marketing strategy, for selecing the most appropriate pricing objectives and strategies, and for calculating the specific price for a given product.

"A Decision-Making Structure for Price Decisions" describes the role of price in a marketing strategy and its impact on the competitive structure of an industry. The next article, "Risk-Aversive Pricing Policies: Problems and Alternatives," discusses various pricing objectives and strategies, as well as problems and disadvantages of cost-based and selling-related price policies. It also suggests alternative policies to correct these problems and make price a more effective marketing tool.

A more detailed discussion of one alternative pricing policy is given in "Flexible Pricing: Industry's New Strategy to Hold Market Share Changes the

Rules for Economic Decision-Making." The misapplication of a new product pricing strategy is illustrated in "A Painful Headache for Bristol-Myers?" which describes the firm's introduction of the product Datril.

The last article of Part Six provides a detailed procedure for determining a specific price. "Price-Cost Planning" describes a process of forming long-term pricing plans and short-term price changes in a competitive industrial market.

The objectives of these articles are to identify the factors that should be evaluated in setting a price and the sequence in which they should be evaluated. Although the articles do not exhaust all the aspects of pricing, they provide a better understanding of the complexity and dynamics of price decisions in a marketing strategy.

1

A DECISION-MAKING STRUCTURE FOR PRICE DECISIONS

Alfred R. Oxenfeldt

This article analyzes the gap between pricing theory and pricing practice in order to explain why pricing had remained largely an intuitive process. A seven-stage framework is developed to guide more rigorous pricing decisions.

Until recently, almost all pricing decisions have either been highly intuitive, as in the case of new product introductions, or based on routine procedures, as in cost-plus or imitative pricing. The proportion of price decisions representing these extreme approaches seems to have declined substantially; yet, many business executives have not altered their pricing methods substantially.[1]

Research continues on how businesses should set prices. Most of these studies attempt to uncover the best methods rather than those in current practice. No researcher has completely overcome the enormous difficulties of learning the basis on which group decisions are made and the "sensitive" reasons underlying many price decisions.[2] This article examines some trends

---

[1] Professor F. E. Gillis writes in 1969, "Joel Dean opines that cost-plus pricing is the most common technique in the United States. The statement is too weak; it is almost universal." See his *Managerial Economics* (Reading, Mass.: Addison-Wesley, 1969), p. 254.

[2] A. A. Fitzpatrick, *Pricing Methods of Industry* (Boulder, Colo: Pruett Press, Inc., 1964); *Decision Making in Marketing—A Description of Decision Making Processes and Its Application to Pricing*, 1971, Report No. 525, National Industrial Conference Board; Kaplan, Dirlam and Lanzilotti, *Pricing in Big Business* (Washington, D.C.: The Brookings Institution, 1958); B. Fog, *Industrial Pricing Policies* (Amsterdam, Holland: North Holland Publishing Co., 1960); W. W. Haynes, *Pricing Decisions in Small Business* (Lexington, Ky.: University of Kentucky Press, 1962); and J. Fred Weston has been reported as directing a major study of this subject. See "The Myths and Realities of Corporate Pricing," *Fortune*, Vol. LXXXV (April, 1972), p. 85.

in pricing and the apparent gulf between pricing theory and practice. A pricing framework is presented to aid practitioners structure their important pricing decisions.

The Gap Between Pricing Theory and Application

The current pricing literature has produced few new insights or exciting new approaches that would interest most businessmen enough to change their present methods. Those executives who follow the business literature have no doubt broadened their viewpoint and become more explicit and systematic about their pricing decisions; however, few, if any, actually employ new and different goals, concepts, or techniques.

The gap between pricing literature and practice may exist because the authors lack extensive personal experience with the practical problems facing executives in a highly competitive and complex business environment. Other explanatory factors include: the number of products for which executives are responsible, the lack of reliable information on product demand, the dynamic nature of technology, and the unpredictable responses from competitors. Because of the large number of highly uncertain and variable factors, executives responsible for pricing closely adhere to methods that they have found to be effective in the past. Economists and practitioners have long recognized that price is a dangerously explosive and complex marketing variable.

This discussion does not suggest that those responsible for pricing should always adhere to traditional methods of setting price, or that those writing about pricing have contributed little of value. The point is that a significant gap exists between the two areas and that this gap must be closed if pricing is to continue to develop as a crucially important area of marketing theory and practice. Pricing specialists have suggested many helpful methods that have not been implemented in practice even after they have [been] demonstrated to be valid.

Literature Trends: A Critique

The field of pricing remains largely the domain of economic theorists who discuss price primarily in relation to the analyses of specific market structures.

Much of the pricing literature deals with tactics and strategems for particular kinds of firms—wholesalers, manufacturers, franchisees, or joblot shops. Special corporate situations such as new product introductions, inflation, declining product, product-line pricing, price-structure problems, and price-cutting are also popular topics in the pricing literature.[3] The current literature on pricing, like that in most other areas of marketing, draws heavily on the behavioral sciences, quantitative tools, and detailed empirical research. Present-day writers employ simulation techniques and other computer applications much more than in the past, and are often concerned with cost computation and demand estimation. Pricing receives far more attention from marketing specialists today than it did when managerial economists such as Joel Dean, Jules Bachman, Arthur R. Burns, Donald Wallace, Edward Mason, Edwin Nourse, Walton Hamilton, Walter Adams, and Morris A. Adelman were the chief contributors to the field.

Recently, pricing specialists have channeled much of their research efforts into the development of approaches designed to aid the accuracy and efficiency of the decision maker. The most promising methods are: use of the computer;[4] simulation as a method for anticipating the effect of price changes on sales and for testing complex strategies;[5] research techniques for obtaining more reliable information about prospective customer responses to price change;[6] and the nature and determinants of price perception.[7]

Nevertheless, large gaps still remain in the pricing literature. Very little is said about reconciling the various price-optima; i.e., the prices that are best vis-à-vis costs, the ultimate customer, resellers, and rivals. Most authors deal with pricing problems unidimensionally, whereas businessmen must generally deal with price as one element in a multidimensional marketing program.

---

[3] The best of these writings are to be found in several collections of articles and talks about pricing. These are: Elizabeth Marting, ed., *Creative Pricing* (New York: American Marketing Association, 1968); Almarin Phillips and O. E. Williamson, eds., *Prices: Issues in Theory, Practice and Public Policy* (Philadelphia: University of Pennsylvania Press, 1967); D. F. Mulvihill and S. Paranka, eds., *Price Policies and Practices: A Source Book of Readings* (New York: John Wiley, 1967); American Management Association, Management Report No. 17, *Competitive Pricing: Policies, Practices and Legal Considerations*, 1958; American Management Association, Management Report No. 66, *Pricing: The Critical Decision*, 1961; Donald Watson, ed., *Price Theory in Action: A Book of Readings* (Boston: Houghton Mifflin, 1965); and B. Taylor and G. Wills, eds., *Pricing Strategy* (London: 1969).

[4] R. E. Good, "Using the Computer in Pricing," in *Creative Pricing*, Elizabeth Marting, ed. (New York: American Marketing Association, 1968), pp. 182-194.

[5] Arnold E. Amstutz, *Computer Simulation of Competitive Market Response* (Cambridge, Mass.: M.I.T. Press, 1967); and D. Kollat, R. Blackwell and J. Robeson, *Strategic Marketing* (New York: Holt, Rinehart and Winston, 1972), Chapter 19.

[6] A. Gabor and C. W. J. Granger, "On the Price Consciousness of Consumers," *Applied Statistics*, Vol. 10 (1961), pp. 170-188; idem, "Price as an Indicator of Quality: Report on an Enquiry," *Economica*, Vol. 33 (1966), pp. 43-70; and idem, "The Pricing of New Products," *Scientific Business*, Vol. 3 (1965), pp. 141-150.

[7] Nystrom, *Retail Pricing: An Integrated Economic and Psychological Approach* (Stockholm: Economic Research Institute of Stockholm School of Economics, 1970), especially Chapters 7 and 8; Brown and Oxenfeldt, *Misperceptions of Economic Phenomena* (New York: Sperr and Douth, 1972).

Price is often dealt with as if it were completely separated from the other elements in the marketing mix. These authors tend to concentrate on the effect of price on immediate marketwide sales without adequately considering long-run or individual market effects. The writers dealing with pricing decisions typically identify variables that are sometimes not considered and suggest conceptual errors that are commonly made, but they typically treat only small, isolated parts of the problem faced by a business executive. Little has been written on innovative approaches to pricing—approaches designed to *increase* demand, rather than *adapt to existing* demand. This failing has been most common in writings that employ quantitative techniques. A price-setter must not merely view his responsibility as that of determining the various demand elasticities (price, promotion, assortment, quality, design, and place) and finding the price that best adapts to them. Attention must be given to measures that alter these elasticities in his firm's favor.

The setting of any price involves: (1) values that particular segments of customers place on a firm's offering; (2) consumer responses to price changes of the product; (3) competitive responses to any price changes; and (4) resellers' sensitivity to price changes. No one has yet developed a completely reliable method to measure the price elasticity of demand for a particular brand. Similarly, little is known about resellers' responses to margin changes or the sales support a brand will receive from distributors and retailers. The specific responses of competitors to both price and nonprice actions is still a matter of great uncertainty in almost all industries.

Pricing should be regarded as a field where the essential elements are quite clear and well known and where the concepts that need to be applied also are widely recognized and within reach of all executives. Practitioners face the problem of measuring a multitude of factors in many different specific situations; that is, they must attempt to quantify the response functions (elasticities) so they can be compared. One of the major problems in pricing is obtaining the data required to measure each of these response functions in different market contexts. Pricing specialists have made very few contributions to the solution of this problem.

Constraints on Pricing Decisions

Many vital price-related decisions made by top management deal with the following issues: Are we willing to drive competitors from business if we can? Should we inflict serious injury upon them when they have been struck by misfortune? Are we willing to violate the spirit or letter of the law to increase sales? At a different level of concern, pricing decisions are related to price strategy and general competitive policy by questions such as: "Should we seek price leadership for ourselves or foster a pattern of price leadership with some other firm as leader? Should we try to shake out the weak firms in the industry to achieve price stability and higher profitability? Should we foster a spirit of cooperativeness among rivals by an avoidance of price competition?"

These decisions are properly made by top executives and do not require a frequent revision. When they are not made explicitly, the executive responsible for pricing decision implicitly makes many of these decisions by default. A complete discussion of these constraints goes beyond the scope of this article.

To manage the complex nature of price-setting, practitioners need an effective, multidimensional model to guide their analysis. Such a pricing model would not only explicitly encourage systemized thinking, but also underscore the differential advantage available to the firm which strategically sets the prices of all of its products.

A Framework for Pricing Decisions

The following discussion of price decisions employs a decision-making framework which identifies the following stages:

1. *Recognize the need for a pricing decision.*
2. *Price determination.*
3. *Develop a model.*
4. *Identify and anticipate pricing problems.*
5. *Develop feasible courses of action.*
6. *Forecast the outcomes of each alternative.*
7. *Monitor and review the outcome of each action.*

These seven stages overlap somewhat and are not strictly sequential.

Recognize the Need for a Pricing Decision

A firm's pricing difficulties and opportunities are related to its overall objectives. Only when a firm is explicit in defining its corporate objectives can the executive specifically evaluate the obstacles and opportunities confronting him. Table 1 provides a partial list of feasible pricing objectives. It is important to note that the objectives of profitability and growth constitute only a small part of this list. The pricing objectives of many different firms are listed below; however, *each firm* must evaluate and determine the priority of these objectives as they relate to the individual firm.

Table 1

POTENTIAL PRICING OBJECTIVES

1. Maximum long-run profits
2. Maximum short-run profits
3. Growth
4. Stabilize market
5. Desensitize customers to price
6. Maintain price-leadership arrangement
7. Discourage entrants
8. Speed exit of marginal firms
9. Avoid government investigation and control
10. Maintain loyalty of middlemen and get their sales support
11. Avoid demands for "more" from suppliers—labor in particular
12. Enhance image of firm and its offerings
13. Be regarded as "fair" by customers (ultimate)
14. Create interest and excitement about the item
15. Be considered trustworthy and reliable by rivals
16. Help in the sale of weak items in the line
17. Discourage others from cutting prices
18. Make a product "visible"
19. "Spoil market" to obtain high price for sale of business
20. Build traffic

From this list of objectives, some of the pricing problems that firms face can readily be inferred. Among the more important are:

1. A decline in sales.
2. Prices are too high—relative to those charged by rivals, relative to the benefits of the product. (Prices might be too high in a few regional markets and very appropriate elsewhere.)
3. Price is too low, again in certain markets and not in others.
4. The company is regarded as exploitative of customers and not to be trusted.
5. The firm places excessive financial burdens on its resellers.
6. The price differentials among items in the line are objectionable or unintelligible.
7. Its price changes are too frequent—or do not take account of major changes in market circumstances.
8. The firm's price reflects negatively on itself and on its products.
9. The price is unstabilizing the market which had finally become stabilized after great difficulty.
10. The firm is offering its customers too many price choices and confusing its customers and resellers.

11. The firm's prices seem higher to customers than they really are.

12. The firm's price policy attracts undesirable kinds of customers which have no loyalty to any seller.

13. The firm's pricing behavior makes customers unduly price sensitive and unappreciative of quality differences.

14. The company has fostered a decline in market discipline among sellers in the industry.

The list of pricing objectives in Table 1 and the illustrative list of pricing difficulties above suggest that prices and price changes do not simply affect current sales, but have more far-reaching effects.

To identify the problems listed, a firm requires a monitoring system or a means of empirically determining the existence of potential problems and opportunities. Table 2 presents indicators a firm might use to suggest the existence of pricing problems. It is evident that some of these indicators are very difficult to measure with accuracy.

Price Determination

A warning system will detect pricing problems and allow the manager to decide how much attention to give to each potential price problem and to

---

Table 2
DATA THAT MIGHT BE USED TO DESIGN A PRICE MONITORING SYSTEM

1. Sales—in units and in dollars
   a. Previous year comparisons
   b. Different markets/channels comparisons
2. Rivals' prices
3. Inquiries from potential customers about the line
4. Company's sales at "off list" price
   a. Measured as a % of total sales
   b. Revenue as % of sales at full price
5. Types of customers getting the most and largest price reductions
6. Market shares—in individual markets
7. Marketing costs; production cost; production costs at nearly output
8. Price complaints
   a. From customers
   b. From salesmen
9. Inventories of finished goods at different levels
10. Customers' attitudes toward firm, prices, etc.
11. Number of lost customers (brand-switching)
12. Inquiries—and subsequent purchases
13. Marketing costs

whom to assign it. In assigning a problem for study, a decision-maker must determine whether to use his own staff or call upon outside resources. Some price problems are self-correcting, in which case the price setter should ignore the warning.

Develop a Model

The primary question that must be addressed here is: What models would help businessmen to best cope with pricing responsibilities? Models developed by economic theorists rarely direct a pricing executive's attention to the key variables. Behavioral science offers far more insight into the factors that determine how price changes will be perceived and reacted to by consumers. The influence of price extends far beyond current sales figures, and behavioral science helps us more fully understand the extensive effect of price decisions.

Some mathematical models deserve a brief mention, even though they are not widely used in practice. The multiple regression model is familiar to most economists and marketing specialists. Based on historical data, this technique determines a linear functional relationship between sales and factors such as price, advertising, personal selling, relative product quality, product design, distribution arrangements, and customer services.

Another technique is the experimental approach to pricing strategy. One type of experimental approach, which may be based on regression analysis, is simulation. Such models allow the pricing specialist to combine wide varieties of inputs (including price) to achieve desired results such as short- and long-run sales together with the costs incurred. The relative merits of different factor combinations can be tested and compared.

A third type of mathematical model emphasizes the situation-specific parameters of a strategy. This approach is referred to as adaptive modeling and combines historical analysis with different environmental situations. A given input mix may have widely divergent results for each situation. This type of approach is particularly helpful in assessing the merits of market expansion, segmentation analysis, and other decisions where contextual analysis is important.

These last two models deal with some fundamental characteristics of price. First, the interdependence and synergy of related model components become key issues in their effective use. Second, the proper mix of variables will differ from occasion to occasion, even for the same product or brand. Third, the outcome of any combination of marketing actions may be perceived differently by different consumers.

To completely understand how and when price works, an executive must understand how potential customers perceive, interpret, and evaluate price changes in making their purchase decisions. These decisions vary with the individual; therefore, an executive must also consider different market segments.

Identify and Anticipate Pricing Problems

When a firm encounters a pricing problem, its manifestations are generally not subtle and obscure; however, executives still have difficulty obtaining information that identifies the source of the problem. Information about customer reactions to a product are extremely difficult to interpret because the responses must be related to their particular market segments. A seller primarily seeks the opinions of those customer segments he wishes to serve, rather than of all prospective customers. Most research data, however, do not match customer responses with the corresponding market segment to which they belong.

Price-setters require an information system to monitor the effects of their pricing arrangements and thus to help make prompt and specific adaptive action in a fast changing market environment. Salesmen's reports, current sales experience, and individual favorite customers are the primary sources of information available to most firms.

Develop Feasible Courses of Action

Traditionally, price setters have considered only a very limited number of alternatives when faced with pricing difficulties. If their price seemed high, they would lower it, and if it was too low, they would simply raise it. Much more complex behaviors are available to most pricers which provide opportunities for novel approaches. In addition to varying the price level, the executive responsible for pricing may also change the following factors: (1) The timing of the price change; (2) the number of price changes (he is not limited to a single change); (3) the time interval to which the price change applies; and (4) the number of items whose price he changes (he could raise some prices while lowering others). In addition, the executive can combine a price change with other marketing actions. For example, he might change the product's package, advertising, quality, appearance, or the after-sale customer service. Even more important, he can change price in some markets and not in others, or change them in different ways. The price-setter may even modify his discount arrangements in such a way as to increase the effectiveness of the price change.

A price-setter must not regard his actions as simply shifting prices on individual product offerings. He must recognize that his firm sells a line of products in a wide variety of geographic markets, and that its offerings embrace many benefits of varying importance to customers. Price is only one of those consumer benefits. A firm rarely makes its very best reaction to a pricing problem or opportunity by simply altering price.

Forecast the Outcome of Each Alternative Action

Once a price-setter has selected the most feasible actions available, he must forecast their consequences to determine which will best achieve his goals. At this stage, the price-setter must be as specific as possible about the expected short- and long-term consequences of his decision.

Successful management of pricing information requires an understanding of the possible consequences of price changes. The more important of these include the effect of price changes on: the customer's ability to buy; the brand image and customers' evaluations of a product's quality; the value of inventories held by resellers; the willingness of resellers to hold inventory; the attitude of ultimate customers and resellers who recently purchased the product at a different price; the company's cash flow; and the need to borrow capital. Price changes can also disrupt or improve market discipline; foster or retard the growth and power of a trade association; instill the trust or suspicion of competitors in the integrity of one's business practices; or increase or reduce the probability of government investigation and criminal prosecution.

The effects of most business actions are extremely difficult to forecast, but an executive must attempt to forecast them. Before selecting an alternative, the executive should consciously consider all possible effects.

If the concept of price elasticity of demand has any value to price-setters, it is in forecasting the effect of price changes. Therefore, the following questions should be asked: Can price elasticity of demand be measured accurately? How much do such measurements cost? How long are such measurements valid? Does price elasticity apply to all geographic markets or only represent an average of all regions? Do elasticity measurements apply equally to all items in a firm's line of products? Is the elasticity of demand the same for all brands of the same product? The emphatic answer is that it is impossible to measure accurately the price elasticity of demand for any brand or product. However, executives responsible for pricing must continue to improve their understanding of the effects of price changes on sales.

Can a measure of demand be developed that is a better indicator than the price elasticity of demand? As implied above, past experience is an unreliable guide to present relationships. Rather than seek a quantitative measure of price elasticity, perhaps a different concept is needed. Businessmen will rarely change price alone, but ordinarily adopt a marketing program coordinated around the proposed price change. A marketing executive wishes to forecast the effects of the total marketing program, rather than the effect of price change alone.

Since most markets are highly dynamic and extremely complex, one cannot expect to develop reliable quantitative measures of the effects of different marketing programs on unit sales. How can a marketing executive forecast the results of alternative price strategies and marketing programs? He must intuitively estimate the effects of the program; however, he will rarely find precisely comparable circumstances in either his own firm's experience or in that of other firms. Specifically, the executive should consider the extent to which his price change will be perceived; the possible interpretations that customers and resellers can attribute to his price change; and the effects of customers' reactions to the price changes.

Select Among Alternative Outcomes

When a price-setter forecasts the outcomes of alternative actions, he selects that alternative which best achieves his objectives. As indicated earlier, an executive actually pursues many objectives; therefore, the selection among alternatives is quite difficult in practice, although it is simple in principle. An index should be developed to indicate the extent to which any set of outcomes achieves the executive's multiple goals—weighing each one according to its importance. Various outcomes of each feasible course of action can then be forecast by assigning probabilities to each one. The action selected should represent the alternative that best realizes product, department, and corporate goals, while reflecting an acceptable amount of risk.

Summary

Pricing involves far more than arriving at a dollar and cents figure for a single product. A price-setter is responsible for managing a complex function, even though pricing involves relatively little effort for the implementation of decisions. To manage the pricing function, a firm must develop a detailed hierarchy of objectives; a monitor system; explicit mathematical models; and, most importantly, new approaches to pricing management.

The corporate pricing function within a decision-making structure is a very complex process. Many components must be integrated and managed as a unit if the firm is quickly to capitalize on its pricing opportunities.

QUESTIONS

1. Has pricing remained an intuitive activity primarily because of a lack of theory in the pricing area? Give reasons for your answer.

2. How closely have the situations and conditions used in pricing research mirrored the situations and conditions managers must face when actually making price decisions?

3. How do economic models of pricing differ from behavioral models?

4. Describe the range of alternative actions a manager could take when faced with a pricing problem.

5. Explain why the author refers to the pricing decision as developing a function rather than arriving at a single dollar figure.

2

RISK-AVERSIVE PRICING POLICIES: PROBLEMS AND ALTERNATIVES

Joseph P. Guiltinan

The author indicates that the usual responses to the riskiness of pricing decisions are cost related or selling related. Since these responses are somewhat ineffective and create many additional problems, more effective alternative responses are suggested.

The marketing manager for a heavy-equipment manufacturing concern in northern Ohio recently suggested that before 1973 he spent no more than three days a year on pricing policy but that currently pricing dominates all marketing policy-making activities in his firm. This experience is not unusual. Decision makers are becoming increasingly aware that pricing policy changes must be made with consideration for possible major shifts in economic conditions such as the prices and availability of raw materials, aggregate demand, interest and exchange rates, and liquidity. Uncertainty regarding these economic forces leads to uncertain and fluctuating gross margins, creates difficulties in planning working capital needs, and impedes budgeting. Since price can influence cash flow and margins more quickly than other marketing variables, the development of policy regarding price levels, changes, and discounts has become of paramount concern in current marketing practice.

This article reviews some current pricing responses to economic uncertainties and identifies key problems associated with the implementation of these responses. In particular, responses that reflect risk-aversive, defensive perspectives are of primary concern. While it is often appropriate for managers to adopt policies that seek to minimize risk, this article contends that such responses may have unanticipated consequences that entail a good deal of risk. Alternative courses of action for developing pricing policies under economic uncertainty are also presented. The analysis is based on concepts, practices, and theories gleaned from marketing theory, general business periodicals, and a series of executive development pricing seminars in which the author has participated with senior pricing executives.

Current Pricing Responses

Most current pricing responses reported in the literature are concerned with reducing the risk of low margins, avoiding bottlenecks, and improving cash flows.[1] In general, these responses are of two types: cost based and selling related.

Cost-Based Pricing Responses

Many current pricing methods and related product decisions are primarily responses to production cost uncertainties and related pressures on margins.

ADOPTION OF "DELAYED-QUOTATION" PRICING. In this approach, which is particularly widespread among manufacturers of custom-made products such as machine tools, the seller sets a final price only when the items have reached the stage of finished goods. This is due to a combination of long production lead times (often because of bottlenecks on key materials) and rapidly escalating prices (typically in metals and petro-chemicals). This approach (which includes the "price at time of delivery" variation) is not novel but has been practiced much more broadly the past couple of years.

ELIMINATION OF LOW-MARGIN PRODUCTS. This policy has also received widespread attention by firms that are uncertain about future cost increases or their ability to pass such increases forward. In addition, the cost and unavailability of working capital have made it unprofitable to maintain inventories of low-margin items.

ADOPTION OF "ESCALATOR" CLAUSES. This policy is simply one in which price increases (frequently across-the-board increases on all items in a product

---

[1] This section was developed based particularly on: Daniel Nimer, "Pricing Capital Goods," *Industrial Marketing*, March 1971, pp. 53–55; "Profitless Boom in Machine Tools," *Business Week*, July 6, 1974, pp. 52–54; "Pricing Strategy in an Inflation Economy," *Business Week*, April 6, 1974, pp. 43–49; and "The Squeeze on Product Mix," *Business Week*, January 5, 1974, pp. 50–55; as well as from discussions with pricing executives.

line) are automatically implemented based on a previously stated formula. The objective is to alleviate the risks involved in cost increases. The bases for such escalations include simple factors such as increases in wholesale price indexes, industry-specific published indexes, listed price increases of raw material suppliers, or highly complex formulas that incorporate increased costs of labor, energy, and several material inputs. The effective use of such escalators depends on the willingness of customers to accept them, and on the firm's ability to change the formula over time as cost structures change and to measure variations in cost changes across products.

Selling-Related Pricing Responses

These responses focus on increasing margins by reducing customer incentives used by the sales force (particularly in industrial firms). While they reflect cost pressures, unlike cost-based responses they have a minimal impact on direct list prices. Rather, they reflect an attempt to redirect sales efforts to nonprice approaches.

UNBUNDLING OF SERVICES.   In this response, a firm that has priced a major product (typically a large, complex piece of equipment) to include special services, peripheral equipment, or replacement parts shifts to a policy in which each element of the product-service mix is priced separately. Typically, the sum of the prices (after unbundling) will exceed the old, single price. Thus, unbundling represents the elimination of a form of product-line discount to buyers purchasing the full mix.

REDUCE CASH AND QUANTITY DISCOUNTS.   Because discounts represent direct reductions in the gross margins earned by sellers, there is a temptation to arbitrarily eliminate many cash and quantity discounts as a means of improving margins. Further, many firms have found that large customers (including many government agencies) often subtract the cash discount but still fail to pay invoices within the stipulated period. The incentive to maintain quantity discounts is also reduced for suppliers who experience shortages of key materials.

ELIMINATION OF PRICE "SHADING."   The concept of varying price policy, or "shading," is one in which reductions from list price are made as the result of negotiations between buyers and salesmen. The recent trend toward a "one-price" policy in many firms can be attributed to the desire to maintain gross margins (as was the case with discounts), to centralize control over pricing (by removing the sales force from this role), and to attempt to generate more sales effort in nonprice attributes of the product.

While pricing is generally a competitive tool for increasing demand for a firm (and often a tool for stimulating industry demand), risk-aversive policies generally do not explicitly consider competitive response and consumer demand as significant inputs to the pricing decision. This appears to result from the knowledge that similar pressures (such as the rising cost of materials) also usually plague competitors, from the expectation that competitors will adopt (or have adopted) similar policies (especially on discounts or escalators), or from limitations in the comparability of products and service among competitors.

Problems Experienced with Current Pricing Responses

For a variety of reasons, an individual enterprise may find that the foregoing responses are difficult to implement or that they lead to unintended consequences. Marketing theory and the experiences of many pricing executives are used in this section to illustrate such difficulties.

Distribution and Sales Force Problems

Distributors may react negatively to the elimination of discounts because in some cases this may eliminate part of their competitive advantage, because it typically violates traditional trade practices, and because it reduces possible bases for promoting the product to final buyers. Similarly, they will react negatively to any changes that influence the total effectiveness of a product line (such as the elimination of an important low-margin, sales-leading product). Consequently, the degree of reseller support may be influenced by such pricing policies.

It is also important to understand the nature of distributors' cost and profit structures before radically changing discount policies. For instance, one St. Louis manufacturer eliminated quantity discounts to improve margins and then learned that many of the firm's distributors relied almost exclusively on the discount for the profit they made on that company's products.

Many of the risk-aversive responses also lead to a serious alteration in the role of the company sales force, often diminishing the role of the salesman while giving him the task of smoothing over customer reactions to price increases and product shortages and backlogs. This role change is likely to lead to increased sales force dissatisfaction and turnover.

Product-Line Problems

Where arbitrary elimination of low-margin items or unbundling takes place, product-line considerations on both the production and demand sides become important. Low-margin items may significantly stimulate sales of complementary, high-margin items, especially where items are bundled. Accordingly, care must be taken to ascertain the competitiveness of each element of the mix when unbundling takes place. For instance, a small institutional services firm in Tennessee found that it was not equally competitive on all components of the product-service mix, and declining sales of part of the line more than offset the revenue gains from price changes.

When a price change significantly affects end prices, buyers' perceptions of the entire line's price/quality image may be influenced.[2] A western manufacturer of special fertilizer products recently introduced a third, middle-of-the-line product. However, pricing executives failed to price it high enough to avoid a perception of similarity in quality to the low-end product, which had just experienced a price increase. Thus, both products appealed to the same market and few new customers were obtained.

Where bottlenecks are a problem, the decision to concentrate on so-called high-margin items may backfire. To the extent that high-margin items require materials, labor, or equipment in short supply, production capacity will be underutilized and total dollar margins may not be maximized.

Escalator Clauses and Cost-Forecasting Problems

Probably no pricing problems are as pervasive as those associated with escalators. Most firms can readily appreciate the problem of spiraling costs and, consequently, industrial buyers appear more willing to accept some sort of escalator provision today.

Problems related to escalators fall into categories typified by the following:

- A California aircraft supplier must bid now on products to be delivered in 1983.
- An Indiana automotive parts manufacturer has had a bid for a large order rejected until the company indicates what percentage of a cost increase it will absorb itself and what portion of its escalator clause is attributable to labor and each of various materials.
- A New England manufacturer in the electronics industry developed a cost escalator based heavily on the price of copper. When copper prices fell, his customers demanded sharp price decreases; yet other cost elements that were not incorporated into the escalator formula had recently increased significantly.

These considerations demonstrate the need for improved and realistic costing. This is true whether a firm is developing an escalator clause for direct use in a contract or for setting a fixed future price.

---

[2] This is treated in detail in Kent B. Monroe, "Buyers' Subjective Perceptions of Price," *Journal of Marketing Research*, Vol. 10 (February 1973), pp. 70–80.

Problems Related to Demand Curve Assumptions

A fundamental problem with all cost-based pricing strategies is the implicit assumption that demand is inelastic. Such assumptions gain credence if recent price increases have not resulted in any major loss of sales. Even where demand curve estimates are developed, however, three factors must be considered: [3]

CUMULATIVE PRICE INCREASE EFFECTS AND CONFOUNDING REAL INCOME EFFECTS.   The presence of either or both of these effects often results in the invalidation of historical price/quantity relationships.

Illustrative of this is the plight of a Texas manufacturer of metal home improvement products. Normally, sales in this industry are booming and demand is inelastic when new construction is down. As the recession began to take shape in mid-1974, however, this firm's home improvement sales began to slide when prices were raised to reflect steel and aluminum cost increases, even though new housing starts remained low.

This situation probably resulted from both of the effects suggested above. As price increases become more frequent, historical relationships become less applicable because the historical range of price/quantity observations is increasingly remote from current price levels. The firm may well have moved into a range where demand elasticity is higher.

Demand estimates may also be confounded when economic forces (such as recessions) result in a downward shift in the demand curve. Smaller quantities are demanded at all (or most) price levels as either the rate of use or number of users diminishes.

In both cases, the failure of historical relationships to hold reduces the usefulness of simple statistical demand curve models and of untempered executive judgments that rely on recent sales history. More complex forecasting models that incorporate economic conditions as well as price variables may reduce confounding effects. Where feasible, the use of experimentation or surveys may provide some information for updating judgments.

POOR SALES FORCE ESTIMATES OF DEMAND.   Sales force estimates of the effect of price changes are considered inadequate by many pricing executives. The tendency to rely on price selling and the desire to be more competitive have generally made subjective sales force estimates of the effects of a price reduction very optimistic and their estimates of the effects of increases very pessimistic. The controller of an Ohio-based equipment manufacturer sug-

---

[3] For a more extensive discussion of demand curve estimation problems and approaches, see Mark Alpert, "Demand Curve Estimation and Psychological Pricing," in *Managerial Analysis in Marketing*, Frederick D. Sturdivant et al. (Glenview, Ill.; Scott, Foresman & Co., 1970), Chap. 10.

gested that his sales force typically overestimates actual sales increases by about one-fourth of unit volume when queried about the effects of prospective price decreases. Consequently, sales force estimates may be ignored if not accompanied by supportive value analysis comparisons, data on customer revenue trends, or other specific customer purchasing constraints.

LIMITATIONS OF THE DEMAND CURVE CONCEPT.   Elasticity and demand curve estimates reflect the impact of price on total revenue only. While revenue may increase as a result of a price increase, reduced unit volume may result in sharply increased average unit costs when fixed costs are a major portion of total costs.

Problems with Cost Orientation in General

In the long run, perhaps the most serious problem facing firms that adopt cost-oriented approaches to pricing is the self-perpetuating nature of the price squeeze that often results—particularly in periods of reduced consumer and industrial demand. Automatic and continual escalation of prices merely to preserve target gross margins is a fundamental culprit in prolonging recessions. When such increases occur in the elastic zone of a demand curve, reductions in demand in response to these changes often lead to increased average unit cost. This, in turn, leads to increased prices by those firms that rely on target margins as a pricing device (even in the absence of further increases in labor, energy, and materials costs).

The foregoing problems in demand curve estimation notwithstanding, pricing executives must consider the unit-sales implications of average-cost pricing. When the pricing objective is to maximize profit, then it is appropriate to use marginal analysis of the incremental costs and expected incremental revenue associated with either a price cut or the attempt to avoid a price increase.

In short, many firms are now realizing that pricing to maintain a given gross margin may not really be a low-risk strategy. In an economy where demand may be increasingly elastic and where fixed costs are very high for most industries, lower margins may be required to maintain adequate demand. Stated alternatively, it will generally prove counterproductive to rely solely on higher prices and margins to deal with problems of cost control and cost forecasting. Since risk-aversive policies may not achieve the objectives for which they were designed, perhaps more positive approaches are needed.

Developing Some Alternative Responses

Given that many of the current pricing responses will not be appropriate for a given firm due to the problems outlined above, some alternative responses do exist that may be more consistent with the actual decision environment. Further, some guidelines are available to help pricing executives evaluate and implement alternative policies.

Developing Price Objectives

Price responses are always made with some objective in mind, at least implicitly. As suggested earlier, objectives such as improving margins, avoiding bottlenecks, and improving cash flow seem to be the dominant forces behind current price responses. However, such objectives may not be mutually consistent. Focusing on high-margin products may lead to increased bottlenecks due to the materials or labor required, or it may lead to reduced total cash flow as a result of reduced sales of items complementary to low-margin items. Accordingly, a clear statement of the objectives of pricing policy is a fundamental requirement for selecting alternatives. Also, the impact of short-term policies and objectives on long-term profit must be clarified. As Kotler suggests, the identification of weak products should consider potential sales growth and annual cash flow generated per dollar of asset tied up in the product.[4]

Positive Pricing Perspective

While most current price responses are risk-aversive, organizations that have clearly defined price objectives, that have carefully analyzed the pricing and cost environment, and that are organized to absorb and act on all appropriate information should be in a position to act positively and opportunistically in creating pricing policy. The following policies illustrate this posture.

- Balance pricing policy on a major product with policy on related items. For instance, by restricting large price increases to replacement parts, services, and complementary items, a West Coast firm was able to hold the line on price increases for the major item.

- Employ a varying price policy (where injurious price discrimination is not a problem) as a tool that permits the sales force to orient demand toward those products that the firm wishes to promote and to obtain a foothold in new accounts for the long run. Maintaining this policy may be especially effective in softening the blow of price increases or reduced cash discounts.

- Rather than reduce quantity discounts and promotional allowances, use them creatively to stimulate demand for products not requiring critical resources, or to partly offset price-level increases. Further, as costs change, frequent review of the quantity discount structure becomes imperative and may lead to the discovery of

---

[4]Philip Kotler, "Marketing During Periods of Shortage," JOURNAL OF MARKETING, Vol. 38 (July 1974), pp. 20–29.

more marketable and more competitive quantity discount policies. (Interestingly, many firms are not even aware of competitors' quantity discount structures.)

- Where cash discounts are under review, be sure to consider both the marketing and financial issues involved (including changes in short-term interest rates). A period of tight money and inflation may present opportunities to obtain new customers and build long-term goodwill. Many firms have countered the trend toward eliminating cash discounts by initiating or expanding them. One California manufacturer reported that the average age of accounts receivable was reduced by over 40 days with the initiation of a 1½% cash discount, thus dramatically reducing working capital binds. (Note that paying 1½% for getting payment 40 days earlier is tantamount to paying: $\frac{360 \text{ days/year}}{40 \text{ days}} \times 1\frac{1}{2}\% = 13.5\%$ annual interest for that money.)

- Where buyers fail to pay invoices on time, several firms have invoked penalty charges at 1% to 1½% per month with some success.

- To spread the financing costs of large-scale capital projects, a Pennsylvania construction firm began to write contracts that included progress payments—with the first payment made at the start of construction.

- Discounts may also serve as an alternative to escalator clauses. An Ohio manufacturer with a large product line has begun to print price lists that are expected to last six months. However, at the start of the period, all products are discounted to all buyers; as cost increases occur, discounts are reduced. This practice reduces the number of price increases and eliminates the problem of delays in buyer notification of changes.

- Cash or merchandise rebates (promotion allowances) may be useful for industrial manufacturers as well as for consumer products manufacturers. As in the case of across-the-board discounting, this avoids a complete overhaul of price lists (and related notification) for short-term pricing policies.

- Conduct periodic audits of the cost structures of all major products or (where joint costs are difficult to separate) major product groups before developing escalator clauses. Such audits would examine possible savings in labor, energy, or distribution costs that might offset cost increases in materials. This approach frequently makes escalators more palatable to buyers by demonstrating the seller's good faith in holding down controllable costs and by developing an up-to-date data base for constructing realistic escalator indexes. Several firms have uncovered previously undetected productivity improvements on some items (often due to learning curve effects) which enabled them to set more competitive prices on those products.

- Exploit the product life cycle.[5] As products go through growth, maturity, and decline, price levels and promotional policy change to meet consumer, competitive, and technological changes. Typically, one would expect practices such as discounts, shading, and product-service bundles to be fundamental aspects of

---

[5] See Chester Wasson, *Product Management* (St. Charles, Ill.: Challenge Books, 1971) for thorough treatment of pricing over the product life cycle.

marketing strategy in the maturity/saturation stages, where price level and technological parity tend to exist.

- Where demand conditions permit, increase the use of long-term contracts to guarantee transactions, in part to reduce costs, but also to guard against multiple ordering by buyers who are attempting to hedge against further inflation and who will likely cancel out at a later time. This is particularly important for products where material shortages and long production backlogs formerly existed.[6]

- Employ new sales force incentives to meet production, cash flow, and margin objectives, to reduce reliance on price shading, and to stimulate more sales force concern with accurate demand estimation.

- Promote distributor cooperation by: expanding cooperative promotions on key items, emphasizing any product improvement associated with price increases, contrasting price increases with either industry averages or the Industrial Wholesale Price Index, and noting that distributors selling on commission or fixed percentage discount will increase their gross income.[7]

Conclusion

Each firm faces a unique set of cost, supply, customer demand, and competitive forces at a given point in time, and each must select its price objectives and policies accordingly. This article has suggested some considerations for making policy selection. Pricing executives should avoid adopting current practices used by other firms without considering the problems that may hinder their implementation or that may lead to unintended consequences. Pricing responses should be developed on the basis of clearly defined price objectives, incorporating research on the anticipated effects of price changes. Further, pricing policy under uncertainty need not consist solely of defensive, risk-aversive alternatives, but can be positive and opportunistic in perspective.

Price has long been one of the most ignored dimensions of marketing policy in both academia and industry.[8] The cost-oriented, risk-aversive trends that are so prominent in current business practice seem to bear this out. Firms are defensive about pricing, probably because its ramifications are not well understood. Improved knowledge of this aspect of marketing may be an unforeseen benefit of attempts to deal with the current problems.

---

[6] "A Reducing Diet for Inventories," *Business Week*, August 3, 1974.

[7] "Is There a 'Best Way' to Tell Distributors of Price Hike?" *Industrial Marketing*, June 1967, pp. 27–32.

[8] See Alfred Oxenfeldt, "A Decision-Making Structure for Price Decisions," JOURNAL OF MARKETING, Vol. 37 (January 1973), pp. 48–49, for an excellent discussion of this problem.

QUESTIONS

1. What are "selling-related" pricing strategies?
2. What are the disadvantages of "cost-based" pricing strategies?
3. Describe the difference between risk-aversive pricing and positive pricing as described by the author.
4. What are some positive pricing alternatives to using escalator clauses?
5. How should competitive price responses be developed?

3

FLEXIBLE PRICING: INDUSTRY'S NEW STRATEGY TO HOLD MARKET SHARE CHANGES THE RULES FOR ECONOMIC DECISION-MAKING

Business Week

Due to the economic pressures of inflation, recession, and foreign competition, firms have moved toward more short-lived and flexible pricing policies. This article describes these tendencies and discusses the reasons for them.

Scissored between soaring costs and sluggish demand at home and under intense competitive pressure from abroad, U.S. companies are overhauling ancient formulas for setting prices:

- To fight Japanese inroads, Ford Motor Co. and General Motors Corp., in an unprecedented move, are charging less for their 1978 subcompacts on the West Coast than elsewhere in the country.
- In a challenge to the industry's traditional price leaders, Armco Steel Co. last month announced plans to cut prices on four stainless steel products by an average of 5%.
- In an industry long sheltered by government regulation of competition, airlines have been slashing prices to hold on to market shares.
- In almost every consumer goods industry where producers had long believed that strong brand identification insulated their products from competition from cheaper makes, scores of famous names—Zenith, RCA, Singer, and even Sony Corp. of

America—are being propelled headlong into a new world of fierce price competition.

The upshot is little short of a revolution in pricing practices that will have ramifications for capital spending, the inflation rate, industrial concentration, and the application of existing antitrust laws. Above all, though, an ability to adapt to the new pricing environment will characterize those companies that succeed in competing over the next decade.

The chief characteristics of the new price strategy are flexibility and a willingness to cut prices aggressively to hold market shares. On the way out the window are many of the pricing traditions of the U.S. industrial giants. Companies no longer try to hang on to fixed markups over cost through thick and thin. The strong no longer hold the umbrella of high prices firmly over weaker competitors. And in many industries, customary price leadership— where competitors passively follow a big company that sets the price for all—is on its way out.

The new practices differ radically from the old in aim and concept. The traditional model for pricing by large industrial corporations was codified in the management system introduced at General Motors by Alfred P. Sloan in the 1920s. Pricing was essentially static. Companies set a price that they believed would provide a desired long-run "target rate of return" at a given production volume. Although management was obviously forced to deviate from this pricing ideal by competition, the aim nevertheless was to create a pricing structure that was programmed to change gradually and predictably and to stick to it. Price changes to meet competition were regarded as the exception rather than the rule. The list price on steel mill products, for example, rose less than 4% from 1950 to 1965; aluminum by about 3%. The prices of industrial commodities and crude materials fluctuated only slightly over these years . . . [Figure 1]. Even though price-cutting occurred at the fringes of the market, the corporate establishment looked on it with disdain as "chiseling" and sometimes disciplined the offender, as happened in steel in 1968, when several small companies tried to undercut the industry price.

Although this may seem like a strategy better suited to industrial pachyderms than the modern managers that Sloan was supposed to have inspired, it was, in fact, well-suited to the climate produced by the rapid growth of the first 2½ decades following World War II. To set a price that will be consistent with meeting profit targets over the long run, companies must be able to count on generally high levels of capacity utilization and predictability in the future course of costs and product demand. Although there were four recessions between 1945 and the end of the 1960s, companies in general found themselves in an atmosphere in which it made sense to gear business decisions, including pricing decisions, to long-run aims. Sloan-style pricing was an integral element in a business environment where companies confidently told securities analysts that they were aiming to iron out earnings fluctuations and were attempting to meet high and steady targets—such as Citicorp's famed 15% per year—for earnings growth.

The New Flexibility

But in this decade, two recessions in five years, price controls introduced by a Republican Administration, and double-digit inflation have undermined the predictability and stability of growth as planning assumptions. And the restrictive policy reaction to inflationary forces—particularly in quadrupling of oil prices in 1974—sealed the doom of the old price strategy, by producing slow growth and excess industrial capacity around the world.

The initial business response was a confused attempt to pass on cost increases in an unthinking way—an effort to retain target rates of return but in an atmosphere requiring higher and higher prices. But with unused capacity around the world, there was just too little demand and too much competition to allow target return pricing to work. Indeed, 1975 and 1976 were marked by repeated retreats from announced industrywide price boosts in steel, paper, aluminum, and chemicals [see Figure 1].

"Target pricing just does not prove to be as viable as it once was," says Robert F. Lanzillotti, dean of the University of Florida School of Business and a member of the commission that administered Phase II of President Nixon's price control program. "Firms are becoming much more flexible in their price thinking now." Businessmen acknowledge that the days of complacent attitudes toward pricing are over. "We were fat, dumb, and happy back in the 1960s," says a top executive of a major chemical company, "but now most companies have been so badly burned that it will be a long time before they commit themselves to a long-run pricing strategy."

Instead, companies throughout the U.S. economy, from mammoth chemical companies to small computer time-sharing complexes, are turning to a pricing strategy that is flexible in every respect. It is a strategy, says Norma Pace, chief economist at the American Paper Institute, that stresses pricing "product by product instead of the whole glob." While companies have always shown some willingness to adjust prices, or profit margins, on specific products as market conditions varied, this kind of flexibility is being carried to the state of a high art.

Long-term contracts that passed on cost increases from sellers to buyers flourished in the 1950s and 1960s. But they are now breaking down in a wide range of industries, including chemicals, where they have been a way of

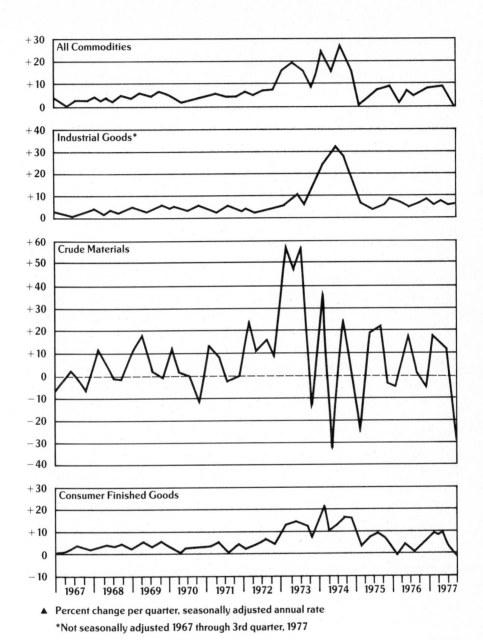

▲ Percent change per quarter, seasonally adjusted annual rate
  *Not seasonally adjusted 1967 through 3rd quarter, 1977

FIGURE 1   *Wholesale prices have become far more volatile.*

life, in favor of short-lived and more flexible—but far less predictable—
arrangements.

Companies are taking several major steps to make their price policies bob and weave like a well-trained boxer dodging the blows of his opponent. They are juggling prices among products—raising some, lowering others—to get the maximum mix of sales and profits.

Marketing Autos

In the automobile industry, for example, companies are "doing a balancing act in pricing that is highly dynamic," says an economist at one of the Big Three auto manufacturers. "And this means a more sensitive effort to assess the competitive relationship of products and the costs of making them." GM still dominates auto pricing and it uses long-range profit targets as a guide. Nevertheless, the auto industry is an excellent example of how a confluence of forces—government-mandated product standards, foreign competition, and worries over slow growth—is generating a new pricing strategy.

For auto makers, a special impetus to be flexible comes in part from an attempt to produce and market a product mix that will maximize profits while on average meeting federal gas mileage requirements. But equally important have been the squeeze from foreign competition and a general industry expectation of slower growth in car sales in the long run. Low-cost subcompact models, especially from Japan, such as Hondas, Toyotas, and Datsuns, have been taking an increasing share of the domestic market—the total import share had grown from less than 15% in 1976 to over 20% last September. Moreover, many auto economists say the market is near saturation with one car for every two Americans.

After raising prices last year on small cars, GM this year has slashed the price of its subcompact Chevrolet Chevette to head off foreign competition. More striking, though, is that GM and Ford have begun to price by geography, with geographic differences in prices exceeding traditional transportation cost differentials. Subcompact models—such as the Ford Pinto—were reduced 10% on the West Coast, where Japanese competition is the stiffest, and 6% in the rest of the country.

To offset the lower profit margins on lower-price, small cars, the industry is already raising the prices of large-size cars. The Cadillac Seville and Lincoln Versailles now sell for more than $14,000—four times the price of the lowest-price model. Ten years ago the top of the line was three times as costly as the lowest-price car. And some industry experts think this trend toward a wider pricing spread will intensify. "GM will be selling a $30,000 Cadillac by 1985," says Eugene F. Jennings, professor of management at Michigan State University.

Of course, such a pricing strategy is beyond the means of American Motors Corp., which does not build large-sized luxury cars. "I'm sure that GM, in its approach to small-car pricing, is awful damn glad it's got Cadillac Sevilles," says AMC Chairman Roy D. Chapin Jr.

In line with the new flexibility, manufacturers are now trying to build models in the low, medium, and high price ranges into each car size—small, intermediate, and full. By adding luxury appointments and optional equipment, companies are able to charge more, even for smaller-size cars. Chrysler Corp.'s intermediate-size Volaré, for example, now has stripped-down and luxury models as well as several special models, such as the high-performance Volaré Road Runner.

The airline industry has plunged into fierce competition as carriers break away from federally regulated, industry-wide fares and initiate flexible pricing to maximize the use of seat space and airliners. Last summer Trans World Airlines Inc. began offering no-frills service on its Chicago to Los Angeles route, with discounts up to 43% off standard fare. Now the three other major airlines on that route—American, Continental, and United—have matched TWA's price cut. Flexible and more competitive pricing on domestic and international routes is fast becoming widespread.

The End of Price Leadership

Sharply rising energy costs, too, can impel companies to price flexibly. In the paper industry, for example, "companies now price selectively to protect profit margins," says economist Pace. The industry is the economy's second-largest industrial consumer of energy. In contrast, prior to the 1973 oil embargo, paper companies were able simply "to price across the board in reaction to overall changes in the economy," says Pace.

The new environment is forcing companies into what would have been regarded as an act of corporate sacrilege only a few years ago: They are violating the price leader-price follower pattern. "The worst thing a company can do now is price identically to its competitors," says Gerard Badler, director of service programs at the Strategy Planning Institute, a nonprofit research center in Cambridge, Mass. "It should either price above or below the competition—anything to set itself apart—but it should never price equally."

Under target return pricing, the price for the industry was set by the industry leader—usually the company with the largest market share, such as a U.S. Steel Corp. or an International Business Machines Corp. Then the smaller companies fell in behind with identical prices. The system was designed to stave off price wars and "predatory" competition, which would force down prices and hurt all parties. Companies that deviated from this norm were chastised by discounting or shaving by the leaders. Price deviation was quickly disciplined. In the steel industry, for example, price discipline was so stringent "that in 1968 Bethlehem Steel came on as the price enforcer," says Eugene J. Frank, vice-president of Shearson Hayden Stone Inc. in Pittsburgh. In this case, Bethlehem announced formal price cuts. Within three months prices were raised back to the accepted industrywide level.

Now, however, smaller companies are taking bold steps to undercut the price leader. For example, while list prices of steel display a semblance of cooperation, companies are discounting prices of steel products more than ever. According to government sources, there is strong evidence that steel companies are offering substantial discounts under pressure from surging steel imports, which now account for nearly 20% of the total domestic market. "When this year's operating results are out, you're going to see that discounts of as much as 15% have been offered," say steel analyst Frank. "They are much bigger than expected." According to Frank, the large discounts have been offered in the Great Lakes market, where foreign imports have jumped by 73% this year.

Steel discounting does not always take the form of pure price reductions but often shows up in the elimination of inventory and freight charges or the knocking down of so-called "extra" charges for special cutting and treating of steel that normally are added to list prices. This kind of surreptitious price-shaving has gone on before, but now it is more intense that ever.

The only company that has publicly admitted to discounting is Armco Steel. Its big structural steel mill in Houston has taken a pounding from Gulf Coast imports, which now account for about 50% of the regional market. Last November the company announced a "foreign fighter" pricing campaign, shaving 20% off list prices and launching a splashy media effort against imported steel. Although the company suspended the discounts in the spring because the Japanese were still undercutting its prices, Armco revived the program this fall and recently announced that it would keep it running through next January. Now other steel makers reluctantly admit that they are meeting the Armco discount. Further, Armco last month announced actual price cuts on four stainless products—an average decrease of about 5% that will put pressure on its competitors to break their price rigidity.

Domestic steel companies are hoping that the so-called "reference pricing" system now being drawn up by the Treasury Dept. will protect them from Japanese competition. The reference price sets a minimum price below which Japanese steelmakers—who account for 50% of all steel imports—cannot sell products in the U.S. market. But reference pricing will help U.S. steelmakers only if the price is set near the current list price for steel. If it is set substantially lower, domestic companies will be forced to either cut prices or continue to lose business to the Japanese competition.

Even if reference pricing succeeds in protecting domestic steel companies from foreign price competition, it still may be too late to resuscitate price discipline. It is widely held that in the past companies would announce to the press their desire to stop price discounting as a way of signaling to the other companies to restore industrywide pricing. Right now industry executives admit they are having problems with such signals because companies have become so accustomed to the competitive environment.

In the chemical industry, price leadership is breaking down under pressure from several forces. Competition from foreign chemical companies, such as West Germany's giant Bayer, is growing steadily, and global demand is flagging. The result has been "a rash of temporary allowances on prices that breaks the industry discipline," says a chemical industry analyst.

Traditional patterns of price leadership also are breaking down in the glass container industry, with smaller companies moving to the fore in pricing. Last year, for example, Owens-Illinois Inc.—which is larger than its next five competitors combined—increased its list prices by 4½%. Fearing that the increase would hurt sales to brewing companies that were just beginning to switch to glass bottles, the smaller companies broke ranks and offered huge discounts. The action not only negated O-I's increase but served notice that the smaller companies were after O-I's market share. "In effect, the smaller companies became the price leaders in order to entice the brewers," says William A. Kerr, president of Kerr Glass Mfg. Corp. in Los Angeles.

Revising the Rules

Indeed, it is often a desperate financial condition that drives many small companies to break the follow-the-leader rule. "The small firms are always the first to feel a dwindling cash flow," says one economist, "so it comes as no surprise that they aren't afraid to go for the jugular."

Price decisions and product decisions are obviously interconnected. In the new environment, companies more than ever either are trying to carve out a niche where they can raise prices without sacrificing sales or cut prices and try to gain a larger market share with aggressive pricing. "We now find that loss of volume has profit implications as significant as price markups on each unit," says John J. Nevin, chairman of Zenith Radio Corp. Zenith was badly burned by Japanese competition in the TV-set market because it insisted on keeping prices up to protect profit margins. "We're making a more aggressive bid to make the maximum use of price to catch up with imports," says Nevin.

The key to securing a niche is for companies to distinguish their product from others on the market. Says the financial vice-president of a large data-processing company: "Because we can no longer depend on forward pricing, we try to find a proprietary enclave where our product has a unique application. This offers us a competitive alternative and helps protect our revenue stream from fluctuations." For this company, the solution lies in tailoring its data-processing services to customers' particular in-house computer requirements—such as inventory and production control. "We look harder now to find services that others just don't yet provide," says the vice-president.

Selecting the proper market segment has led many companies to centralize pricing decisions in corporate headquarters, taking the authority out of the hands of division heads and sales representatives. For example, at U.S. Elevator Corp., a subsidiary of Cubic Corp., top management now allows its salesmen to bid only on jobs priced under $100,000. All other bidding is handled by a headquarters "estimating group" that has doubled its staff in the last two years.

And to avoid cutthroat competition in the sluggish construction industry, says U.S. Elevator President George C. Tweed, "we try to find something to sell where we have a unique edge. Then pricing isn't quite so traumatic." Tweed has increased his service business by 40% in the last year and is now emphasizing so-called "special projects" such as shipboard elevators and nuclear-plant elevators. "The secret is seeking out business that nobody else wants," says Tweed.

Along the 'Learning Curve'

The best example of a successful "market niche" pricing strategy is provided by the Hewlett-Packard Co. In the highly competitive pocket calculator market, where price-cutting is rampant, H-P has been able to thrive by offering high-priced products for a select segment of the market. H-P equips its products with special features and then offers its calculators at an average price higher than the industry average. To stay in the market with this strategy, H-P must continually vary its product line and offer new models as the competition rushes in to undercut H-P's price. So far, the strategy has been successful: H-P's pretax income has grown by a staggering 400% since 1967.

While H-P follows the market niche strategy, its major competitor follows a market share strategy. Texas Instruments Inc. employs a pricing system based on high sales volume for a limited product line. It is called "design-to-cost" planning and relies on the concept of the learning or experience curve. The concept holds that production costs will decline as output rises, partly because of economies of scale, but—more important—because machines and workers "learn" with time how to produce standard products faster. TI prices along its learning curve, which means steadily lower prices at higher levels of output for a relatively unchanging product. "We perform a careful study of the market to see how it expands as the price of the product is lowered," says Charles H. Phipps, TI's head of strategic planning and corporate development.

Pricing along the learning curve to maximize market share "has been a strategy of the Japanese for years in gaining a hold on U.S. markets," says Harvard Business School professor Steven C. Wheelwright. "They have used it in everything from steel, to textiles, to electronics." Now, U.S. companies are finally using this aggressive price strategy against the Japanese in the burgeoning new market for TV-set tape recorders. RCA Corp. made the first major price move in August when it set a suggested price of $1,000. Last month Zenith cut its suggested price to $995 from $1,295. Under pressure from these price cuts, Sony recently announced it would lower the price of its Betamax model by $200, to $1,095. However, most analysts agree that Sony will have to lower its price further to stay in the market.

Basic processing industries such as steel and chemicals have been the slowest to learn the market share strategy. But these are the industries that need it the most, according to marketing expert Bruce D. Henderson of Boston Consulting Group Inc. "These companies have been too concerned with earnings and short-term cash flow," he argues. "They have to be willing to give up short-run profits to gain market share."

Contending that "once market share shifts, it rarely shifts back," Henderson says that companies in these industries must build capacity faster than their competitors. "Once capacity is in place, the competition can't enter the market at the same price," says Henderson.

The problem, he says, is that companies in the past have followed a "pricing mythology," attempting to predict costs and pass them through to the consumer no matter how high they go. He cites the case of U.S. Steel, which "kept prices high enough to allow 10 to 12 smaller companies to take a substantial share of the market." As a result, Big Steel has watched its market share dwindle from 48% in 1910 to 34% in the mid-1950s and to 23% today.

Dow Chemical Co. offers the contrasting example of a mammoth company that prices aggressively. "This company is trying to price on a flexible basis, while U.S. Steel is trying to be the industry statesman and hold prices steady in good times and bad," says Henderson. Unlike U.S. Steel, Dow will not hesitate to slash prices when and where demand is slack and raise them as high as possible when and where demand is strong, he says.

According to the Strategy Planning Institute (SPI), market share is a major determinant of profitability. SPI's computer analyses show that companies with larger market shares tend to have bigger profit margins. The reason, says SPI's

Badler, is that "companies with larger market share realize economies of scale and are more clearly identified by customers."

Profits and Cost Control

With financial support from 150 major corporations, including General Electric Co. and Control Data Corp., SPI has developed a computerized system, called profit impact of market strategy (PIMS), that pinpoints a company's market position. Then, depending on that position, SPI recommends an appropriate pricing strategy.

If excess capacity in the U.S. has contributed to the new price strategy, excess capacity abroad is making it vital to survival. Demand has been weak at home, but it has been moribund elsewhere in the industrialized West and in Japan. Growth rates in West Germany and Japan, for example, have slowed dramatically since the mid-1960s. The upshot is even more excess capacity in these countries than in the U.S. and intensification of industrial competition. Because the U.S. is the least unhealthy of these economies, foreign companies are rushing to capture ever-larger shares of its market.

Sustained periods of excess capacity have occurred before, most notably during the Depression of the 1930s. Then, in a highly protectionist atmosphere, the only real option that seemed open to industrial companies was to try to preserve what was left of profit margins by rigid adherence to target return pricing enforced by static follow-the-leader pricing patterns. While a huge deflation took place in agricultural, raw material, and service prices, industrial prices were characterized by a rigidity that was often noted and that was described in the voluminous report of the Temporary National Economic Committee.

But something new has been added to the pricing scene—if not to antitrust attitudes—since the 1930s. The growing sophistication of computer technology has provided the means for flexible pricing. Using computers, companies are now able to continuously monitor costs of inputs such as labor, raw materials, and energy across a wide range of product lines. In fact, computerized cost review has spread so fast that virtually all moderate-size companies use some kind of data-processing system for this purpose. U.S. Elevator, for example, initiated a cost-monitoring system earlier this year that follows daily and monthly cost fluctuations. The purchase price of every component or raw material is compared with its last purchase price and entered into a price book that the company president reviews daily. Every month a computer prints out how prices look in terms of 30-day periods.

And 18 months ago, International Telephone & Telegraph Corp., began a system of cost review that provides the company's controller at New York headquarters with monthly cost monitoring for each of the company's divisions. The system tracks deviations of actual from budgeted production costs.

The Impact on Federal Policy

The new pricing strategy is almost certain to change the structure of U.S. business and force changes in government policy designed to foster competition, such as antitrust policy.

A giant company following a flexible price strategy aimed at effective competition with foreign producers can no longer be counted on to hold a high-price safety net under its weaker domestic competitors. In the past, says economist Lanzillotti, the giants in such industries as automobiles and steel preferred target return prices partly because these companies feared antitrust action if price-cutting forced smaller companies out of business. Now, as flexible prices gain steam, "it will make the positions of marginal companies like American Motors all the more precarious," he says. Indeed, AMC is already weakening under the new competitive pressure, even though the auto market in general has remained strong. The industry's smallest domestic producer recently announced the shutdown of its assembly plant in Kenosha, Wis., for one week because of declining sales. At the same time, both Ford and General Motors were working double shifts at their production plants.

What is happening in the auto industry is suggestive of what is almost bound to become a new trend toward more industrial concentration. As the U.S. industrial giants begin to price more efficiently to meet competition from the foreign industrial giants, it seems almost inevitable that the weaker, high-cost domestic producers will either fall by the wayside or be gobbled up in mergers. In effect, U.S. industry is being asked to choose between competing more effectively in a world of industrial giants, or hanging on to old price practices that allowed efficient and inefficient producers to coexist comfortably using price strategies that did not rile the antitrust enforcers.

In the case of the steel industry, economist Hendrik Houthakker, a former member of President Nixon's Council of Economic Advisers, says that the Justice Dept. may have to fundamentally change the way in which it approaches antitrust activity so that U.S. companies will be able to "achieve the economies of scale necessary to match the foreign competition."

Most companies appear to have decided to compete instead of coexist. And this could mean that the giants will soon be running into new battles with the Justice Dept. and the Federal Trade Commission, unless these agencies change their posture in a way that recognizes what life is really like in an internationally competitive world.

The new price strategy also appears to have some implications for policies designed to stabilize the economy. It is true that "profits inflation"—inflation caused by business attempts to push up profit margins in periods of declining demand—is less likely under flexible than under target rate of return pricing. But flexible pricing also means that any surge in demand is likely to lead to quicker and bigger price boosts than it has in the past, while lower demand will result in quicker price cuts. This strongly suggests that a flexible price economy is likely to be a relatively unstable economy.

But it is also likely to be a more vigorous economy. Companies that use flexible pricing to build market shares are apt to be more willing to undertake new capital spending projects, despite the presence of excess capacity, than are companies that are wedded to achieving hard and fast target rates of return. "Pricing feeds back into investment decisions in a powerful way," says Henderson of the Boston Consulting Group. "And the company with foresight to expand will gain the benefits of added market share."

The move to a flexible pricing may eventually shake business investment out of the catatonic state it has been in for the past 2½ years.

The new competitiveness also makes business far riskier. Profits will be much more dependent on nimble decision-making than in the past. Companies in the same industry are much more likely to show diverse profit performance than any time during the past 25 years. It has been fashionable for commentators and economists to argue that U.S. executives have become averse to taking risks. This may still be a correct assessment of their psychology. But the new competitive atmosphere is likely to force companies that wish to be successful to take more risks, like it or not.

QUESTIONS

1. What are some factors that have contributed to the increased use of flexible pricing?
2. How does flexible pricing differ from the traditional pricing model?
3. Describe some of the techniques that automobile manufacturers have used to introduce flexibility into their pricing. How could these techniques be used by a packaged-goods producer?
4. What must firms do in this new competitive environment to raise prices without fear of losing sales or share?
5. What federal regulations might be created as a result of flexible-pricing strategies? Do you agree that they should be created? Why?

4

A PAINFUL HEADACHE FOR BRISTOL-MYERS?

Business Week

This article illustrates the possible consequences when a penetration pricing strategy is inappropriately used. It also shows how a firm can effectively respond to a new, low-price competitive entry.

When Bristol-Myers Co. decided to challenge Johnson & Johnson for a piece of the $61-million market for nonaspirin headache remedies, it based its tactics on only one marketing difference—lower price. It is proving to be a costly mistake and Johnson & Johnson, which controls 90% of the market, seems to be coming out ahead.

Bristol-Myers' carefully-laid program to introduce its acetaminophen-based Datril to the public was untracked almost immediately, and there are signs that the company is floundering in trying to set things right. Advertising men and marketing executives are shaking their heads in disbelief at the company's problems: One TV network, CBS, is refusing to run its ads and two others are running them only after three debilitating revisions. Magazine schedules have been delayed. And the National Advertising Div. of the Council of Better Business Bureaus is about to rule on Bristol-Myers' ethics.

In challenging Johnson & Johnson's Tylenol on price, the experienced $1.5-billion-a-year marketer of Bufferin, Excedrin, Vitalis, Ban, and dozens of other household names ignored some basic tenets of modern marketing. One is that price is seldom successful as an advertising tool. Another is that cut-throat price competition is all too easily met by the company challenged.

Still, Bristol-Myers moved ahead and, in doing so, weakened J&J's immediate profit picture, forced J&J to revise its own marketing policies, disrupted the profit potential of the entire market, and frustrated others about to enter the field with their own acetaminophen products. At this point, the question is unanswered as to whether B-M has carved a niche for itself in a fast-growing market or has committed a marketing blunder that could cost it upwards of $20 million.

ROOM FOR TWO.   Marvin H. Koslow, vice-president for marketing services, radiates confidence as he fends off questions aimed at determining if B-M has "done an Edsel." The company, he contends, carefully studied the growing acetaminophen market before it exploded Datril nationally this summer "and determined there was room for a second product at a lower price." The basis for this belief was a five-month test of Datril that began last October in Peoria, Ill., and Albany, N.Y. There, when advertised as costing $1 less than Tylenol, Datril racked up huge sales. "Not every product category is open to us with a marketing opportunity like this," notes Koslow.

Of particular interest is the fact that Bristol-Myers in two earlier tests apparently had proved to its own satisfaction that there was not room for a Tylenol-like "me, too" product at a comparable price. In the test markets, with advertising based solely on the benefits of a nonaspirin pain reliever, sales were sluggish.

The reason lies in the history of Tylenol. Made and marketed by J&J's McNeil Laboratories, Inc., for more than two decades, the product was originally a prescription analgesic recommended for people who experience side-effects from aspirin: primarily stomach upset, irritation of the stomach lining, or allergic reaction. When the product was made an over-the-counter drug in the early 1960s, McNeil continued to market it carefully through the medical profession. A few rival makers of ethical drug products were in the field, but the market attracted little attention from the giants because of its limited size: Sterling Drug, whose Bayer brand name is on the preponderance of 100-million aspirin tablets taken daily in the U.S., cites studies showing that only one out of 100 people suffer stomach upset from aspirin.

Because Tylenol was a specialty type of product usually recommended by name by a physician, it was priced at roughly twice the cost of aspirin. This, coupled with the fact that its advertising and promotional costs were extremely low, made it extremely profitable, says a McNeil spokesman. The product was ideally situated when, a few years ago, some highly publicized studies began questioning consumers' almost blind dependence on aspirin as a pain reliever.

Suddenly, sales of acetaminophen products shot upward, going from 5% of the total analgesic market ($550 million) in 1972 to about 13% of a $680-million market last year. With acetaminophen sales now growing at an annual rate of 50% while sales of aspirin and aspirin compounds are climbing 9%, Bristol-Myers executives opened their eyes. What they saw was one $1.9-billion company, Johnson & Johnson, sitting comfortably with almost all of the acetaminophen business to itself, with a product unfamiliar to the great majority of Americans.

FRONTAL ATTACK. "We decided to use our great strength as a mass marketer, offering the consumer a significant price difference—which is very important in today's economy," says Koslow in explaining B-M's all-out frontal attack on Tylenol. Huge ads to the trade last May promised "a hard-hitting advertising campaign" of commercials "on all three TV networks," plus magazine ads in *Reader's Digest, Ladies' Home Journal,* and others, along with newspaper ads and heavy TV spots in the top 50 markets, and medical promotion—all based on the idea that "the 100-tablet size of Datril sells for as much as a dollar less than the same quantity of Tylenol . . . . Since they are both the same, there is no reason to keep paying more for Tylenol." The campaign, one rival estimates, would cost $6 million over six months.

On June 3, shortly before the network ads were scheduled to run, J&J pulled the rug out from under its new competitor. James E. Burke, president and chairman of the executive committee, personally telephoned Richard L. Gelb, president and chief executive officer at B-M, to notify him that Tylenol's price to the trade was reduced 30%, effective immediately. Thus, there would be no significant differences in retail prices of the two products—and any ads saying so would be misleading.

Bristol-Myers, perhaps figuring that it would take some months for J&J's price change to filter down to all of the nation's 165,000 retail outlets, launched its ads anyway. The taped commercials, featuring a housewife talking about Tylenol for $2.85 on the left side of the screen and one talking about Datril for $1.85 on the right, were immediately met with a J&J protest that sent B-M's ad agency, Young & Rubicam, scrambling to revise the copy and produce new commercials. In the revisions, the talk of a $1 lower price was changed to a statement that "Datril can cost less, a lot less." Another protest from J&J brought deletion of "a lot less."

CBS refused the ads altogether, agreeing with J&J's contention that Tylenol is now priced so that a store taking a standard markup can sell it profitably at $1.99, and that promotional allowances offered to the trade resulted in some stores selling 100 tablets for 79¢ or even 49¢. The Datril ads, in their fourth versions on ABC and NBC, now make the weak claim that "Datril can cost less, depending on where you shop"—a claim that J&J continues to label as false and misleading, and one currently being scrutinized by network lawyers.

Even before the Datril ads broke, J&J had organized "Operation Team-work" to blunt their effect on Tylenol. Although McNeil Laboratories had recently had a small group of sales specialists working with supermarkets on expanded distribution, the product now was taken on by J&J's own Health Care

Div., which markets Band-Aid bandages, Micrin mouthwash, and Shower-to-Shower body powder, among others. Within weeks, says Edmund G. Vimond, group vice-president for J&J's domestic operating company, Tylenol had 90% distribution in the food field to go along with its 98% distribution in drug outlets. Datril, as a new item on the shelves, had considerably less.

MOVING FAST.   At McNeil, a crash program saw a new executive named to establish a consumer products division to handle future sales of an expanded Tylenol line. Compton Advertising, Inc., was asked to devise a consumer ad campaign for Tylenol, and some test TV spots went on the air almost immediately. Meanwhile, a videocassette presentation on Tylenol's new price policy and strategy was shown simultaneously in 16 major cities to 700 sales managers and territorial salesmen, who immediately fanned out to contact their customers.

"Bristol-Myers may have thought it would take a long time for us to get the word," says Maurice Badway, owner of Lawrence Pharmacy in Brooklyn, N.Y. "But my Tylenol man was in here before Datril really got rolling, to tell me about the new price and give me a rebate in stock."

Probably Bristol-Myers underestimated J&J's willingness to retaliate so swiftly and decisively. Having established Tylenol with the medical profession almost as an ethical drug, J&J might have been thought reluctant to promote it directly to the consumer—and thereby lose its franchise with doctors. Or B-M may have reasoned that J&J would let Datril have a slice of its market as a lower-profit product, while it continued to make a greater profit on Tylenol at a higher price.

The evidence points to a miscalculation. B-M's own ads give as much exposure to Tylenol as to Datril, saving J&J a considerable sum—and if the consumer sees no price difference of signficance at retail, or sees one actually favoring Tylenol, he most likely will buy the established, proven product. B-M, meanwhile, is being forced to spend ad dollars, spend more than it budgeted originally in order to make copy revisions, and "deal" Datril heavily to the trade in order to meet Tylenol's deals.

FIRST CASUALTY.   There are two major suppliers of acetaminophen to the drug industry, Mallinckrodt and S. B. Penick. At one, a sales executive says that 100 tablets contain about 20¢ worth of the chemical and 20¢ worth of binders and other inert ingredients. "Toss in your bottle, your box, your instruction sheet, advertising costs, sales costs, and the rest," he says, "and it's pretty obvious that nobody is making a profit selling at 79¢."

One small company already has decided to clear out of the acetaminophen war. Thompson Medical Co., which was test-marketing Dantol, sees no profits for a little fish in a pond of big sharks. But some of the sharks themselves are seemingly stunned by the Tylenol-Datril confrontation. American Home Products has advertised an acetaminophen called Trilium in test markets and was about to go national with it. Miles Laboratories was readying Actron for a full-scale introduction. Sterling Drug, which is the world's largest marketer of acetaminophen products by virtue of overseas sales, is planning to put Bayer Non-Aspirin Pain Reliever into national distribution this fall. Several of the companies have the pipelines filled with millions of dollars worth of product and ad campaigns ready to go—but they cannot proceed until the price situation stabilizes.

"It's one thing to make less than you expected on each bottle sold, but it's something else altogether when you have to spend heavily at the same time," says one bewildered executive. "That's where J&J has the big advantage over all of us. They don't have to advertise. We do."

Claiming that Bristol-Myers foresaw various counter-strategies that J&J might employ, B-M's Koslow refuses to concede any advantage to the competition. "It's too early to have market-share figures in yet," he says, "and the consumer will ultimately decide the merits of the products. Naturally, each will have to make a profit to stay in the market. All I know at this time is that we got in ahead of several other competitors, we've established our brand with millions of consumers—and we'd rather be where we are right now than anywhere else."

The question, of course, is just where are they?

QUESTIONS

1. How would you characterize Tylenol's pricing strategy before Datril?
2. Were the market conditions appropriate for Datril's use of a penetration pricing strategy? How?
3. What did Datril do wrong in implementing its strategy? What should it have done?

5

PRICE-COST PLANNING

C. Davis Fogg
Kent H. Kohnken

This article provides a detailed description of the roles of marketing and manufacturing in a price plan. Steps are described to develop a plan that establishes appropriate market share goals, profit goals, price goals, and unit-cost goals. In addition, guidelines are given on how to implement a pricing plan to achieve these goals.

Developing a financially healthy business for each distinct product line requires the formulation of a realistic price-cost plan. Specifically, such a plan should:

1. Establish *market share goals* appropriate to the firm's competitive strengths and the stage of the product line's life-cycle.
2. Define *profit goals* appropriate to the market share goals.
3. Structure a *pricing plan* to achieve the market share goals.
4. Establish *unit cost goals* which will achieve targeted profitability.
5. Develop a *manufacturing or cost reduction plan* that will result in targeted unit costs.

This article will focus on steps 1–4 and will describe a systematic process that has been successfully used to: (a) evaluate the competitiveness of an established price structure and make necessary short-term price changes, and (b) define a long-term price-cost plan for an established industrial product line in a highly competitive market.

First described are the roles of marketing and manufacturing in establishing a price-cost plan, and then each stage in the planning process—the

352

information required to accomplish it and, where appropriate, a numerical example of the output.

Companies should consider using this process under the following key circumstances:

- A significant change in a competitor's price structure or product offering renders the company's price structure obsolete.
- Feedback from the marketplace indicates that the current price structure needs revision because significant volume is being lost on price, or quotations are frequently lower than that judged necessary to obtain desirable business.
- The firm is considering a significant change in profit strategy for the business which will result in substantial changes in market share goals and subsequent pricing policy.
- Manufacturing cost reductions have not been sufficient to maintain or attain the desired level of profitability.
- The firm is re-examining pricing policy at the time of the annual or periodic marketing plan development.

Roles of Marketing and Manufacturing

Marketing should be, and often is, the lead function in establishing a price-cost plan. The marketing function is normally responsible for defining product policy, marketing strategy, market share goals, and subsequently, development of pricing policy and product line profit targets. In highly competitive industrial markets, marketing has little leverage over the key profit determinants such as product mix and pricing, once basic marketing strategy and the pricing policy necessary to implement it are established.

Manufacturing has the responsibility for taking market-directed cost goals and establishing a long-term plan to meet them. The manufacturing function often has more leverage to control cost, and, consequently, profitability than does marketing. Manufacturing's ability to reduce cost is bound only by the resources available for cost reduction programs; the technologies available to effectively implement them; and manufacturing's ability to combine them to produce lower costs with an acceptable return on any capital investment involved.

If manufacturing, in fact, cannot meet marketing-directed cost goals, then the goals must be revised to those that can be realistically achieved; or the total market share—price-cost-profit plan—must be varied until a satisfactory option is found.

Time Frame

The price-cost plan often will cover a period of 1–3 or 1–5 years. Typically, modest cost reductions can take place in one year, while necessary major cost reduction programs take 2–5 years to implement, particularly if significant breakthroughs are required in process, equipment, or product design and construction technologies.

The Price-Cost Planning Process

Exhibit [Figure] 1 is a schematic overview of the process of developing a price-cost plan. The process assumes that the product line is already established in the marketplace, with well-defined price schedules that are consistent with the currently defined marketing strategy.

As shown in the exhibit, the process is divided into seven major stages, each of which will be described.

I. Evaluating the Current Price/Cost Structure

The purpose of evaluating the current product line price/cost structure is two-fold: *First*, to evaluate current pricing versus competition and to identify items where prices could be lowered to become competitive, or could be successfully raised to improve profitability. *Second*, to establish the profitability of each item in the product line—to identify items that are not sufficiently profitable and those items that require consideration of immediate cost reduction and/or price increases. The six steps in this stage are:

1. *Define the Current Price Structure* by obtaining unit prices for each product style and quantity break (line item) for *each* channel of distribution such as direct sales, sales to distributors, readily available from published and internal price lists.

2. *Establish Competitive Prices* by line item where possible. A comprehensive list of competitive pricing information should be collected, recognizing that a large body of accurate information is extremely difficult to obtain.

   This information is normally obtained not only from published competitive price sheets from distributors or industrial buyers, but also through inputs from salesmen who collect such information as a matter of routine, i.e., during contract negotiations. Other sources for such information are lost business reports maintained by the sales or sales service organizations, or direct market research among customer purchasing personnel. Because of the difficulty of obtaining competitive pricing information, there will be many gaps in the data requiring intelligent interpolation.

   The output of this step is the simplified three-product matrix shown in [Table 1] . . . comparing company prices with prices of key competitors.

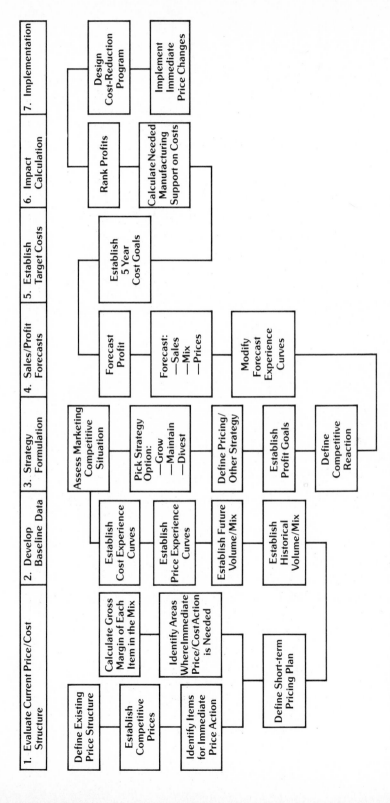

FIGURE 1   *The Process of Developing a Price-Cost Plan*

Table 1	CURRENT PRICE STRUCTURE		
		Quantity	
	1–10	*100*	*1000+*
Product A			
Our price	.90	.80	.70
Comp. price	.90**(C)**	.80**(C)**	.65**(L)**
% difference	0%	0%	+7%
Product B			
Our price	.85	.75	.60
Comp. price	.85**(C)**	.65**(L)**	.60**(C)**
% difference	0%	+15%	0%
Product C			
Our price	.70	.60	.45
Comp. price	.70**(C)**	.60**(C)**	.50**(R)**
% difference	0%	0%	−10%

Strategy Implications:
(L) Consider lowering price/losing share.
(R) Opportunity to raise price without losing share.
(C) Competitive—hold price.

3. *Identify Items Where Specific Price Increases or Decreases Should Be Considered* in light of the current or tentatively proposed marketing strategy. Items subject to change are identified in [Table 1] . . .

4. *Calculate the Profitability of the Current Company Product Mix* by establishing current unit costs for each product and calculating the gross margin for the total product line and each item. Prices are obtained from Step 1 above. Costs from actual manufacturing cost records can only be used if they are available in sufficient detail. Detail cost estimates for each major segment of the product line must often be specially developed to provide sufficient data for this analysis. The output of this stage [Table 1] . . . is a summary of current product line profitability. Note that this is a simple matrix with only 9 line items. An actual analysis may contain 50–300 line items.

5. *Identify Items of Unacceptable Profit* where immediate price increases or cost reductions should be considered, as indicated in [Table 2] . . .

6. *Tentatively Define the Short-Term Pricing Structure.* Raising prices should be considered where the current structure is below competition or profitability is unacceptable. Where the item is priced significantly above competition, another option may be lowering prices. All proposed changes in price and their magnitude must be considered in light of (a) their effect on current and future unit and profit volume, (b) any advantages over competition, in service, quality, and distribution (which might command a price premium), (c) the firm's tentative future plans for growth,

Table 2

CURRENT PRODUCT PROFITABILITY

	Quantity			
	1–10	*100*	*1000+*	*Total Product*
Product A				
Price	.90	.80	.70	.75
Cost	.61	.56(X)	.46	.51
G.M. %	32%	30%	34%	32%
Product B				
Price	.85	.75	.60	.75
Cost	.56	.51	.41	.51
G.M. %	32%	32%	32%	32%
Product C				
Price	.70	.60	.45	.60
Cost	.48	.43(X)	.33(X)	.43
G.M. %	32%	28%	26%	28%
Total				
Price	.82	.72	.58	.70
Cost	.55	.50	.40	.48
G.M. %	32%	31%	31%	31%

General Competitive Assessment: No significant product or nonproduct (service, quality, and so on) advantage over competition, but considered equal to top two competitors.
Strategy Implication:
  (X) Consider price increase/cost reduction to immediately improve profitability, as below 31% current profitability average.

maintenance, or divestiture of market share. If, at the end of this step, profitability, the revised price structure, and the market strategy are deemed adequate, the remainder of the analysis need not be completed. [Table 3] . . . summarizes proposed actions if the firm chooses not to change market share.

If, however, changes in marketing and pricing strategy are contemplated, the short-term price plan is set aside, pending completion of the long-range analysis described below.

II. Developing Base Line Data

The purpose of this section is to develop the basic market and price forecasts needed to effectively evaluate proposed long-term alternate marketing strategies. The four steps in this process are:

Table 3

ACTION SUMMARY: PROPOSED SHORT-TERM ACTION TO MAINTAIN MARKET SHARE

| | Quantity | | |
	1–10	100	1000+
Product A			
Price	**(C)**	**(C)**	**(L)**
Profitability	OK	**(X)**	OK
Action	None	Price cannot be raised—cost must be lowered ASAP by 5% to get to acceptable profit.	Not losing share. No need to lower price.
Product B			
Price	**(C)**	**(L)**	**(C)**
Profitability	OK	OK	OK
Action	None	Losing share—need to lower prices 10% requiring additional 6¢ cost reduction to maintain acceptable profit.	None
Product C			
Price	**(C)**	**(C)**	**(R)**
Profitability	OK	**(X)**	**(X)**
Action	None	Cost must be reduced by 3¢ to get acceptable profitability.	Price can be raised 10% to improve profitability.

1. *Establish Historical Unit Market Volume and Product Mix* for the company and the market, if it deviates significantly from the company's product mix. Overall market volume is readily available from published or industry association data, from internal market research reports, or by estimation of company market share and "scaling up" company sales accordingly to estimated total market volume. Product mix, if not available from industry reports, can be estimated by adjusting the firm's actual product mix to account for observed deviations from the "typical" product mix.

2. *Forecast Market Volume and Mix* for a five-year period. Overall market volume forecasts are obtained from any of a number of suitable forecasting techniques—trend analysis, input/output analysis, modeling, Delphi studies, and market research among customers.

   Establishing the future product mix is more difficult, but it is normally accomplished by one or more of a number of methods: "eyeballing" the current mix and adjusting it for perceived changes; establishing trends in the company's historical mix into the future; input/output analysis or market research among customers to forecast expected changes in mix, and, particularly the need for new products which might radically alter future mix.

[Table 4] . . . shows the results of these steps—a five-year forecast of market volume and mix, and the cumulative volume produced to date. In this example, the company mix and market mix are assumed to be the same.

3. *Establish Historical and Forecast Market Price Experience Curves* for the total product line and for any significant subsegments. An experience curve is constructed by plotting, on log-log coordinates, the cumulative unit volume produced by all producers at a number of historical points in time versus the constant dollar market price at each chosen point in time. Historical industry volume and market prices can usually be obtained from industry association production and pricing reports. Where such data are not available, they can be obtained through market research or extrapolation from the firm's price, volume, and market-share history.

The expected future market prices, assuming that competitive strategies and relative market shares remain constant, are obtained by extending the experience curve as shown in the simple example in [Figure 2] . . . Extrapolation of experience curves is sometimes difficult, and the shape of the curve often depends upon the stage of market development, degree of competition, and competitive product and pricing strategies.[1]

4. *Establish the Cost Experience Curve* for the firm by plotting the firm's unit cost in constant dollars versus its cumulative unit volume at a number of points in time. Extend this experience curve to establish what the firm's costs will be if it continues to reduce costs at historical rates.

---

[1] See *Perspectives on Experience* (Boston: MA: Boston Consulting Group, 1969).

Table 4

CURRENT AND FUTURE MARKET UNIT VOLUME AND MIX BY PRODUCT STYLE

Product Style	Current Mix	% Unit Sales Year 1	2	3	4	5
A	50	48	47	45	43	40
B	20	20	20	20	20	20
C	30	32	33	35	37	40

Total Market (units)	Total Market (cumulative units)
Current year—32 (M)	140
1—35	172
2—38	207
3—42	245
4—46	287
5—51	333

The firm's unit costs, past and forecast, can then be appropriately transferred to market price experience curves to establish historical and future profitability, if the price or cost curves or the firm's market share, or the volume continues to accumulate at the current annual rate, are all held constant. (See [Figures 2 and 3] . . .)

III. Strategy Formulation

The purpose of this stage is to examine or re-examine basic alternative long-term marketing strategies and their profit implications, establish or confirm a strategy and its pricing implications, and construct basic profit goals consistent with the chosen strategy. There are five steps:

1. *Situation Analysis.* The summary of the current business situation along key market and competitive dimensions is shown in [Table 5] . . . Significant, but normally available knowledge about non-product competitive strengths—service, distribution, pricing, provision of customer assistance—is required to complete this analysis.

2. *Strategic Options.* A strategic option is chosen based on the current and future competitive situation and the basic goals established for the business by top management. [Table 6] . . . summarizes basic strategic options, when they are used, and the pricing and financial implications of each option. Note that the

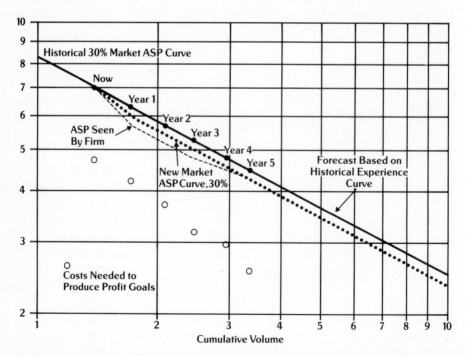

FIGURE 2 *Market ASP Experience Curve*

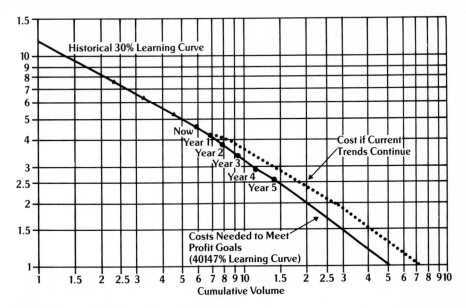

FIGURE 3 *Cost Experience Curve*

option dictated by the market situation may be in conflict with legitimate management goals. For example, marketing strategy may dictate growth in share at the expense of current profitability, while management may want maximum profit now to invest in other projects or businesses. In the example presented here, it is assumed that the option selected is growth in share from 25% to 40%.

3. *Strategy Definition.* To accomplish selected goals, such as introduction of new products, correction of any service deficiencies, special promotions, etc., a strategy must be defined for pricing (and any other necessary strategic moves). In this example, it is assumed that share gain will be accomplished through price alone; that pricing 5% below competition for three years will accomplish that goal; that the price reductions will be implemented immediately; and that prices need not be reduced on the single item currently priced sufficiently below the competition to accomplish share goals.

Table 5	BASIC SITUATION ANALYSIS	
Dimension	**Our Situation**	**Comments**
1. Market	High Growth	
2. Competitive Position	No. 2 by Narrow Margin	
3. Competitive Strengths	Equal to Top Two Competitors	
4. Current Profit	Low ⎫	Cost Reduction
5. Forecast Profit	Low ⎬	needed/possible
6. Pricing	Inconsistent	Easily Reconciled

Table 6

BASIC STRATEGIC/PRICING OPTIONS

Option	When to Use It	Pricing Strategy	Financial Implications
1. Significantly increase market share	• Growth market • Have or can get equal or superior competitive strength • No. 1 in market or good position to take it	Pricing at or below market, depending on competitive strength	• Low profit now • High profit later • Low cash flow now
2. Hold share	• No. 1 in market • Non-growth market • Very strong competition	Maintain or increase price	• Profits/cash flow now
3. Divest share	• Dying market • Inordinately high competitors' strength	High price premium	• Maximum profit/cash flow in near term

4. *Profit Goals.* A top-level management decision considering (a) the business's historical profitability, (b) the industry's profitability, (c) the pricing and market share strategy chosen for the business, and (d) management expectations— establishing profit goals for the business.

   In this example, a target of 40% gross margin, consistent with achievement of leadership market share was selected for Year Five. Lower margins of 28%, 31%, 34%, 37% were targeted for the four earlier years, reflecting the need for cost reduction and the necessity of lowering prices to gain market share.

5. *Definition of Competitive Reactions.* Such a definition will result from the proposed strategy, in this case, a decrease in price. Effectively assessing a competitor's reaction to a firm's marketing strategy requires some basic information and assessment of the competitor's financial and technical strengths and weaknesses, nonproduct strengths and weaknesses in the marketplace, his marketing strategy, and his historical reaction to competitive moves.

   This information is normally kept as part of any first-rate marketing effort and is obtained from analysis of public financial data, and other internal sources.

   In this instance, it is assumed that the two competitors from which market share is to be taken will follow price cuts during the first two years of the company's, forcing an abnormal 3% reduction in each year and temporarily depressing the marketplace experience curve from its historical trend level. This will result in an overall 8% reduction experienced by the firm, which intends to keep prices 5% below competition.

IV. Forecasts

The sales price and profit forecasts will be used to establish long-range cost goals and are obtained through the following three steps:

1. *Price Forecast,* where the price experience curve is modified to account for the firm's pricing action and competitive reaction. Two curves are shown in [Figure 2] . . . presented earlier: (a) the competitive prices, 3% below normal trend; and (b) the price seen by the firm—8% below trend. It is assumed that the market stabilizes after three years, establishing a new starting point for the experience curve, while continuing to diminish at the pre-price reduction rate.

2. *Sales Forecast,* where a forecast of unit sales, overall price, sales mix, and mix price for each of five years is obtained by (a) applying market share figures to the market estimates (see [Table 4] . . .), (b) adjusting the company mix to reflect any planned mix changes, and (c) establishing the mix price by lowering current competitive prices by the percentage decrease dictated in each year by the price experience curve. The resulting five-year price-volume forecast for the firm is shown in [Table 7] . . .

3. *Price Forecast,* where overall gross profits are obtained (assuming historical cost reduction trends continue) by multiplying the forecast sales volume by the difference between the forecast prices and the forecast experience curve as shown in [Figure 2] . . . In this instance, forecast profits do not meet established profit goals.

V. Establishing Target Costs

Target unit costs are calculated for the total product line and for each item in the product mix for each year by discounting the mix price structure by the margin desired in each year. These costs then become manufacturing cost goals (see [Table 7] . . .).

VI. Impact Calculation

There are two stages:

1. *Calculate the Cost Reduction Impact Required* in total and for each item in the mix by multiplying total volume for Years 1 through 5 by the difference between current costs and target costs in Year 5. This assumes that target costs will decrease steadily, which may not be the case if feasible cost reduction programs are expected to have the bulk of their impact in later years.

2. *Rank Priorities.* Each line item in the product line is then ranked in order of cost reduction impact required to single out items requiring the most immediate attention, as shown in [Table 8] . . .

Table 7	OVERALL FORECAST FOR PRICE (IN CONSTANT 1976 DOLLARS)				
Products	**Pieces**	**$**	**ASP**	**Cost**	**G.M. %**
Product A					
Now	4,000	$3000	.75	.51	32%
Year 1	4,536	2812	.62	.45	28%
Year 2	5,358	3054	.57	.39	31%
Year 3	6,237	3306	.53	.36	33%
Year 4	7,121	3703	.52	.33	36%
Year 5	8,160	3917	.48	.29	40%
Product B					
Now	1,600	$1200	.75	.51	32%
Year 1	1,890	1157	.61	.44	28%
Year 2	2,280	1295	.57	.39	31%
Year 3	2,772	1448	.52	.35	33%
Year 4	3,312	1734	.52	.33	36%
Year 5	4,080	1958	.48	.29	40%
Product C					
Now	2,400	$1400	.60	.43	28%
Year 1	3,024	1512	.50	.36	28%
Year 2	3,762	1693	.45	.31	31%
Year 3	4,851	2037	.42	.28	33%
Year 4	6,127	2512	.41	.26	36%
Year 5	8,160	3101	.38	.23	40%
Overall					
Now	8,000	$5640	.71	.48	32%
Year 1	9,450	5481	.58	.42	28%
Year 2	11,400	6042	.53	.37	31%
Year 3	13,860	6791	.49	.32	34%
Year 4	16,560	7949	.48	.30	37%
Year 5	20,400	8976	.44	.26	40%

	Years					
	Now	*1*	*2*	*3*	*4*	*5*
Mkt. Pcs.	32	35	38	42	46	51
Mkt. Share	25%	27%	30%	33%	36%	40%

VII. Implementation

The final and critical stages in the process are designing and implementing the cost reduction program, a lengthy subject itself, and implementing the short-term price structure.

Table 8	COST REDUCTION/$ SAVING						
	A	**B**	**C**	**D**	**E**		
					$\frac{A-B}{2}$	Yrs. 1–5[1]	
	Actual	Cost Needs	Avg. Units	Avg. Units		Average	
	Cost	Yr. 5 For	% Mix Yrs.	Sales/Yrs.	Avg. Cost		
Product	Now	40% G.M.	1–5	1–5	Reduction	Savings	Priority
A	.51	.29	44.6%	6282	.11	$ 691	1
B	.51	.29	20.0%	1518	.11	$ 167	3
C	.43	.23	35.4%	2171	.10	$ 217	2
Total			100.0%	9971	.1070	$1075	

[1]Average cost reduction necessary in constant $, assuming increased market share from 25% to 40%, and increasing G.M. % from 32% to 40%.

1. *Design the Cost Reduction Program*, normally a function of the manufacturing organization, in collaboration with the R&D function. During this phase, engineering and technical personnel examine the product construction and process for every conceivable means of reducing costs, frequently focusing on elimination of expensive material or construction techniques; improving the manufacturing process where there are sub-par selection rates or manufacturing rates, or mechanizing high labor content operations.

    Once the cost reduction programs are proposed, their impact calculated, and the cost and capital expenditure necessary to implement them estimated, then those with sufficient return on investment can be implemented.

    If the proposed pricing strategy coupled with the cost reduction program does not produce targeted profit margins, or if the return on incremental capital spent or cost reduction is not sufficient, then the proposed marketing and pricing strategy will have to be revised.

2. *Short-Term Price Structure*. The modified short-term structure proposed in Stage 1 is changed, if necessary, to be consistent with proposed strategy changes and the subsequent pricing strategy presented in [Table 6] . . .

Practical Considerations

There are a number of practical considerations that should be taken into account in using and implementing this system:

- Computer programs are necessary to quickly do the complex calculations needed to complete the price-cost analysis presented earlier.
- Manufacturing and marketing must work together closely and frequently in both completing and implementing the analysis. They must philosophically be committed to *joint* management of the price-cost structure, a commitment that is often

difficult to obtain in a company dominated by either the marketing or manufacturing function.

- Product line prices and costs must, obviously, be carefully tracked versus goals to insure that immediate action is taken to correct deviation from plan.
- There must be a commitment to spend sufficient money and resources on cost reduction over a long time period, and not on urgent or as needed basis, if cost goals are to be met.
- Cost-price analysis should be done on a regular basis, preferably annually, to insure that goals, price structure, and cost reduction programs are adequate and up-to-date.

Summary

Manufacturing and marketing equally share the responsibility of producing acceptable profits by effectively managing the product line price-cost structure. Marketing is responsible for establishing the firm marketing and pricing strategy and establishing reasonable long-range cost goals. Manufacturing is responsible for achieving these goals. The most successful firms will aggressively manage the price-cost structure rather than let it evolve in response to competitive pressures or as a result of normal cost reduction or process improvement efforts. This article presents a systematic process for effectively establishing price-cost goals in the context of long-range marketing strategy, and the firm's relative competitive strengths.

QUESTIONS

1. When should the price-cost planning process be used? When, if ever, would it be appropriate for a consumer goods producer?
2. Describe the interrelationships between marketing and manufacturing.
3. What steps are involved in the first stage of the price-cost planning process?
4. What are the responsibilities of the strategy formulation stage of the process?
5. What is the most critical stage in the price-cost planning process?
6. What organizational activities and structures are required to successfully implement the price-cost planning process?

PART SEVEN

Other Marketing Considerations

The previous parts of this text have focused on the traditional functional areas of marketing management. However, marketing is a dynamic discipline; and as environmental conditions and consumer needs and wants change, the nature and focus of marketing must also change. For example, as the competitive activity within industries has taken on more of a world perspective, the attention given to international marketing has also increased. As the influence on society of large corporate organizations has increased and the structure of the economy shifts away from manufacturing, marketers have increased their study of marketing's social responsibilities and marketing's role in nonprofit and service industries. Part Seven focuses on these areas of marketing. The objective is to render an overview of the issues and state of knowledge in these developing areas. Specifically, the topics covered are international marketing, marketing's social responsibility, and marketing in the service and nonprofit sectors, which correspond to the central issues of the decade as identified in "Marketing Issues," the first article in Part Seven. Also discussed in this article are marketing's role in strategic planning and its interrelationship with the other functional areas of the business.

The issues associated with expansion into foreign markets are addressed in "Market Expansion Strategies in Multinational Marketing." In "Responsible Marketing in an Expanded Marketing Concept," the marketing concept and the functional areas of marketing (such as product, distribution, promotion, and price) are expanded to include societal goals. "Strategies for Introducing Marketing into Nonprofit Organizations" examines marketing activities in the nonprofit sector.

In order for a firm to grow and prosper, all the theories, concepts, and issues in marketing that have been discussed in this text must be coordinated into a single plan, and that plan must be integrated with the other functional areas of the organization. Procedures for accomplishing these tasks are provided in the articles that conclude Part Seven. The nature and requirements of planning are described in "Are You Really Planning Your Marketing?", and an example of a coordinated marketing plan is given in the final article, "Coke's Big Marketing Blitz."

1

MARKETING ISSUES

Stephen Greyser

Based on discussions by some 40 senior management executives, this article identifies the central issues that marketing scholars must address in this decade.

- Improving marketing productivity
- Government regulation and marketing practice
- Effective corporate communications with a variety of constituencies
- Integrating marketing and strategic planning within a companywide marketing orientation.

These are the principal areas of future concern in marketing, as seen by marketing executives. (Perhaps because they were asked explicitly for issues of broad interest, they chose to devote relatively little emphasis to individual elements of the marketing mix.)

Here is a summary of executive thinking on these major issues, including illustrative comments and questions.

Marketing Productivity

The most central issue is that of improving marketing productivity—for business and for the U.S. economy. The concerns expressed by marketing executives encompass the productivity of marketing expenditures within the firm, the marketing decision process, and marketing as a contributor to U.S. economic growth. There is widespread recognition of the growing inflationary pressures for greater efficiency in marketing. At the same time, some executives pointed to marketing as a major contributor to increasing the competitiveness of U.S. business throughout the world.

Some specific comments and questions illuminate the importance of the challenges for improving marketing productivity:

Within the Firm

"Senior management is concerned with evidence on the effectiveness of high marketing and advertising levels. The CEO with a non-marketing background wants more rigorous demonstration of what return he gets from the marketing investment and is more likely to expect marketing to be a *science* rather than an *art*."

"We are constantly wrestling with the long-standing questions of marketing effectiveness. Where is the most effective deployment of (additional) marketing dollars—advertising, sales promotion, lower prices, or a stronger sales force? There is a need for more testing, experimenting, evaluating."

The Marketing Decision Process

"The basic question still remains of how to measure the productivity of the marketing team or of marketing decisions."

"We need to learn more about increasing marketing skills in order to increase productivity. What are the internal corporate roadblocks? There seems to be a career planning/organizational behavior problem in which a number of companies using the product management system tend to reward managers for becoming general managers rather than marketing managers; thus, over the long term, the marketing skills of the corporation can be substantially reduced."

"Marketing people must confront the question of measuring productivity by 'knowledge' workers. We also need better thinking about the marketing implications of decisions made to increase productivity in manufacturing and operations areas."

The Impact of Marketing on Economic Growth

"Marketing can make a contribution to economic growth and to U.S. exports. But can this role be documented? What is the impact of rising marketing expenditures on economic growth? The underlying theory is that marketing activities speed the process by which resources are allocated to the most economically productive industries, products, and companies. Similarly, how can marketing help increase exports? The idea is that better applications of marketing skills to exporting could be considered a 'national resource' via beneficial effects on unemployment and capital utilization in the United States and the balance of payments problems. A side benefit of demonstrating marketing's contribution would be to increase the credibility of business as a source of economic strength for the country."

Marketing and Inflation

"Given high rates of inflation in marketing costs (but with differing rates for different components), how can companies better organize to understand the changing cost/return ratios for various elements of the marketing mix—price, promotions, advertising-media vehicles, sales force, etc.—in order to shift tactics to more cost efficient mixes?"

Regulatory Impacts on Marketing

Of almost equal concern (and for many, greater intensity of feeling!) is the challenge of regulation. As one person put it, "Business seems to have so little control in this area, yet regulation has major effects on our daily activities." While the growth of regulation in marketing is widely recognized, executives think that not enough is known about the process by which public needs, desires, and perceptions at the grass-roots level evolve into legislation or regulatory action and about the extent to which the end result of this process reflects the concerns of the public at large. In order to try to influence the regulatory environment, executives think the sources of regulation and the factors which influence its development need to be more fully understood. They also believe the consequences of both more and less regulation should be examined, particularly in situations where "deregulation" has occurred. Finally, they cite the challenge of determining how business can or should respond to regulatory initiatives and their underlying roots in changing social trends.

Here are illustrative comments and questions reflecting each of these three concerns:

Reflecting the Public's Needs and Demands for Regulation

"The regulators say the public demands more regulation. How accurate is this perception of public demands?"

"*Why* is the public demanding more regulation and what could industry do to offset that in marketing areas?"

"It would be useful to illuminate how well consumer groups actually represent the public."

The Consequences of Regulation and Deregulation

"Once the regulation process is 'in place,' how does it affect the conduct of business, particularly in the areas relevant to marketing?"

"Companies feel government is increasingly having an impact in defining the framework of competition in ways not in industry's interest. A major challenge to marketing is whether it can continue to be effective in the wake of these changes."

"We need to examine the effects of *de*regulation on both industry structure and consumers."

Business Response to Government Regulation

"Regulation reflects changing social demands/trends. But business should be able to assess these trends and adapt to them. Where in the business should the appropriate information in this area reside and how is it best transferred to marketing and product decision makers?"

"We must learn faster and better about how to carry out marketing in an environment of government regulation. This involves studying whole industries as well as individual companies within an industry to assess both common and differential patterns."

Corporate Communications: New Messages and Media

Another major challenge of a changing environment affects corporate communications. This extends beyond the traditional functions of advertising. Executives recognize new roles for advertising and new channels of communications for reaching both traditional audiences and special groups in the public at large. One key question for the business community, as executives see it, is how to present and communicate its views on many issues of public policy which transcend traditional product advertising. In addition to new messages, the variety of communication channels has been expanding and will expand even more in the 1980s. Marketing executives think increasing complexity of the communications process—due to changes in media vehicles, consequent changes in audience size and composition, and the impact of these changes on the cost of reaching product prospects (and other target groups)—poses a substantial challenge for marketing planning.

Despite the challenges of these new and expanded roles for advertising, such basic tasks as creating and changing brand images will, of course, continue to be essential to the marketing process. Finally, in order to communicate effectively about products or public policy issues, marketing executives see the need to be informed about changes in social values, consumer behavior, and consumer demographic/life-style characteristics. Early indications and forecasts are particularly important.

Some of the specific observations made and questions raised by executives on these communications areas include:

Effective Communication of the Business Side of Public Policy Issues

"Advocacy advertising—speaking out on issues apart from product advertising—is increasing. We need to learn more about the effects of such advertising in influencing decision makers and on the attitudes of influential target groups, as well as any impact on the advertiser's products."

"How can American business most effectively communicate its side of issues to the government, media, opinion leaders, and the public at large? How can business communicate to the public the concept of 'trade-off'? What elements work best in such communication?"

New Media Opportunities and Problems

"Changing media environments and media roles, higher costs, and the communication of adversary positions represent challenges for marketing and prospectively productive areas for research."

"There will be problems for mass advertising in the future, when TV audiences are likely to become increasingly fragmented due to developments such as cable, video recorders, etc."

Traditional Tasks of Advertising

"Methods and costs of changing the image of a brand or company represent a continuing challenge."

"We need to assess better the trade-off between the presumed longer-term brand-building effects of advertising versus the shorter-term impacts of promotion."

Changing Environment for Corporate Communications

"We need to improve the process of measuring social change and assessing the impact of such change on consumer behavior. This includes consideration of the inputs of people in the futurist business."

"Consumer preferences for product types may change quickly, but forecasting has to be done well ahead because it often takes a long time to 'grow the right grapes.' There is a need for better study of life-style and demographic changes as an aid to such forecasting."

Integrating Marketing and Strategic Planning Within a Companywide Marketing Orientation

Many of the issues already described have dealt with the nature and influence of *external* pressures on marketing planning and programs. Executives also have a continuing concern with attitudes and experiences *internal* to the business organization which influence its basic orientation and strategic direction. A frequently cited goal among marketing managers is the desirability of developing and encouraging a *companywide marketing orientation*. Directly related to a "marketing orientation" influencing corporate practices, organizational structure, allocation of resources, and decision making is the process of strategic planning. The *integration* of marketing planning and strategic planning was a focal point in many executive comments. Further, the management of corporate resources for effective marketing performance in the context of a strategic plan normally implies support of the development and introduction of new products. An issue of enduring concern is how to evaluate the results of new product activities.

Specific concerns executives express in these areas include:

Developing a Marketing Orientation

"What is the process by which a company makes a shift to or from a marketing orientation versus a production, finance, or sales orientation? How is the need to make a shift discovered—what kinds of organizational and/or culture-changing steps are undertaken?"

"A particularly challenging organizational issue is the role and organization of marketing in a high-technology company that doesn't think of itself as a marketing company."

"An age-old (but common) problem is finding a positive way to establish a positive marketing attitude throughout the company rather than having marketing regarded as merely a department. There is an obvious need for the internal marketing of 'marketing.'"

Linking Marketing Planning and Strategic Planning

"We must develop ways to relate corporate strategic planning and marketing effectively. The broadest issue here is how do/should marketing considerations affect corporate strategic planning and how does/should strategic planning affect marketing planning? Some specific questions are:

(a) How should a company best integrate its strategic and marketing planning to cope with dramatic environmental changes—such as a sudden shift in the market (e. g., from big to small cars), a significant change in the cost or availability of key materials or services (e. g., the energy crunch), or major changes in regulatory or tax laws affecting the corporation. The implication of this issue is that big changes affecting one part of a corporation's portfolio of businesses can have major consequences for existing business and marketing plans. Big organizations often have difficulty coping with this.

(b) How can we improve our ability to decide what new businesses/segments we should be in and how best to enter them. This is directed at corporate diversification planning rather than traditional new product planning.

(c) How can a big company organize itself to compete profitably with small companies that have developed a 'niche' in the market?"

Evaluating New Product Activities

"Organizing resources to provide a flow of new products is a perennial problem. How should a company audit its new product activitiy? How can top management decide whether the function is doing a good job?"

Further Issues

Finally, several additional problems of concern to specific clusters of industries or groups of companies facing a common competitive situation were identified. One of particular importance to industrial marketers is the management of national or corporate account selling. Another is worldwide marketing competition as described by one executive:

"Established, high quality, full-service companies have problems holding onto strong positions against inroads of foreign competitors trying to buy market share through low price without regard to short-run profit.

Foreign companies with different goals and a high debt structure compete in ways to which American companies are not accustomed. This phenomenon is occurring in both U.S. and international markets, where U.S. firms seem to operate at a disadvantage."

A further concern relates to the marketing aspects of decisions about new marketing facilities:

"We need to learn how to assess the marketing dimensions of manufacturing decisions involving trade-offs between using old and building new plants. The older plants are substantially less flexible in terms of product innovation and productivity, but they are cheaper and faster to put into operation than are new, more productive plants. This is partly due to accounting rules and partly due to environmental issues and other governmental regulations."

Conclusion

These are some of the major challenges for marketing and more broadly for business in the years ahead, as seen by current marketing executives. Personally, I believe these challenges will call for increased *effectiveness* in marketing programs, increased *efficiency* in marketing operations, and increased *responsiveness* by marketing to the changing expectations of society.

Whether these problems in fact turn out to be central for practitioners, whether research inputs from academics and/or marketing research professionals can effectively be mounted to help address them, and whether they can be confronted successfully by the marketing and business community as a whole—only time will tell.

QUESTIONS

1. Do you agree with the panel's ranking of importance of the central marketing issues? Why? List several other important issues.
2. Discuss the economic and environmental conditions that existed in the early years of this decade that probably influenced the selection of these issues.
3. Identify any common factors or aspects among the issues identified by this article. What are the possible areas of conflict? (That is, when would addressing one issue cause problems concerning another issue?)

2

MARKET EXPANSION STRATEGIES IN MULTINATIONAL MARKETING

Igal Ayal
Jehiel Zif

This article compares a diversification strategy with a concentration strategy for entering a new foreign market. Factors that should guide the selection of these two strategies are presented.

Any firm attempting to expand international operations must decide on the number of countries and market segments it will attempt to penetrate at any given period. Given a fixed marketing budget the firm must also decide how to allocate its efforts among different markets served. One can conceive of two major and opposing strategies for making these decisions: market diversification and market concentration. The first strategy implies a fast penetration into a large number of markets and diffusion of efforts among them. The second strategy is based on concentration of resources in a few markets and gradual expansion into new territories.

After a number of years, both strategies may lead the firm to export into the same number of markets. The alternative expansion routes may generate, however, totally different consequences in terms of sales, market shares, and profits over time. In this paper, these two strategies are compared and the factors impinging on the choice between them are analyzed. Within the framework of the two major strategies, a number of more detailed strategic choices are identified, and alternative measurements of market expansion are discussed. Application of the framework for the choice of strategy is discussed and illustrated by a brief case study.

The Research Literature

Questions of market expansion in multinational marketing have received limited attention in the literature. Most of the research has concentrated on questions of national rather than international marketing, and on the allocation of promotional budgets among sales territories. No published attempt for systematic identification and choice of market expansion strategies has been found.

Nordin (1943) applied a basic marginal approach for allocating sales effort between two geographical areas subject to a budget constraint. Zentler and Hyde (1956) considered the allocation of advertising expenditures among a given number of countries. Their model takes into account an S-curve response function to promotion, and time-lag in the effect of promotion. A graphic solution is proposed to solve the complex mathematical problem. Hartung and Fisher (1965) used a model of brand switching and mathematical programming for market expansion in locating new gasoline stations.

Hirsch and Lev (1971; 1973) influenced our research by their empirical study of sales stability and profitability of two alternative penetration strategies into foreign markets. Their findings were supported by data from 200 exporting firms. Their identification of strategies was based on the direction of change in a market concentration index of sales between two periods.

Shakun (1965; 1966) attacked the related problem of promotional effort allocation between products through a game-theoretic approach. Luss and Gupta (1973) concentrated on the mathematical problem of designing an algorithm for solving the sales maximization problem, when marketing effort is allocated between products and sales territories. More recently, Beswick (1977) studied the allocation of selling effort via dynamic programming.

The various research papers mentioned above contribute important points to the analysis of market expansion and resource allocation. None of the papers however, presents a comprehensive framework for identification and analysis of alternative market expansion strategies over time. The purpose of this paper is to help fill this gap.

The Major Strategic Alternatives

The choice of a market expansion policy is a key strategic decision in multinational marketing. To develop such a policy, a firm has to make decisions in the following three areas:

- Identification of potential markets and determination of some order of priorities for entry into these markets.

- Decision on the overall level of marketing effort that the firm is able and willing to commit.
- Selection of the rate of market expansion over time, and determination of the allocation of effort among different markets.

This paper concentrates on the third area, assuming that decisions in the first two areas have already been made. In practice, the process will frequently be iterative; analysis of the third area will be helpful in clarifying and reviewing the first two areas.[1] The major strategic alternatives of market expansion, within the third area, are market concentration versus market diversification.

A strategy of market concentration is characterized by a slow and gradual rate of growth in the number of markets served. On the other hand, a strategy of market diversification is characterized by a fast rate of growth in the number of markets served at the early stages of expansion. It is, therefore, expected that a strategy of concentration will result in a smaller number of markets served, at each point in time, relative to a strategy of diversification. Expected evolution of the number of markets served, for a strategy of concentration versus a strategy of diversification, is presented graphically in Figure 1. The functional forms of the two strategies in Figure 1 represent a family of possible curves, showing the relative changes in the number of markets served over time.

In the long run, a strategy of diversification will frequently lead to a reduction in the number of markets, as a result of consolidation and abandonment of less profitable markets. A fast rate of market expansion is usually accomplished by devoting only limited resources and time to a careful study of each market prior to entry. The firm is, therefore, bound to make a few mistakes and is more likely to enter unprofitable markets and drop them later.[2]

The different patterns of market expansion are likely to cause development of different competitive conditions in different markets over time. The profitability of a late entry into new markets is affected by these competitive conditions and by the length of the product life cycle. As a result, the optimal

---

[1] Analysis of the third area requires identification of some markets with sufficient potential for entry and a preliminary idea about available budget. The results of the analysis may lead to a reevaluation of the order of entry priorities and provide more definite guidelines for the budget.

[2] In their empirical study, Hirsch and Lev (1973) have used the direction of change in a market concentration index of sales between two periods in order to identify the two major strategies. Figure 1 demonstrates, however, that this measure is insufficient for strategy identification. The direction of change for the two strategies is different only during a limited range of time. A more positive identification can rely on the rate or the shape of market expansion over an extended period of time.

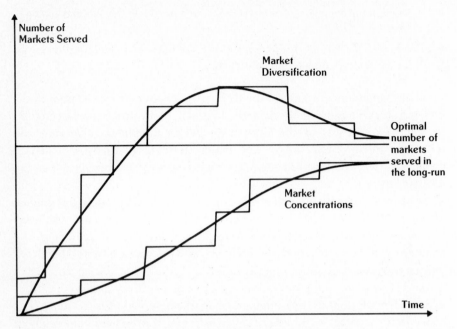

FIGURE 1   *Alternative Market Expansion Strategies Over Time*

number of markets served in the long run is not necessarily the same for both strategies.

The two strategies of concentration versus diversification lead to the selection of different levels of marketing effort and different marketing mixes in each market. Given fixed financial and managerial resources, the level of resources allocated to each market in a strategy of diversification will be lower than with concentration. The size of the budget gives an indication about possible selection of means or marketing mix. Specifically, a lower level of marketing effort implies less promotional expenditures, more reliance on commission agents, and a stronger tendency for a skimming approach to pricing. A strategy of concentration, on the other hand, involves investment in market share. This implies heavy promotional outlays, a stronger control of the distribution channel and, in some cases, penetration pricing.

Detailed Strategic Options

A strategy of market expansion is characterized not only by the rate of entry into new national markets. Two additional considerations are of particular importance for more detailed identification of optional strategies: (1) market segments within national markets and (2) allocation of effort to different markets (and market segments).

A number of strategic options can be derived based on the consideration of market segments and effort allocation; these are introduced and briefly discussed in this section. The full range of considerations affecting the choice of market concentration versus market diversification is treated in the following section.

MARKET SEGMENTS WITHIN NATIONAL MARKETS.   Four major market expansion alternatives can be identified when market segments are examined. These alternatives are presented in Table 1.

Strategy 1 concentrates on specific market segments in a few countries and a gradual increase in the number of markets served. This dual concentration is particularly appropriate when the product (or service) appeals to a definite group of similar customers in different countries, and the costs of penetration into each national market are substantial in relation to available resources. To be successful with this strategy, the segments served must be sufficiently large and stable.

Strategy 2—characterized by market concentration and segment diversification—requires a product line which can appeal to different segments. The strategy is particularly effective when there are significant economies of scale in promotion (e. g., umbrella advertising) and distribution, and when the sales potential of the home market and other national markets served is large. Under such conditions, a firm can achieve growth objectives by concentrating on many submarkets within a limited number of national markets.

Strategy 3—characterized by market diversification and segment concentration—is suitable for firms with a specialized product line and potential customers in many countries. With this strategy, a firm frequently can use a similar product and promotion strategy in all markets. The strategy is particularly effective when the cost of entry into different markets is low relative to available resources. For strategy identification, it is important to note that two firms may follow different expansion strategies with respect to countries and segments (strategy 2 versus strategy 3) yet serve the same total number of market segments at each point in time.

Strategy 4 is based on dual diversification in both segments and markets.

Table 1

MARKET EXPANSION STRATEGIES BASED ON COUNTRIES AND SEGMENTS

		SEGMENTS	
		Concentration	Diversification
Countries	Concentration	1	2
	Diversification	3	4

This aggressive strategy can be employed by firms with a product line appealing to many segments, and sufficient resources to accomplish a fast entry into many markets. Large international firms with sales offices in many countries frequently use this strategy when they introduce a newly developed or acquired product line. A poorman's version of strategy 4 can sometimes be employed by small firms with limited resources, based on superficial coverage. The commitment of resources in market expansion is the subject of the following paragraphs.

ALLOCATION OF EFFORT TO DIFFERENT MARKETS. Marketing expansion can be achieved by different means. Even a small firm with limited resources can achieve market diversification quickly by using independent commission agents in each market, with little or no investment. In order to identify a specific strategy of market expansion it is, therefore, necessary to specify the overall marketing effort as well as the allocation of effort to different markets.

Some researchers have defined resource commitments to international markets on the basis of a stepwise expansion of operations (Johanson and Wiedersheim 1975). A sequence of three stages demonstrates successively larger commitments of resources and marketing involvement:

- Export by independent agents
- Sales subsidiary
- Manufacturing subsidiary

The marketing expansion of Volvo into 20 countries between 1929 and 1973 is presented graphically in Figure 2. This figure separates expansion by the three stages above and shows the gradual increase in territorial coverage and resource commitments. Two periods of relatively fast diversification, prior to and after World War II, are indicated.

The first two stages above specify an essential element of distribution strategy in market expansion. Extensive use of independent agents is frequently associated with market diversification; and a resource commitment to sales subsidiaries is a more likely strategic element of market concentration. Many firms like Volvo prefer to employ independent agents in some markets and sales subsidiaries in others. The relative share of each distribution method is an important strategic option of market expansion.

Distribution strategies do not always portray a correct picture of effort allocation. A firm may invest the same resources in two markets using a different marketing mix and distribution setup. In one market the firm may employ an independent agent backed by substantial promotional activity. In another market the firm may establish a sales subsidiary with a limited promotional budget. A quantitative measure of effort allocation would be more precise for analytical purposes.

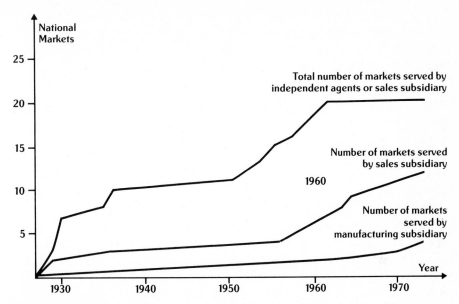

FIGURE 2   *Market Expansion of Volvo into Twenty National Markets*
Source of data: Johanson and Wiedersheim (1975).

Managers inside the firm can determine the overall marketing investment in each market, based on internal accounting. With this information, it is possible to calculate a diversification index that takes into account both the number of markets served and the uniformity of effort distribution.[3]

Considerations Affecting The Choice of Market Expansion Strategy

The selection of market expansion strategy is influenced by characteristics of the product, characteristics of the market, and decision criteria of the firm.

---

[3] An effort diversification index for period t, D_{et}, is given by:

$$D_{et} = 1/\sum_{i=1}^{n_t} ME^2_{i,t}$$

where:

$ME_{i,t}$ = Marketing effort in market i and period t, expressed as a fraction of the firm's total marketing effort for period t.

n_t = total number of markets served in period t.

This index is equal to the total number of markets served $D_{et} = n_t$ when efforts are equally distributed; it approaches a lower bound $D_{et} = 1$ when the firm concentrates most of its effort in a single market.

Table 2 summarizes 10 key product/market factors affecting the choice between market concentration and market diversification. The following discussion explains the effect of each factor on the adoption of market expansion strategy.

(1) **SALES RESPONSE FUNCTION.**   Two alternative classes of sales response functions—a concave function and an S-curve function—are common in the literature (Kotler 1971). Graphic examples of these functions are presented in Figure 3.[4] If the firm believes that it faces a concave response function, there will be a strong motivation to follow a strategy of market diversification. On the other hand, when the response function is assumed to be an S-curve, a market concentration strategy usually is preferred.

The concave response function implies that the best return on marketing effort (x) is at lower levels of effective effort (see Figure 3). This is based on the assumption that the markets under consideration include a number of clients

---

[4] For a given initial market size, the sales response function can be separated into a market share response function and a rate of market growth; the first is directly influenced by the firm's marketing efforts while the second is usually more dependent on product life cycles, environmental conditions in the market, and the combined marketing efforts of all competitors.

Table 2
PRODUCT/MARKET FACTORS AFFECTING CHOICE BETWEEN DIVERSIFICATION AND CONCENTRATION STRATEGIES

Product/Market Factor	Prefer Diversi-fication if:	Prefer Concen-tration if:
1. Sales response function	Concave	S-curve
2. Growth rate of each market	low	high
3. Sales stability in each market	low	high
4. Competitive lead-time	short	long
5. Spill over effects	high	low
6. Need for product adaptation	low	high
7. Need for communication adaptation	low	high
8. Economies of scale in distribution	low	high
9. Program control requirements	low	high
10. Extent of constraints	low	high

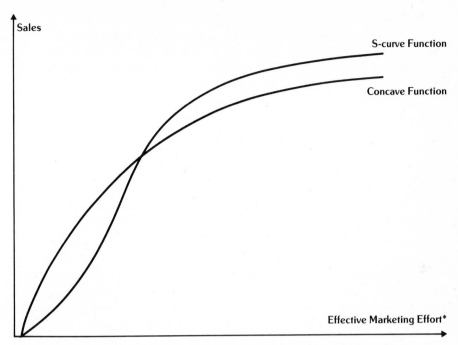

*Effective marketing effort takes into account current marketing effort as well as carry over effects of previous efforts.

FIGURE 3 *Alternative Market Share Response Functions*

or submarkets which are particularly interested in the firm's products. Such interest is frequently generated by a unique product or marketing program, possibly the result of substantial investment in R&D. As additional effort is spent, market share increases, but the firm faces stiffer resistance, more skeptical buyers, and increased effort by competitors. Therefore, market response is characterized by diminishing marginal returns and diversification of effort is more productive. It is interesting to note that most empirical studies of advertising effectiveness support the hypothesis of concave market response functions (Simon 1971; Lambin 1976).

The S-curve response function assumes that small-scale efforts of penetration to a new market are beset by various difficulties and buyers' resistance and will not count for much. Increases in market share and profitability will be achieved only after a substantial concentration in marketing effort is made. This type of response function is likely for products that do not enjoy obvious advantages—which is, of course, the case for most products. There are a number of reported cases of geographical market expansion which support the premise of an S-curve response function (Cardwell 1968; Hofer 1975).

A quantitative example of the choice of market expansion under the two sales response assumptions is presented in a footnote below.[5]

(2) **GROWTH RATE OF EACH MARKET.**   When the rate of growth of the industry in each market is low, the firm can frequently achieve a faster growth rate by diversification into many markets. On the other hand, if the rate of market growth in present markets is high, growth objectives can usually be achieved by market concentration.

When the rate of growth of the industry in many markets is high, there are occasional opportunities for diversification with limited resources. Penetration to many markets can be accomplished by relying on marketing efforts of independent sales agents and licensees who are interested in promoting the firm's products in their own growing markets. The case of Miromit, an Israeli producer of unique solar collectors, serves as an example. Following the energy crisis, the firm was flooded by requests for sales representation from interested parties in many countries. In this case, the firm followed a mixed strategy by concentrating its resources in a few markets and diversifying to other markets with little or no investment. By this strategy the number of markets served would increase rapidly, but the effort diversification index would show a slow rate of growth.

(3) **SALES STABILITY IN EACH MARKET.**   When demand in each market is unstable, the firm can spread the risk through judicious diversification. To the extent that markets are independent with respect to demand, an increase in the number of markets is likely to increase sales stability. This was demonstrated empirically by Hirsch and Lev (1971). When sales stability in each market is high, the firm can concentrate its market expansion effort while still satisfying the need for stability.

---

[5] Let us assume that the functional form of Figure 5 is expressed quantitatively, in the following table.

Marketing effort	Concave function. Sales $	S-curve. Sales $
100,000	1,000,000	600,000
200,000	1,800,000	1,200,000
300,000	2,400,000	2,400,000

What is the preferred market expansion strategy for a firm which is planning to invest $300,000 of marketing effort in three identical markets? Under consideration are two strategic alternatives: (1) Concentrate all marketing effort in one market (2) Diversify marketing efforts equally among the three markets (invest $100,000 in each). The outcome of each strategy, depending on the assumed sales response function, will be the following: (preferred strategy indicated by *)

Expansion Strategy	Concave function	S-curve function
1. Concentrate on one market	$2,400,000	$2,400,000*
2. Diversify into three markets	$3,000,000*	$1,800,000

(4) COMPETITIVE LEAD-TIME. The lead-time that an innovative firm has over competitors and potential imitators is an important consideration in selecting a market expansion strategy. When competitive lead-time is short and there is a major advantage to being first in a market with a new innovation, there is a strong motivation to follow the route of diversification. In this situation, the firm faces a favorable response function for a limited period. The urgency to enter many markets quickly is diminished if the innovative firm has a long lead-time, or when there is no innovative advantage. This argument of competitive lead-time was expressed by an executive of a small computer equipment company: "The compelling reason for entering Europe now . . . was to capitalize on our innovative advantage. We consider our products to be well ahead of competitors' . . . but in our fast moving field—data entry systems and input equipment—this could change rapidly" (Sweeney 1970).

(5) SPILL-OVER EFFECTS. Spill-over of marketing effort or goodwill from present to new markets is another factor favoring diversification. This spill-over effect can be the result of geographical proximity, cultural influence, or commercial ties. It is common in TV and radio coverage of close national markets. There is obviously a strong motivation to take advantage of spill-over effects by diversifying into new markets which are influenced by current and past effort in presently-served markets.

(6) NEED FOR PRODUCT ADAPTATION. The experience curve phenomenon of systematic reduction in variable cost with an increase in accumulated production volume has a major impact on international market share strategy (Rapp 1973). Firms that grow faster than their competitors are able to reduce production costs faster and as a result enjoy a major competitive advantage. When the same product is sold in different international markets, market expansion is not only a vehicle for diversification and new profit opportunities, but it also can increase profits by reducing costs in currently-served markets.

Frequently, a company cannot sell the same product in all international markets. There is a need to adapt the product to the standards and regulations of a new country, as well as to the special tastes and preferences of new consumers. The magnitude and nature of the adaptation costs are an important consideration in choosing an expansion strategy. In particular, a firm should assess whether adaptation to new markets requires only a small fixed investment or whether a major change is necessary. If entry into new international markets requires major changes in the production process, the company will not only have to invest a significant amount before entry, but will probably be unable to enjoy the full cost advantage of accumulated experience. In this case there will be a lesser motivation to expand geographically than in the case of an investment that has positive effects on potential economies in production.

(7) **NEED FOR COMMUNICATION ADAPTATION.**   Adaptation may be necessary not only for the product, but also for the marketing or communication program. In many situations, the communication program is more important than the technical specifications of the product. In a recent study of international expansion of U.S. franchise systems, 59% of the 80 respondent firms indicated alteration in strategy upon entry into international markets (Hackett 1976). Twenty-five percent of the firms reported a change in product (or service) to fit local tastes, while all other changes were related to communication adaptation. If communication adaptation requires a large investment in consumer and advertising research and in production of new programs, the temptation to follow a diversification strategy is diminished.

(8) **ECONOMIES OF SCALE IN DISTRIBUTION.**   When distribution cost is a significant expense and there are economies of scale with increased market share, there is motivation to follow a concentration strategy. A strategy of rapid expansion into many new markets can frequently increase distribution costs substantially as a result of increased transportation distance and a low level of sales over a large territory. Efficient distribution can, however, be achieved in different ways depending on the product and specific channels. For example, it is possible that diversification with respect to countries and concentration with respect to segments (strategy 3 in Table 1) can lead to an efficient distribution system.

(9) **PROGRAM CONTROL REQUIREMENTS.**   Extensive requirements for control are typical of custom-made and sophisticated products and services which require close and frequent communication between headquarters (R&D, production, marketing) and clients. The cost of managerial communication with clients and agents, per unit of sales, is likely to increase with the number of markets served. A comparison of average contact costs in concentrated and diversified markets suggests that the difference in favor of a concentrated market is increasing with the number of contacts (Bucklin 1966). We can, therefore, expect that when the program control requirements are extensive, a concentrated strategy of market expansion will have an advantage.

(10) **CONSTRAINTS.**   There are a number of constraints on management action in international markets. External constraints include import and currency barriers created by government authorities in the target markets. There may also be difficulties in finding or developing an effective sales and distribution organization. Internal constraints are based on the availability of resources in order to function in new markets. Trained managers and salesmen

may be limited, financial resources may be scarce, and production factors may be in short supply.

In the previously mentioned study of international expansion of franchise systems, respondents were asked to rank problems encountered in international markets (Hackett 1976). The five most important problems were: (1) host government regulations and red tape, (2) high import duties and taxes in foreign environments, (3) monetary uncertainties and royalty retribution to franchisor, (4) logistical problems inherent in operation of international franchise systems, and (5) control of franchisees. The spectacular rate of international market expansion, and the reported plans for further expansion by the respondent firms, indicate that these obstacles were surmountable in most cases. This was partly due to a strategy based on franchisee-owned outlets, which is a form of diversification with limited resources.

External or internal constraints place a limit on the capability or the profitability of market diversification. While some constraints can be overcome, extensive barriers in many markets will lead to market concentration.

Decision Criteria

The expected value and the variance of the net present value of each expansion alternative are common decision criteria. To use these criteria, it is necessary to estimate and express the product/market factor considerations in quantitative terms of sales, prices, costs, and timetable.

Many firms frequently will supplement these profitability estimates with other criteria based on the multiple objectives of the firm. Objectives of international market standing and prestige are frequently stated as major causes for fast diversification with limited regard to profitability consequences. For example, Koor, the largest industrial concern in Israel, established a trading company and decided to enter the European Common Market with a strategy of fast diversification by setting up sales offices in seven European countries within one year (Perry 1977). The major objective was: "to become the largest and most important Israeli commercial organization in Europe." It is interesting to note that profitability results in the short-term were quite disappointing.

The criteria used by business firms to select alternatives for action are outside the scope of this study. We merely suggest that these criteria can be another major cause for preference of one market expansion strategy over another.

Application

Selecting a market expansion strategy based on the product/market factors of Table 2 is bound to raise a few application questions. These questions can be clarified by reviewing the case of a leading electronics manufacturer in Israel (name withheld at request of company executives). The firm is a subsidiary of a large and internationally known American firm. Two relatively sophisticated product lines are being exported: communication equipment and control systems. The communication equipment was developed by the parent company while the control systems were developed in Israel. Table 3 and Figures 4 and 5 present, for each product line, a summary analysis of the product/market factors, market expansion graphs, and international sales.

One question of application is illustrated by Table 3. The 10 factors do not point in one direction; some imply market diversification, while others imply market concentration.

Two explanatory remarks can clarify the dilemma: (1) Management must weigh the relative importance of the product/market factors in selecting a strategy. Although some factors such as the sales response function will be important in all cases, the relative importance of other factors such as distribution cost are likely to change from case to case. (2) The concepts of market concentration and market diversification should be viewed in relative terms. Occasionally, the choice between concentration and diversification is not clear-cut in absolute terms and a middle course should be selected. In comparison with extreme alternatives, however, the strategic choice is clear.

Table 3

CASE STUDY: ANALYSIS OF PRODUCT/MARKET FACTORS BY PRODUCT LINE

Product/Market Factor	Communication Equipment		Control Systems	
	Direction	*Implied Strategy*	Direction	*Implied Strategy*
1. Sales response function	Concave	D	S-curve	C
2. Growth rate of each market	High	C	High	C
3. Sales stability in each market	Low	D	High	C
4. Competitive lead-time	Long	C	Long	C
5. Spill-over effects	High	D	Low	C
6. Need for product adaptation	Low	D	High	C
7. Need for communication adaptation	Low	D	High	C
8. Economies of scale in distribution	Low	D	Low	D
9. Program control requirements	High	C	High	C
10. Extent of constraints	High	C	Low	D

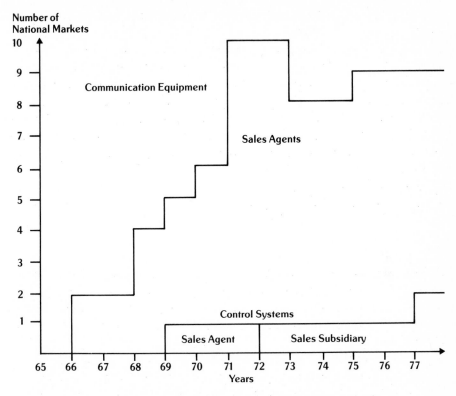

FIGURE 4   *Case Study: Market Expansion Graphs by Product Line*

In the case of control systems most factors point to a concentrated strategy (Table 3); the firm followed this strategy with respect to both markets and segments. The direction implied by the factors for communication equipment is more mixed, and the firm followed a middle of the road strategy of "prudent" diversification, or fairly rapid concentrated expansion. The strategy was diversified with respect to segments. Figure 4 demonstrates that the expansion of the communication equipment is much more diversified relative to the concentrated expansion of the control systems.

A second question of application also can be clarified by reference to the case. A summary analysis like Table 3 assumes that the markets under consideration are quite similar and that the effects of the product/market factors can be estimated prior to entry. This is not always the case, as can be seen by the withdrawal from two communication equipment markets in 1973 (Figure 4).

A few points should be made in response to this question: (1) A summary table, like 3, is applicable to a group of similar markets. When different

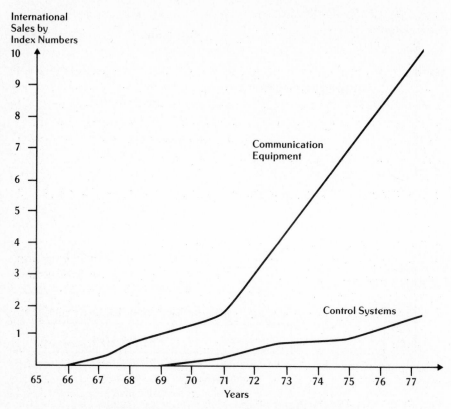

FIGURE 5 *Case Study: International Sales by Product Line*

groups of markets are being considered, it is advantageous to analyze each group separately, since a different expansion strategy may be appropriate for each group.

(2) An investment in market research prior to entry can reduce uncertainty, but not eliminate it. Penetration into international markets which are politically and economically unstable is liable to produce surprises with changing events. This was the case with the communication equipment that was introduced into developing Asian and African markets.

(3) A firm may prefer to acquire information by actual testing in the marketplace, rather than by costly and prolonged market survey prior to entry. This policy is particularly applicable when quick entry is important, or when market diversification with limited resources is employed. Abandonment of some markets, following testing, is quite likely under this policy.

(4) Market expansion is a discrete process based on a market by market entry. It is therefore possible and desirable to view it as a learning process, and to correct strategic decisions as more information becomes available. This learning process can explain the expansion curve of the control systems

(Figures 4 and 5). After three unsatisfactory years in one market, the firm decided to switch from a sales agent to a sales subsidiary, and a second market was penetrated only after eight years of international experience with the product line. It is interesting to note that in spite of necessary corrective action, a different and distinct long-term strategy for each product line was pursued, and that these strategies were consistent with the evaluation of the product market factors.

Conclusion

This paper presents a framework for planning and evaluation of market expansion strategies. In particular it focuses on the rate of entry into new markets and the allocation of effort among markets. The framework can be used in national or regional marketing, but has special relevance for international expansion. A careful review of the literature did not reveal any other framework which serves the same purposes.

This framework aids managerial action in multinational marketing in the following ways:

- It helps management specify market expansion alternatives for decision making purposes. In addition to the comparison of the two major and opposing strategies—market concentration and market diversification—the paper aids in defining additional strategic options. By considering market segments within national markets, four viable market expansion strategies are identified (see Table 1). By considering resource commitments to new markets, three strategic options are specified and many more are implied.

- It helps management to systematically analyze the problem of choice among the major alternative strategies. Ten key factors affecting this choice are summarized in Table 2, discussed in some detail in the body of the paper, and illustrated by examples and a case study. In each application it will be necessary to separately assess each factor and its relative importance for comprehensive evaluation of the alternatives.

- It offers guidance for measuring market expansion. Two specific measures suggested are the number of countries and market segments served, and an effort diversification index, both as a function of time. Measuring market diversification can be used not only for evaluating the firm's own expansion policy, but also for evaluating competitive moves. The factors affecting the choice of strategy can be used to interpret competitive assumptions.

A systematic approach to identification of alternatives, analysis of choice, and performance evaluation will clarify managerial planning and help reduce mistakes and disappointments in expansion to new markets.

We hope that this paper will aid in directing research attention to this important and interesting area. Further research can benefit by the following points:

- Comparison of market expansion strategies based on the direction of change between two static measurements—as used in past empirical research (see 4)—may not be sufficient. Figure 1 and the following discussion of dynamic measures point out the complexities of identification and offer some direction.
- Decision making models based on one kind of response function (see 2) are useful in some situations, but can be quite misleading in others. Only by exploring alternative response functions and examining their assumptions and implications, can reliable guidance to action be provided.
- The framework of this paper is useful for planning additional research. Identification of a marketing expansion strategy can be used as an explanatory variable for other marketing decisions. As an example, we have used this framework for studying the related problem of competitive market-choice in multinational marketing (Ayal and Zif 1978). Specific priorities for additional research include further empirical investigation of the relationships among the product/market factors, strategies followed, and business outcomes. There also is room for model building that will offer quantitative analysis of the product/market factors.

References

Ayal Igal and Jehiel Zif (1978), "Competitive Market Choice Strategies in Multinational Marketing," *Columbia Journal of World Business,* 13 (Fall).

Beswick, C.A. (1977), "Allocating Selling Effort via Dynamic Programming," *Management Science,* 23 (March), 667–678.

Bucklin, L.P. (1966), *A Theory of Distribution Channel Structure,* IBER Special Publications, Berkeley, CA: Graduate School of Business Administration, University of California, 49–50.

Cardwell, John J. (1968), "Marketing and Management Science—A Marriage on the Rocks," *California Management Review,* 10 (Summer), 3–12.

Hackett, D.W. (1976), "The International Expansion of U.S. Franchise Systems: Status and Strategies," *Journal of International Business Studies,* 7 (Spring), 71.

Hartung, P.H. and J.L. Fisher (1965), "Brand Switching and Mathematical Programming in Market Expansion," *Management Science,* 11 (August), 231–243.

Hirsch, Seev and Baruch Lev (1971), "Sales Stabilization Through Export Diversification," *The Review of Economics and Statistics,* 53 (August), 270–279.

——— (1973), "Foreign Marketing Strategies—A Note," *Management International Review,* 13, 81–88.

Hofer, Charles W. (1975), "Toward a Contingency Theory of Business Strategy," *Academy of Management Journal,* 18 (December), 804.

Johanson, J. and Paul F. Wiedersheim (1975), "The Internationalization of the Firm—Four Swedish Cases," *The Journal of Management Studies*, 12 (October), 306–307.

Kotler, Philip (1971), *Marketing Decisions Making—A Model Building Approach*, New York: Holt, Rinehart and Winston, 31–37.

Lambin, J.J. (1976), *Advertising, Competition and Market Conduct in Oligopoly Over Time*, Amsterdam: North-Holland Publishing, 95–98.

Luss, Hanan and Shiv K. Gupta (1973), "Allocation of Marketing Effort Among P Substitutional Products in N Territories," *Operational Research Quarterly*, 25 (March), 77–88.

Nordin, J.A. (1943), "Spatial Allocation of Selling Expenses," *Journal of Marketing*, 3 (January), 210–219.

Perry, Michael (1977), Koor-Trade Europe, a Case Study presented in a Management Seminar on International Marketing, Tel-Aviv: Graduate School of Business, Tel-Aviv University.

Rapp, William V. (1973), "Strategy Formulation and International Competition," *Columbia Journal of World Business*, 8 (Summer), 98–112.

Shakun, M.G. (1965), "Advertising Expenditures in Coupled Markets, A Game Theory Approach," *Management Science*, 11 (February), B42–B47.

———— (1966), "A Dynamic Model for Competitive Marketing in Coupled Markets," *Management Science*, 12 (August), B525–B530.

Simon, Julian L. (1971), *The Management of Advertising*, Englewood Cliffs, NJ: Prentice-Hall, Inc., 55–76.

Sweeney, James K. (1970), "A Small Company Enters the European Market," *Harvard Business Review*, 48 (Sept.-Oct.), 126–132.

Zentler, A.P. and Dorothy Hyde (1956), "An Optimal Geographical Distribution of Publicity Expenditure in a Private Organization," *Management Science*, 2 (July), 337–352.

QUESTIONS

1. What decisions are required for selecting market expansion policies?

2. Compare the level of marketing effort and the general types of marketing mixes associated with a concentrated expansion program versus a diversified program.

3. What product and market characteristics should be evaluated by the manager when choosing a market expansion strategy?

4. Under what conditions or situations should a concentrated strategy be selected?

3

RESPONSIBLE MARKETING IN AN EXPANDED MARKETING CONCEPT

Leland L. Beik
Warren A. French

This article expands basic marketing principles, such as exchange, the marketing concept, and marketing goals, to reflect a social responsibility. The importance of this social responsibility and its impact on marketing strategy are also discussed.

While societal aspects of marketing have frequently been expressed, the operational responsibilities necessary to deliver satisfaction and well-being to both the transacting parties and the community have not been treated in full. A reexamination of the functions and goals of the parties participating in, and affected by, exchange will help to formulate these responsibilities. By incorporating goals and responsibilities in the format of an expanded marketing concept, this article will delineate a mode of operation which should contribute to public welfare and to responsible evolution of marketing as an institution.

New Dimensions for Marketing

In a substantive article, Lazer suggested that a broader definition of marketing is necessary in order to meet the goals of society. An emerging view recognizes the influence of marketing on our life styles, on the ethical and moral attitudes we bring to the process of exchange, on our very philosophy of consumption. Marketing, in Lazer's estimate, must extend beyond the realm of profit and be recognized as an instrument of social control.[1]

A provocative companion article by Kotler and Levy suggested that principles of marketing are transferable to similar non-business situations. Any organization must undertake strategic marketing functions such as formulating a generic product or service policy and defining target groups. Marketing concepts and tools may be used to foster marketing activities in many kinds of social or political groups or institutions.[2]

The broader view is apparent in adjustments to key definitions in the second edition of Kotler's text. Marketing management is "an action science consisting of principles for improving the effectiveness of exchange." Exchange is considered a normalized set of transactions—not necessarily limited to the transfer of money or goods. Societal marketing incorporates long-run consumer welfare in its objectives. And marketing, the general case, is the "set of human activities directed at facilitating and consumating exchange."[3]

Extending the definition of exchange and therefore the applicability of marketing functions to nonprofit organizations, adds breadth to previous concepts of marketing. (See Figure 1.) Societal goals add a dimension of depth to the context of marketing. A third important dimension, that of time, comes into play when considering the long-run implications of transactional activity. A legitimate expansion of these dimensions, though, has its costs. It implies the acceptance of corresponding areas of responsibility as an integral part of the functions and scope of marketing thought and practice.

Incorporating an Added Function

Given expanded boundaries, basic marketing functions require clarification to account for objectives not directly related to purchasers and profit. Most traditional functions start with buying and selling or are otherwise tied to transfer of title as the end result of commercial transactions. Even the purpose-oriented functions of obtaining and servicing demand are stated as

---

[1] William Lazer, "Marketing's Changing Social Relationships," *Journal of Marketing* (January, 1969), p. 3.

[2] Philip Kotler and Sidney J. Levy, "Broadening the Concept of Marketing," *Journal of Marketing* (January, 1969), p. 10.

[3] Philip Kotler, *Marketing Management* (2nd ed.; Englewood Cliffs, N.J.: Prentice-Hall, Inc., 1972), pp. 12 and 13; See also Philip Kotler, "A Generic Concept of Marketing," *Journal of Marketing* (April, 1972), p. 46.

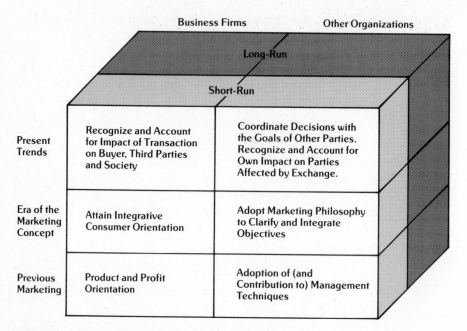

FIGURE 1   *Expanded Dimensions of Marketing*

managerial objectives.[4] Yet, such analyses do not describe tasks inherent in an expanded view of marketing.

Although Kotler does not use the term, aspects of his generic marketing can be interpreted as functions. Market analysis and product analysis are basic analytical tasks. Through these, value is created and offered to the market by means of configuration (designing the social object), valuation (establishing terms of exchange), symbolization (associating meaning with the object), and facilitation (making the object accessible).[5] The language now encompasses marketing activities in non-business organizations.

An insightful analysis of functions was earlier developed by McGarry.[6] By generalizing his language, McGarry's functions as well as Kotler's analytical tasks can provide the underpinning for added breadth. To accommodate

[4] Theodore N. Beckman and William R. Davidson, *Marketing Management* (8th ed.; New York: The Ronald Press Company, 1967), p. 423 for criteria and p. 424 for a standard list. See also Richard J. Lewis and Leo G. Erickson, "Marketing Functions and Marketing Systems: A Synthesis," *Journal of Marketing* (April, 1972) p. 10.

[5] Philip Kotler, "A Generic Concept of Marketing," *Journal of Marketing* (April, 1972), pp. 50 and 52.

[6] Edmund D. McGarry, "Some Functions of Marketing Reconsidered," in Reavis Cox and Wroe Alderson, *Theory in Marketing* (Chicago, Ill.: Richard D. Irwin, Inc., 1950), p. 269.

societal goals and responsibilities, added depth, it is necessary to insert one additional function, designated as propriety. The adapted list becomes:

1. Contractual or market analysis—searching out reciprocal interests in exchange,
2. Matching or configuration—fitting goods, services, communications, etc., to clientel requirements,
3. Promotion or symbolization—cultivating attitudes favorable to both current and future transaction,
4. Bargaining or valuation—selecting conditions considered beneficial by both parties to a present transaction,
5. Propriety—considering the impact of the transaction on other individuals and groups; conforming to evolving moral, ethical, and legal standards,
6. Distribution or facilitation—completing communication, transportation, storage and other arrangements requisite to the transaction,
7. Termination or facilitation—consummating the transaction; however, note the time dimension influences on all the parties affected by the transaction.

The adapted functions encompass the strategy of formulating and enacting product or service policies for selected target segments, while accounting for the impact on other groups. These generalized definitions serve to emphasize client or patron actions and responsibilities which, in fact, constitute half of the marketing process.

Recognizing Added Goals

Expanding the boundaries and functions of marketing requires reconsideration of marketing goals. While admitting that any one of the parties engaged in or influenced by exchange has multiple goals and that any combination may be temporarily dominant, it is important to identify divergent goals and responsibilities. [Table 1] . . . presents an array of short and long-run goals held by marketing management, top management, competitive firms, consumers, third parties or organizations, regulatory agencies, and the public in general. Both cooperative and competitive conditions are implied by this array.

To establish a rough hierarchy among the major goals using societal criteria, one would have to name long-run social welfare as predominant and assume that it is attained by evolution of social and cultural norms. Second in order of importance, and an accessory to social evolution, are the fundamental goals of government. In the long-run, widespread political, economic and social well-being are pursued through legislative, judicial, and administrative actions. Specifically, this involves (1) chartering the autho-

Table 1

THE GOALS OF EXCHANGE

Party	Short-run Goal	Means	Long-run Goal
Buyer, client or patron	Want satisfaction	Purchase of goods or services; membership privileges, etc.	Personal well-being, a continuity of want satisfactions in line with a pattern of personal goals
Seller or organization	Profit, R.O.I., contributions, participation, etc.	Delivery of goods, services, communications, etc.	Survival, growth, favorable image, social impact, etc.
Third parties or organizations	Subsidiary benefits; avoidance of detrimental effects	Communication of interests; social, economic, political, or legal pressures	Personal well-being in face of actions by others; survival, growth, image, impact, etc.
Government interface	Minimal friction in exchange	Monitor rules of exchange; legislate or recodify rules as needed; arbitrate controversies via FTC hearings or courts	Promote widespread political, economic, and social well-being, i.e., communal welfare
Society at large	Satisfaction among parties to exchange	Exchange in accord with social and cultural norms	Enhancement of communal welfare

rized activities of organizations in line with public interests, and (2) setting the conditions under which exchange takes place. In the short-run, the government objective reduces to supervising the system of exchange, including the search for benefits for and prevention of harm to third party individuals or organizations affected by exchange.

Separate acts of exchange among individuals and/or organizations, although they may be critical to the parties involved, must be considered of lesser importance from a societal point of view. Even here, the search for long-run well-being is of greater importance than short-run want satisfaction, although the latter may dominate individual transactions. Then too, the aggregate of transactions contributes strongly to social welfare as sought by society at large and its agent, the government.

Present marketing strategy, even if consumer oriented, substantially fails to account for the goals or rights of any parties not participating directly in exchange. Public criticism and action (e.g., the consumer movement, civic and social sensitivities, and attention to ecological considerations) stridently recognize the need for new directions.

Accompanying Rights and Responsibilities

To some degree, all transaction decisions are moderated by the context in which they are made. Specifically, important rights and responsibilities may be cited for the individuals involved in transactions which have an impact on any of the goals noted in the array of [Table 1] . . .

Certain rights such as the right to life are considered absolute or unqualified. They require no correlative duties in order to be respected. Few such rights are acknowledged by society. More common are a second class of rights, relative rights, which do imply correlative responsibilities.[7] Most rights apparent in the marketing process, e.g., the right to fair exchange, fall under this second classification.

Certain reciprocal responsibilities are embedded in the laws and customs of exchange. In addition to protecting third parties who might be directly harmed, responsibilities may need to be extended to society in general in instances where the quality of life is at stake or the communal resources are endangered as through pollution or exploitation.[8]

Consumers' and Marketers' Rights and Responsibilities

The consumer (buyer, client, patron), in seeking value from a transaction, has rights which must be respected by the seller and the community. The right to a fair exchange implies the rights to be heard, to a safe product, to honest information, etc. These rights are currently well publicized under the consumerism label. Equally basic to our system of exchange are the rights to freedom of choice and to negotiate as an equal party to a transaction.

---

[7] D. D. Raphael, *Political Theory and the Rights of Man* (Bloomington: Indiana University Press, 1967) and Heinrich A. Ronimen and Thomas R. Hanley, *The Natural Law* (St. Louis: B. Herder Book Company, 1959), pp. 207, 208, and 243.

[8] Laurence P. Feldman, "Societal Adaptation: A New Challenge for Marketing," *Journal of Marketing* (July, 1971), p. 54.

Along with these rights are coincidental responsibilities. A buyer is responsible for making a reasonable search and comparison of offerings as prerequisite to an intelligent decision. In undertaking this task, the buyer is obligated to respect the marketer's rights. He is expected to live up to customary as well as contract conditions of any transaction in which he participates. Nor should third party impacts and the common good of the community be ignored in his search for satisfaction.

Like the consumer, the marketer (individual, business, or other organization) has the right to engage in exchange of goods, services, or communications for motives ranging from profit to propaganda. Subsidiary rights include substantial freedom of choice in selecting market targets, in determining the nature of product, service, or communication, and in marshalling resources to advance organizational goals through meeting the goals of the individuals or groups served.

Responsibilities to the consumer include an honest attempt to provide needed information, fair value in exchange, reasonable mechanisms for adjustment, etc. Since trusting consumers place their economic and sometimes their physical and mental safety in the hands of the marketer, responsible management becomes a crucial obligation. Custom, legal precedent, and codified law express the reciprocal rights and responsibilities inherent in exchange.

Managements are developing an increased sensitivity to the rights of third parties and the public. Although managers sometimes react only to preclude adverse publicity, judicial review, or strict legislation, they are often aware of the impact of their decisions through fundamental legal, moral, and ethical standards.

Rights and Responsibilities of Third Parties and Society

Although third parties have some protection under law, the general assumption is that other members of society benefit as long as a transaction operates to the mutual advantage of those directly involved. As an aggregate of individuals and an amalgamation of groups, the rights widely accorded to individuals, groups and organizations become those of society. Freedom of choice and equality in a transaction are rights illustrating the special interest which members of the public should maintain in the laws and customs of exchange.

Effective social responsibility is difficult to attain because of its dispersion. Each of us shares responsibility for social structure and, in a democracy, especially for its political arm. Added responsibility is inherent to various degrees in the nature of managerial positions in business as well as in government. To preserve freedom and equality, societal interests must, on occasion, override those of individuals where it is necessary to protect individuals or social components from each other. Because our society places a premium on individual values, perhaps the chief societal responsibility is to preserve what social, economic, and political equality we have and to work toward improving it and making it more widespread.

Managing Augmented Responsibilities

It is clear that the locus of interest, authority, and responsibility for marketing activity varies radically and is not well specified, especially with respect to the societal arena. The goals of the parties involved, however, are not totally incompatible. Friction does arise due to the competitive aspects of transactional behavior, but other factors are working to preserve the cooperative benefits expected from exchange.

Because of the diverse goals and responsibilities, some common rule for decision-making is needed to work toward coordination of decentralized decisions. Massive cost benefit or systems studies might be used to evaluate societal impacts as well as the direct results of decision alternatives. But even such techniques run into nonquantifiable data and cannot comprehend other independent or broader systems. Consumers, even businessmen and administrators, are not generally competent in using the more sophisticated decision techniques, nor would such techniques apply to the majority of day to day decisions.

The Relational Theory of Value

The broadened concept of marketing with its propriety function requires operational guidelines to gain repute. The addition of breadth and depth to the context of marketing calls for a revised decision framework which accounts for the goals of all the parties affected by the transaction. The relational theory of value provides a guideline that is general and simple. Through expression in the field of philosophy, it has a rational foundation.[9] It also accords well with the outlines of decision theory and with behavioral analysis of human decision-making. Most of all, it provides a credible description of how day-to-day decisions are, or could be, handled.

---

[9] The relational theory of value is expressed in D. W. Gotshalk, *Patterns of Good and Evil* (Urbana, Ill.: University of Illinois Press, 1963), Chapter 7.

Briefly described, the relational theory of value implies that any transaction provides an alignment between human satisfactions and the attributes existing in or imputed to a product, service, communication or other entity.[10] Value in exchange is estimated in prospect when the parties involved anticipate that attributes of the things exchanged will fulfill expected satisfactions. Value is realized only when the satisfactions are actually experienced.

Under the relational theory, short-run, self-centered, decisions are moderated by two factors endogenous to the transacting parties. Aside from impulsive, trivial, misguided, or coerced decisions, the parties to a transaction consciously or unconsciously compare expected consequences with potential long-run satisfactions, values and well-being. This modifies the primacy of short-run satisfactions. Concurrently, the well-being of an individual and of his associates requires mutual restriction of conflicting desires—the recognition of overlapping value structures. Similar comments apply to profit as the goal of the firm, or to short-run, self-seeking goals of other organizations.

Although some transactions may be detrimental to third parties or to the transactors themselves, more comprehensive adjustments take place among individuals, firms, and organizations throughout society. Under the relational theory, individual and social value structures, which evolve through bargaining, act as one exogenous moderating factor; the competition among consumers for products or services and among firms or organizations for patronage, acts as a second; and the laws and conventions of exchange provide a third factor working in the interest of a socially acceptable aggregate of transactions.

The New Marketing Concept

If the marketing concept is to be more than "evangelistic rhetoric," as Barksdale and Darden have pointed out, better ways must be found to make it operational.[11] Bell and Emory suggest that to prevent the concept from faltering, it is necessary to integrate criteria of social responsibility with profit goals.[12] Kelley, among others, has explored the concept of social indicators

---

[10] The theory's applications are explored by Warren A. French and Leland L. Beik, "Marketing: An Area of Value," a paper presented before the Fall Educators' Conference, American Marketing Association, Boston, 1970. Measurement of value is approached by Ralph E. Anderson, "Consumer Dissatisfaction: The Effect of Disconfirmed Expectancy on Perceived Product Performance," *Journal of Marketing Research* (February, 1973).

[11] Hiram C. Barksdale and Bill Darden, "Marketers' Attitudes Toward the Marketing Concept," *Journal of Marketing* (October, 1971), p. 29, quote p. 36.

[12] Martin L. Bell and C. William Emory, "The Faltering Marketing Concept," *Journal of Marketing* (October, 1971), p. 37. These authors note that a few firms use such criteria.

with a view to incorporating them in managerial decisions.[13] The need for a practical approach, and expansion, is apparent in these citations.

The traditional concept centers on the marketer, on the consumer, and on integrating activities within the firm by recognizing the dominance of consumer orientation. Profit via consumer satisfaction, however, remains primarily a managerial objective. Although the status of one seller and one buyer may be improved by a transaction, any additional benefits to society are realized only through the rationing process of competition in a free enterprise economy.

To become operational, an expanded concept will have to be activated in the goal-setting and functional decisions of all parties engaged in, or influenced by, exchange and thus in the conventions of exchange themselves. The alternative to decentralized, negotiated decisions is an increase in central control and law—a diminution of freedom of choice and, potentially, of equality. An increasingly centralized system of exchange would become less flexible in adapting to the rapid change which marks the modern world, and change, when essential, would tend to be increasingly disruptive.

Revitalizing the marketing concept is necessary to attempt a consistent framework for expanded boundaries of marketing. The responsibilities of the respective decision-makers must be integrated into the discipline and must be responsibly managed if marketing is to remain viable as an institution. The relational theory of value supplies the mechanism for incorporating added goals and the propriety function in responsible decision-making under an expanded marketing concept. Normative decision-making, integrating the relational theory, is illustrated in Figure [2] . . .

Logically, a firm's managers would think first in terms of immediate, internal objectives such as profit or return on investment, while modifying the present decision for expected long-run impacts on such goals as growth and survival. These internal goals can be satisfied only by offering both immediate and long-run consumer satisfactions, thus accounting for the key element of the traditional marketing concept. Under the expanded concept, consumer satisfaction and welfare would become explicit, rather than implicit, goals. In addition, decision-makers should consider impacts on third parties, and ethical, legal, and environmental standards as integral to their judgments.

Similarly, consumers and nonbusiness organizations should act in accord with the normative model of [Table 1] . . . to seek greater coordination of individual transactions, greater common welfare from exchange, and favorable evolution of the rules of exchange. As information inputs to exchange,

---

[13] Eugene J. Kelley, "Integrating Social Feedback into Business Decisions: Value System Conflicts and Corporate Planning," a paper presented at the Social Indicators Conference, American Marketing Association, Washington, D.C., February 18, 1972.

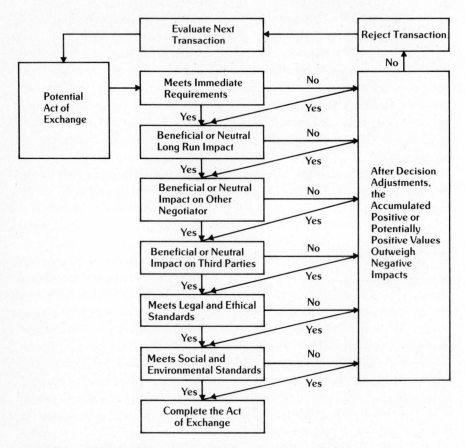

FIGURE 2   *Filtering Decisions for Public and Societal Impacts*

third parties, the public, the press, and government agencies have the responsibility of expressing their interests, formulating issues, and working toward coordinated solutions.

The Marketing Institution

Day-to-day transactions may be conducted in accord with a normative model which integrates the relational theory of value in the marketing concept and extends the concept to use by nonbusiness organizations and by consumers. The model is actually a fair description of what we now do in a haphazard way. Provided publicity and education promote deliberate use in more transactions, the normative model—like the original marketing concept—could begin to permeate and improve the process of exchange.

Integrating the relational theory of value in an expanded marketing concept, encourages a balancing of value structures on the part of each negotiator before adopting a limited set of goals for a transaction. Exogenous goals and constraints condition decisions to a greater degree, and decisions are more likely to accord with consumer and social requirements. By considering the full range of relationships inherent in exchange, use of an expanded marketing concept, by consumers and organizations alike, can begin to moderate among conflicting goals and work toward the general welfare.

While mutual benefits are anticipated by the parties directly participating in a transaction, their decisions should in some way advance, or at least not hinder, the welfare of others. Transactions provide the tactical matching of the needs and wants of individuals and groups, while development of the rules and customs of exchange operates to match these needs and wants strategically. Marketing, as the set of functions which facilitates transactions, acts to normalize the process of exchange. Formalizing current decision practices in line with an expanded marketing concept, can contribute to responsible evolution of the marketing institution.

QUESTIONS

1. What is meant by "social marketing"?
2. Should corporations actively pursue policies of social responsibility? Why?
3. How can the objectives of exchange be adjusted to include the goals and objectives of social responsibility?
4. What rights and responsibilities do consumers possess in the marketplace? List several others that the consumer should expect.
5. How could an expanded marketing concept that embraced social-responsibility goals be implemented in a firm?

4

STRATEGIES FOR INTRODUCING MARKETING INTO NONPROFIT ORGANIZATIONS

Philip Kotler

This article suggests that one of the ways that our economy fulfills its social responsibilities is through its large nonprofit sector. In order to operate more effectively, these organizations need to obtain greater marketing capabilities. The advantages and disadvantages of alternative ways to introduce marketing capabilities into a nonprofit organization are discussed.

In most societies of the world, economic activity is a function of the actions and interactions of a profit sector and a governmental sector. The American economy, however, contains an important third sector made up of tens of thousands of private, not-for-profit organizations ranging from The Society for the Preservation and Encouragement of Barber Shop Quartet Singing in America to major foundations, colleges, hospitals, museums, charities, social agencies, and churches.

This strong third sector constitutes a *middle way* for meeting social needs, without resorting to the profit motive on the one hand or government bureaucracy on the other. Third sector organizations tend to be socially responsive and service-oriented. They specialize in the delivery of social services that are not adequately provided by either business or government.

While Big Business is healthy and Big Government continues to grow, the third sector, unfortunately, is in trouble. Third sector organizations depend upon the support of private citizens and upon grants from the other two sectors. Many colleges, hospitals, churches, social agencies, performance groups, and museums are increasingly feeling the pinch of rising costs and stable or declining revenues. Consider the following:

- More than 170 private colleges have closed their doors since 1965, unable to get either enough students or funds or both. Tuition at Stanford and Yale is now over $6,000; if college costs continue to climb at the current rate, the parents of a child born today will have to put aside $82,830 to buy that child a bachelor's degree at one of the better private colleges (Pyke 1977).

- Hospital costs continue to soar, leading to daily room rates of $300 or more in some large hospitals; many hospitals are experiencing underutilization, particularly in the maternity and pediatrics sections. Some experts have predicted the closing of 1,400–1,500 hospitals in the next 10 years.

- The Catholic Church drew as many as 55% of all adult Catholics under 30 years of age to church in a typical week in 1966. By 1975 the figure had fallen to 39% and further declines in weekly attendance were expected.

- Many performance groups cannot attract large enough audiences. Even those which have seasonal sellouts, such as the Lyric Opera Company of Chicago, face huge operating deficits at the end of the year.

- Many third sector organizations that flourished in earlier years—the YMCA, Salvation Army, Girl Scouts, and Women's Christian Temperance Union— presently are reexamining their mission in an effort to reverse membership declines.

In a word, these third sector organizations have marketplace problems. Their administrators are struggling to keep them alive in the face of rapidly changing societal needs, increasing public and private competition, changing client attitudes, and diminishing financial resources. Board members and supporters are asking administrators tough questions about the organization's mission, opportunities, and strategies. Unfortunately, many administrators are mere "Monday-morning quarterbacks" when it comes to strategic planning. At a time when these organizations face uncertain prospects, the lack of management depth poses a serious threat to survival.

Let us examine a major requirement for such survival: third sector administrators must begin to think like marketers. Ten years ago, Sidney J. Levy and I advanced the thesis that marketing is not just a business function— it is a valid function for nonbusiness organizations as well—and that all organizations have marketing problems and all need to understand marketing (Kotler and Levy 1969). The article created considerable controversy. Many academic marketers attacked it, saying that marketing made sense only in profit-oriented enterprises. However other marketing professors found the idea stimulating and, without necessarily agreeing that it was valid, began to study and experiment with it. Initial interest was confirmed to academia. The issue was of little concern to businessmen, and was largely ignored by administrators of nonprofit institutions.

More articles followed in the 1970s, reporting applications of marketing technology to such areas as college recruiting, fund raising, membership development, population problems, public transportation, health services, religion, and arts organizations.[1] Benson Shapiro's article in the September-October 1973 issue of the *Harvard Business Review* elicited many favorable comments, published in the following issue of *HBR*. The only textbook on the subject, *Marketing for Nonprofit Organizations*, appeared in 1975 and has enjoyed a growing readership (Kotler 1975). Recently Gaedeke (1977) published a book of readings, Lovelock (1977) a bibliography of over 100 cases, and Nickels (1978) a general marketing textbook giving equal attention to business and nonbusiness marketing. It appears that marketing for nonprofit organizations is an idea whose time has come.

How have administrators of nonprofit organizations responded? Are they interested or aware? Enthusiastic? Do they know how to use marketing? Is it making a difference anywhere? On this tenth anniversary of the idea's launching, we are in a position to supply some answers.

Enter Marketing

Of all the classic business functions, marketing has been the last to arrive on the nonprofit scene. Some years earlier, nonprofit managers began to get interested in accounting systems, financial management, personnel administration, and formal planning. Marketing lagged, except where the nonprofit institution experienced a decline in clients, members, or funds. As long as institutions operated in a sellers' market—as colleges and hospitals did throughout the 1960s—marketing was ignored, but as customers and/or resources grew scarce the word "marketing" was heard with increasing frequency, and organizations suddenly discovered marketing or reasonable facsimiles thereof.

Colleges

Colleges provide a good example of this development. By the mid-1970s, they were reading this grim scenario: (1) the annual number of high school graduates would decline from a peak of 3.2 million in 1977 to 2.8 million in 1982–83; (2) the proportion of high school students electing to go to college

---

[1] A relevant 43-page bibliography lists over 600 references. See Rothschild, Michael L. (1977), *An Incomplete Bibliography of Works Relating to Marketing for Public Sector and Nonprofit Organizations*, Second Edition, Boston, MA: Intercollegiate Case Clearing House 9-577-771.

might decline; (3) a higher proportion of the college-bound students would elect to attend community colleges instead of four-year colleges; and (4) the absolute and relative future level of tuition would deter college-going in general and hurt private colleges in particular.[2]

What are college administrators doing about this? One group is doing nothing. Either enrollment hasn't slipped, or if it has, the administrators believe the decline is temporary. Many believe it is "unprofessional" to go out and "sell" their colleges.

A second group has responded with "marketing," which in too many cases means aggressive promotion unaccompanied by any real improvements in competitive positioning, teaching quality, or student services. For example:

- The admissions office at North Kentucky State University planned to release 103 balloons filled with scholarship offers.
- The admissions staff of one college passed out promotional frisbees to high school students vacationing on the beaches of Fort Lauderdale, Florida during the annual Easter break.
- St. Joseph's College in Rensselaer, Indiana achieved a 40% increase in freshmen admissions through advertising in *Seventeen* and on several Chicago and Indianapolis rock radio stations. The admissions office also planned to introduce tuition rebates for students who recruited new students ($100 finders fee), but this was cancelled.
- Bard College developed a same-day admission system for students who walk into their office and qualify.
- Worcester Polytechnic Institute offers negotiable admission in which credit is negotiated for previous study or work experience to shorten the degree period.
- The University of Richmond has spent $13,000 to create a 12-minute film for showings to high school students and other interested publics.
- Drake University advertised on a billboard near Chicago's O'Hare Airport that "Drake is only 40 minutes from Chicago" (if one flies).
- Duke University paid for a supplement in *The New York Times* to tell its story.

Promotional competition has not yet led to premiums given to students for enrollment (free radio, typewriter) or offers of "satisfaction guaranteed or your money back," but these may come.

In equating marketing with intensified promotion, there are several dangers. Aggressive promotion tends to produce strong negative reactions among the school's constituencies, especially the faculty, who regard hard selling as offensive. Also, such promotion may turn off as many prospective students and families as it turns on. Aggressive promotion can attract the

---

[2] See *A Role for Marketing in College Admissions*, New York: College Entrance Examination Board, 1976, 54 and elsewhere.

wrong students to the college—students who drop out when they discover they don't have the qualifications to do the work or that the college is not what it was advertised to be. Finally, this kind of marketing creates the illusion that the college has undertaken sufficient response to declining enrollment—an illusion which slows down the needed work on product improvement—the basis of all good marketing.

Promotion alone doesn't always work. Briarcliff College, a long-established women's college, faced an enrollment drop from 688 in 1969 to 280 in 1973. The college president scrambled to find ways to "sell" Briarcliff to prospects, including advertising and more high school visits. He personally went on the road to talk up Briarcliff, managing to raise enrollment to 350. But his effort was too little and too late. Briarcliff's finances continued to deteriorate and the college finally closed its doors in 1977.[3]

A genuine marketing response has been undertaken by a relatively small number of colleges. Their approach is best described as *market-oriented institutional planning*. In this approach, marketing is recognized as much more than mere promotion, and indeed, the issue of promotion cannot be settled in principle until more fundamental issues are resolved. These issues are shown in [Table 1]. By doing its homework on market, resource, and missions analysis, a college is in a better position to make decisions that improve student and faculty recruitment and institutional fundraising.

As an example, the University of Houston recently completed an intensive institutional audit using several faculty task forces. The final report presented recommendations on the university's mission, strategy, and portfolio. The portfolio section recommended which components of the university's "product mix" (schools and departments) should be built, maintained, phased down, or phased out. The criteria included: (1) the centrality of that academic program to the mission of the university, (2) the program's academic quality, and (3) the program's marketing viability. Thus, a department of women's studies that is marginal to the mission of the school, of low national reputation, and unable to attract an adequate number of students, would be slated for phasing down or out. A few other schools such as New York University, Northwestern University, and Kent State University are taking marketing initiatives to bring strategic planning and marketing into their operating frameworks.

Hospitals

Hospitals are beginning to treat marketing as a "hot" topic. A few years ago, health professionals scorned the idea of marketing, imagining that it would

---

[3] See "Rest in Peace," *Newsweek*, April 11, 1977, 96.

| Table 1 | **ISSUES IN MARKET-ORIENTED INSTITUTIONAL PLANNING FACING COLLEGES AND UNIVERSITIES** |

Market Analysis

1. What important trends are affecting higher education? (Environmental analysis)

2. What is our primary market? (Market definition)

3. What are the major market segments in this market? (Market segmentation)

4. What are the needs of each market segment? (Need assessment)

5. How much awareness, knowledge, interest, and desire is there in each market segment concerning our college? (Market awareness and attitude)

6. How do key publics see us and our competitors? (Image analysis)

7. How do potential students learn about our college and make decisions to apply and enroll? (Consumer behavior)

8. How satisfied are current students? (Consumer satisfaction assessment)

Resource Analysis

1. What are our major strengths and weaknesses in faculty, programs, facilities, etc.? (Strengths/weaknesses analysis)

2. What opportunities are there to expand our financial resources? (Donor opportunity analysis)

Mission Analysis

1. What business are we in? (Business mission)

2. Who are our customers? (Customer definition)

3. Which needs are we trying to satisfy? (Needs targeting)

4. On which market segments do we want to focus? (Market targeting)

5. Who are our major competitors? (Competitor identification)

6. What competitive benefits do we want to offer to our target market? (Market positioning)

lead to ads such as "This week's special—brain surgery, only $195." Hospital administrators also argued that patients didn't choose hospitals, their doctors did; so marketing, to be effective, would have to be directed to doctors.

Thus, it came as a surprise when a single and tentative session on marketing for hospital administrators, sandwiched between several other sessions during the 1975 convention of the American College of Hospital Administrators, drew about one-third of the 2,000 attendees. Perhaps they were tired of hearing panels on rising hospital costs and money collection problems, but more probably they were beginning to sense an opportunity, in marketing, to halt their declining occupancy rates.

As did many colleges, some hospitals rushed into marketing with more enthusiasm than understanding, believing it to consist of clever promotional gimmicks. For example:

- Sunrise Hospital in Las Vegas ran a large advertisement featuring the picture of a ship with the caption, "Introducing the Sunrise Cruise, Win a Once-in-a-Lifetime Cruise Simply by Entering Sunrise Hospital on Any Friday or Saturday: Recuperative Mediterranean Cruise for Two."
- St. Luke's Hospital in Phoenix introduced nightly bingo games for all patients (except cardiac cases) producing immense patient interest as well as a net annual profit of $60,000.   .
- A Philadelphia hospital, in competing for maternity patients, let the public know that the parents of a newborn child would enjoy a steak and champagne candlelight dinner on the eve before the mother and childs' departure from the hospital.
- A number of hospitals, in their competition to attract and retain physicians, have added "ego services," such as saunas, chauffeurs, and even private tennis courts.

Fortunately, some hospitals are now beginning to apply marketing to a broader set of problems. Where should the hospital locate a branch or ambulatory care unit? How can the hospital estimate whether a new service will draw enough patients? What should a hospital do with a maternity wing that is only 20% occupied? How can the hospital attract more consumers to preventive care services, such as annual medical checkups and cancer screening programs? How can a hospital successfully compete in the recruitment of more highly trained specialists who are in short supply? What marketing programs can attract nurses, build community goodwill, attract more contributions?

The marketing naivete of the typical hospital is well-illustrated by a hospital in southern Illinois that decided to establish an Adult Day Care Center as a solution to its underutilized space. It designed a whole floor to serve senior citizens who required personal care and services in an ambulatory setting during the day, but who would return home each evening. The cost was $16 a day and transportation was to be provided by the patient's relatives. About the only research that was done on this concept was to note that a lot of elderly people lived within a three-mile radius. The Center was opened with a capacity to handle thirty patients. Only two signed up!

Not all hospital administrators launch new services without research and testing of market size and interest. An increasing number are now attending marketing seminars to learn more about marketing research and new service development. The Evanston Hospital, Evanston, Illinois, a major 500-bed facility, appointed the world's first hospital vice president of marketing. Recently, MacStravic (1977) published an entire book devoted to hospital marketing, and many articles are now appearing on health care marketing.[4]

Other Institutions

In addition to colleges and hospitals, other institutions are paying more attention to marketing, The YMCA is taking a fresh look at its mission, services, and clients in order to develop new services and markets for the 1980s. Major charities like the Multiple Sclerosis Society, the American Heart Association, and the March of Dimes are investigating marketing ideas that go beyond selling and advertising. Marketing successes have been reported by arts institutions,[5] family planning associations (Roberto 1975), and energy conservation groups (Henion 1976). It is likely that within 10 years, much of the third sector will have some understanding and appreciation of the marketing concept.

Implementing Marketing

The interesting thing about marketing is that all organizations do it whether they know it or not. When this dawns on a nonprofit organization, the response is much like Moliere's character in *Le Bourgeois Gentilhomme* who utters: "Good Heavens! For more than forty years I have been speaking prose without knowing it." Colleges, for example, search for prospects (students), develop products (courses), price them (tuition and fees), distribute them (announce time and place), and promote them (college catalogs). Similarly, hospitals, social agencies, cultural groups, and other nonprofit organizations also practice marketing, wittingly or unwittingly; whether they do it well is a separate issue. For institutions which would like to improve their marketing effectiveness, I recommend consideration of the six steps shown in . . . [Table 2]. The "steps" really represent alternative approaches to the introduction of marketing into a nonprofit institution rather than a rigid sequence of steps.

Marketing Committee

As early as possible, the head of the institution should consider appointing a marketing committee to examine the institution's problems and look into the

---

[4] See, for example, the special issue on marketing of hospitals, *Journal of the American Hospital Association*, June 1, 1977.

[5] See, Newman, Danny (1977), *Subscribe Now! Building Arts Audiences through Dynamic Subscription Promotion*, New York: Theatre Communications Group, Inc. This book deals primarily with the use of promotion as a marketing tool rather than with overall marketing strategy.

Table 2	APPROACHES TO INTRODUCING MARKETING IN A NONPROFIT INSTITUTION
1. Appoint a Marketing Committee	
2. Organize Task Forces to Carry out an Institutional Audit	
3. Hire Marketing Specialist Firms as Needed	
4. Hire a Marketing Consultant	
5. Hire a Director of Marketing	
6. Hire a Vice President of Marketing	

potentialities of marketing. In a college, for example, such a marketing committee might consist of the president, vice presidents of faculty and development, director of admissions, dean of students, and one or two school deans. The committee should also include a marketing professor and/or a marketing practitioner. The marketing committee's objectives are (1) to identify the marketing problems and opportunties facing the institution; (2) to identify the major needs of various administrative units for marketing services; and (3) to explore the institution's possible need for a full-time director of marketing.

Task Forces

The chief administrator should consider appointing task forces to carry out various phases of an institutional audit. The aim is to discover how the institution is seen by key publics, what its main constituencies want that institution to be, which programs are strong and which weak, and so on. The task force's reports should adduce a consensus on institutional goals, positioning, and strategies. Even when task forces fail to find dramatic solutions, the members usually gain a deeper appreciation and understanding of the institution's problems and the need to work together to solve them.

Marketing Specialist Firms

From time to time, the organization should engage the services of marketing specialist firms, such as marketing research firms, advertising agencies, direct mail consultants, and recruitment consultants. A marketing research firm might be hired to survey the needs, perceptions, preferences, and satisfaction of the client market. An advertising agency might be hired to develop a corporate identification program or an advertising campaign. High quality marketing specialist firms bring more than their specific services to the client; they take a total marketing viewpoint and raise important questions for the institution to consider concerning its mission, objectives, strategies, and opportunities.

Marketing Consultant

As a further step, the organization should seek a marketing consultant to carry out a comprehensive *marketing audit* on the problems and opportunities facing that organization. The marketing consultant could be someone affiliated with the institution—such as a marketing professor, or a board member who is a marketing specialist. However, volunteers tend to give less attention than is necessary to the project, and often lack objectivity. It is usually preferable to engage a professional marketing consultant, one who has experience in that nonprofit subsector of the economy. In education, for example, several consulting firms have emerged specializing in college marketing and management. Alternatively, the institution could seek the services of a general consulting firm. In any event, the institution should make an effort to invite at least three proposals from which to select the best consultant. A contract should be written which specifies the objectives, the time frame, the research plan, and the billing. A liaison person within the institution should be assigned to work with the consultant, arrange interviews, read and comment on the emerging reports, and make arrangements for the final presentation and implementation of proposals.

The marketing consultant will interview representative sets of people connected with the institution. In the case of a college, he or she will interview the president, members of the board of trustees, major vice presidents, directors of admissions and public relations, several school deans, several department chairmen, several professors, several students, representative alumni, and outside opinion leaders. The marketing consultant would seek to answer the following questions for each *academic program* studied:

What is happening to student size and quality?

How successful is the program in attracting qualified students?

What are the main competitive programs and their positions in the market?

What is the image and reputation of this program?

What is the mission and what are the objectives of this program over the next five years?

What budget is needed to accomplish these objectives?

What fund raising potentials exist in the program?

What marketing problems face the program and what marketing activities are being pursued?

What useful services could a marketing director contribute to this program?

On the basis of this survey, the marketing consultant will develop and present a set of findings and recommendations regarding the institution's operations, opportunities, and needs in the marketing area. One of the recommendations will specifically deal with whether the institution is ready to effectively utilize a marketing director or vice president of marketing.

Marketing Director

Eventually the organization might become convinced of the need to appoint a director of marketing. This requires the development of a job description which specifies to whom this person reports, the scope of the position, the position concept, the functions, responsibilities, and major liaisons with others in the institution . . . [Table 3] presents a job description in a university context. The job is conceived as a middle management position, one in which the occupant primarily provides marketing services to others in the institution.

A major issue is where this person should be located in the organization and his or her relationships with kindred functions. Specifically, what is the marketing director's relationship to planning, public relations, and fund raising? A good case could be made for locating the marketing director within the planning office and therefore reporting to the vice president of planning. It would not make sense for the marketing director to report to public relations or fund raising because this would overspecialize the use made of marketing. The solution used by a large, eastern hospital consisted of appointing a vice president of institutional relations to whom directors of marketing, public relations, fund raising and planning reported.

Some public relations directors have been uncomfortable about the emergence of marketing directors, out of fear that they may eventually be reporting to the latter. Some public relations directors argue that marketing isn't needed, or that it is being done, or that they can do it. To the extent that marketing is thought to be aggressive promotion, public relations people feel they are best equipped to carry out this function. To the extent that marketing is seen to consist of marketing analysis, new services development, marketing strategy, product line evaluation, and so on, public relations personnel are not equipped insofar as their training is basically in the fields of journalism and communications, not economics and business analysis. However, public relations persons can, of course, take courses in marketing and attempt to promote the concept of a combined office of marketing and public relations.

Marketing Vice President

The ultimate solution is the establishment of a vice president of marketing position. This is an upper level management position which gives more scope, authority, and influence to marketing. A vice president of marketing not only

Table 3

JOB DESCRIPTION: DIRECTOR OF MARKETING FOR A UNIVERSITY

POSITION TITLE: Director of Marketing

REPORTS TO: A vice president designated by the president

SCOPE: University-wide

POSITION CONCEPT: The director of marketing is responsible for providing marketing guidance and services to university officers, school deans, department chairmen, and other agents of the university.

FUNCTIONS: The director of marketing will:

1. Contribute a marketing perspective to the deliberations of the top administration in their planning of the university's future
2. Prepare data that might be needed by any officer of the university on a particular market size, segments, trends, and behavioral dynamics
3. Conduct studies of the needs, perceptions, preferences, and satisfactions of particular markets
4. Assist in the planning, promotion, and launching of new programs
5. Assist in the development of communication and promotion campaigns and materials
6. Analyze and advise on pricing questions
7. Appraise the workability of new academic proposals from a marketing point of view
8. Advise on new student recruitment
9. Advise on current student satisfaction
10. Advise on university fundraising

RESPONSIBILITIES: The director of marketing will:

1. Contact individual officers and small groups at the university to explain services and to solicit problems
2. Prioritize the various requests for services according to their long run impact, cost saving potential, time requirements, ease of accomplishment, cost, and urgency
3. Select projects of high priority and set accomplishment goals for the year
4. Prepare a budget request to support the anticipated work
5. Prepare an annual report on the main accomplishments of the office

MAJOR LIAISONS: The director of marketing will:

1. Relate most closely with the president's office, admissions office, development office, planning office, and public relations department
2. Relate secondarily with the deans of various schools and chairmen of various departments

coordinates and supplies analytical services but also has a strong voice in the determination of where the institution should be going in terms of its changing opportunities.

The vice president of marketing would be responsible for planning and managing relations with several publics. The person's title may be altered to that of vice president of institutional relations or external affairs to avoid unnecessary semantic opposition. Thus far, only a few nonprofit organizations have gone this route.

The top marketing job should be tailored to the specific institution. Consider the YMCA, often called "the General Electric of the social service business." The YMCA is in not one, but several "businesses:" recreation, education, camps, physical fitness, hotels, and so on. Central headquarters must wrestle with decisions on where to build new facilities, what new programs to introduce, what programs to drop, how to promote membership, and dozens of other matters. Were a vice president of marketing appointed, this person would be responsible for defining better ways to serve various constituencies. Reporting to the vice president would be functional marketing specialists (marketing research, pricing, promotion, and planning), product managers (recreational programs, educational programs, camps) and market managers (teens, young marrieds, senior adults). These people would design programs and offer services to the various YMCA units throughout the country. There is no question that marketing decisions are being made all the time throughout the YMCA system but they are made, unfortunately, without professional marketing expertise.

Let us assume that an institution decides to hire a marketing vice president. This person's contribution will be carefully scrutinized. The new appointee will have to develop a strategy to make marketing visible and useful.

The marketing executive is not likely to be immediately swamped with requests for services, because many administrators initially will not understand marketing. The marketing executive should spend the first few months meeting various groups within the institution to learn about their problems. For example, Evanston Hospital's new marketing vice president arranged separate meetings with senior physicians, residents, interns, senior nurses, and others. At each meeting he described his job position, explained the nature of marketing, indicated the kinds of problems he could solve and services that he could offer, and then opened the meeting to discussion. He sought suggestions of projects that he might conduct. At the end of two months, he found more than enough useful projects. His problem, in fact, was to set priorities for the many projects, and he did so by rating each potential project using the following criteria (on five-point scales): (1) the importance or centrality of the project to the future of the institution; (2) the magnitude of the improved service or cost savings that it might effect; (3) its probable cost;

(4) the difficulty of carrying it out; and (5) the length of time it would take to complete. An ideal project was one that was very important, would effect great cost savings, would cost little to do, could be easily carried out, and could be completed in a short time. It became clear which projects went to the top of the list, and he concentrated his efforts in the first year on these projects.

The marketing executive will be expected to prepare an annual marketing plan listing major projects and a required budget. Much of the budget will go toward buying the services of outside marketing research firms and advertising agencies for needed projects. At each year's end, the executive will prepare a report summarizing levels of accomplishment and savings. Eventually, the nature of this position will become well understood within the organization and easy to assess its contributions toward institutional survival and growth.

Conclusion

At the present time, the marketing idea is beginning to attract the interest of administrators in the third sector. This is evidenced by the growing literature on college, hospital, and other third sector marketing, as well as by increased attendance at specialized marketing conferences for nonprofit organizations. Interest is not likely to abate; indeed, it is likely to increase as more administrators come to see their institution's future in marketing terms. For an institution, marketing offers a much richer understanding of what is happening and throws light on new opportunities.

Despite the growing interest in marketing, however, many nonprofit organizations still resist it. Many groups within these organizations see marketing as a threat to their autonomy or power. Eventually, out of necessity, marketing ideas will filter into these organizations. Marketing will initially be viewed as advertising and promotion rather than as a revolutionary new way to view the institution and its purposes. A few institutions will lead the others in developing an advanced understanding of marketing. They will start performing better. Their competitors will be forced to learn their marketing. Within another decade, marketing will be a major and accepted function within the nonprofit sector.

The issue that frightens some observers is not that marketing will be ineffective but that it may be too effective. They see funds and clients flowing to institutions that are willing to spend the largest sums of money on advertising and promotion. They fear that large scale promotional warfare will ruin the smaller institutions that cannot afford marketing, and will create a competitive stalemate among the larger institutions. This fear is based, once again, on the fallacy of viewing marketing as primarily promotional.

The real contribution of marketing thinking is to lead each institution to search for a more meaningful position in the larger market. Instead of all hospitals offering the same services, marketing leads each hospital to shape distinct service mixes to serve specific market segments. Marketing competition, at its best, creates a pattern of varied institutions, each clear as to its mission, market coverage, need specialization, and service portfolio.

Administrators and businessmen who have a stake in the third sector are beginning to recognize the contributions that marketing thinking can make. Marketing will lead to a better understanding of the needs of different client segments; to a more careful shaping and launching of new services; to a pruning of weak services; to more effective methods of delivering services; to more flexible pricing approaches; and to higher levels of client satisfaction. Altogether, marketing offers a great potential to third sector organizations to survive, grow, and strengthen their contributions to the general welfare.

References

Gaedeke, R.M. (1977), *Marketing in Private and Public Nonprofit Organizations: Perspectives and Illustrations*, Santa Monica, CA: Goodyear Publishing Co.

Henion, Karl E. (1976), *Ecological Marketing*, Columbus, Ohio: Grid, Inc.

Kotler, Philip (1975), *Marketing for Nonprofit Organizations*, Englewood Cliffs, NJ: Prentice-Hall, Inc.

———— and Levy, Sidney J. (1969), "Broadening the Concept of Marketing," *Journal of Marketing*, 33 (January), 10–15.

Lovelock, Christopher H., ed. (1977), *Nonbusiness Marketing Cases*, 8-378-001, Boston, MA: Intercollegiate Case Clearing House.

———— and Charles B. Weinberg (1977), *Cases in Public and Nonprofit Marketing*, Palo Alto, CA: The Scientific Press.

———— and Charles B. Weinberg (1978), "Public and Non-profit Marketing Comes of Age," in *Review of Marketing 1978*, Gerald Zaltman and T. Bonoma eds., Chicago, IL: American Marketing Association, 413–452.

MacStravic, Robin E. (1977), *Marketing Health Care*, Germantown, MD: Aspen Systems Corp.

Nickels, William G. (1978), *Marketing Principles*, Englewood Cliffs, NJ: Prentice-Hall, Inc.

Pyke, Donald L. (1977), "The Future of Higher Education: Will Private Institutions Disappear in the U.S.?" *The Futurist* 374.

Roberto, Eduardo (1975), *Strategic Decision-Making in a Social Program: The Case of Family-Planning Diffusion*, Lexington, MA: Lexington Books.

Shapiro, Benson (1973), "Marketing for Nonprofit Organizations," *Harvard Business Review*, 51 (September-October), 123–132.

QUESTIONS

1. What are some of the marketing problems of a nonprofit organization?
2. Are the objectives of the "marketing concept" and the objectives of a nonprofit organization inconsistent? Give reasons for your answer.
3. Would marketing planning differ in a nonprofit organization from that in a profit-oriented organization? If so, how? If not, why not?
4. Give an example of how marketing planning could aid an organization like a blood bank.
5. When would contracting an outside marketing consultant be more appropriate than hiring a marketing specialist?

5

ARE YOU REALLY PLANNING YOUR MARKETING?

Leon Winer

*The marketing planning procedures
commonly used by firms are reviewed in
this article and found to be inadequate.
More effective procedures are presented
with examples to illustrate their
implementation.*

The biggest problem in marketing planning is the *planning.* Many companies have a marketing "plan," yet few of these plans represent any real planning. To demonstrate this point, five steps will describe practices encountered frequently. These practices were observed through intensive interviews with manufacturing firms and their advertising agencies, and have been reported by executives at meetings and seminars attended by the author.

STEP 1. Set the market share objective of your brand by adding to its present market share, depending on how ambitious you are.

STEP 2. Project total sales volume, for *all* brands of the product, in dollars, for the following year.

STEP 3. Multiply the result of Step 1 by the result of Step 2. (Market share objective X projected total dollar market.) This gives the dollar sales objective for the brand.

STEP 4. Subtract from the dollar sales objective: (a) total factory cost, (b) an allocated portion of the company's fixed marketing costs, and (c) desired profit. What is left, if anything, is "planned" marketing expenditure.

STEP 5.   Compose a "marketing mix" of advertising, marketing research, personal selling, price concessions, public relations, package design, point of sales materials, dealer aids, and so on, that will (a) just use up all the marketing funds and (b) yield exactly the forecasted sales volume.

These five steps represent the procedures of many companies, yet they are thoroughly unsound, for three reasons:

First, this procedure assumes that an increase in market share is profitable or, for that matter, possible. By definition, not *all* brands of a product can increase their market shares.

Second, this method of marketing planning reverses the cause-and-effect relationship between marketing effort and sales volume. Clearly, the sales volume forecast should depend on the amount of effort expended on marketing, not the other way around.

Third, this method requires the manager to select the "right" marketing mix from among the hundreds, or thousands, of possible marketing mixes. In other words, the manager is given a sales volume objective and a fixed amount of money for marketing, and he is expected to devise the combination of advertising, price reductions, personal selling, marketing research, public relations, point of sale materials, and so on, that will just use up the available money and will attain the sales objective. No human being has the knowledge or the calculating ability to do this, even if it were *theoretically* possible.

If the argument presented above is correct, and widely-followed practice is inadequate, what alternatives are available?

To answer this question, a study was made of the marketing planning practices of companies recognized as leaders in this area, and of planning books and articles. The conclusion was that while a certain amount of adaptation is required in each case, a general procedure exists that is applicable to marketing planning. This procedure is presented as a flow model in Figure 1. The discussion of the steps in the model will follow the sequence shown, except that "assigning responsibility for planning" will be discussed last instead of first.

Setting Marketing Objectives

In setting marketing objectives, planners should keep in mind three properties of objectives: (1) multiplicity, the fact that organizations have many objectives; (2) time, objectives need to be set for varying lengths of time; and (3) level, the firm should have many levels of objectives, or a hierarchy of objectives.

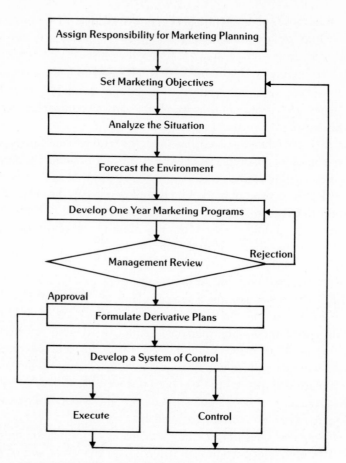

FIGURE 1   *Flow Model of a Marketing Planning Procedure*

Multiplicity

Generally speaking, marketers tend to focus on maximizing next year's profits as being the only proper objective for their efforts. Actually a company may be equally interested in stabilizing profits, or in seeking opportunities for investments for the longer term. Therefore, before doing any marketing planning, it is necessary to explore thoroughly with the company's management what *it* views the company's objectives to be and to derive marketing objectives from those of the company.

Objectives and Time

Given the company's objectives, it does not necessarily follow that these can be realized directly. A firm may not be able to capture a larger share of the market, economically, unless it has an improved product. Therefore, in order to attain a more distant objective of increasing its market share, it will set an intermediate objective of developing an improved product.

Since the firm possesses only limited management and financial resources, in setting the objectives described above, it will very probably have to forsake such alternative objectives as entering a foreign market or acquiring a potentially profitable competitor.

Therefore, in setting long-range objectives, and the intermediate objectives that will lead to their attainment, the firm must consider the alternatives it is forsaking, and select those most suitable to its circumstances.

Hierarchy of Objectives

Even though a firm sets long-term objectives and determines the appropriate intermediate objectives, that may not be enough. It does not do much good to tell the advertising department that the objective of the company is to increase its rate of return on investment unless this objective is translated into specific strategies. Therefore, it is necessary to develop a hierarchy of objectives.

Development of such a hierarchy of objectives is not a simple task. Careful study is required to make sure that sufficient alternatives are considered at each level and that suitable criteria are discovered for deciding which alternatives are to be selected, or emphasized.

An example, showing how a hierarchy of objectives may be derived through flow-modeling, is shown in Figure 2. This is the case of the business market (offices, factories, stores, hospitals, and so on) of the Interstate Telephone Company (a fictitious name for a real company). At the top of the chart is one of the Company's permanent objectives, that of increasing return on invested capital. A rate of return of 7½% is believed to be attainable. Two possible objectives were derived from this one: (1) increase return, or net profit, and (2) reduce the investment base on which return is computed. The second possibility was not believed to be attainable because of (1) population growth, (2) rapidly growing communication needs, and (3) trend toward mechanization and automation. Therefore, attention was focused on the first.

To increase profits, two objectives may be set, following the reasoning of the Interstate Company: (1) increase billings, or (2) reduce costs. Again, the second objective is unlikely to be attained because one of the important sources of the return on investment problem is the rising cost of labor and materials. (One exception should be noted, however. Costs may be reduced by reducing the rate of disconnections due to customer dissatisfaction, since the cost of installing complex equipment often exceeds installation charges.) This leaves the alternative of increasing billings.

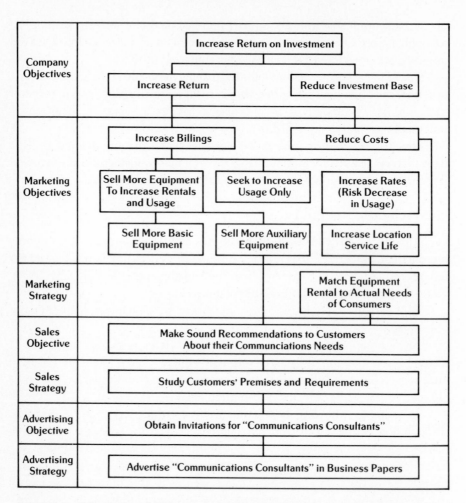

FIGURE 2   *Hierarchy of Objectives for the Interstate Telephone Company*

To increase billings, the Interstate Company may (1) try to raise rates and risk reduction in usage, (2) persuade customers to increase usage of existing equipment, or (3) sell additional equipment and services in order to increase equipment rentals and, to some extent, usage. However, a public service commission will not grant a rate increase unless return on investment is *below* a certain minimum, say 5½%. Then a commission is not likely to grant a raise that will increase return by as much as two percentage points. The next alternative objective, persuading customers to increase usage, has been used as an objective for promotional efforts of the Company. The third objective, that of selling additional equipment and services, has been selected for particular emphasis. In particular, because of the saturation of the business market with respect to basic equipment, the marketing effort has focused on the sale of auxiliary services and equipment, such as "Call Directors," teletype units, modern switchboards, and interior dialing.

To achieve the objective of selling more auxiliary services and equipment, and reducing disconnections due to customer dissatisfaction, the Company needs to match equipment and services to the *needs* of the customers, by making recommendations based on careful study of these needs. To do this, it seeks to persuade customers, through advertising, to invite "Communications Consultants" to survey their communications problems. In this way, by deriving a hierarchy of objectives, Interstate identifies the specific marketing strategies that will lead to attainment of the Company's highest objectives.

Analyzing the Situation

Once the planner has a well-developed set of objectives, the next step is to begin discovering ways of attaining them. To do this, he has to form some ideas about what *actions* of the firm, under what *environmental conditions*, have brought about the *present* situation. He will then be able to identify courses of action that may be used in the future.

Logan[1] has suggested a four-step procedure for conducting the situation analysis:

INVESTIGATION.   A wide range of data that may be relevant should be sought, with care being taken to distinguish between facts and opinions.

CLASSIFICATION.   The planner sorts the data collected during the investigation.

GENERALIZATION.   Classes of data are studied to discover relationships. Statistical techniques such as correlation analysis are used to determine whether dependable associations exist between types of events. For example, a distributor may find that leased outlets are more profitable than owned outlets to a degree that prevents attributing the differences to chance.

ESTIMATE OF THE SITUATION.   Causes are sought for the associations discovered in the previous step. The planner now has some ideas about what actions under past conditions have resulted in the present situation. In this way he has learned several courses of action that he may follow to achieve his

---

[1] James P. Logan, "Economic Forecasts, Decision Processes, and Types of Plans" (unpublished doctoral disseration, Columbia University, 1960), pp. 14–19, 76.

objectives. In the example cited previously, the distributor may find, on searching further, that the higher profitability of leased outlets is caused by the superior location of the leased outlets. In other words, the fact that the outlet was leased was *not* the cause of the higher profitability. Rather *both* the leasing *and* the higher profitability were caused by a third factor—superior location. (Owners of well-located outlets were not willing to sell them and therefore the distributor had been forced to lease.) Consequently, the appropriate strategy for the future would not be to prefer leasing to owning, but to seek good locations and leasing, if necessary. Inadequate search for causes might have led to very poor results.

Ideally, the situation analysis should cover other firms in the industry, so that the company may benefit from their experiences, both successes and failures.

Forecasting the Future Environment

The forecasting problem, from the viewpoint of the planner, is to determine *what* conditions he should forecast and *how* to do it. In this article we will limit ourselves to the first part of the problem because the literature of forecasting techniques is too vast to be reviewed adequately here.

Frey[2] has listed five factors that may affect purchases of a product:

1. Population changes.
2. Improvements in, and new-use discoveries for competing types of products.
3. Improvements in, and new-use discoveries for the company's own type of product.
4. Changed consumer attitudes and habits.
5. Changes in general business conditions.

Howard[3] suggests four criteria for identifying *key* factors:

1. Variability. If a factor is stable over time, there is no need to make a forecast of it.
2. Co-variation. There must be a relationship between changes in the factor and changes in demand.
3. Measurability.
4. Independence. The factor must not be closely related to another factor already considered.

---

[2] Albert W. Frey, *The Effective Marketing Mix: Programming for Optimum Results* (Hanover, New Hampshire: The Amos Tuck School of Business Administration, 1956), p. 11.

[3] John Howard, *Marketing Management* (Homewood, Illinois: R. D. Irwin, Inc., 1957), Chapter VI.

Essentially, this means that the planner has to find out *which* uncontrollable factors, such as personal income, occupation of consumers, educational level, attitudes, affect sales of his brand, and then he has to forecast the future of these factors. Here, as in situation analysis, statistical methods must be used with care, to avoid erroneous conclusions.

Developing One-year Marketing Programs

Development of marketing programs requires three steps: (a) formulating alternative courses of action, (b) examining these alternatives, (c) comparing alternatives and selecting the ones to be recommended.

Formulating Alternatives

The first step in conceiving alternative courses of action was described in an earlier section on situation analysis. We reviewed a four-step process for discovering factors that had brought about the present situation, and presumably could be manipulated to achieve future objectives. However, in addition to the cause-and-effect relationships discovered in situation analysis, there is usually room for innovation, or the development of new courses of action.

The importance of the creative process cannot be under-estimated, because a plan can only be as good as the best of the alternatives considered. Therefore, it is highly rewarding to spend time evolving alternatives. Unfortunately, there is a strong human tendency to stop the search for alternatives as soon as an apparently acceptable course of action is discovered. This is a tendency that planners must guard against.

Examining Alternatives

This step consists of projecting all the outcomes of each alternative course of action evolved above. The outcomes considered should include (1) desirable and undesirable; (2) immediate and long range; (3) tangible and intangible; and (4) certain and only possible.[4]

Clearly, one of the outcomes that must be projected in every case is sales volume and/or profit. In making this projection, errors in both directions are possible. Eldridge[5] discusses the probable consequences of these errors and suggests a solution to the problem.

---

[4] William H. Newman and Charles E. Summer, Jr., *The Process of Management* Englewood Cliffs, New Jersey: Prentice Hall, Inc., 1961), p. 302.

[5] Clarence E. Eldridge, "Marketing Plans," in E. R. French (editor), *The Copywriter's Guide* (New York: Harper & Bros., 1958), pp. 3–28, on pp. 24–25.

"If (the marketing manager) overestimates his sales volume and gross profit, and bases his marketing expenditures on that overestimate . . . he is likely to find . . . that profits are running well below the forecast. . . .

"If he underestimates his volume and gross profit, he runs the risk of spending less than the product needs—and thereby . . . makes certain that the results are less than hoped for.

"Nevertheless, it is probably preferable for the marketing manager, when weaving his way perilously between the devil and the deep sea, to err on the side of conservatism in budgeting sales, his marketing expenditures, and his profits. . . .

"For himself, his associates, the advertising agency, and the field sales department, it is wholly desirable that objectives should be set on the high side, in order that the attainment of those objectives shall require 'reaching . . .'"

In other words, Eldridge suggests "keeping two sets of books." The implications of this suggestion will be discussed subsequently.

Comparing and Selecting Alternatives

In this step the planner compares the projected outcomes of the various alternative courses of action. The purpose is to rank the alternatives on the basis of the extent to which they achieve objectives and avoid undesirable results. Then the most desirable alternatives are recommended to management.

This point, after programs are prepared, and before they are reviewed by top management, is suitable for writing down the plans.

On the basis of the argument presented here, the written plan should discuss the following topics, if it is to enable management to evaluate it:

1. Specific objective(s) of the plan.
2. Relationship between the specific objective(s) and the objectives of the firm, or an explanation of the extent to which this plan will advance the higher-level and longer-term objectives of the firm. Quantitative measures should be included, if possible.
3. Other specific objectives considered, and the planner's opinion of the relative values of these specific objectives. This evaluation should also include quantitative measures, if possible.
4. Costs of executing the plan.
5. Forecasts of the firm's environment.
6. Course of action recommended: first, briefly, then in detail.
7. Alternative courses of action and reasons why they were considered inferior to the action recommended.

8. Projected results of the plan, if it is executed.

9. Listing of control standards and procedures to be used for controlling execution of the plan.

Before leaving this discussion of preparation of programs, an important point should be emphasized:

Marketing planning should not be done function by function, as has been the tradition for a long time and still is the practice in many firms. (By "functions" we mean the activities normally performed by a marketing department, such as advertising, personal selling, pricing, marketing research, and product and package development. *Within* these functions are many sub-functions. For example, within personal selling is recruitment, selection, and training of salesmen; assignment of territories; design of compensation systems; sales analysis, and so on. At least 50 functions and sub-functions could easily be listed.)

Marketing planning should be oriented to achieving objectives. Of course, if objectives may be fulfilled entirely within one function, the objective-directed plan will also be "functional." But the approach, even then, will still be from objectives to means rather than from means to objectives.

Management Review

Criteria of reviewing executives may be grouped conveniently as follows: (1) economic, or financial; and (2) subjective.

Economic or financial criteria, such as return on investment, present discounted value of future income, alternative uses of funds, and cut-off rates, are sufficiently well known that they do not require comment here.

Subjective criteria, on the other hand, may require some discussion. Smith[6] has commented on the role of management as follows: "Management may simply accept the goals indicated. . . . More frequently . . . management's reaction will be one expressed by such comment as: 'Surely we can do better than that. . . .'"

In the case of the National Paper Company (a fictitious name for a real firm), during one year, management reduced the recommended marketing expenditures by 23%, *without* reducing the sales volume objective. Other, similar, reviewing actions could be cited. Therefore, it appears that management, in reviewing marketing plans, asks itself: "How much 'fat' does this plan contain?" and answers the question somehow, probably subjectively.

---

[6] Wendell R. Smith, "A Rational Approach to Marketing Management," in Eugene J. Kelley and William Lazer (editors), *Managerial Marketing* (Homewood, Illinois: R. D. Irwin & Co., 1958), p. 154.

Are such reviewing actions justified? In other words, is it fair to the planner to suspect him of "padding" his plan? We have noted earlier the view that: ". . . when it comes to budgeting (setting sales, profit and marketing expenditure goals), the situation is different (from setting objectives for the advertising agency, the sales force, and the like). The forecasts for financial budgeting should be sufficiently conservative that . . . they are certain to be made. . . ."[7] This commentator appears to be suggesting that the planner should overstate consistently the expenditure needed to achieve the goals of the plan. This appears to recognize that a conflict may exist between the objectives of the planner and those of the firm.

The management literature has emphasized repeatedly that differences exist between the objectives of the employee and those of the employing organization. Therefore, it seems fair to conclude that the planner, in trying to achieve his personal goals of continued employment and approval of his superiors, may undermine organizational objectives such as maximum return on marketing expenditures. Following this, the problem of the reviewing manager would then appear to be not to decide *whether* there is "fat" in the plan, but rather to estimate the percentage.

Formulating Derivative Plans

Ultimately, at the lowest level in the hierarchy, the result of planning has to be a list of actions, or a program, to be carried out.

For drawing up this program, Newman and Summer[8] suggest six steps:

1. Divide into steps the activities necessary to achieve the objective.
2. Note relations between each of the steps, especially necessary sequences.
3. Decide who is to be responsible for each step.
4. Determine the resources needed for each step.
5. Estimate the time required for each step.
6. Assign definite dates for each part.

In formulating its derivative plans, the Finchley (a fictitious name for a real company) Drug Company, uses the individual plans prepared for each of 50 products. The pertinent information is pulled out of each product plan and reassembled in three derivative plans: (a) detailed (personal selling) schedule,

---

[7] Eldridge, same reference as footnote 5, p. 25.

[8] Newman and Summer, same reference as footnote 4, pp. 415–416.

(b) advertising program, and (c) financial summary. These derivative plans are described below:

DETAILING SCHEDULE. The Detailing Schedule is structured very much like a calendar. For each month, three products are listed in the order in which they are to be presented to physicians. The schedule serves as a working document for the sales force. As the year passes, 500 copies of each page are made and distributed to Finchley's detail men to be carried out.

ADVERTISING PROGRAM. The Advertising Program describes several thousand items of direct mail and journal advertising to be prepared during the course of the year. The items are arranged by month and by day of the month when they are to appear, or to be mailed. As the year progresses, this information is used by technicians and artists in the Advertising Department and the Company's agency to prepare advertisements, buy space and materials, and so on.

FINANCIAL SUMMARY. The Financial Summary, unlike the other two documents, is not used by any functional department as a basis for action. Instead, it is essentially a communication and control device. Probably the best way to describe the contents of this document is to list the information presented for *each* actively promoted product:

1. Total market ($).
2. Company's share (%).
3. Company's sales ($).
4. Advertising expenditure ($).
5. Allocated detailing cost ($).
6. Total marketing cost ($).
7. Marketing cost as a % of sales.
8. Gross profit ($).
9. Gross profit as a % of sales.

This information is presented both for the current year and the following year.

As plans are executed, the Financial Summary is used for comparing actual results with plans, or controlling the execution of the plan. The point is that advertising, sales, and financial plans are derived from objective-directed product marketing plans and *not* prepared independently by the separate functions: Advertising, Sales, and Finance.

Developing a System of Control

A system of control should (1) establish standards, (2) measure activities and results (3) compare these measurements to standards, and (4) report variances between measurements and standards.

Control is relevant to planning because control standards have a greater effect in determining actual results than the objectives of the plan. Therefore, it is necessary that the standards which *are* set, reflect very closely the objectives of the plan.

In addition, a system of control informs the planner of the results obtained from execution of his plans. This is helpful because it becomes possible to change plans if they are found to be ineffective either because (1) the cause and effect premise on which they were based turns out to be faulty, or (2) the actual environment is sufficiently different from the forecast environment.

In the first instance, the objectives are still valid, but the method of attaining them needs to be changed. In the second instance, the objective may no longer be appropriate. Therefore, new objectives and strategies may be required, and with them, new courses of action.

Assigning Responsibility for Marketing Planning

In practice, the management decision of assigning responsibility for marketing planning is the first step performed. In this paper, we have postponed discussion of this topic until the end, because organization of the planning function may depend on the kind of planning to be done. Therefore, it was necessary to describe first the steps in marketing planning.

Writers on the subject of marketing planning organization have described several alternatives:

1. Delegation of planning to functional executives, such as managers of the advertising, sales, pricing, sales promotion, marketing research divisions of the marketing department.
2. Planning done by a planning staff group.
3. Planning done by everyone who has a part to play in marketing the brand, including outside organizations.
4. Planning done by brand, or product managers.

However, criteria are lacking in the literature for selecting the appropriate planning organization.

Leading firms often rely on product, or brand managers for planning, although the practice is not universal, and where such managers are used, their responsibilities are not always the same.

To illustrate this point:

1. At the drug company discussed earlier, product managers plan advertising of two kinds, and personal selling.
2. At the household paper products company, brand managers plan consumer advertising and temporary reductions in price charged to retailers and consumers.
3. The telephone company, on the other hand, does not employ product managers. Instead, planning is assigned to sales and advertising executives, for their individual functions.

Possibly these differences in planning organization can be attributed to differences in the means used for communicating with the market. The telephone company needs to communicate with business market customers (that is, business firms, government agencies, and so on) on an individual basis. The reason is that no two customers (other than the very smallest) are likely to need exactly the same combination of products and services. Therefore, a centrally-conceived, uniform approach, used alone, would not be suitable. The household paper products company and the drug company deal with mass markets where the potential profit made from individual customers is small. This rules out the possibility of tailoring a specialized approach to each customer. In addition, the needs and desires of large numbers of potential and actual customers are relatively similar. Therefore, grouping large numbers of customers into a market for a brand is an economical way of approaching the planning problem.

It follows that the "brand" manager is really a *market* manager, the market being the totality of actual and potential consumers of the brand. We may conclude, therefore, that a brand or product manager has a role to play whenever there is an opportunity to use standardized appeals in communicating with numerous customers.

Nevertheless, not all firms require brand managers, even though they may use mass communication media. For example, the Interstate Telephone Company permits all the advertising planning to be done in its advertising department, and delegates the major part of its sales planning to sales executives. The question arises then: what are the key differences that cause such marked differences in planning organization?

The answer that suggests itself is that there are important differences in the marketing objectives of these firms. Two illustrations can be given.

1. At the paper company, two of the important objectives are increase in market share, and product distribution in certain areas. Programming for

these objectives requires crossing of functional lines. Therefore there appears to be a need for a special planning executive.

2. At the telephone company the important marketing objectives are: (1) to increase auxiliary equipment and service billings; and (2) to increase location service life of auxiliary equipment. These objectives are interpreted to require that "communications consultants" survey the operations and promises of business market customers. To achieve this, the company tries to persuade customers to avail themselves of the free services of these consultants. Thus, we have three levels of objectives: (a) persuade the customer to invite the communications consultant, in order to (b) have the communications consultant advise the customer, in order to (c) increasing billings and service life.

Achieving objectives (a) and (b), the objectives that can achieved by direct action—(c) obviously cannot—does not require any coordination among functions. Objective (b) is achieved by the Sales Department, and objective (a), by the Advertising Department.

The conclusion is that the planning organization should mirror the hierarchy of objectives: a planning manager is needed wherever there is an objective whose achievement requires coordination of, or selection from among, several functions. In practice, the existing organization may satisfy this requirement, in which case, no new responsibilities need be assigned. However, if existing planning responsibilities do not allow for this type of selection, or coordination, new ones need to be created.

Implications for Marketing Managers

When a new idea or concept is presented to the business world, its *form* often receives more attention than its *substance*. While attempts are made to adopt the new concept, old habits of thought, and procedures, are continued even though they may not be consistent with the new idea.

The central idea of marketing planning is to develop marketing objectives that will lead to attainment of the objectives of the firm, and then to devise programs and controls that will help to achieve these marketing objectives. In deciding to plan its marketing activities, a business firm has to stand ready to scrap its traditional budgeting and functional planning procedures and to re-think and reorganize its marketing. Only those methods and procedures should be retained that fit logically with the pattern of starting with the highest objectives of the firm and refining successive steps of instrumental objectives until courses of action are specified. Any other approach, or procedure, will give inferior results.

Admittedly, it is much easier to go through the five steps outlined in the first few paragraphs, and say that marketing is being planned, than to follow the procedure described in the body of this paper. However, in this instance, as in most, there are no easy short-cuts to the development of good, effective, and profitable plans. Also, there really is no escape from the need to plan conscientiously. Leading companies *are* planning in this way, with obvious financial success. Those who wish to attain similar success will have to apply themselves equally. Successful procedures will not be developed overnight, or even in one year. Most likely, it will take from three to five cycles of planning to establish an effective, smoothly-working procedure. However, nothing will be accomplished if a sincere beginning is not made.

QUESTIONS

1. Given the reasons why the commonly used planning process is inappropriate, list the capabilities that a good planning procedure should possess. Does the planning procedure recommended in this article possess these capabilities? Justify your answer.
2. What steps are involved in formulating marketing objectives?
3. What is the role of planning in the marketing process of a firm?
4. What factors should be evaluated in assigning the marketing-planning responsibility to a particular part of the organization?
5. Does the planning model suggested in this article adequately allow for marketing's integration with the other areas of the firm, such as finance and production? Justify your answer.

6

COKE'S BIG MARKETING BLITZ

Business Week

Coke's intensive competitive response to the market inroads by PepsiCo Inc. and other soft-drink companies is outlined in this article, and their strategy is presented.

An era of tumultuous change has been uncapped in the U.S. soft-drink industry, now coming alive after several years of slow growth and desultory product innovation. Diet and caffeine-free drinks have captured the public's fancy, and retailers' shelves are overcrowded with new entries. But few companies have the resources to finance and distribute a steady stream of new beverages successfully. The result, say industry executives, will be a shakeout during the next few years among producers and bottlers alike. Only one thing is now certain about the industry's future: Coke will still be "it."

Few would have bet five years ago that Coca-Cola Co. would be so firmly in charge. Although the Atlanta-based company has dominated the soft-drink business for most of its 97-year life, lately its power has derived more from sheer size than savvy marketing. Coke seemed content to watch consumers reach for the "real thing" in supermarkets, food-service outlets, and vending machines, while jealously guarding its brand name. But that complacency vanished in 1977 when PepsiCo Inc.'s Pepsi-Cola brand rudely threatened Coke's cherished title as king of food-store sales and challenged its leadership of the $20 billion domestic industry.

Stung into action, a revitalized Coke has responded with uncharacteristic speed. The company has become a true powerhouse, and under the prodding of Roberto C. Goizueta, who became corporate chairman in 1981, it has embraced a new operating philosophy: all-out attack. Not only is Coke willingly—some say eagerly—continuing the fierce price and promotion war touched off by Pepsi's challenge, but it has embarked on a policy of resolute market segmentation, bringing out no fewer than four major new colas in less than a year.

SPREADING ITS NAME.   Last July, the company introduced diet Coke—the first time it has allowed the world's best-known trademark to be put on another product. Coke and industry observers predict that diet Coke will top the success of its category-leading Tab brand in about three years. And on Apr. 28, the soft-drink giant catapulted into the exploding market for caffeine-free sodas by introducing decaffeinated versions of best-selling Coke, diet Coke, and Tab.

Coke executives say this is only the beginning. "We're a changed company," declares Brian G. Dyson, president of Coca-Cola USA, which accounted for 29.7% of the parent's 1982 revenues of $6.2 billion and 23.4% of its $512 million earnings. "You can expect to see a lot of new concepts, new products, and packages from us," he promises. "This marketplace wants, needs, and responds to innovation."

Adds one longtime Coke manager: "Goizueta's message to us is loud and clear. He says that for too long we treated Coke as a warehouse of equity and that we better realize that what we are is a factory."

Coke has ample financial resources to back up its new aggressiveness. The parent has little debt, a $2.3 billion overseas soft-drink business boasting 26% operating margins, and a hefty cash flow from Columbia Pictures Industries Inc., which it acquired a year ago.

To make sure the production line keeps moving briskly, Coke has spent the past two years recasting its bottler network into one of the most powerful sales organizations in the world. Bottlers are crucial to the soft-drink industry, since they are the ones who actually manufacture and package the drinks, then sell and stock them to retail outlets. Through a strategy of cajoling, counseling, and helping to arrange financing, the syrup-manufacturing parent has managed the transfer of about 50% of its bottling capacity to larger, better-financed companies able and eager to battle Pepsi and all other rivals. It is further aiding its bottlers in their quest to acquire larger, contiguous territories, which will give them significant economies of scale and marketing might.

Coke's new determination is likely to drain sales from smaller competitors rapidly—even bottlers. "The small bottler is in dreadful shape," says Van Myers, chief executive of Miami-based Wometco Enterprises Inc., a major Coke bottler. "If you don't have high-speed lines, you can't be the low-cost producer—and at $1 million a line, the smaller guys just can't afford them."

SHELF-SPACE DUEL.   But the increasing number of new brands—especially in the cola category, which accounts for 63% of all soft drinks—will put the biggest squeeze on producers. The battle for shelf space is already a duel to the death. Companies without the financial resources of Coke and Pepsi will find themselves off the bottlers' minds and off the retailers' shelves. "Some of the weaker-flavor brands will be the first to go," says Bart S. Brodkin, president of Westinghouse Electric Corp.'s Los Angeles-based Beverage Group, which handles Seven-Up Co. products, A&W root beer, and Orange Crush, among others.

"ON A ROLL."   Dr Pepper Co. has already been forced to turn from a national to a regional strategy. And observers wonder how long Royal Crown Cola Co. can hold on without a cash-rich parent. Even strong No. 2 Pepsi [see Figure 1], which has gathered momentum through its highly successful taste-challenge ads and promotions, is feeling the heat. "Coke is a very tough competitor, and their new bottler network poses a challenge to us," concedes Roger Enrico, the new head of Pepsi-Cola USA. Agrees Richard Q. Armstrong, president of Dr Pepper: "Coke is on a roll, and Pepsi is going to have a very tough year."

Much of the upheaval stems from producers' attempts to spur the industry's sagging growth rate. As recently as the early 1970s, carbonated beverages were growing at a heady 10% clip, as millions of baby boomers guzzled gallons of fizzy drinks. But growth moderated as those younger adults aged. During recession-plagued 1982, the business gained only about 2%, and most industry insiders agree that growth will be in the 3% to 4% range for the remainder of the decade.

While soft-drink producers are cheered by the fact that overall annual per capita consumption has grown from 33 gal. in 1975 to 40 gal. today, other trends are giving them pause. A number of different beverages—notably wine, bottled waters, and juices—are being consumed in greater quantities than ever before. Part of the reason is that as the population matures, health and fitness are its new bywords. Calorie-counting accounts for the surge in diet drinks, which grew at a 10% rate last year, far outpacing the 1.4% rise that sugared products eked out. And the public's perception that caffeine is harmful has given rise to a host of decaffeinated drinks.

Executives agree that new products aimed at specific consumer groups will be the industry's only real chance of boosting soft-drink intake to 50 gal. a year by 1990. "We have to stay on top of changing demographics because as the population ages the needs and wants will change, and that will give us the keys to segmentation," says Enrico, who knows all about market segmentation from his days as marketing vice-president at PepsiCo's Frito-Lay Inc. unit, which has dominated the snack-food business through adroit positioning.

Dyson agrees: "We'll probably go after smaller segments than we have in the past, maybe bringing out juice-based drinks or noncarbonated ones, or even getting into the area of nutritive beverages. Everybody's looking for ways to increase their breakfast business, and that may be the ticket."

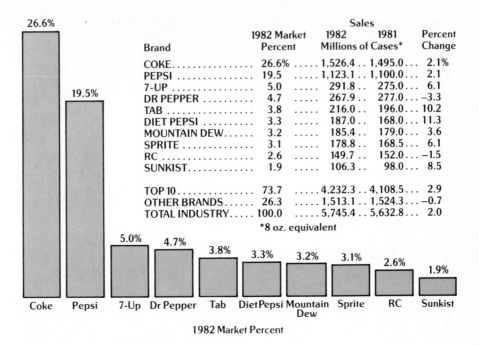

Brand	1982 Market Percent	Sales 1982 Millions of Cases*	Sales 1981 Millions of Cases*	Percent Change
COKE	26.6%	1,526.4	1,495.0	2.1%
PEPSI	19.5	1,123.1	1,100.0	2.1
7-UP	5.0	291.8	275.0	6.1
DR PEPPER	4.7	267.9	277.0	−3.3
TAB	3.8	216.0	196.0	10.2
DIET PEPSI	3.3	187.0	168.0	11.3
MOUNTAIN DEW	3.2	185.4	179.0	3.6
SPRITE	3.1	178.8	168.5	6.1
RC	2.6	149.7	152.0	−1.5
SUNKIST	1.9	106.3	98.0	8.5
TOP 10	73.7	4,232.3	4,108.5	2.9
OTHER BRANDS	26.3	1,513.1	1,524.3	−0.7
TOTAL INDUSTRY	100.0	5,745.4	5,632.8	2.0

*8 oz. equivalent

1982 Market Percent

FIGURE 1 *The Top 10 Soft Drink Brands*
Data: *Beverage World*

STAND-BACK STYLE. Coke might well be expected to lead the charge into new segments. But that is not its strategy. "The high ground is that we [Coke] should be leading the way," admits Allen A. McCusker, senior vice-president for marketing operations. "But that's not our style. We like to let others come out, stand back and watch, and then see what it takes to take the category over."

That wait-and-watch style has produced winners. For example, Royal Crown was the first company to score a hit in the diet-cola category when it brought out Diet Rite Cola in 1962. A year later, Coke swung in with Tab, snaring the top slot in the segment and leaving tiny RC chugging far behind.

Today the diet category attracts 20% of total soft-drink sales and is expected to grow to 30% by the end of the decade as better-tasting sweeteners come on stream. Last year, Coke increased its grip on the area by appealing to male drinkers with diet Coke. "Tab has a very narrow consumer base—largely weight-conscious females—and we saw that the Diet Pepsi brands were pulling in a lot more men drinkers than we were, which told us there was a good opportunity there," explains R. Bruce Kirkman, the vice-president responsible for marketing diet Coke and developing the caffeine-free drinks.

THE QUICKENING PACE OF NEW PRODUCTS

1961: **SPRITE** (Coca-Cola)

1962: **DIET RITE** (Royal Crown)
DIET DR PEPPER

1963: **TAB** (Coca-Cola)

1964: **DIET PEPSI**
MOUNTAIN DEW* (Pepsi-Cola)

1970: **DIET 7UP**

1971: **SUGAR FREE DR PEPPER**

1974: **SUGAR FREE SPRITE**

1977: **PEPSI LIGHT**

1980: **RC 100** (Royal Crown)

1982: **RC 100 REGULAR**
LIKE (Seven-Up)
SUGAR FREE LIKE
PEPSI FREE
SUGAR FREE PEPSI FREE
DIET COKE

1983: **PEPPER FREE**
CAFFEINE FREE COKE
CAFFEINE FREE DIET COKE
CAFFEINE FREE TAB

*Acquired from Tip Corp.

Diet Coke is now available in 80% of the U.S. and is a phenomenal success, with a 3.3% market share and sales running 50% ahead of plan.

SHARING WITH TAB.   Initially, Coke was concerned about hurting its own Tab. "Most of our bottlers wanted diet Coke for a long time, but we had to convince them and ourselves that a three-cola strategy would work," says Kirkman. "We didn't want our bottlers to overlook Tab." By showing them how the two drinks appeal to two separate but growing markets, the company has been able to execute its strategy—so far. But the cost may be dear. Coke was prepared to accept a staggeringly high rate of switchers from its existing brands—it estimated that 50% of the new drink's sales would come from former Tab users. A surprised Roy G. Stout, Coke's senior vice-president for market research, has found instead that only 30% to 35% of diet Coke's sales have come from its sister brand. "Frankly, I'm not sure we're analyzing these numbers right," he says.

One brand that has been hurt is Diet Pepsi. "There's no question that in their [Coke's] initial test markets, our brand has been impacted," admits Enrico, who quickly adds that "the unusual amount of price promotions Coke put behind it made the cost differential enormous." But Pepsi is no slouch in the diet market, either. Its Diet Pepsi is still aimed at female drinkers, but Pepsi Light, which has a lemon flavor, has been repositioned to appeal specifically to males.

Cannibalization of existing brands has Coke worried about its new caffeine-free drinks, too. Once again, RC pioneered this segment in 1980. However, it was not until Seven-Up, the cash-rich Philip Morris Inc. unit, repositioned its flagship brand into the segment and brought out Like, a similar cola, that the big guns sat up and took notice. "We knew we'd be followed," sniffs Edward W. Frantel, president of Seven-Up. "The only questions we had were when, where, and what were they going to call it."

He didn't have to wait long. Mindful of how PM's Miller Brewing Co. subsidiary had pulled off a coup with its Lite beer when the beer industry was slumbering, Pepsi rushed no-caffeine brands to market last July with its Pepsi free regular and diet entries. By spending at a $100 million national rate and speeding its rollout to take advantage of Coke's absence, Pepsi free can now claim 50% of the caffeine-free segment—which is running about 7% of the total market—and distribution across 90% of the U.S. A Coke bottler says Pepsi has done a sterling job getting consumer attention. "Coke was late getting into caffeine-free," he says. "If they hadn't had diet Coke out there to slow Pepsi, it would have been a disaster."

Coke claims it deliberately delayed moving into the area. "We wanted to give diet Coke a chance to see itself before we came out with something new again," explains Kirkman. Indeed, the company is trying to discourage bottlers from taking the three newest entries until diet Coke has been in their territories at least three months. Nevertheless, in typical Coke fashion, Dyson asserts that "we fully plan to have 50% of this market by the end of 1984."

Not, of course, if Pepsi can help it. "Our job is to establish a leadership position and prevent them [Coke] from achieving their stated goal," vows Enrico. "It will be a real gladiator contest."

While Coke is certain the caffeine-free category presents a marketing opportunity, it also recognizes the dilemma. "This company was built on colas with caffeine, and with no evidence that the ingredient presented a real health problem, we didn't want to do anything that might hurt them," says Kirkman. "But once we saw how many people were aware of the issue—whether or not the medical facts said otherwise—the perception that caffeine is a problem became our marketing reality."

A BURDEN?   Yet the arrival of decaffeinated drinks, plus the crowding of the cola section—10 brands last May have turned into 18 this month—almost guarantee heavy cannibalization of sales. How much real incremental growth is to be gained from all this segmentation remains to be seen. Coca Cola's projections concede that market shares for Coke, diet Coke, and Tab may slip, but they optimistically predict that the total Coke family share will increase 3.1%, to 34%.

"All the new brands place a tremendous burden on bottlers," says Harry M. Hersh, president of PepCom Industries Inc., which handles Pepsi, 7UP, A&W, Schweppes, and Dr Pepper in New Jersey and North Carolina. "It means changes all through your line, and your marketing costs go up dramatically."

Bottlers are also facing the harsh reality of a finite amount of supermarket shelf space. The popularity of the 12-can pack and the 2-liter plastic bottle has squeezed that space to the limit. Pulling the slowest movers from the shelves is the retailer's only real solution. Harland L. Polk, merchandising vice-president at Southern California's 41-store Hughes Markets Inc., is considering dropping Coke's fading Fresca brand to make room for the new line of decaf sodas. Adds Jane Armstrong, a vice-president at $5.6 billion supermarket operator Jewel Cos.: "All of the companies are into new products, but they're not willing to drop anything. It looks like it will be up to us, and we're at the point now where we have to delete."

DISCOUNT WARS.   So producers and bottlers must convince consumers to buy enough products to show retailers it is worth their while to stock them. Following Coke's lead, other soft-drink companies have turned to "trade deals"—a mixture of volume discounts, limited-time price reductions, and free product for bulk buyers. Where bottlers normally gave retailers a hefty 25% off list on new products and 15% on mature lines, these numbers are often being doubled.

The sheer magnitude of these promotions—which also have the potential of destroying brand loyalty—is giving most of Coke's competitors a bad time. "We took our biggest hits when discounting got really heavy, and a lot of our bottlers, who also distribute Coke and Pepsi, put their big promotions behind those brands," grouses W. W. "Foots" Clements, chief executive at Dr Pepper. Clements says his bottlers are beginning to support the brand again, but adds, "We will probably spend more money in discounting this year than last simply because the market demands it."

Even Pepsi, which up to now has been able to match Coke dollar for dollar, wants out of the pricing free-for-all. The company had a disappointing year in 1982: Its domestic soft-drink earnings grew only 4%, and it has been embarrassed by publicity about accounting irregularities in its overseas soft-drink business, which caused the parent to take an extraordinary charge of $79.4 million for the reduction in net assets of the unit last year. Pepsi attempted to raise prices in its company-owned bottling territories last year, but it had to cut them again when Coke bottlers kept on slashing prices and Pepsi lost share. "Pricing as a strategy has been overutilized," argues Enrico. "It's a short-term mentality. . . . The last three years have not been healthy for the industry."

Although some Coke managers are not happy with discounting, Dyson makes it clear there will be no change in posture. "If someone believes price promotions will abate dramatically, they're very wrong. Discounting is not going to disappear into blue smoke fast."

NEW CONTRACTS.   Discounting is part of Coke's bet that its refitted bottler network is now rich enough to beat Pepsi's challenge. In a 1979 strategic plan, Coke decided for the first time to take an active role in franchise transfers, including acquiring minority interests as they occurred. "[We] decided that who our bottlers were was a matter of vital interest to us and that it was important that we be actively involved in the process when there was a change," says Lawrence C. Cowart, Coke's executive vice-president for finance and operations.

At that time, unrest was running high in the family ranks. Coke was trying to counteract Pepsi's threat and knew it needed to increase its marketing outlays, both nationally and locally. It moved to change the terms of its 58-year-old bottler contract, which—except for increases in the price of sugar—guaranteed the price of Coke syrup "in perpetuity." While Coke managed to push the new contract with its raised prices through (bottlers representing about 8% of its volume have yet to ratify it), there were some hard feelings. "A lot of Coke bottlers got used to living in a clublike atmosphere, and they resented the changes Coke wanted them to make," says one Coke franchisee. The company says that for many reasons, including tax and estate problems, some of its distributors decided to cash in their chips.

SWAPPING.   That was fine with Coke, which set out to bring in well-financed, well-managed bottlers. Coke's part in the sale of its former Crass Bottling Co. franchise for Washington, D.C.; Richmond, Va.; and Harrisburg, Pa., is representative of its new facilitator role. In that 10-month-long deal, Coke helped match a West Coast management firm that wanted to enter the soft-drink business with experienced beverage operators. Then it arranged financing from Citicorp Venture Capital Ltd. To give the new bottler, renamed Mid-Atlantic Coca-Cola Bottling Co., better economies of scale, Coke also sold it the contiguous, company-owned Baltimore franchise.

Whenever reorganization is possible, Coke has been trying to create large marketing groups. For example, Beatrice Foods Co. purchased the Coke franchise in Los Angeles late in 1981 and then bought the San Diego territory in January, 1982. Coke helped it buy neighboring San Bernardino county from its large, Texas-based bottler, JTL Group, giving Beatrice control over a huge swath of Southern California. "There are a lot of bottlers swapping areas to round out their territories," says Dyson. "It just makes a great deal of operating sense." It also increases the marketing clout. For instance, John R. Atwood, president of Beatrice's bottling operations, points out that in Southern California "we can now offer a major supermarket like Ralph's a promotion that can be run in all the stores' trading areas. A small bottler can't do that."

With so many new bottlers on board, Coke has used the opportunity to make its franchise contract more specific. A Phase 2 amendment was sent to its 422 bottlers on Apr. 28. Its most important points set out syrup and concentrate pricing levels for all current and future products, establish what part of sweetener costs the parent will pick up (and provide a cap on these prices), and uphold bottlers' rights to all future Coke products. Bottlers handling about 60% of Coke's volume have already signed the new contract.

THE CORN-SYRUP EDGE.   Such radical changes at Coke have elicited various strategic rumblings from its rivals. Pepsi is trying to counteract its chief competitor's new bottling network by "doing a lot more cooperative things like purchasing and joint marketing programs with our group," says Enrico. Pepsi owns far more bottlerships than Coke: About 23% of its gallonage is derived from its own bottlers vs. 11% for Coke. The decision in early May to allow up to 50% high-fructose corn syrup (HFCS) in Pepsi should also give the company and its bottlers some welcome savings. Coke has permitted the practice for several years, giving its bottlers a 30¢-per-gal. price advantage over local Pepsi franchisees. The revenue was usually plowed back into local marketing.

PM's Seven-Up unit is counting heavily on segmentation strategies to shield it. The company's total soft-drink share jumped to about 7% last year—reversing a six-year slide—after the flagship brand turned to a strong product-differentiation campaign that was designed to proclaim its no-caffeine advantage.

But in the cola area, Seven-Up will have hard work with Like. While a handful of bottlers—primarily from RC—have dropped other colas to pro-duce Like, some of its larger franchisees will not carry the brand. General Cinema Corp., Seven-Up's fourth-largest franchisee and a major Pepsi bottler, is not carrying Like in any of its 26 markets. "Pepsi is our major brand, and we've been successful with Pepsi free," explains J. Atwood Ives, GC's senior vice-president. Such reluctance by its bottlers to carry Like has sparked speculation that PM will turn to alternative distribution avenues. But Frantel denies Seven-Up will abrogate the traditional store-door delivery by indepen-dent bottlers.

HEALING DR PEPPER.　　After its flagship brand's market share took a slide and its 1982 earnings dived 58%, to $12.5 million, a hurting Dr Pepper is retreating to its marketing strongholds in the South and Southwest, where it hopes concentrated advertising and promotion will allow it to compete more effectively. "We can't let [the cola giants] get us playing their game," says Clements. "We have to capitalize on our drink's unique flavor and its strong customer loyalty."

And troubles lie ahead for Royal Crown. The fifth-ranked producer has continually lost out as the better-financed powers captured most of the markets RC pioneered. Now that both Coke and Pepsi are spending heavily in the decaffeinated area, RC's growth outlook has dimmed.

Fred M. Adamany, RC's president, remains doggedly optimistic. He believes that RC can continue to compete if it "stays one step ahead in anticipating what consumers want, and really works the niches." But rumors abound that RC will soon become an acquisition target, since it offers a well-known cola brand and has a national distribution network already in place. "RC's good, but there's no way they can go it alone," observes one of its bottlers.

The only major soft-drink franchisor to sidestep the bruising cola battle so far has been General Cinema, which has made its Sunkist orange soda the 10th most popular drink after only five years on the market. The company realized that there was no nationally distributed, strongly promoted brand in that category, although orange-flavored drinks snare about 8% of the total market.

Capitalizing on its expertise as a major Pepsi and 7UP bottler, GC purchased the rights to the Sunkist name and assembled a bottling force made up primarily of the leading bottlers in each market. "We knew that these guys would have the clout to get us on the shelves and into vending machines before Coke and Pepsi could try to preempt us," explains Ives.

Now, however, the strongest-bottler strategy could slow Sunkist's growth for a while as those bottlers concentrate more on the new primary products. Explains Ives: "If your local bottler is introducing diet Coke, you don't expect him to load up on Sunkist."

ALMOST UNBEATABLE.　　Almost nothing happens in the soft-drink business without a similar accommodation to Coke and its bottlers' actions. And Coke's overpowering strength outside the supermarkets—only about 35% of its sales come from food stores vs. 50% for Pepsi—has made it almost unbeatable.

For example, Coke owns about 60% of the fountain business in fast-food outlets and convenience stores. It will probably continue to hold that lead, despite Pepsi's attempts to make inroads, because of the limited number of dispensing taps in each location. Fountain outlets usually have only five taps from which to squeeze a full complement of flavors, and most operators choose category leaders so they can please the most customers. McDonald's Corp., for instance, lists Coke as its only approved cola. And while it currently allows franchisees to choose between Tab and Diet 7Up for the single diet slot on its machines, it will be adding diet Coke as the third competitor for that tap.

Coke is also beginning to roll out diet Coke—or Coke light, in countries that restrict use of the word diet—in its overseas markets. Internationally, there is little doubt that Coke is champ. In Europe alone, Coke outsells Pepsi four to one, and it is even putting pressure on its archrival in the Pepsi-dominated Philippines and Venezuela markets.

Coke's competitive push will come in the U.S., especially in the already brutal food-store arena, where Coke plans to grab whatever it can. "We've got this huge fundamental base, and if we did nothing more than concentrate on doing better than what we have been doing for the next three to four years, we'd get respectable growth," asserts Dyson. "But we plan on doing much more than that—and we're very capable of it."

QUESTIONS

1. Do you agree with Coke's new strategy? If so, why? If not, what would you change?
2. How would you expect competitors to respond to Coke's new strategy?
3. Which element of the marketing mix is most important for a firm in this industry? Why?

Copyrights and Acknowledgments

"Don't Sell Food, Sell Peace of Mind" by Anne Bagamery. Reprinted by permission of *Forbes Magazine*, October 11, 1982. © Forbes, Inc., 1982.

"Dollars from Doodads" by William Baldwin. Reprinted by permission of *Forbes Magazine*, October 11, 1982. © Forbes Inc., 1982.

"The Retailer's Changing Role in the Marketing Channel" by Bert Rosenbloom. Reprinted from *Educator's Conference Proceedings 1979*, published by the American Marketing Association.

"Logistics: Essential to Strategy" by James L. Heskett. *Harvard Business Review*, November-December 1977. Reprinted by permission of the *Harvard Business Review*. © 1977 by the President and Fellows of Harvard College; all rights reserved.

"A Decision Sequence Analysis of Developments in Marketing Communication" by Michael L. Ray. Reprinted from *Journal of Marketing*, January 1973, published by the American Marketing Association.

"A New Look at 'Old' Advertising Strategy" by Dodds I. Buchanan. Reprinted by permission from *Business Horizons*, Winter 1965. Copyright 1965 by the Foundation for the School of Business at Indiana University.

"Confession of a Creative Chief: 'I Squeezed the Charmin'" by John V. Chervokas. Reprinted by permission from the December 25, 1972 issue of *Advertising Age*. Copyright 1972 by Crain Communications, Inc.

"Sales Promotion—Fast Growth, Faulty Management" by Roger A. Strang. *Harvard Business Review*, July-August 1976. Reprinted by permission of the *Harvard Business Review*. © 1976 by the President and Fellows of Harvard College; all rights reserved.

"Manage Your Sales Force as a System" by Porter Henry. *Harvard Business Review*, March-April 1975. Reprinted by permission of the *Harvard Business Review*. © 1975 by the President and Fellows of Harvard College; all rights reserved.

"A Decision-Making Structure for Price Decisions" by Alfred R. Oxenfeldt. Reprinted from *Journal of Marketing*, January 1973, published by the American Marketing Association.

"Risk-Aversive Pricing Policies: Problems and Alternatives" by Joseph P. Guiltinan. Reprinted from *Journal of Marketing*, January 1976, published by the American Marketing Association.

"Flexible Pricing: Industry's New Strategy to Hold Market Share Changes the Rules for Economic Decision-Making" reprinted from the December 12, 1977 issue of *Business Week* by special permission, copyright © 1977 by McGraw-Hill Inc.

"A Painful Headache for Bristol-Myers?" reprinted from the October 6, 1975 issue of *Business Week* by special permission, copyright © 1975 by McGraw-Hill Inc.

"Price-Cost Planning" by C. Davis Fogg and Kent H. Kohnken. Reprinted from *Journal of Marketing*, April 1978, published by the American Marketing Association.

"Marketing Issues" by Stephen Greyser. Reprinted from *Journal of Marketing*, Winter 1980, published by the American Marketing Association.

"Market Expansion Strategies in Multinational Marketing" by Igal Ayal and Jehiel Zif. Reprinted from *Journal of Marketing*, Spring 1979, published by the American Marketing Association.

"Responsible Marketing in an Expanded Marketing Concept" by Leland L. Beik and Warren A. French. Reprinted by permission from *Business and Society*, Spring 1973.

"Strategies for Introducing Marketing into Nonprofit Organizations" by Philip Kotler. Reprinted from *Journal of Marketing*, January 1979, published by the American Marketing Association.

"Are You Really Planning Your Marketing?" by Leon Winer. Reprinted from *Journal of Marketing*, January 1965, published by the American Marketing Association.

"Coke's Big Marketing Blitz" reprinted from the May 30, 1983 issue of *Business Week* by special permission, copyright © 1983 by McGraw-Hill Inc.

15060037

DATE DUE

GAYLORD			PRINTED IN U.S.A.